REGGAETON

Refiguring American Music
A series edited by Ronald Radano and Josh Kun
Charles McGovern, contributing editor

REGGAETON

Edited by Raquel Z. Rivera,
Wayne Marshall, and
Deborah Pacini Hernandez

Duke University Press
Durham and London
2009

© **2009 DUKE UNIVERSITY PRESS**
All rights reserved
Printed in the United States of America
on acid-free paper ∞
Designed by Amy Ruth Buchanan
Typeset in Minion by Keystone Typesetting, Inc.
Library of Congress Cataloging-in-Publication
Data appear on the last printed page of this book.

Frontis: *Plátano Pride* (2006) by Miguel
Luciano. Chromogenic print, 40 x 30
inches (101.6 x 76.2 cm).

A German language version of "Reggae in
Panama: *Bien* Tough" appeared in *Riddim*
magazine, March 2004.

An earlier version of "How to Make
Love with Your Clothes On" appeared as
"Dancing Back to Front: Regeton, Sexual-
ity, Gender, and Transnationalism in
Cuba" in *Popular Music* 25(3): 2006.

"Chamaco's Corner" originally appeared
in Spanish, yet under the same English
title, in *Barrunto* (San Juan / Santo Domingo, Isla Negra Editores, 2000).

"Black Pride" was originally printed in
New York Post (February 15, 2007).

CONTENTS

ILLUSTRATIONS

FOREWORD

What's All the Noise About?

My late friend Johnny Ramírez used to call it "racketón." "Apaga ese racketón" (Turn off that racketon) he would shout as the thumping cars shattered the peaceful quiet of his little house, *campo adentro* in the hills of Puerto Rico. For him, music was El Trío Los Panchos, *Ramito*, a little salsa maybe, an occasional tango, and a lot of boleros, Daniel Santos, Pedro Flores, Rafael Hernández, and of course, Felipe Rodríguez, "La Voz." Even after spending forty of his seventy years in New York City, Johnny's whole system was geared to "la música de ayer," the trusty old melodies and familiar cadences of yesteryear. The insistent boom and incoherent vocal gibberish of reggaeton was a "racket," nothing but meaningless, ear-grating noise. It's just not music.

Reggaeton is to this extent no different than other new styles or modes of popular music as they take hold among the young generation and conquer the soundscape of its place and time. The history of emergent genres and practices of music making illustrate time and again how the new language is greeted with widespread disdain among those with a stake in perpetuating what's been accepted and taken for granted as "the real stuff." Often what is at stake is social privilege, the wealth and power of the tastemakers and gatekeepers. But in the case of Johnny, who spent his whole life poor and uneducated, it's obviously not about privilege or wealth or power. His rants against "racketón" were backed by another kind of power, the weight of tradition and generational authority. Music is what music has "always" been. The rest is simply not music; it's noise, a racket.

Of course music is never just about music, and the social judgments it faces are always about the people who create it and love it. Johnny's responding not only to the sounds he hears but to the wayward, good-for-nothing young people these days, with their drugs and sex and the contaminating influence from outside, in this case meaning from the inner-city jungles of the United States. The sonic intrusion he feels is the invasion of generational degeneration, the moral decline of young people today "que no valen ná' " (who are worthless). Again, this is a familiar clash, the story of modern-day popular music, a story with countless examples around the world.

What is new about reggaeton—and the editors and authors of this anthology point up this novelty in multiple ways and from many angles—is how it came into being. Previously, what made the new style "popular" and immediately recognizable in all its novelty, was that it was rooted in a certain place, whether that local point of origin be defined in terms of geography, ethnicity, nationality, or simply grounding in certain ancestral traditions. Think of jazz, tango, blues, *plena*, reggae, salsa, samba, hip-hop—we can trace with some precision where the form started and by whom and why then and there. All those styles diffuse throughout the country and around the world, but it is always possible to say from where and how they spread and became relocalized in the many settings where they take hold. Controversies generally swirl over proprietary rights and issues of authenticity and corruption, but the power of roots and local groundedness, the "down-homeness" of the emergent style, remains decisive in establishing its place in music history.

Reggaeton may well go down in that history as the first transnational music, in the full sense of the term. Not only that it becomes transnational by its massive and far-flung spread in the world, a process that has become more rapid and intensive with every new generation of technology and global shrinkage. Hip-hop, in that sense, has outpaced and surpassed even rock, salsa, and reggae in becoming a musical lingua franca of world reach and proportions. But reggaeton kicks that remarkable process up still another notch by being an eminently popular form of music without any single specifiable place of origin, with no *cuna* (cradle) in the sense of a " 'hood" or even national setting from which it sprang. The contention over whether it's Panamanian, Jamaican, Puerto Rican, or Nuyorican will most likely seethe on, since it seems to be a style brewed in a multilocal, transnational cauldron from the beginning. All of these parental claims are valid, yet none of them are, because the "location" of origin in this elusive, perhaps unprecedented case is at the very crossroads of many diasporic, migratory, and circulating communities of taste and generational solidarity.

The twist, though, and what belies this seemingly disembodied, unrooted genesis, is that reggaetón (and here I use the accent mark) is in Spanish. Unlike hip-hop, whose English-language lyrics attest to its South Bronx birthplace even when it finds expression in Turkish, French, Swahili, Hebrew, or Cantonese, the Spanish rhymes of reggaetón (or is it "reguetón"?) signal a reassertion of cultural and national specificity within a thoroughly trans- (not to say post-) national field of musical and poetic expression. It's almost like a kind of Latino revenge against the doggedly Anglophone nature and official narrative of early hip-hop, with its erasure of the powerful Boricua (Puerto Rican) presence and input from the outset. And it's an in-your-face at the nervous gatekeepers of "Hispanic" culture who would deny the overriding presence of hip-hop in the lives of a whole generation of young Latinos, a massive public that will not stop insisting that "this is the culture I grew up with, it's *my* culture." This anthology opens a chapter in hip-hop history that brings it all back home, back to our transnational Afro-Spanish-speaking countries and diasporas and 'hoods where young people are going through their hip-hop ecstasies and traumas, but in their own language, and in their own unique and hitherto-unknown style. And let's be clear: some of these lyrics are also vibrant, fresh poetry as well. Check out Gallego's street-corner chronicle, "Chamaco's Corner," included in this pioneering book, for a good example.

Maybe what freaked out "old Johnny" the most, even more than old-school rap ever seemed to bother him, was just that, that it's in Spanish, his own language, too close to home and too undeniably Caribbean to be waved off as "de allá" (from over there). A reappropriated sound that was incubated somewhere else finally comes home to roost. Such is the blast that shattered Johnny's rural tranquility, not "racketon" but "raquetón"!

Bring on the Racket!

ACKNOWLEDGMENTS

An anthology like this one is by definition a collective endeavor, but in addition to the contributors, many other people and institutions were crucial to its development, and we would like to thank them. Tufts University's Mellon Postdoctoral Fellows Program can take credit for creating the intellectual context for an interdisciplinary approach to reggaeton. While Raquel Z. Rivera was at Tufts in 2004–6 as a Mellon Post-Doc, she co-taught with Deborah Pacini Hernandez a course entitled Music, Blackness and Caribbean Latinos that generated so much excitement from the students when the conversation turned to reggaeton, that the need for a volume like this one became apparent. Tufts's Mellon Program also provided Rivera with the funds for a symposium on reggaeton, which brought Wayne Marshall into the discussion, and eventually into the editorial collective. Rivera later received generous support from the Center for Puerto Rican Studies at Hunter College through a research fellowship as well as funding and logistical assistance in securing images and permissions. Tufts University also provided publication support via a Faculty Research Award to Pacini Hernandez.

We were also fortunate to find exceptional translators for the articles submitted in Spanish and German: Juan Flores, Héctor Fernández L'Hoeste, Noah Dauber, and Maritza Fernández. Marisol Rodríguez and Melinda González provided valuable assistance by compiling the bibliography. Cambridge University Press, *Riddim* magazine, Editorial Isla Negra, and the *New York Post* also contributed by granting us permission to reprint articles.

Each of us also benefited individually from the support and generosity of friends and collaborators. Raquel Z. Rivera would like to thank Bryan Vargas of Mofongo Music & Media, Jorge "Georgie" Vázquez and Jonathan "J-Blak" Troncoso, for the many, many musical consultations, and Anabellie Rivera, Sabrina Rivera, and Marisol Rodríguez for research assistance. Wayne Marshall is grateful to Mario Small, Anton Kociolek, and DJ El Niño for their insightful answers to his oddball queries and especially to all the kids in Boston and Cambridge who put him on to this "Spanish reggae" thing back in 2002–3. Rebecca Nesson and Jesse Kriss both deserve props for their assistance with the transcriptions that appear in his essay. He would also like to acknowledge the support of the University of Chicago Department of Music, where he enjoyed a postdoctoral fellowship during the preparation of this anthology. Deborah Pacini Hernandez thanks those who generously shared their time and thoughts on Dominicans and reggaeton in Puerto Rico and New York, among them Jorge Duany, Jorge Giovannetti, Juan Otero, Welmo Romero Joseph, Andrés Ramos (aka DJ Velcro), Karin Weyland, Jorge Oquendo, Orquídea Negra, Boy Wonder, and Jeanette Luna.

Finally, our heartfelt thanks to Ken Wissoker, Mandy Earley, Neal McTighe, and Sonya Manes, who so skillfully helped shepherd the manuscript through the editorial and production process.

WAYNE MARSHALL, RAQUEL Z. RIVERA,

AND DEBORAH PACINI HERNANDEZ

INTRODUCTION

Reggaeton's Socio-Sonic Circuitry

In a January 2006 article published by the *Village Voice*, Jon Caramanica ended a largely celebratory piece on reggaeton with a somewhat sudden, cryptic remark: "Fuck a Slim Shady," he quipped, "Hip-hop's race war begins here."[1] Caramanica thus suggests that the most prominent "racial" tensions around hip-hop are not between African Americans and whites (represented by prominent white rapper, Slim Shady, a.k.a. Eminem) but between African Americans and Latinos. Similarly, blogger Byron Crawford's tongue-in-cheek March 2006 post for xxl magazine's website, "Ban Reggaeton: Fight the Real Enemy of Hip-Hop," makes one wonder how exactly—snide and enigmatic remarks aside—the perceived rivalry between hip-hop and reggaeton is informed by extramusical tensions between African Americans and Latinos.[2] What seems clear is that reggaeton has emerged in recent years as a prominent, potent symbol for articulating the lines of community. Its suggestive sonic and cultural profile has animated contentious debates around issues of race, nation, class, gender, sexuality, and language. That the genre's commercial rise and mainstream presence in the United States have coincided with increasingly tense rhetoric and anxiety centering on immigration—rhetoric which in turn informs the reception and production of the music—makes an analysis and understanding of reggaeton's social, historical, and political dimensions all the more important, if not urgent.

Drawing on reggae, hip-hop, and a number of Spanish Caribbean styles and often accompanied by sexually explicit lyrics and a provocative dancing style known as *perreo* (doggy style), reggaeton emerged from Puerto Rico in the late 1990s but only recently crossed over into the U.S. mainstream and public consciousness. According to Nielsen SoundScan, while overall album sales declined close to 8 percent in the first six months of 2005, Latin music albums grew almost 18 percent. Though reggaeton was not the only genre driving the increase, reggaeton artists generated great enthusiasm in an industry concerned with boosting waning record sales. Dozens of Latin music stations across the United States switched to a reggaeton or "hurban" (Hispanic urban) format—for example, La Kalle, a franchise of the Mexican media conglomerate, Univision—while numerous record companies established new label imprints under the Latin urban music umbrella where reggaeton plays a starring role.

During reggaeton's meteoric rise to mainstream prominence in 2005–6, major U.S. newspapers and magazines such as the *New York Times*, *Los Angeles Times*, *Village Voice*, and *Rolling Stone* published articles heralding and interpreting the phenomenal success of the genre. More recently, in the wake of relatively disappointing sales figures, industry excitement and media coverage has grown more measured, and several journalists have wondered whether the genre is "running out of gasolina," referring to the Daddy Yankee song that served as the genre's (first and only?) mainstream anthem.[3] Reggaeton-format radio stations have broadened their playlists to include urban *bachata* and other Latin pop, and reggaeton subsidiaries of major record labels—Roc La Familia and Wu Tang Latino, for instance—have closed shop. Leila Cobo, in a January 2007 *Billboard* article taking stock of the multiple and contradictory interpretations regarding the period 2005–6 in Latin music sales, explained how dire predictions and disappointment over reggaeton might have less to do with its impending demise and more with the high expectations initially placed on the genre: "Those 2005 numbers were misleading, inflated by overly ambitious shipments of reggaeton releases. The numbers plunged during the first six months of the year when returns started coming in and factors like gasoline prices and immigration issues cut into Latin music sales."[4]

At the same time, other accounts seem to affirm the genre's continued rise and future potential. After attending a Radio City Music Hall concert in February 2007, during which the duo Wisin and Yandel "kept a packed audience on its feet, screaming for nearly two hours," the *New York Times'* Kelefa Sanneh cautioned against premature eulogies: "The concert certainly didn't secure the future of reggaetón, or even the future of Wisin and Yandel. But it was impressive proof of what this genre and this duo can do."[5]

Some observers have explained reggaeton's success as the result of demographic changes in the wake of record levels of immigration from Latin America, but the significance of the reggaeton phenomenon goes well beyond the similarly hyped but ephemeral "Latin boom" that attracted media attention a few years ago: for the first time since the "mambo craze" of the 1950s, a music whose lyrics are in Spanish and whose aesthetics are Latin Caribbean has been embraced not only by pan-Latino but mainstream audiences as well—both African American and Anglo-American. (The commercial hits of Ricky Martin and the other "boom" artists, such as Shakira and Christina Aguilera, were primarily in English, and their aesthetics were mainstream pop rather than "Latin.") Moreover, reggaeton differs from earlier Latin pop or dance "explosions" in its widespread grassroots popularity, especially among Spanish speakers, as the genre's basis in digital tools of production and distribution has facilitated a flowering of aspiring producers and performers across the United States and Latin America.

Whether or not reggaeton reached its commercial apex in 2005 with Daddy Yankee's "Gasolina," its resonance continues as localized versions emerge from Santo Domingo to Springfield, Massachusetts, from Chicago to Cartagena. Reggaeton's significance thus extends beyond its commercial success, which offers but one measure of the genre's cultural and social footprint. Although we might wonder how a more modest mainstream profile for reggaeton might affect the discussions and debates around, for example, Latino, Puerto Rican, American, and/or black identities, we might also ask whether reggaeton's moment in the mainstream suggests a more profound reordering of mainstream and margin, center and periphery.

NAMING REGGAETON

Readers may notice that the spelling of *reggaeton* in the anthology takes a number of forms. Because we have decided to respect the individual contributors' decisions about spelling the term, it appears throughout the text as *reggaeton*, *reggaetón*, *reguetón*, *regeton*. Even so, as editors, we have our own ideas about which rendering best represents the public discourse. The title of the anthology and many of the essays employ the unaccented *reggaeton*. There are a number of reasons for preferring this spelling.

Since the music has been embraced—and indeed, shaped—to such a degree in the United States and is so often referred to as *reggaeton* in newspapers and on album covers and websites, it seems most appropriate to spell it without the accent. Several influential mixtapes by DJ Blass, for example, spell the term *sin acento* (see, e.g., the *Reggaeton Sex* series), and along with the work of DJ Nelson and others, these releases are largely responsible for popularizing the term itself as well as its "Anglicized" spelling. Although the term dates to the late '90s, *reggaeton* did not circulate as a popular descriptor until the early years of the new millennium. Before the music attained a presence in the U.S. mainstream in 2004—a process which may have been facilitated by the advent of the term itself—practitioners and devotees frequently held on to such terms as *rap*, *underground*, *dembow* (or *dembo*), *melaza*, or simply *reggae* to describe the music and to place it in social and cultural context. As a neologism emerging from a circuit of production, performance, and distribution between Puerto Rico and the United States—sometimes understood as conjoining *reggae* and *maratón* (in order to describe the genre's staple of nonstop, long-playing mixes)—the unaccented spelling thus expresses the genre's increasing, if not inherent, Spanglish orientation. In his essay, Wayne Marshall explores this changing nomenclature along with its accompanying shifting musical aesthetics.

Moreover, despite the appearance of a more properly Spanish form, *reggaetón* (with an accent) does not follow standard Spanish orthographic rules: hence the current debate within *con acento* circles about whether to spell it *reguetón*, rather than *reggaetón*.[6] The Academia Puertorriqueña de la Lengua Española (APLE; Puerto Rican Academy of the Spanish Language) has announced that it will submit a proposal suggesting that the next edition of the Real Academia Española dictionary include an entry on *reguetón*. This well-meaning approach seems problematic, however, in its erasure of the term's and the genre's relationship to Jamaican reggae (which is rarely rendered as *regue* in Spanish), as well as its Spanglish constitution. Aware of these objections, APLE's Maia Sherwood Droz has said that "orthography does not require that type of fidelity" to the original Jamaican term and argues, instead, for the advantages of having phonetics match orthography, as is typical in Spanish.[7] We prefer *reggaeton*—particularly for this English-language anthology—not only as the more popular spelling, but because it best embodies the music's transnational and multilingual character.

DEFINING REGGAETON

Spelling reggaeton, for all the problems it poses, is a simpler endeavor than attempting to define reggaeton and hence to extricate it from related genres and from a direct stylistic genealogy in which the term is but the latest and most widely used label to date. As noted above, before it was called reggaeton, artists and audiences referred to the music simply as *reggae* or sometimes as *Spanish reggae* or *reggae en español*. The latter term, however, more often describes Panamanian recordings from the 1980s and early 1990s than the Puerto Rican productions that eventually coalesced into reggaeton. Other terms, especially as used in Puerto Rico during the 1990s—such as *dembow, underground,* or *melaza*—are not interchangeable with *reggaeton*; they describe stylistic pre-cursors which depart from reggaeton in their sonic and sociocultural profile, as Marshall explains in his essay. Even more confusing, discussions of reg-gaeton frequently make reference to other genres, especially hip-hop (and/or rap) and reggae (and/or dancehall), which are themselves the sites of a great deal of discursive contest, their meanings (and division into subgenres) vary-ing depending on the speaker and the context. Although we attempt to exercise some clarity with regard to these labels across the anthology, their various shades merit some discussion here, especially for readers less acquainted with the range of meanings and debates over dominant nomenclature among these genres' practitioners, devotees, and documenters.

We might begin by unpacking a commonplace characterization of reg-gaeton in all its hybrid glory. Take, for example, a description of reggaeton's musical style offered by Puerto Rican hip-hop pioneer Vico C: "Musically, reggaetón was born in a hip-hop environment, with a little bit of Jamaican dancehall and Puerto Rico's own tropical flavor and ritmo."[8] At first glance, this definition would seem apt enough, though the emphasis here on hip-hop—understandable given Vico C's perspective—might be transferred by an-other narrator to Jamaican or Panamanian sources, or to the Puerto Rican or more broadly "tropical" input often glossed as an essentialized "Latin" *sabor*. All of these connections are important, of course, opening out into significant social and cultural articulations and disarticulations. It is imperative, however, to interrogate this laundry list of genres contributing to reggaeton's hybrid style, and to examine the ways that its links to the United States, the wider Caribbean, Latin America, and the African diaspora serve to inform the cul-tural work that reggaeton does. Toward this end, it is necessary to be clear about what we mean here by certain well-worn terms.

Hip-hop and reggae might both be understood as umbrella terms describ-ing a range of styles and subgenres (and cultural practices more generally), not unlike rock, R&B, or salsa for that matter. Hence, while hip-hop includes such subgenres as Miami bass, Atlanta "crunk," and Bay Area "hyphy" (not to mention "extra-musical" practices such as breakdance and "graffiti"), reggae often refers to everything from dub and dancehall (sometimes called "ragga" or "raggamuffin"—two terms that turn up in a good deal of '90s-era "proto-reggaeton") to ska and "rocksteady," stylistic precursors of reggae which none-theless are sometimes grouped under the reggae umbrella by listeners and practitioners. The term *rap*, often used interchangeably with hip-hop, intro-duces additional ambiguity. For many, *rap* and *hip-hop* are synonyms, both describing a U.S.-based musical style marked by rhythmic, spoken-sung declamation over prerecorded backing tracks or *beats*. *Rap* was the more dominant term in the late '80s and early '90s, especially as record companies began to market the music to a mainstream audience. Alongside this practice, *hip-hop* was often used—erroneously according to some torchbearers—to describe a sort of nonhardcore rap, a derivative style marked by elements of R&B and other pop forms. *Hip-hop*, however, had long described the wider set of cultural practices which included rap as well as breakdance, graffiti, and the art of the DJ, and the work of hip-hop journalists, historians, artists, and connoisseurs during the '90s served to revise the dominant discourse, in many cases making hip-hop the more common term for the genre. In this book the terms will appear interchangeably to describe the U.S.-based genre wherein rappers or MCs declaim over beats, though the term *rap* may also be used to refer to the more general practice of performing speechlike vocals (whether in dancehall, reggaeton, or hip-hop). Although musically speaking, hip-hop embraces a variety of forms, it is most easily distinguished from reggaeton in its embrace of the downbeat and the backbeat, emphasizing duple divisions of the meter rather than the 3:2 cross-rhythms that mark reggaeton and other Caribbean genres.[9] This form of sonic organization is one reason, for instance, why Vico C is more commonly regarded as a rap or hip-hop artist rather than a reggaeton performer, despite his occasional collaborations with reggaeton producers.

Dancehall reggae—frequently referred to simply as *dancehall* and sometimes as *reggae*—emerged as a distinctive subgenre of reggae in the early '80s, deriving its name from the social spaces where the music was played. It has tended toward a rhythmic minimalism, and a moral "slackness," that causes many observers to wonder how the music of Buju Banton, Beenie Man, or Bounty Killer could possibly be related to that of Bob Marley and other proponents of "roots" reggae. Though we do not have the space to indulge such a genealogical exposition here, it is important to note that while dancehall is strongly marked by a symbiotic engagement with hip-hop, especially audible in vocal style, most Jamaicans hear dancehall as another form of reggae, in part thanks to dancehall's familiar polyrhythms, dub aesthetics, and the occasional "skanking" keyboard accent on the offbeat—reggae's hallmark if any.[10] Moreover, many of the same artists and producers bridge roots and dancehall approaches, many classic "riddims"—or accompanimental tracks—have been versioned for dancehall remakes, and the two styles continue to coexist in the social spaces of the dancehall.[11] It is significant, however, that long after roots reggae was embraced by mainstream Jamaican society, due in part to its transcendent themes and international success, dancehall has continued to fuel local "culture wars," dismissed and denigrated by the middle and upper classes as rude, crude, and bound up with gun violence and explicit sexual content. For all its continuities with roots reggae, then, dancehall tends to be associated with a militant blackness and a particular class position and critique, characteristics which have boosted its appeal in "foreign" contexts such as the United States, Panama, and Puerto Rico. Musically speaking, dancehall's prevailing rhythmic pattern from the late '80s and early '90s has served as reggaeton's backbone—the *boom-ch-boom-chick* that now resounds from cars and clubs worldwide.

If dancehall is indeed a latter-day form of reggae and can properly be referred to simply as *reggae*, other historical factors in Puerto Rican cultural development complicate attempts to explain why and how the term *reggae* was conflated locally with reggaeton. As Jorge Giovannetti has explained elsewhere,[12] roots reggae enjoyed considerable popularity in Puerto Rico as early as the 1970s, although interestingly, it was middle- and upper-class youth, who tended to be white and whose musical preferences were for rock, who became reggae's most avid fans. While many of these *blanquitos* fancied themselves as Rastas or at least fervent admirers of Rastafarianism,[13] they were much more interested in the superficial trappings of Rastafarianism—wearing red, gold, and green clothing, smoking ganja, and attending reggae concerts—than they were in the trenchant social critiques that characterized Jamaican reggae artists such as Bob Marley and Peter Tosh. In contrast, when Spanish language dancehall reggae appeared in Puerto Rico in the 1990s, it was adopted primarily by the same lower-class youth listening to rap (and who, increasingly, had also been listening to Jamaican dancehall, as Welmo E. Romero Joseph chronicles in his essay). Though there was porosity between roots reggae, rap, dancehall reggae, and *underground*, Giovannetti explains that there were "clearly marked" boundaries between the upper- and middle-class *blanquitos* who were roots reggae devotees and the lower-class *raperos* who preferred rap, dancehall, and *underground*. These class distinctions (which were also heavily racialized, as the essay by Raquel Z. Rivera illustrates) regarding the consumption and production of popular music in Puerto Rico were certainly nothing new and had been most immediately preceded by the *cocolos* versus *roqueros* (salsa fans vs. rock fans) antagonisms of the 1980s.[14]

The sharp class and racial cleavages that separated roots from dancehall reggae in Puerto Rico, as well as the routes that the music traveled to get there from Jamaica, were quite different from the ways in which reggae and its social meanings traveled to and were incorporated into Panama's cultural landscape.

While Puerto Rican youths' identification with reggae was heavily mediated by the global music industry, the development of reggae in Panama—though still related to the global music industry—was also rooted in a history of West Indian immigration and a resulting social context where Jamaican music, patois, and Rastafarianism were not trendy affectations but an integral part of Panamanian vernacular culture. These issues are explored closely in part II of this volume, which is devoted to Panama and includes an overview by Christoph Twickel, as well as Twickel's interview with the reggae en español luminary El General, and Ifeoma Nwankwo's interview with the seminal Panamanian reggae performer Renato.

Similar to the anachronistic use of *reggae* to describe precursors such as rocksteady and ska, the term *reggaeton* is now applied, especially in journalistic discourse, to such earlier instantiations as reggae en español and *dembow*. This kind of elision, however, can mask the moment of reggaeton's emergence as well as its significant departures from earlier forms of sonic and economic organization. Attention to historical context is hence of crucial importance here, especially since a focus on reggaeton to some extent requires an emphasis on the contemporary. By *reggaeton*, then, we refer to a relatively new genre (and related set of cultural practices) strongly marked both by a particular approach to musical style (e.g., dancehall's *boom-ch-boom-chick* as reshaped by urban Puerto Rican sensibilities and informed by a fusion with hip-hop) and a relation to the market (i.e., explicitly commercial, courting a wide audience).

In addition to teasing out reggaeton from reggae and hip-hop, dancehall and rap, it is important also to extricate the genre from the pool of putatively "Latin" styles with which it is frequently conflated. Representations of reggaeton often tie the music to salsa, bachata, merengue, plena, *bomba*, and other "tropical," Afro-Latin, Latin-Caribbean, Puerto Rican, and Latin forms more generally. As noted in Pacini Hernandez's and Marshall's essays, however, for all the interaction and resonance with these forms, including more recent trends toward infusing reggaeton with sonic markers from bachata, merengue, *cumbia* and *vallenato*, to emphasize reggaeton's "Latin" character serves to overlook its stronger connections to hip-hop and reggae, connections crucial because of their links with a cultural politics based more around race and class and transnational linkages than national or pan-Latin identities.[15] Ultimately, we hope to make clear that reggaeton is neither hip-hop nor dancehall nor Latin nor tropical in the traditional sense, yet it draws from all of these (and forges imagined connections with them) in projecting a distinctive, resonant sound.

Reggaeton and its most immediate precursor, *underground*, have been embroiled in multiple culture wars. Debates rage over charges of appropriation, ethnic and racial tensions, sexuality and sexism, questions of profanity, and fears that the genre is inextricable from drugs and violence. Some of these debates have involved media-propelled moral panics, state regulation and even censorship, as chronicled in Raquel Z. Rivera's and Alfredo Nieves Moreno's essays. Other indictments against reggaeton have centered on the genre's purported lack of aesthetic merit, whether in comparison to Jamaican reggae,[16] or to music considered more "traditionally" Puerto Rican, Caribbean, or Latin American.[17] However, the reggaeton-driven dispute best engaged by this anthology is that which pits the genre against hip-hop.

Though reggaeton is indebted—historically, aesthetically, discursively—to hip-hop, there are nevertheless deep rifts that separate the genres in the minds of consumers, critics, practitioners, and music industry insiders. The strain between reggaeton and hip-hop in Puerto Rico is the backbone of Welmo Romero Joseph's essay Titled "From Hip Hop to Reggaeton: Is There Only a Step?," Romero Joseph offers an overview of the development of reggaeton in Puerto Rico from the perspective of a hip-hop artist who continues to resist the pressure to embrace the upstart genre which now dominates the island's soundscape. As we explained earlier in the introduction, the perceived differences and rivalries between reggaeton and hip-hop in the United States are related to tensions between Latinos and African Americans—the U.S.-based ethnic or racial communities each genre supposedly represents. But as illustrated by the anthology contributors Wayne Marshall, Geoff Baker, Jose Davila, and Welmo Romero Joseph, the connections and contentions between reggaeton and hip-hop have widely different underpinnings, manifestations, and interpretations, depending upon the context and the observer in question. For example, while Baker proposes that "revolutionary" ideals and the Cuban government play a key role in the opposition between the genres in Cuba, Davila suggests that aesthetics, language choices, and market forces drive the rivalries in Miami.

One of the most prominent reasons reggaeton (as well as reggae en español and *underground*) has been valued by fans and devalued by detractors is the genre's defiant embrace of blackness and its insistent connections to hip-hop's and reggae's race-based cultural politics. Christoph Twickel's essay and his interview with El General, as well as Ifeoma Nwankwo's interview with Renato, explore these connections in the Panamanian context, while Raquel Z. Rivera's essay addresses them within the Puerto Rican milieu.

Tego Calderón is, undoubtedly, the reggaeton artist whose celebrations of blackness and indictment of Latino and/or Latin American racism—manifest in his music, lyrics, video imagery, interviews—have had the most visibility, depth, and consistency. His essay, titled "Black Pride," was originally published in the *New York Post*. It is a rare intervention in printed public discourse by a reggaeton artist, both because it is not crafted as an interview (though it is based on one) and also because it is such a detailed and cogent political statement on race. Calderón contradicts the myth of racial democracy in Latin America and proposes the U.S. civil rights movement as a model for black Latin Americans to follow.

Reggaeton's engagement with blackness has been neither simple nor static. As argued in Wayne Marshall's essay, one can hear a shift in the genre's identity politics "from música negra to reggaeton Latino"—from a race-based "black music" to a pan-ethnic musical expression. Alexandra Vazquez's essay also grapples with these ethnoracialized tensions manifest in reggaeton's engagement with blackness and pan-*latinidad*, while paying particular attention to the intersections between race, ethnicity, and gender.

MAPPING REGGAETON

The genre known today as reggaeton is the product of multiple and overlapping musical circuits that do not comply with geographic, national, or language boundaries, nor with ethnic or pan-ethnic expectations. And yet, reggaeton's history is most often explained in linear fashion, abiding by and affirming these very boundaries. The genre's ascribed point of departure may vary—Panama and Puerto Rico being the most often cited—yet these historical narratives tend to name a single origination point and to run in only one direction. For example, as stated by many of the artists interviewed in *The Chosen Few: El Documental*, reggaeton originated in Panama; was adopted, transformed and popularized in Puerto Rico; and from there was exported to other countries in Latin America, the United States, and, eventually, the rest of the world.

But how, exactly, can we map reggaeton? In fact, how can we map any genre? Do we privilege sonics or social context? In terms of social context, do we privilege place of origin or location of development? In terms of sonics, do we give more definitional weight to the *beats* or to the lyrics? To the lyrics' meanings and language choices or to the musicality of their delivery? How is our mapping affected by the changing nomenclature and musical aesthetics of the genre? Because we understand the careful balancing of all these factors as paramount in the mapping of reggaeton, we propose reggaeton as best understood through the image of overlapping and multidirectional circuits rather than a bipolar axis.[18]

Perceptive observers have long noticed that reggae en español, *underground*, and reggaeton are best described as trans-Caribbean genres whose history and aesthetics do not abide by nation and language as chief organizing principles.[19] Yet, the two most popular competing discourses regarding reggaeton's origins locate the genre in one of two Spanish-speaking countries: some point to Panama's reggae en español of the 1980s as reggaeton's genesis, while others insist on locating its origins in Puerto Rico's early 1990s *underground* music. Both camps bring crucial points to the discussion, and it seems unlikely that reggaeton would have ever emerged without the inputs of both Panamanian reggae en español and Puerto Rican *underground*. But these nation-based narratives are extremely limiting considering how much reggae en español as well as *underground* consisted of "versioning" dancehall reggae hits coming out of Jamaica in the 1980s and 1990s.[20] Indeed, if anything is certain in the reggaeton narrative, it is that without Jamaican dancehall reggae there would be no reggaeton.

There is yet another key locale in the development of reggaeton that, though rarely surfacing in popular discussions of reggaeton's origins, will not surprise those acquainted with the last hundred years of Caribbean and Afro-diasporic music history: New York City. In this sense, reggaeton joins such genres as calypso, *jíbaro* music, mambo, reggae, salsa, and hip-hop as products of New York's distinctive intercultural dynamics.[21] Not only has the city served as a place where different Caribbean groups come into intense social, cultural, and musical contact; New York has also been a center for the recording and international diffusion of Caribbean music.[22] This complex and multidirectional circuitry of musical production and dissemination was acknowledged in the earliest academic articles dedicated to the early *underground*/reggaeton scene in Puerto Rico: Mayra Santos's "Puerto Rican Underground" and Jorge L. Giovannetti's "Popular Music and Culture in Puerto Rico: Jamaican and Rap Music as Cross-Cultural Symbols."[23] This anthology builds upon their work, and many of its essays contribute to the complex project of mapping and making sense of reggaeton's geographical contours and local significations.

Several essays in this book concern themselves directly with reggaeton's geographical and cultural cartography. Wayne Marshall explores reggaeton's historical, translocal socio-sonic circuitry, taking into account the drawing and crossing of national and social boundaries via musical, linguistic, and visual aesthetics. Deborah Pacini Hernandez's essay places Dominicanness—in its national as well as transnational dimensions—at the center of her remapping efforts. Similarly, Christoph Twickel's essay and his interview with El General, alongside Ifeoma Nwankwo's interview with Renato, bring into relief the important role that Panama and its historical connections to Jamaica played in the genesis of new reggae styles. Marshall and Twickel both discuss New York City as a key locale in the development and diffusion of reggae en español, while Jose Davila explores reggaeton's resonance and interplay with hip-hop and *crunkiao* in Miami. Although neither Geoff Baker nor Jan Fairley make claims for Cuba in the genesis and development of the genre, their ethnographic perspectives show how the island nation fits into reggaeton's cultural geography, providing an intriguing vantage point—within a Spanish-speaking, semi-socialist society—from which to view the genre's international development and significance.

In contrast, Welmo E. Romero Joseph, Félix Jiménez, Alfredo Nieves Moreno, Frances Negrón-Muntaner, and Raquel Z. Rivera focus on reggaeton in local Puerto Rican contexts, reading what reggaeton tells us about contemporary Puerto Rican culture and society. Although, as discussed above, we have given careful consideration to representing reggaeton as a transnational phenomenon, considering the genre's strong, if not prevailing, Puerto Rican character, such an emphasis not only seems reasonable but necessary. Moreover, this geographical focus enables a breadth and depth of analysis, especially along the axes of such important dimensions as race and class, gender and sexuality, aesthetics and poetics. Rounding things out, Alexandra Vazquez's essay considers reggaeton's racial and gender politics as grounded in Puerto Rican social mores and practices but resonating in wider contexts. Finally, "Chamaco's Corner," by Gallego (José Raúl González), a Puerto Rican poet and recent *reggaetonero*, serves as a bridge between the literary/academic world, and the sphere of popular music; this critically acclaimed poem is featured in Gallego's award-winning first book, *Barrunto*, and served as the introduction to Daddy Yankee's 2000 debut album *El cartel de Yankee*.

ANTHOLOGIZING AND READING REGGAETON

The editorial collaboration that has produced this volume is the result of several converging trajectories. As scholars, each of us has been analyzing Caribbean popular music and culture—in both U.S. and island contexts—for many years. Rivera has written extensively in both academic and journalistic forums about Puerto Rican and Caribbean Latino music—particularly hip-hop and reggaeton—focusing on the intersections between nation, ethnicity, class, race, and gender. Marshall's research has centered on the interplay between hip-hop, reggae, reggaeton, and other (pan-)American urban genres as giving musical shape and form to social and cultural processes in and across the United States, the Caribbean, and the greater Americas. Pacini Hernandez has also done extensive work on musical circuits in the Spanish Caribbean: with particular attention to how globalization and transnational migration have altered patterns of music production and consumption typically bounded by common language and nationality, she has examined how these changes have "re-Africanized" Spanish Caribbean cultural identity.

Beyond our converging research interests, we were moved to compile this anthology after observing that despite extensive media attention, reggaeton had not yet received scholarly analysis commensurate with its musical and cultural significance. To date, there have been few academic articles on the topic, and no book that takes reggaeton as its primary subject.[24] Given our strong, abiding interests in the region's musical, social, and cultural dimensions, and our overlapping but distinct disciplinary orientations, we felt both motivated and well positioned to take on the complex task of "reading reggaeton" and thinking about how an anthology of essays might attempt such a project.

While we sought to provide an appropriate balance of thematic and location-specific coverage, we ultimately selected the most insightful and provocative essays, even if that meant some aspects of reggaeton are not fully covered here. For example, while Jan Fairley offers her interpretation of reggaeton dance in Cuba from the perspective of a British feminist, the cultural meanings of the perreo (doggy-style) dance associated with reggaeton might be understood quite differently in other Caribbean locations, such as Jamaica and Trinidad, with long traditions of sexually explicit dances.

Most of the essays in this anthology are new and examine reggaeton's history, musical and poetic aesthetics, discourses and images, dance styles, and technologies, as well as issues such as migration and globalization, from the multiple perspectives of production, dissemination, consumption, and performance.[25] Because of its historical importance, one of the earliest articles on the emerging genre (even before it had become known by the term *reggaeton*) is reproduced here (Raquel Z. Rivera's essay).[26] We also include here two essays that were previously published in English: Jan Fairley's and Tego Calderón's. Christoph Twickel's essay was published in Germany and translated for this volume. Gallego's poem was also translated specifically for this publication from its original Spanish by Juan Flores. The fourth part in this anthology,

"Visualizing Reggaeton," offers alternative strategies for "reading reggaeton": these include a gallery of still photographs from Carolina Caycedo's video/performance piece about reggaeton dance, *Gran Perretón*; selected pieces from visual artist Miguel Luciano's series *Pure Plantainum*, a meditation on identity politics in the "bling-bling" era, and from *Filiberto Ojeda Uptowns—Machetero Air Force Ones*, a customized pair of Nike sneakers that explore the intersections between hyperconsumerism and revolutionary ideals; and, finally, photographs by the noted reggaeton videographer Kacho López that document Tego Calderón's life-changing experiences in Sierra Leone during the 2006 filming of the VH1 documentary *Bling'd: Blood, Diamonds, and Hip-Hop*.[27]

Although we do not entertain the notion that this anthology will serve as the final or most authoritative word on reggaeton, it is our hope and intention that it might provoke, as it focuses, further discussion of the genre's vistas, borders, meanings, and significance. The vibrant and varied discourses around reggaeton neither start nor end here, but the collected contributions in this book should serve to guide future conversations about how and why we value, name, and map reggaeton in the ways that we do.

NOTES

Translations of Spanish-language quotations are those of this essay's authors.

1. Jon Caramanica, "Grow Dem Bow," *Village Voice*, January 10, 2006.

2. Byron Crawford, "Ban Reggaeton," *Bol's Saturday Night Workout by Byron Crawford*, entry posted March 29, 2006, http://xxlmag.com/online/?p=767 (accessed February 6, 2006).

3. See, e.g., Agustin Gurza, "When the Fad Goes Fizzle," *Los Angeles Times*, April 16, 2006; Jordan Levin, "Reggaeton's Unrealized Dream," *Miami Herald*, May 20, 2007; and Leila Cobo, "Reggaeton No Longer Translates to Automatic Sales," *Monsters and Critics*, May 21, 2007, under "Music News," http://music.monstersandcritics.com/news/arti cle_1307425.php/Reggaeton_no_longer_translates_to_automatic_sales (accessed May 23, 2007).

4. Leila Cobo, "What the Numbers Tell Us: Latin Retail. Not as Rosey, or Maybe Not as Dire, as You Think," *Billboard*, January 20, 2007, 12 (col. 1).

5. Kelefa Sanneh, "Celebrating the Sweet Beat of Reggaetón Success," *New York Times*, February 5, 2007.

6. Maia Sherwood Droz, "Reguetón: Una propuesta ortográfica," *El Nuevo Día (Revista Letras)*, May 2006.

7. Iñaki Estívaliz, "Academia Puertorriqueña propondrá que se escriba 'reguetón'," *Terra/EFE*, November 7, 2006, http://www.terra.com/ocio/articulo/html/oci154833 .htm (accessed June 7, 2007).

8. Raquel Cepeda, "Riddims by the Reggaetón," *Village Voice*, March 28, 2005.

9. These musical relationships are clarified further in Wayne Marshall's essay.

10. For more on the relationship between dancehall and roots reggae, and between these related forms and hip-hop, see, e.g., Norman Stolzoff, *Wake the Town and Tell the People: Dancehall Culture in Jamaica* (Durham, N.C.: Duke University Press, 2000); and Wayne Marshall, "Routes, Rap, Reggae: Hearing the Histories of Hip-Hop and Reggae Together" (Ph.D. diss., University of Wisconsin, Madison, 2007).

11. For more on reggae's concept of "riddims" and practice of "versioning," see, e.g., Peter Manuel and Wayne Marshall, "The Riddim Method: Aesthetics, Practice, and Ownership in Jamaican Dancehall," *Popular Music* 25, no. 3 (2006): 447–70.

12. Jorge L. Giovannetti, "Popular Music and Culture in Puerto Rico: Jamaican and Rap Music as Cross-Cultural Symbols," in *Musical Migrations Volume I: Transnationalism and Cultural Hybridity in Latin/o America*, ed. Frances R. Aparicio and Cándida F. Jáquez (New York: Palgrave Macmillan, 2003), 89.

13. *Blanquito* is the diminutive form of the word *blanco* (white). Though it can be used as a purely descriptive term for someone who is phenotypically white, in this case, though using the language of color, *blanquito* is a term that is class based as much as it is race based.

14. Frances Aparicio, *Listening to Salsa: Gender, Latin Popular Music and Puerto Rican Cultures* (Hanover, N.H.: University Press of New England, 1998), 69–82; *Cocolos y Roqueros*, film recording, directed by Ana María García (Pandora Films, 1992).

15. For an early elaboration of this argument, see Mayra Santos, "Puerto Rican Underground," *Centro* 8, nos. 1 and 2 (1996): 219–31.

16. As noted in Wayne Marshall's essay, reggaeton has been derisively described by some as "polka reggae." See also the 2005 thread "Reggaeton Smeggaeton," http://www.blackchat.co.uk/theblackforum/forum4/15744.html (accessed February 1, 2007); or any number of contentious discussions at dancehallreggae.com, e.g., http://dancehallreggae.com/forum/archive/index.php?t-51080.html (accessed January 25, 2008).

17. Jaime Torres Torres, "De espaldas a la tradición," *El Nuevo Día*, October 10, 2004; Jaime Torres Torres, "Ojo crítico al ritmo del reggaeton," *El Nuevo Día*, October 10, 2004.

18. Numerous other genres, such as salsa, have also generated spirited arguments regarding their origins and trajectory. See, e.g., Peter Manuel, "Puerto Rican Music and Cultural Identity: Creative Appropriation of Cuban Sources from Danza to Salsa," *Ethnomusicology* 38, no. 2 (spring/summer 1994): 249–80; Marisol Berríos-Miranda, " 'Con Sabor a Puerto Rico': The Reception and Influence of Puerto Rican Salsa in Venezuela," in *Musical Migrations Volume I: Transnationalism and Cultural Hybridity in Latin/o America*, ed. Frances R. Aparicio and Cándida F. Jáquez (New York: Palgrave Macmillan, 2003), 47–67; and Angel Quintero Rivera, *Salsa, sabor y control: Sociología de la música tropical* (Mexico City: Siglo XXI, 1998), 87–104.

19. Santos, "Puerto Rican Underground."

20. Again, for more on the practice of "versioning," see, e.g., Manuel and Marshall, "The Riddim Method."

21. For more on hip-hop's Caribbean influences and participation, see Raquel Z. Rivera, *New York Ricans from the Hip Hop Zone* (New York: Palgrave Macmillan, 2003); and Jeff Chang, *Can't Stop Won't Stop: A History of the Hip-Hop Generation* (New York: Picador, 2005), 7–88.

22. Kenneth Bilby, "The Caribbean as a Musical Region," in *Caribbean Contours*, ed. Sidney W. Mintz and Sally Price (Baltimore: Johns Hopkins University Press, 1985), 181–218; Ray Allen and Lois Wilcken, eds., *Island Sounds in the Global City: Caribbean Popular Music and Identity in New York* (Urbana: University of Illinois Press, 2001).

23. Santos, "Puerto Rican Underground"; Giovannetti, "Popular Music and Culture in Puerto Rico."

24. The exception is the cursory and independently published volume in Spanish by Raúl Moris García, *El rap vs. la 357: Historia del rap y reggaeton en Puerto Rico* (N.p., n.d. [2005]).

25. Ideally, we would have wanted to reprint many of the few existing essays on reggaeton, but space constraints have forced us to prioritize the publication of unpublished manuscripts. These previously published texts are listed in the bibliography, along with some key journalistic pieces on the subject.

26. This paper was presented at the Puerto Rican Studies Association Conference in 1998 and served as the basis for various journalistic articles by the author, but, as an academic paper, it remained unpublished.

27. *Bling'd: Blood, Diamonds, and Hip Hop*, film recording, directed by Raquel Cepeda (Article 19 Films and Djali Rancher Productions, 2007).

PART I
MAPPING
REGGAETON

From Música Negra to Reggaeton Latino

The Cultural Politics of Nation, Migration, and Commercialization

When Daddy Yankee's "Gasolina" galloped up the charts on a catchy chorus, some shifty snares, and a riff befitting a bullfight, it expressed as much a sense of where reggaeton had come from as where it might go. Though some detractors heard it as little more than the latest quasi-Caribbean commercial confection (and a rather sexist bit of ear and eye candy at that),[1] a closer listen, with ears attuned to the genre's aesthetic history, reveals a number of ways that the song embodies a complex history of social and sonic circuitry. In particular, if one attends more carefully to the *pista*, or track, propelling the lexically and musically suggestive vocals of Daddy Yankee and his eager foil, Glory, one can hear Luny Tunes' sleek, powerful production not only as a quintessential example of contemporary, commercial reggaeton style but as a musical text engaging with a long history of circulating sounds, people, and ideas about self and other, race and place.

One might hear such social and sonic circuitry in the explicitly electronic sounds of "Gasolina," which include brittle, chintzy, "preset" virtual instruments from such popular music software as Fruity Loops (or, as it has rebranded itself, FL Studio) as well as more sophisticated "synth patches" offering sounds, such as orchestral strings, with a greater verisimilitude. Ranging from bright and needling to low and buzzy, the track's interwoven synthesizer lines evoke engagements with contemporary hip-hop, pop and R&B, dancehall reggae, and even techno as they provide a dense harmonic texture for Yankee's sing-song, rapid-fire rap. Conjuring club culture, the track's crescendoing kick drums and periodic "breakdowns" seem more clearly borrowed from "trance" and dance anthems than from any of reggaeton's more typically cited "tropical" sources.[2] The harmonic movement of the track, shifting a semitone or half-step every other measure—especially with its galloping figures, adding 32nd note flourishes to propel the pista forward—may suggest to some, including listeners who first heard such clichés via the producers' namesake (i.e., Looney Tunes cartoons), the classic contours of bullfight music or pasodoble, as typified by Pascual Marquina Narro's well-worn sporting anthem, "España Cañí." Appearing to affirm such associations, Yankee boasts, "En la pista nos llaman los matadores" (On the track they call us the matadores). Figuring Spain in this manner, or Spanish colonial legacies (as mediated by pop culture fantasies), "Gasolina" not only features the harmonic movement and marchlike figures associated with bullfight music, it also employs, as do many contemporary reggaeton productions, a I-V or "oompah" style bassline, hence gesturing as well to the polka and other social dance forms that have long resounded across the colonial Americas (as can also be heard in Mexican *banda*).

Daddy Yankee's vocal style similarly embodies a range of forebears, from the nasally tinged projections of salsa *soneros* (or, for that matter, of *bomba* singers), to the double-time deliveries and lilting melodies of dancehall DJs, to the more complex rhyme schemes and speechlike flows of hip-hop MCs.[3] Accordingly, Yankee's lyrics touch on themes resonant with the race- and class-based concerns so central to these stylistic forebears—genres which, as we shall examine, have long informed reggaeton. The song's blatant sexual innuendo and apparently asymmetrical gender relations, for instance, could be heard as celebrating simple pleasures, affirming patriarchy, and challenging middle-class mores in a similar manner to hip-hop, reggae, or salsa. Suffice to say, though, for all its obvious qualities, Yankee's suggestive, central metaphor has been interpreted by audiences and observers to mean any number of things, from synecdoche for speed to an allusion to oral sex. Indeed, the song's inclusion on the compilation *Reggaeton Niños* (EMI Latin 2005) would seem to confirm its inherently multivalent character.[4] Unsurprisingly, in an era of gas hikes and instability in the Middle East, many heard "Gasolina" as a rather literal reference, including some surprisingly empathetic listeners in Iraq.[5]

But all these potential meanings only scratch the surface of the track's suggestive figurations. Indeed, for many listeners and dancers, it is no doubt the steady kick drum and syncopated snares, marking out reggaeton's trademark, bedrock rhythm, which primarily catches their ears and hips. Sometimes referred to as the *dembow*—recalling a connection to Bobby Digital's and Shabba Ranks's early '90s dancehall reggae recording "Dem Bow" (1991), a song and a *riddim* (i.e., backing track) which has profoundly shaped the sound of reggaeton—the snares in "Gasolina" play against the steady four-on-the-floor kick pattern, creating a 3 + 3 + 2 groove that cross-cuts as it reaffirms the downbeat emphasis of the track: *boom-ch-boom-chick boom-ch-boom-chick.*[6] Overlapping in rhythmic orientation (and embodied dance movement) with a wide variety of Caribbean genres, from salsa to *son* to reggae to soca, reggaeton's prevailing pattern allows the genre, for all its connections to hip-hop and reggae, to circulate as a regionally inflected form of global pop.

Attending more closely to the snares, the production also takes on a more particularly Puerto Rican character. Not only do the snares play a rhythmic role; perhaps more crucially they delineate the song's form while making direct, timbral connections to such foundational source materials for the genre as the *Dem Bow* and *Bam Bam* riddims—Jamaican dancehall "versions" (or instrumental sides) which became staples of the "proto-reggaeton," self-proclaimed *underground* scene in Puerto Rico during the 1990s. Rather than employing a single snare drum sample for the duration of the track, as most pop songs tend to, Luny Tunes alternate between a couple of particular, familiar snare sounds, shifting the sample every four measures to create a subtle, stylistically grounded sense of movement against the otherwise repetitive structures of the track (though it should be noted that the duo also manipulate the layers of synths in a similar, regular manner). By directly indexing the classic building blocks of reggaeton, the snares in "Gasolina" suggest connections to a long history of pistas and mixtapes which preceded the breakthrough pop smash and which remain as audible, palpable, if subtle remnants of an unbridled, underground, sample-based past in a genre that has since embraced slick synthesizers and commercial channels.

By beginning with this close reading of what many might dismiss as a disposable, overly commercialized example of the genre, I hope to have suggested some of the ways that contemporary reggaeton style emerges from a long-standing, technologically enabled practice of culturally charged musical engagement. Given how fraught discussions of reggaeton's origins and history tend to be, especially along the lines of nation and style (often putatively cast as national provenance), it is worth taking a closer look at the particular ways that so many social and sonic flows coalesced in Puerto Rico in the 1990s, connecting North, South, and Central America and the Caribbean in symbolic, sensual form. The aim of this essay is to examine reggaeton's aesthetic history to date, tying its shifting shapes and enduring forms to articulations of community relationships amidst shared living spaces and soundscapes. Considering such processes as migration, mediation, identification, and commercialization, I attempt to tease out how the social and sonic have been deeply intertwined in the history of the genre, dialectically informing each other in the music's production, circulation, and reception. Although I analyze verbal and visual texts in order to explore the correspondence between musical style, sartorial and linguistic symbolism, and the politics of culture, my focus here is on musical texts—primarily, the genre's pistas, the underlying tracks which propel reggaeton into the global mediascape and so suggestively embody its complex twists and turns. Reggaeton's driving rhythms and dense textures, I contend, give shape and form to myriad movements across the Western Hemisphere, with metropoles and labor centers serving as crucial sites for the music's creation and dissemination. Connecting musical style to cultural politics (as historically grounded and complexly cross-cut by race- and class-commitments, ideologies of color, gender, and nation, and market forces), I seek to lend you my ears—admittedly, the ears of an engaged outsider—as I hear the genre's musical development reflecting and informing the sonic and social flows of the postcolonial Americas.

FROM WHERE? THE LOADED QUESTION OF ORIGINS

Despite some serious contention, reggaeton's publicly negotiated narrative has tended to locate the music's genesis in Panama, while other places—from Jamaica to New York to Puerto Rico—remain significant, if secondary, sites for the genre's genealogy.[7] On the one hand, all of these places have played a pivotal role in the music's development. On the other, a number of important figures in the music's history have moved back and forth between various sites over the course of their careers, and so to some extent the most well-worn arguments about national provenance tend to overlook the imbrications of these places due to (circular) patterns of migration and the reach of mass media. The established narrative also tends to proceed in far too linear a fashion, for the interplay between hip-hop and reggae in Panama, Puerto Rico, and New York was rather simultaneous. As I will attempt to tease out, each of these symbolic sites might better be understood as representing both distinctive, local contexts as well as mobile, fluid sociocultural constellations. Depending on where one draws the lines around reggaeton, one draws different lines of community, and various observers, enthusiasts, and participants have sought to circumscribe or expand the genre's geographical-cultural borders according to incompatible if overlapping ideologies of race, class, nation, and the like. Given how heated such debates can become, it is imperative to attempt to clarify the relationships between these various central sites of reggae/ton history.[8] In this section, I will consider and appraise some of the more common connections made between the current, ascendant sound of the genre and its alleged antecedents, namely *reggae en español*, "meren-rap" and

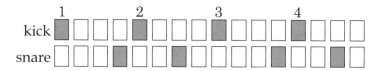

1. A skeletal sketch of reggaeton's *boom-ch-boom-chick*.

"merenhouse," bomba and *plena*, salsa and merengue, (Latin) hip-hop, and reggae itself.

Journalists and cultural nationalists (or pan-nationalists) alike have been eager to tie the sound of reggaeton to other Latin (or "tropical," to use the music industry term), Puerto Rican genres, or a combination of them. The explicit, if exceptional, appearance of Afro–Puerto Rican folk forms such as bomba on the recent recordings of Tego Calderón and La Sista has helped to encourage this perception. Similarly, the increasing presence in the last few years of musical figures (and direct digital samples) from salsa, merengue, and *bachata*—as will be discussed in some detail later in this essay—serves to fuel fantasies about reggaeton's inherent *latinidad*. Such perceptions of Latin or Afro-Latin musical identity in reggaeton are not without merit, though one would have to propose a more general theory of Latin-Caribbean musical influence and Afro-American (in the broadest sense) musical unity in order to reconcile history with the imaginary.[9] It is telling that some observers hear reggaeton's musical structures not as "Latin" at all, but as essentially Jamaican or African American in constitution, while others make reference to concepts such as *clave* in order to place the genre firmly in an Afro-Latin-Caribbean tradition. If we consider the prevailing, if not crucial, rhythmic template of reggaeton, we can see and hear how it overlaps with various regional styles (figure 1).[10]

The rhythmic pattern in figure 1—accenting a steady 4/4 pulse with 3 + 3 + 2 cross-rhythms—is ubiquitous in the Caribbean and, given some differences in emphasis and arrangement, can be heard in such diverse genres as reggae and *mento*, soca and calypso, salsa and son, merengue and "meringue," "konpa" and zouk.[11] Such overlapping structural features allow some listeners to hear reggaeton less as a "Yankee" thing, as a symbol of cultural imperialism, than as a return to Afro-Latin roots. With specific regard to Puerto Rican traditions, one could understand how reggaeton's persistent kick drum and polyrhythmic snares might dovetail in the musical imagination with plena's steady pulse and playful syncopations or with similarly structured, propulsive bomba rhythms such as *sicá, cuembé*, or *seis corrido*.[12]

In this sense, we might compare articulations between reggaeton and various Afro-Latin traditions with Jamaican poet Linton Kwesi Johnson's proposal for hearing the minimal rhythms of 1980s and '90s dancehall reggae—the very rhythms that underpin reggaeton—not so much as an example of a tech-heavy, northward-leaning corruption of Jamaican style but as a modern return to Afro-Jamaican folk forms:

> With the discovery of digital recording, an extreme minimalism has emerged—in the music of people like Steelie and Clevie, for example. On the one hand, this music is totally technological; on the other the rhythms are far more Jamaican: they're drawn from Etu, Pocomania, Kumina—African-based religious cults who provide the rhythms used by Shabba Ranks or Buju Banton. So despite the extent of the technology being used, the music is becoming even rootsier, with a resonance even for quite old listeners, because it echoes back to what they first heard in rural Jamaica.[13]

Whether or not one agrees with Johnson or, if you will, his hypothetical Puerto Rican brethren, this rhythmic resonance between dancehall's ultramodern rhythmic minimalism and traditional Afro-Caribbean forms seems at best a subconscious phenomenon. At worst, especially with regard to reggaeton, it encourages the uncritical reproduction of stereotypes about an essential Latin *sabor*, or "flavor," "hot" rhythms for "hot blooded" people, and so on. Such ideas can support strategic mobilizations of racial or ethnic identities in particular contexts and moments, but the historical record—not to mention the musical record—offers a much more precise, and less problematic, account of the connections between Jamaican reggae and reggaeton.

For all the resonance with Afro-(Latin-)Caribbean music and with Afro-diasporic music more generally, the predominant rhythmic orientation of reggaeton is derived directly, and quite audibly, from dancehall reggae (sometimes referred to as *ragga*, short for "raggamuffin," connoting the music's rough-and-tumble environs). Thus Jamaica—or more accurately, Jamaica via Panama and New York—merits no small acknowledgment in a genealogy of reggaeton aesthetics. (Explicit tribute is paid, of course, in the derivative name of the genre itself.) One can hear the direct link between these genres quite clearly in the dancehall-derived rhythms and riddims underlying both Panamanian and Puerto Rican recordings and in the borrowed melodies that propel so many of the "proto-reggaeton" recordings from the early and mid-1990s. Although "roots" reggae maintains a degree of popularity in the same sites where reggaeton now rules—such that one still finds "purist" scenes in which Bob Marley is the model—dancehall reggae's synthetic textures, dance tempos,

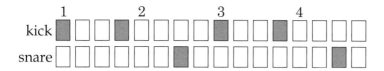

2. Dancehall reggae's minimal "bomp bomp."

rapid-fire rap, and minimalist focus on 3 + 3 + 2 cross-rhythms starkly de-marcated by heavy, synthesized drums, have much more strongly influenced what is today called reggaeton. Indeed, demonstrating a continued engage-ment with contemporary dancehall style, one occasionally hears in reggaeton pistas, rather than the rhythms illustrated in figure 1, a stripped-down pattern more characteristic of dancehall riddims from the mid- to late 1990s. Some-times referred to as the *bomp bomp*—an onomatopoeic phrase gesturing to the proclivity for tracing out the 3 + 3 + 2 by employing two kicks followed by a snare—dancehall's distinctive rhythmic profile might be represented as in figure 2.

In contrast, roots reggae's predominant groove, often called the "one-drop" in order to describe the spare but regular accent of the kick drum, leaves room for plenty of polyrhythmic activity around the downbeats (and, indeed, one can feel a great deal of 3:2 cross-rhythms in roots reggae's live band interplay and studio-engineered effects), but the prevailing feel is more duple—more easily counted in groups of 2s (or 4s) than 3s and 2s, as depicted in figure 3.

Beyond these structural rhythmic relationships, however, dancehall's up-take among young Panamanians and Puerto Ricans was no doubt related to its cultural connotations: its newness, its rudeness, and its close relationship to rap or hip-hop (and thus to the sounds and images of modernity, urbanity, and blackness). Whereas roots reggae preached pan-African liberation and consciousness raising, often couched in the millenarian language of Rastafari, dancehall reggae embraced more earthy and local concerns, themes resonant and in close conversation with contemporary hip-hop: crime, drugs, violence, sex, poverty, corruption. Indeed, affirming their relational character, dancehall and hip-hop have tended to travel together, heard outside their principal sites of production as two sides of the same coin.[14]

It is no mere coincidence that dancehall exploded in popularity in San Juan around the same time that the genre was enjoying one of its periodic crests of "crossover" popularity in New York and in the United States more generally. Dancehall's presence in urban soundscapes was strongly mediated by hip-hop, and the new sounds of Jamaica arrived in Puerto Rico less via Kingston than

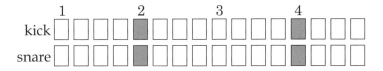

3. A (very) skeletal sketch of roots reggae's "one-drop."

from New York. Connected to the remarkable growth and influence of New York's Jamaican community during the 1980s—a decade during which Jamaican drug-trafficking posses dominated the trade across the Eastern Seaboard and representations of Jamaicans (in hip-hop and Hollywood alike) constructed a fearsome, ruthless, exotic portrait of the place and people— by the early 1990s dancehall reggae had become a ubiquitous and culturally charged feature of the New York soundscape.[15] Because of (and adding to) its resonance with contemporary hip-hop, videos by such Jamaican artists as Shabba Ranks and Super Cat appeared on *Yo! MTV Raps* and BET's *Rap City* alongside popular rap videos, while blocks of dancehall favorites worked their way into the sets of hip-hop DJs. It is worth noting that the very dancehall tracks which found favor among hip-hop DJs at this time—including such hits as "Murder She Wrote" (1992) by Chaka Demus & Pliers, "A Who Seh Me Dun" (1993) by Cutty Ranks, and "Hot This Year" (1993) by Dirtsman—not only tended to employ the *boom-ch-boom-chick* drum pattern which would become reggaeton's bedrock (again, see figure 1), but also popularized a set of riddims and other sonic signposts (from basslines to drum timbres to vocal melodies) which Puerto Rican producers and performers would incorporate into the deeply, densely referential *underground* recordings of the early 1990s, laying the musical foundations for what is today called reggaeton.

As will be discussed in the next section, the "proto-reggaeton" of the early and mid-1990s, as called by a number of other names, draws almost equally on reggae and hip-hop. Notably, many *reggaetoneros* (some of whom formerly called themselves *raperos* or *rapeadores*) cite hip-hop or rap as their primary point of reference, rather than reggae, and some go so far as simply to declare reggaeton a subgenre of hip-hop. The 2004 documentary *Chosen Few*, for example, includes a segment in which various reggaeton artists name hip-hop artists they consider to be important influences on their own development, among them Run DMC, Heavy D, Big Daddy Kane, and Kool G Rap, as well as— for Puerto Rican rap pioneer Lisa M—MC Lyte, Queen Latifah, and Salt-N-Pepa.[16] Notably these influences all date to the mid and late 1980s, marking a particular generational orientation and a formative period for the artists interviewed. The segment, as well as other testimony to reggaeton's hip-hop roots, stands in stark contrast to the conspicuous absence of any similar testimonials about the influence of (Jamaican) reggae artists. This somewhat lopsided genealogy might be explained, in part, by the fact that many current reggaeton stars began as aspiring hip-hop artists, rapping over hip-hop beats rather than reggae riddims, and only switched to a reggaeton format when it became clear that the burgeoning genre would provide a path to greater success. Thus, Polaco professes that hip-hop is "what I love to do and what I learned to do." Master Joe contends that the biggest influence on reggaeton has come from hip-hop artists who rap "en americano."[17] And Tego Calderón feels little compunction about describing himself in the following manner: "I sing hip-hop on top of a reggaeton beat. I don't know how to write in any other way." Tego's additional commentary on the tensions between hip-hop and reggaeton in Puerto Rico, accusing some local hip-hoppers (and reggaeton detractors) of wanting "to be real" while acting "blacker than Big Daddy Kane," shows that issues of race remain central to the discourse around urban popular music in Puerto Rico. Despite foregrounding negritude and racial solidarity in his own music and public image, Tego implies that reggaeton is something that Puerto Ricans of all stripes can embrace un-self-consciously ("This is our music," he adds), whereas hip-hop remains strongly marked as the domain of African Americans and thus tied to a particular notion of blackness (as he puts it, "You can't be more of a priest than the Pope").

Any discussion of reggaeton's relationship to hip-hop, however, would be incomplete without an acknowledgment of what is often referred to as "Latin rap" or "Latin hip-hop"—a subgenre distinguished not so much by musical style, which can vary widely within hip-hop's broad sonic palette, but by language. As Juan Flores and Raquel Z. Rivera have noted, rap in Spanish (and Spanglish), especially as performed by Puerto Ricans (and/or Nuyoricans), has long played a part in New York's hip-hop scene despite its marginalization in the hip-hop narrative.[18] Significantly, however, a good number of the most prominent exponents of Latin rap—including Mellow Man Ace, Kid Frost, and Cypress Hill—have been based in Los Angeles, with family ties to Mexico rather than (or as well as) the Latin Caribbean. The popularity of such acts in the early '90s served to validate Spanish-language rap at a crucial moment, offering inspiration for aspiring artists across the Spanish-speaking United States and Latin America more widely. Other ostensibly "Latin rappers" such as Big Pun, Fat Joe and the Terror Squad, and (more recently) N.O.R.E.—all based in and around New York—have acknowledged their latinidad as a significant part of their cultural, ethnic, or national identity, but they tend to rap predominantly, if not entirely, in English. Nevertheless, their popularity among Spanish-speaking and non-Spanish-speaking audiences has further affirmed the place of Latin rap in hip-hop, in some cases—and for some observers—"proving" that Latin MCs "could rhyme."[19] And yet, despite their common articulations of solidarity among people of color (e.g., freely employing the "n-word"), such performers have also consistently registered strong ambivalence around issues of race, often drawing or redrawing lines between New York's Latino and black communities despite the common racialization of Nuyoricans as black.[20] Lyrics such as the following fragment from Big Pun, for example, seem to reaffirm both hip-hop's putative blackness as well as the assumed nonblackness of "Latin rappers": "I'm the first Latin rapper to baffle your skull/master the flow/niggas be swearin' I'm blacker than coal [Cole]/like Nat King."[21]

In contrast to U.S.-based rappers of Latino heritage, many of whom might be better described as peppering their rhymes with Spanish words and phrases than actually rapping in Spanish, Puerto Rico's Vico C stands as a foundational figure, as the artist who first demonstrated that one could rap entirely and compellingly in Spanish (if perhaps peppered with the occasional English phrase or hip-hop slang). Although other Puerto Rican rappers, including Rubén DJ, also emerged in the mid- to late 1980s, far and away Vico C is cited by raperos and reggaetoneros alike as the pioneer of *rap en español*. In addition to releasing a number of popular recordings of his own (including the 1989 touchstone, "La Recta Final"), he also played a strong role as a producer and ghostwriter, assisting in the early careers of other performers in the Puerto Rican rap (and pop) scene, including Lisa M, Francheska, and El Comandante. It is additionally notable that Vico C has participated in the reggae/ton movement since its underground days—appearing, for example, on *The Noise 7* and its accompanying video (1997)—showing again the degree to which reggaeton not only engages with but emerges from (and blurs into) the local hip-hop scene in Puerto Rico, despite deep and enduring fissures between the two scenes.[22]

Not surprisingly, Vico C shares his compatriots' ideas about reggaeton's basis in hip-hop, describing the genre (in the *Chosen Few* documentary) as "essentially hip-hop but with a flavor more compatible to the Caribbean." While maintaining that the two are of the same essence, he demonstrates the main difference between hip-hop and reggaeton by beatboxing brief examples of each genre's quintessential musical style.[23] In contrast to the 3 + 3 + 2 cross-rhythms that underpin reggaeton, Vico C's representation of a standard hip-hop rhythm is, rather accurately (and audibly), more "duple" in character—that is, more oriented toward a metric accent heard and felt in groups of 2 or

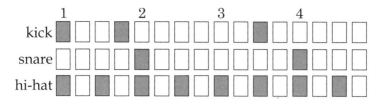

4. Vico C's version of a standard hip-hop beat.

4—a "feel" produced by the steady snares on the backbeat, anchoring the groove against the syncopations of the kick drum, as shown in figure 4.

This essential difference is not an insignificant one. Reggaeton's prevailing rhythmic orientation derives rather directly from dancehall reggae and as such overlaps with a great number of other Caribbean (dance) genres. Indeed, it is reggaeton's danceability, its dance-centric character—as achieved through the genre's 3 + 3 + 2 snares and 4/4 kicks—which distinguishes it from hip-hop for a good number of fans and practitioners and which often serves crucially to "Caribbeanize" what otherwise would be heard simply as Latin hip-hop. A number of interviewees in the *Chosen Few* documentary, for example, distinguish reggaeton from hip-hop by noting that the former is more of a *baile*-centric genre, more appropriate for couple dancing than "b-boying" or break-dancing, where the focus (for many listeners or clubgoers) is more often the beat than the lyrics.

The conventional story of reggaeton typically follows Vico C's towering example with a discussion of another exemplar of Spanish-language "rap," a Panamanian-born dancehall DJ (i.e., a rapping vocalist, in reggae parlance) who, in a nod to the power of Panama's military dictators, dubbed himself El General.[24] Panama's links to Jamaica, and hence to reggae, have long passed into reggaeton lore, with El General serving as a prominent symbol of Panama's important place in the story despite the ways that his own transnational narrative complicates too neat an account of origins and outposts. Invocations of the Panamanian roots of reggaeton are, often, all too facile. Typically taking the form of a brief mention of migrant laborers moving from Jamaica to Panama around the turn of the twentieth century, such citations bolster some rather bold assumptions about the transmission of culture between these places, often ignoring the fact that Jamaicans worked and lived side by side with large numbers of people from across the Anglo- and Franco-Caribbean. Many accounts erroneously imply that Jamaicans "brought reggae" to Panama in the early twentieth century, well before the genre came into being, or, similarly anachronistic, that they emigrated to work on the Panama Canal during the 1970s.[25] In contrast to such conjecture, studies of Jamaican migration and nationhood might better inform an understanding of the movements and connections between the Caribbean and Central America, as well as the sociocultural implications thereof. Indeed, for all the claims (and dismissals) that reggae purists level at reggaeton, it is important to note that cultural influence is rarely unidirectional and that longstanding circuits of migration to the Latin Caribbean and to North, Central, and South America have strongly shaped Jamaican culture.[26] In his influential work on Jamaican national identity, *Mirror Mirror*, Rex Nettleford notably names Panama as a salient site in the modern Jamaican imagination. "Jamaicans are a people who are constantly exposed to external influences," argues Nettleford,

> whose economic system traditionally depends on the caprice of other people's palates, whose values are largely imported from an alien set of experiences, and whose dreams and hopes have, at one time or another, been rooted either in a neighboring Panama, Cuba or Costa Rica, in big brother America and sometimes in Canada, a Commonwealth cousin.[27]

Shoring up this assertion with yet another reference to the country, Nettleford contends that Jamaicans have been "a migrating people ever since the late nineteenth century when the first Panama Canal project was started." He marshals some striking comparative evidence for such a claim: "Between the 1880s and 1920, net emigration from Jamaica amounted to about 146,000—46,000 went to the U.S.A., 45,000 to Panama, 22,000 to Cuba (to work in sugar), and other countries like Costa Rica (for railroad building and banana cultivation) drew some 43,000."[28] Similarly, the anthropologist Deborah Thomas, in discussing the role that Jamaicans' "increased mobility" played in local notions of nation, notes that prior to 1911, when Cuba and the United States began to attract the majority of migrant workers, Panama received 62 percent of all Jamaican emigrants.[29]

For all the assumptions about the primacy of Jamaican cultural influence in Panama, the degree to which Afro-Panamanian musical culture has been shaped by Jamaican forms and practices is striking, especially given that the canal construction projects first led by France and then by the United States attracted migrant labor from across the Caribbean, including significant numbers of workers from Trinidad and Tobago, Barbados, Martinique, and Guadeloupe. Such a remarkable degree of influence, however, is not incommensurate with what might be seen as a kind of late twentieth-century Jamaican cultural hegemony across the Anglo-Caribbean and the African diaspora more generally, especially with regard to youth culture and counterculture.[30] Even so, it is important to note that prior to reggae's global heyday in the 1970s, when the genre found favor even outside the major sites of Jamaican migration, Afro-Panamanian popular music was heavily based around calypso (popularized by Trinidadians and Jamaicans alike), as performed by such local favorites as Lord Cobra and Lord Panama, whose names nod to the calypso tradition in the same way that Panamanian reggae artists would later crown themselves after various dancehall DJs. By the late 1970s, calypso in Panama had been largely supplanted by soca—a more modern version of the Trinidadian sound, engaging with American R&B as well as Indo-Trinidadian styles—and by reggae, which at that point was still defined by roots-style "one-drop" rhythms.[31] Largely based in the urban contexts of Colón and Panama City, some of the earliest proponents of Panamanian reggae—and hence some of the first to perform Spanish-language reggae—included such touted pioneers as Renato y las 4 Estrellas (one of whom was Edgardo Franco, a.k.a. El General), Nando Boom, and Chicho Man.[32]

Because of such strong, direct links to Jamaica and the Anglo-Caribbean, the embrace and transformation of reggae in Panama are in some sense rather different from the parallel processes in Puerto Rico, where reggae's presence was largely mediated via New York (and hip-hop). Such a crucial difference, however, should not obscure the degree to which reggae in both places has served a local cultural politics based on a similar articulation of race, class, and generation. Nor should it efface the ways that Puerto Rican reggae/ton has influenced the Panamanian scene—in circular fashion—since itself emerging, in part, out of engagements with the reggae recordings of such performers as El General. Typically referred to in Panama simply as "reggae" or localized as *plena* (not to be confused with the Puerto Rican genre) or *bultrón*, Panama's Jamaican-derived popular music was also sometimes called *petróleo*, a descriptor—not unlike *melaza* in Puerto Rico (discussed in detail in the next section)—which strongly signified the perceived and projected blackness of the genre and its adherents.[33] Although roots reggae remains popular in Panama, since the early '80s dancehall reggae, as in Jamaica, has dominated the scene. Indeed, this roots-to-dancehall dynamic illustrates the degree to which reggae in Panama has proceeded in step with reggae in Jamaica, often quite audibly—that is, through the consistent production of Spanish-language cover versions of contemporary reggae hits (typically over replayed versions of the original Jamaican riddims).[34] In comparison, one finds far fewer cover songs, melodic allusions, or re-licked riddims in, say, today's Puerto Rican reggaeton scene than in contemporary Panamanian reggae or plena. This would seem to confirm Tego Calderón's assertion, even as he acknowledges the inspiring models of such "purists" (as he calls them) as Nando Boom and El General, that the Panamanian scene is "more an emulation of dancehall" than Puerto Rico's reggae-derived music.[35]

Panamanian reggae's "emulation of dancehall" is certainly audible in the early '90s recordings of El General and his compatriots, and it is worth noting that such reverent remakes would play a strong role in shaping the nascent (dancehall) reggae scene in Puerto Rico. A compilation issued by Columbia Records at the peak of New York's Panamanian-led reggae en español movement, *Dancehall Reggaespañol* (1991), serves as an instructive document, emphasizing the role that cover versions played in this realm of production by pairing "Spanish reggae" tracks by the likes of El General, Nando Boom, Marcony, and Rude Girl (La Atrevida) with the Jamaican recordings (by Super Cat, Cutty Ranks, Ninja Man, Little Lenny, and others) which provided the models for these Panamanian performers' faithful translations.[36] Hence one hears quite clearly how El General's "Pu Tun Tun" adapts Little Lenny's "Punnany Tegereg" or how Marcony's "Mini Mini" translates Fab 5's song by the same name. Typically, the riddims over which these covers were performed sound almost identical to the accompanimental tracks underlying the originals, but a closer listen reveals that they are often very convincing rerecordings of the riddims—"re-licks" or "do-overs," in reggae parlance. Sometimes the only distinction is a slight timbral difference in the synthesizer or drum sounds. In other cases the riddims are clearly pitched up or down into another key, presumably to suit the vocal range of the artist performing the cover, while the layers of the riddim—the basslines, keyboard chords, and drum tracks—are manipulated in a different manner in order to highlight certain passages in the new versions. Although such *versioning* is consistent with the reggae tradition in general and had been put into practice in Panama for some time, the use (and licensing) of such riddims on these New York recording sessions was facilitated by producer Karl Miller, a Jamaican New Yorker who had formerly worked at the Queens-based reggae label, VP Records. Indeed, a year before being reissued by Columbia and Prime/BMG respectively, El General's "Pu Tun Tun" and "Te Ves Buena" (a remake of Shabba Ranks's "Gal Yuh Good") were both released on Miller's own imprint, Gold Disc Records, and distributed by VP.[37]

The tracks on *Dancehall Reggaespañol* not only attest to a close engagement with contemporary Jamaican reggae; they also bear witness, yet again, to the crucial role that New York has played throughout the history of the music now known as reggaeton. As a major Caribbean "cosmopole," to invoke Orlando Patterson's description of the place's "ecumenical" and Caribbeanized culture,

Little Lenny

Rude Girl (La Atrevida)

Marcony

Arzu

La Diva

5. Image from *Dancehall Reggaespañol* liner notes.

New York offered aspiring artists such as El General various opportunities for recording and performing, and its status as a major media hub facilitated the broader circulation of such music, including to Puerto Rico.[38] Across the soundscapes of New York's boroughs—where Panamanians, Puerto Ricans, Jamaicans, and African Americans often lived (and were racialized) side by side—such genres as reggae and hip-hop resonated powerfully as "black musics" which, for all the lines still drawn between such groups, could embody and express new articulations of community. The liner insert for *Dancehall Reggaespañol* underscores the strong Afro-Latin orientation of early New York–based Spanish reggae, depicting, alongside Jamaican artist Little Lenny, the black-and-proud faces of Afro-Panamanian and Afro-Honduran reggae artists, including a shot of Marcony sporting the sort of Afrocentric headgear very much in vogue at that time in New York (figure 5).

And yet, despite such obvious connections between, as the liner notes put it,

"bilingual brethren," a quotation from Rude Girl implies that contested notions of national cultural propriety—which continue to animate discussions of
reggaeton today—could still prove a potent source of division: "Jamaicans like
to think they're the only ones to come off with reggae, but we in Panama have
been chanting deejay music for years."[39]

It is somewhat perplexing that the question of reggaeton's Panamanian
"roots" remains such a sensitive, hotly debated topic, especially given the
degree of documentation and firsthand testimony confirming the connection.
Panama remains an originary touchstone in the established reggaeton narrative, of course, as countless journalistic accounts and popular documentaries
such as the *Chosen Few* consistently reaffirm by starting with the story of
Jamaican workers in Panama. As the *Chosen Few* bears witness, plenty of
Puerto Rican reggae/ton innovators celebrate the foundational influence that
artists such as El General had on the scene there, including DJ Negro, who
recounts spinning the instrumental versions of reggae en español recordings
while local vocalists performed new lyrics over them—a practice he says developed by necessity since Panamanian performers proved too difficult to contact
in order to book for shows. Tellingly, for some Panamanian reggae enthusiasts,
reggaeton is simply "la plena Puertoriquena," a reaccented version of an essentially Panamanian cultural product.[40] And while this may not be an invalid
interpretation, it does tend to underplay the degree to which Puerto Rican
vocalists and producers radically revisioned (and re*versioned*) Panama's more
reverent approach to the reggae tradition.

Beyond nationalist chauvinism, one reason for such prolonged contestation and confusion may be the various ways in which these New York–based
Spanish reggae recordings, largely performed by Panamanians, came to circulate in Puerto Rico. In addition to finding their way into the island's soundscape via such ear-to-the-ground cultural arbiters as DJ Negro, who began
operating the Noise nightclub in 1990, the sounds of Spanish reggae were also
brokered in a somewhat top-down manner by the promoter and producer
Jorge Oquendo and his "meren-rap" project. Released in 1991 on the heels of
Karl Miller's Gold Disc releases of El General's Spanish reggae hits, Oquendo's
Meren-Rap compilation brought together established merengue musicians
and rising Puerto Rican rap stars. Issued on his own label imprint, Prime
Entertainment (and, significantly, distributed by BMG), the disc was less a
representation of actual, on-the-ground musical practice than a calculated
attempt to develop a Latin pop/rap hybrid which might appeal to a wide
audience—not just rap and reggae fans, but devotees of merengue as well
as Latin pop, freestyle, house, and other "Latin" or "tropical" urban dance

genres.[41] Notably, the majority of songs on *Meren-Rap* were written and produced by Vico C.

In addition to tracks that simply add rap vocals and electronic drums to otherwise typical merengue arrangements (e.g., "Meren Rapero") and a number of merengue numbers with seemingly no rap or reggae referents ("Otra Vez"), other songs present a more explicit attempt to fuse contemporary pop and "black" music with merengue. Alongside merengue-inspired piano figures and horn blasts, Brewley M.C.'s "Nena Sexy," for instance, employs a number reggae's sonic signatures, from a "skanking" keyboard pattern (i.e., accenting the offbeat) to the vocalist's dancehall-inflected, double-time rap style. And Lisa M's "El Pum Pum," a response record in the tradition of reggae's "counteraction tunes," not only recontextualizes the melody from El General's "Pu Tun Tun" (i.e., Little Lenny's "Punnany Tegereg") over a merengue piano riff; it begins by invoking the drum-break introduction to Bell Biv Devoe's R&B hit "Poison" (1990). Significantly, *Meren-Rap* also includes a breakbeat-propelled hip-hop remix of El General's "Te Ves Buena," juxtaposing synthesized handclaps playing a 3:2 clave, a chunky sample marking the offbeat in reggae style, a dominant "dubby" bassline, and various sampled vocal interjections.[42] Notably, as a dense, sample-based, hip-hop-inflected attempt at a reggae-style track, the remix of "Te Ves Buena" perhaps comes closest to sounding like the productions soon to emerge from the parallel, grassroots development of rap-reggae fusions in San Juan's clubs and barrios and no doubt helped to affirm the possibilities of such a hybrid genre.

Because of meren-rap's veritable popularity but debatable influence, the studio experiment might best be understood as playing a paradoxically important yet marginal role in the story of reggaeton. The *Meren-Rap* album indeed made a splash on the island, and the artists associated with Oquendo's experiment became visible and audible in the Puerto Rican mainstream. At the same time, meren-rap proved an utterly ephemeral and artificial phenomenon.[43] Without grassroots support the hybrid genre was soon supplanted, at least in what came to be known as the *underground* scene (in contrast to the mainstream), by a similar sort of fusion which, instead of Latin or "tropical" signifiers, tended to foreground the black, urban, transnational sounds of hip-hop and reggae. In contrast to the vibrant if raw recordings produced by and for lower-class youth and circulated locally and informally via mixtapes (as will be discussed shortly), *Meren-Rap* sounds overproduced, too "slick" and too "clean," and rather bourgeois despite the involvement of reputable rappers such as Vico C. Targeted primarily at a commercial, middle-class market rather than a street-level audience, meren-rap failed to inspire a new generation of

Puerto Ricans (and Nuyoricans) who had grown up with hip-hop and for whom the sounds of Jamaica provided a sufficiently Caribbean anchor for their urbane articulations. Nonetheless, Oquendo's experiment presented possibilities that would later be embraced, a full decade later, by yet another generation of producers, who—following hip-hop's ascension to global pop—would reverse their focus from the underground to the commercial sphere and seek to reach, once again, a mainstream, pan-Latin audience in part by invoking the "tropical."

But before discussing reggaeton's turn (back) toward signifiers of Latinness, such that it could eventually project itself into the U.S. and global mainstream as "Reggaeton Latino," it is imperative to appreciate how the genre first crystallized in Puerto Rico in the early and mid-1990s as *música negra* and *melaza*, *dembow*, and *underground*—terms which directly marked and promoted the music as connected to a particular racial and class formation. Although the various antecedents considered above inform and resonate to varying degrees with the San Juan *underground* scene of the 1990s, the unique and pronounced mix of hip-hop and reggae which defined the nascent genre and provided the basis for what would come to be called reggaeton offers the strongest evidence for Puerto Rico's claims on the genre—Jamaica's and Panama's notwithstanding—as a locally inflected and in some ways quintessentially Puerto Rican cultural product. By exploring the distinctive character of early to mid-1990s Puerto Rican reggae-rap fusions, I hope to clarify some of the genealogical relationships which remain the subject of intense debate in public discourse around reggaeton.

FROM "DEM BOW" TO DEMBOW:
MELAZA CRYSTALLIZES UNDERGROUND

Listening to Puerto Rico's underground music of the 1990s, one hears a series of "flip-tongue," sing-song vocalists performing risqué rhymes over dense collages made from contemporary reggae riddims and hip-hop beats.[44] A number of familiar loops and more fragmentary samples cycle in and out of the half-hour to hour-long mixes put together by pioneering producers such as DJ Playero, DJ Negro, DJ Nelson, and their colleagues.[45] Combining dozens of resonant samples, the pistas that drive such nonstop sessions tug constantly at the strings of musical memory, in many cases providing a suggestive, propulsive alternation between the distinctive "feels" of hip-hop and dancehall grooves (see figures 2 and 4)—an approach to form still faintly audible in the shifting snares of today's synth-driven hits.[46] Such chopped-and-rearranged loops of recognizable fragments hence provide a rather resonant, dynamic sort of accompaniment. Adding to the allusive mix, such local, Spanish-slanging MCs as Ranking Stone, Alberto Stylee, Maicol and Manuel, O.G. Black and Master Joe, Baby Rasta and Gringo, Ivy Queen, and Daddy Yankee, among others, frequently propel their verses by intoning one of the many familiar melodic contours that Jamaican dancehall DJs have endlessly reworked since the early to mid-1980s.[47] Especially for San Juan youth, these deeply referential recordings thus engage and embody, as they directly index, the popular and no doubt political *música negra* (as it was called in song lyrics), or "black music," which so powerfully resounded across the shared soundscapes of Puerto Rico and New York, of home and home-away-from-home (though which is which, of course, becomes increasingly difficult to tease out in the contexts of circular migration and "commuter nationhood").[48]

It is no surprise that the terms artists and audiences used to describe the Spanish-language rap-reggae hybrids produced in Puerto Rico during the 1990s themselves index a number of significant, overlapping relations and positions. Such terms as *música negra* and *melaza* (i.e., "molasses," signifying race as sugar products do in postplantation societies) served to express an explicit cultural politics of blackness within a context of enduring racism and *blanqueamiento*.[49] Calling the music *underground* and *dembow*, on the other hand—not to mention *rap* or *reggae* (both of which were also common)—signaled an articulation with such putatively non–Puerto Rican forms as hip-hop and dancehall and therefore to New York, the Afro-Caribbean, and the African diaspora. Moreover, the term *underground* also embodied the music's marginalized (and proud!) status vis-à-vis mainstream Puerto Rican economy, culture, and society. But although terms such as *underground* and *dembow* were derived from hip-hop and reggae, they took on rather local meanings, signifying that San Juan's distinctive musical fusion was, as Raquel Z. Rivera observed in early 1995, "una fusión tan intensa de rap con reggae que no puede ser clasificada como una cosa o la otra" (such an intense fusion of rap and reggae that it could not be classified as one or the other).[50]

Despite being derived from other genres, the terms used to describe the distinctive yet emergent genre necessarily took on expanded and enriched meanings in Puerto Rico. The term *underground* (sometimes shortened to *under*) came directly out of hip-hop discourse, where it already enjoyed some currency as a militant mode of self-identification for artists eschewing the commercialization of rap music (associating such "selling out" with a capitulation to mainstream aesthetics and a movement away from a hardcore stance vis-à-vis copyright, local and national politics, or street authenticity). But whereas self-proclaimed *underground* hip-hop groups in New York often still participated in the commercial economy via "independent" labels (frequently distributed by major labels), in San Juan *underground* referred not simply to musical style or ideologies of authenticity but to actual market position. In the early '90s, Puerto Rican *underground* recordings literally circulated outside of formal commercial channels and centralized modes of mass production. Dubbed from cassette to cassette after an initial, small run of master tapes, the mixes moved somewhat easily through an informal economy until late 1994, when their appearance in certain "aboveground" stores allowed the authorities, spurred by Christian "watchdog" organizations such as Morality in Media, to commence a series of high-profile, controversial, and essentially illegal seizures.[51] (Raquel Z. Rivera cites DJ Playero as noting that he produced only around twenty copies of each mixtape in the early days; of course, these "masters" were rapidly reproduced within and outside the scene, e.g., in New York, Connecticut, the Dominican Republic, etc.)[52] Moreover, even after flirting with local commercial channels, reggaeton's reputation as the "obscene" music of the underclass meant that it had little access to mainstream media channels (i.e., radio and television) before it proved itself commercially viable beyond the underground market. Although the San Juan–based *In the House* magazine offered regular coverage of the music beginning in 1995, for example, as with reggae in Jamaica (which did not have a dedicated place on local airwaves until the launch of Irie FM in 1990) it was not until much later that the genre was embraced by mainstream media: San Juan's Mix 107.7 FM began its "24/7" reggaeton format in 1999 through the efforts of DJ Nelson and DJ Coyote.[53]

The term *dembow* offers a similar example of resignification. A minimal drum track with a hint of Latinesque percussion and a unique timbral profile, Bobby "Digital" Dixon's *Dem Bow* riddim—i.e., the instrumental underlying Shabba Ranks's "Dem Bow" (1991), performed and recorded by the production duo Steely and Clevie—became such a ubiquitous feature of *underground* mixes that, especially in the mid- to late 1990s, one of the most common terms used to describe the genre was simply *dembow*. Before long, at least for some, the term came to refer more generally to the music's prevailing rhythmic structure, the *boom-ch-boom-chick* that has defined Puerto Rican reggae/ton since the early '90s (see figure 1). Notably, the term has been so resignified that it has also, for the most part, lost much of its connection to the idea of "bowing" or giving in to the forces of oppression and corruption—ranging from the forces of neocolonialism to "deviant" sexual practices (e.g., oral and anal sex)—which Shabba Ranks decries on the original recording. Hence, while early Spanish cover versions of the song such as Nando Boom's "Ellos

Benia" (1991) or El General's "Son Bow" (1991) appear to endorse Shabba's conflation of macho sexuality and racialized social struggle, later versions, such as Wisin and Yandel's "Dem Bow" (2003), seem to imply that the term simply signifies dancing to the distinctive beat or otherwise participating in the reggaeton scene.[54] The concatenated form I employ here (after popular use, though orthographies vary widely) is thus meant to signify this transformation of the term's meaning: from a specific allusion to a Jamaican precedent, to a rather resonant bit of local argot describing San Juan's unique approach to reggae production (with a hip-hop twist).

This is an approach and transformation signaled sonically as well, for the instrumental from Shabba's "Dem Bow" has, aside perhaps from early club and home-studio jam sessions, rarely been employed for *underground* productions in its original form. Abstracted instead into a particular rhythmic pattern (slightly altered from if faithful to the original) and a set of specific drum timbres (as directly sampled from the *Dem Bow* riddim and, tellingly, its reggae en español variations[55]), the *Dem Bow* came to stand as a flexible set of musical tools which could be used in combination with other resonant signifiers while retaining a distinctive sonic profile (hence remaining audible in the vast majority of reggaeton productions, even today). Contemporary collections of reggaeton instrumentals such as *Pistas de Reggaeton Famosas* (Flow Music, 2005), for example, often contain one or more versions of the *Dem Bow*: the "original" or "classic" version—a two-bar loop based closely on Dennis "the Menace" Thompson's version of Bobby Digital's dancehall instrumental (as heard on Nando Boom's "Ellos Benia") but often reduced to pure percussion (i.e., not containing the keyboards or bass from the original); and a more recent version, e.g., "Dembow 2004," which might employ different sounds and other effects but audibly maintains the riddim's well-worn rhythms and timbres. Notably, part of what makes the *Dem Bow* distinguishable from other reggae sources is an element often identified, especially in its digital and Internet circulation, as the *timbal* (presumably from *timbales*), a short percussion sample that plays an easily recognizable, two-measure rhythmic pattern which some might hear as congruent with a 3:2 clave (see figure 6).

As indicated in figure 6, the standard *Dem Bow* pattern in reggaeton productions also features a tonally rich bass drum, accenting beats 1 and 3 atop an underlying, "dryer" kick drum which marks each beat of every bar. Together or in various combinations, these musical signifiers can suggest the presence of the *Dem Bow* in a particular pista. Depending on the whims of producers and the extent to which they want to foreground the riddim's familiar sound, the component elements of the *Dem Bow* might take more or less pronounced forms.

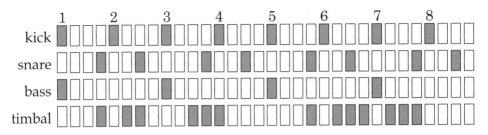

6. The basic elements of Puerto Rico's localized *Dem Bow*.

Like the terms themselves, then, the sounds of *underground, dembow, melaza*, and so on, also served to signal, for all their putative foreignness, a local orientation (if always already transnational). Embodying the process of localizing the foreign-but-familiar, the influential mixtapes issued by DJ Negro for *The Noise* album series and by Playero for his eponymous franchise offer a set of sonic snapshots vividly illustrating the ways melaza crystallized in San Juan in the mid-1990s. The two series are remarkably similar in aesthetic approach. Indeed, the creation of reggaeton's foundational style and its veritable canon of samples, including the elevation of the *Dem Bow* to basic building block, can largely be attributed to the long shadows cast by Playero and *The Noise*. Mixing song into song, on beat and without pause, their mixtapes resembled live DJ sets, not unlike the sort that might be played by a hip-hop DJ or a dancehall selector. In contrast to hip-hop or dancehall, however, songs recorded by outside producers would not be featured (though they could be sampled); instead the mixtapes showcased the work of the producers and DJs who made them. Accordingly, the mixes were often identified simply by the name of the producer or series and given a number, though sometimes each side of the tape would also get its own, more suggestive title, in many cases gesturing to dancehall or hip-hop (and, yet, often signaling a certain distance via minor misspellings): for example, "Dance Hall Mix" and "Ragga Moofin Mix" are the individually labeled sides on *Playero 37* (ca. 1992), while "Non Stop Reegae" and "Raagga Mix to Mix" describe the contents of *Playero 38* (ca. 1994). Affirming and informing the music's projections of a modern, urban, Afro–Puerto Rican aesthetic, the artwork promoting the tapes often employed graffiti-style lettering and featured city skylines (as on *Playero 37*; see figure 7) and lots of images of stylish, and often dark-skinned, denizens of the underground. On the cover of *Playero 38* (figure 8), for instance, a dreadlocked character sports an Africa pendant, a rather popular hip-hop accoutrement in the early '90s (as also depicted, you might recall, on Marcony's headgear in figure 5).

7. Artwork for *Playero 37*.
8. Artwork for *Playero 38*.

As truly underground music (economically speaking), based on live performance practice (where instrumental reggae recordings provided the accompaniment for MCs), and deeply informed by the musical ethics of reggae's version-based "riddim method" as well as hip-hop's sample-based collages, the recordings produced by the likes of DJ Playero, DJ Negro, and DJ Nelson advanced an approach utterly unconcerned with the strictures of copyright or bourgeois attitudes toward ownership. The music brims with references to resonant musical texts. In measure after measure, one hears layer upon layer of samples from the hip-hop and dancehall hits of the day. Taken together with the allusive tunes and texts of vocalists who often quote lyrics or borrow melodies from the same familiar sources being sampled, the music directly and suggestively indexes New York. Remixing the sounds of home-away-from-home for San Juan youth, *underground* could thus express forms of Puerto Rican–ness commensurate with the vistas (and pistas) of a new generation. The degree of intertextuality on such recordings is not only rather remarkable in its own right, then; it is also charged with significance. A brief guided tour of an early, representative production by DJ Playero, I hope, may suffice to impart some sense of this deeply meaningful intertextuality.[56]

Given that *Playero 38* is sometimes cited as having cemented the centrality of the *Dem Bow* in San Juan's "Spanish reggae" scene, the "Raagga Mix to Mix" side's hip-hop-inflected opening offers a telling reminder of the genre's strong connections to rap as well as reggae.[57] Beginning with a "wah-wah" guitar figure and the telltale snaps-and-crackles of aged vinyl (and thus explicitly embodying a sample-based approach), the introduction bears the unmistakable sound of early 1990s, New York–style hip-hop, especially when a jazzy bass riff and then a truncated siren and dusty breakbeat bring the song into a solidly swinging funk. Along with the bass enters a looped voice, slightly distant in the mix and punctuated by the siren sound: "La gente sabe/que somos de la calle" (the people know/that we're from the streets), it repeats, insistently, before delivering a rhyming punch line, "mira como goza/cuando traigo un mensaje" (see how they like/when I bring a message). Before long the vocalist, Manuel, begins rapping in a "flip-tongue" style, as it is sometimes called in Jamaica, doubling up the syllabic syncopation in the manner of dancehall DJs. His change in flow accompanies the appearance of a short but recognizable snippet from "900 Number," a two-measure saxophone loop and a rather familiar reference for hip-hop devotees. Produced by Mark the 45 King, a hip-hop producer based in New York, the riff—as sampled from Marva Whitney's funky R&B single "Unwind Yourself" (1967)—became well-known in hip-hop after being featured repeatedly on *Yo! MTV Raps* from 1989 to 1995 as the backing for the "Ed Lover Dance." Although the sample here is but a beat long, it would be unmistakable for many listeners, especially as a recurring favorite of *underground* producers at this time. As Manuel's partner-in-rhyme, Maicol, makes an entrance, the duo begin trading off rhymes which directly link "la casa" (with its connotations of hip-hop and home alike), "la raza" (signifying racial commitments), and "melaza."[58] Highlighting the articulation of such symbols, the texture of the music changes radically, dropping everything out save for the dusty wah-wah loop and placing the refrain in the foreground: "en la casa, para la raza" they repeat three times, before delivering the punch line, "Maicol y Manuel que te canta melaza" (Maicol and Manuel who sing melaza).

Notably, the punch line—and, significantly, the reference to *melaza*—is followed immediately by the entrance of *dembow*-style drums, and the dancehall-derived *boom-ch-boom-chick* propels their chant forward. As the duo continue their enthusiastic interplay, alluding to dancehall reggae melodies (e.g., Shabba Ranks's "Ting-a-Ling")—as well as, in another nod to hip-hop and reggae tradition, nursery rhymes (i.e., "London Bridge")—the underlying track mixes reggae style with hip-hop style, augmenting the relatively sparse 3 + 3 + 2 drum pattern and synthesized bassline with the sort of truncated siren sample popularized by Cypress Hill, as heard in the introduction. Playero (and in this case, his coproducer, Nico Canada) create a fair amount of variation in the track by pulling the discrete layers—kicks, snares, bass, and other samples—in and out of the texture, a technique for manipulating form rather related to dub-mixing in reggae.[59] In the meantime, Maicol and Manuel string together various routines and, indeed, employ some of the same lyrics they would also record on contemporary mixtapes issued by The Noise, demonstrating once again a notion of originality closer to reggae's and hip-hop's traditions of reuse, allusion, and versioning than, say, the status quo for other pop music—and perhaps even more liberal about reusing materials than such antecedents. About five minutes into the track, after a spirited exchange between the MCs, one hears the repeated line—lest one miss it—"esta (es) la música negra" (this is black music).

To fast-forward a bit, Maicol and Manuel are followed by a series of vocalists who perform their own allusive, resonant rhymes over a constantly but often subtly shifting backing. For instance, elements from the similarly popular *Bam Bam* riddim (as produced by Sly and Robbie and popularized on Chaka Demus & Pliers' crossover hit, "Murder She Wrote" [1992]), especially a recognizable guitar "chop," appear soon thereafter in the mix, accenting the 3 + 3 + 2 snare pattern while a pair of performers interpolate the melody from "Old MacDonald," changing the text to signify again the importance of New

York in the *underground* imagination: "Yo me voy para New York/E-I-E-I-O" (I'm going to New York/E-I-E-I-O). Not long after, we hear an interpolation of "Action" (1993), a contemporary dancehall reggae track by Nadine Sutherland and Terror Fabulous and another crossover hit in the New York hip-hop scene. Notably, the performance is not quite a cover of "Action" in the sense that, say, Panamanian reggae artists might version an extant song, but instead, as a Jamaican dancehall artist might do, it loosely alludes to the main melody of "Action" over a new backing. Similarly, rather than replaying (or re-licking) the *Fever Pitch* riddim that underlies the original, the pista brings together a number of different layers and fragments, among them the *Bam Bam* guitar sample which itself served to inspire elements of the *Fever Pitch* (via Sly Dunbar's *Pitch* riddim, popularized by Cutty Ranks's "Limb by Limb" [1993], another favorite in the *underground* scene), as well as drum samples drawn from various sources and a heavy, newly synthesized (rather than sampled) bassline.

Before long, that mélange gives way to a reversed loop of a breakbeat sampled from (or at least gesturing to) Slick Rick's "Mona Lisa" (1988), a notably older but rather common musical reference in *underground* productions, which is soon unreversed and augmented by 3 + 3 + 2 snares (once again juxtaposing hip-hop and reggae grooves in a striking manner). Cementing the connection to Slick Rick's "Golden Age" hip-hop track, the next vocalist employs melodies, affectations, and other formal features from "Mona Lisa" in order to sing, "Oye Lisa," while a stomping, four-on-the-floor kick drum enters and the hip-hop break is teased in and out of the mix. As the pista changes once again, returning to the bright *Bam Bam/Pitch* guitar sample, the same vocalist shifts to new melodic and textual references, alluding to El General's "Pu Tun Tun" by chanting "boom boom marijuana" as well as to Super Cat's "Don Dada" (which was similarly covered, incidentally, around the same time, on El General's "El Gran Pana"), all in the space of about thirty seconds. From there the mix moves to another resonant sample—the distinctive drum break from Audio Two's 1988 hip-hop classic "Top Billin," which had recently been sampled for Mary J. Blige's 1992 hit single "Real Love"—while two female vocalists rap to the tune of "Ten Little Indians," followed by yet another sly reference to "Action" over a *Bam Bam* guitar propelled *dembow* pattern. But perhaps you get the picture: the degree of intertextuality on these foundational mixtapes is truly remarkable. The sheer number of references surely rivals, if not exceeds, such pastichelike, sample-based masterworks as Public Enemy's *It Takes a Nation of Millions to Hold Us Back* (1988) or the Beastie Boys' *Paul's Boutique* (1989).

Despite bringing together such a wide variety of sources and hence suggesting a rather ecumenical outlook for the genre, the influential mixtapes of Playero, The Noise, and other innovators also established, not insignificantly, a fairly stable canon of resonant references by reusing their favorite samples over and over again. As I have argued, such an approach serves to directly index reggae and hip-hop (and hence, "black music" and New York) even as it advances a rather distinctive take on both traditions—and, notably, violates a number of aesthetic conventions in the process. For one, reggae producers rarely employ samples, preferring instead to version or re-lick previous riddims by replaying (and reshaping) their distinctive elements. Yet Puerto Rican *underground* producers, for all their fidelity to reggae tradition, employ a primarily sample-based approach and demonstrate no compunctions about sampling whatever source seems appropriate. And whereas sample-based hip-hop producers tend to take a fairly liberal attitude toward the direct sampling of other recordings, the *underground* practice of sampling hip-hop tracks, especially recent releases, contravenes (at least for some U.S. producers) a tacit but widespread ban on "jacking" other producers' beats or the same samples used to produce such beats (with the exception of well-worn breakbeats).[60] It is worth noting, then, that Puerto Rican producers and vocalists also depart from the same traditions they so closely engage, extending even further hip-hop's and reggae's central practices of reuse and allusion and attendant notions of ownership or originality. In its own way, the ubiquitous use of the *Dem Bow* (as well as such staples as the *Bam Bam* or *Drum Song* riddims) offers a parallel to other digital age genres, several of which have demonstrated the ability for a single sample to serve as the basis for hundreds, if not thousands, of distinct, discrete tracks: for example, the "Amen" break for UK "jungle" and drum'n'bass, the "Dragrap" or "Triggerman" for New Orleans "bounce," the "Volt" mix for Brazilian funk, or even, though less demonstrably, the constitutive role such breakbeats as the "Funky Drummer" played in late 1980s hip-hop. Puerto Rican producers thus take reggae's "riddim method" and hip-hop's omnivorous approach to sampling to an unprecedented extreme.

The samples most commonly employed by *underground* producers offer a telling profile of the specific sorts of sounds—namely, hip-hop and reggae—that proved resonant for certain Puerto Ricans living in San Juan and New York in the mid-1990s. For the sake of illustration, allow me to provide a short list of the most frequently referenced samples during this period. Notably, the hip-hop-related sources range from well-worn breakbeats (e.g., Bob James's "Take Me to the Mardi Gras" or Lou Donaldson's funk-soul recording of "Ode to Billie Joe"), to classics from the genre's so-called Golden Age (e.g., such late 1980s favorites as Slick Rick's "Mona Lisa," "Children's Story," and "Hey Young

World"; Special Ed's "I Got It Made" and "The Magnificent"; Marley Marl's "The Symphony"; Mark the 45 King's "900 Number"), to contemporary hits and obscurities alike (e.g., Cypress Hill's "Insane in the Membrane," especially, and often only, its squealing siren; House of Pain's "Back from the Dead"; Craig Mack's "Flava in Your Ear"; and De La Soul's "Talkin' Bout Hey Love," i.e., Stevie Wonder's "Hey Love"; as well as various other tracks by such New York–based *underground* hip-hop groups as Gang Starr, Wu-Tang Clan, and Das EFX). Raggamuffin rapper Mad Lion's "Take It Easy," produced by KRS-One, also became a heavily sampled staple shortly after its release in 1994. The resonance of such an already hybrid rap-reggae hit in Puerto Rico calls attention again to the broader currency of such fusions at the time; thus, for all its departures, one can hear the particular mélange of melaza as coherent with simultaneous movements in New York and across the Caribbean-U.S. cosmos.

With regard to reggae, as catalogued to some extent above, the dancehall riddims most commonly sampled, replayed, and reconstructed in Puerto Rico at this time were such recent, popular productions (in Jamaica and New York) as the *Dem Bow*, *Bam Bam*, *Fever Pitch*, and *Poco Man Jam*, as well as older but enduring riddims dating from the '60s, '70s, and '80s: *Drum Song*, *Real Rock*, *Stalag*, *Tempo*, to name a few.[61] DJ Playero and his colleagues and competitors either directly sampled (and "chopped and stabbed") these riddims or alluded to them—especially those defined by their basslines (such as *Drum Song* or *Stalag*)—by replaying the melodies on synthesizers, which had long been used by *underground* producers to augment their sample-based productions. It is also worth noting, as has been mentioned above, that vocalists frequently added yet another layer of intertextuality either by employing melodies drawn directly from dancehall songs (as well as from hip-hop or pop hits) or by borrowing some of the more generic melodic contours that dancehall DJs have long used to propel their lyrics. Shabba Ranks, Tenor Saw, Buju Banton, Super Cat, and Cutty Ranks appear to be favorite models in this regard. (And the names of many *underground* artists—with such appellations as Ranks, Stylee, Notty, and Daddy—pay explicit tribute to such figures.) Even when specific melodies do not appear, *underground* MCs' flows tend to closely resemble dancehall's sing-song, staccato, double-time, end-rhyme orientation. Many *underground* vocalists seem also to have adopted dancehall DJs' frequent disregard for conventional key relationships—what some might brand "off-key" singing—which could be heard as both an expression of these vocalists' "lack" of formal musical training as well as an aesthetic orientation consistent with oral/aural approaches more broadly.[62]

The dense, distinctive intertextual mix of hip-hop and reggae embodied in mid-1990s *underground* recordings thus supported a youth- and class-inflected cultural politics of blackness and did so, significantly, by embracing (if not amplifying) the Nuyorican dimensions of Puerto Rican culture. Taking a hip-hop hatchet to reggae's pop-will-eat-itself aesthetics, *underground* producers and vocalists crafted a rich musical fusion which gestured to New York as the cultural crucible where Puerto Ricans, Panamanians, Jamaicans, and African Americans, among others, encountered each other and contributed to a shared, contested, and culturally charged soundscape. Moreover, as noted above with regard to the mixtapes' artwork, the transnational character of melaza emerged not only in the sounds of the productions but in the images that accompanied them. Significantly, similar articulations of race and place can be seen in the promotional videos for the mixtapes. The video for *The Noise 6*, for instance, with its shots of goose-down jacket wearing MCs hopping turnstiles in the New York subway and posing in front of the Unisphere in Queens, offers a vivid illustration of what Juan Flores describes as a "notable reverse in the direction of social desire for the geographical other":

> While traditionally the translocal Puerto Rican sensibility was characterized by the emigrant longing for the beauties of the long-lost island, in some rap texts and among street youth it was the urban diaspora settings of the Bronx and El Barrio that became places of fascination and nostalgia.[63]

In this sense, the expressive forms of reggaeton (and its rap-reggae precursors) might be heard, seen, and read as embodying the "cultural remittances" of "transnationalism from below," perhaps even promising a rediscovery of Puerto Rican negritude and a reconciliation of Puerto Rican national identity.[64] Nodding to historian Frank Moya Pons, Flores compares such a potential shift to the ways in which notions of Dominican self- and nationhood have been reshaped by returning migrants. "Racial and cultural denial worked for many years," argues Moya Pons, "but migration to the United States finally cracked down the ideological block of the traditional definition of Dominican national identity."[65] Even so, as Tego Calderón contends, despite some encouraging signs—such as Don Omar's self-identification (and projection) as "el negro"—any real change in racial ideologies on the island and across Latin America more widely remains painfully slow: "There is ignorance and stupidity in Puerto Rico and Latin America when it comes to blackness," Calderón bluntly states in a recent piece published in the *New York Post*, and reprinted in this volume.

Resistance to hip-hop, reggae, and reggaeton in Puerto Rico is thus consistent with certain cultural-national parochialisms which fail to come to grips with what Flores calls "the full force of diaspora as source and challenge in Caribbean music history." The communities living in diaspora, Flores contends, "need to be seen as sources of creative cultural innovation rather than as repositories or mere extensions of expressive traditions in the geographic homelands."[66] This is by no means new cultural terrain for Puerto Rico, as the examples of *danza* and salsa demonstrate a similar process of engaging with putatively "other" music (marked, say, as black, Nuyorican, or Cuban), and of nationalizing as quintessentially Puerto Rican expressive forms once coded as foreign.[67] And yet, as the "creole" character of danza or the blanqueamiento of salsa demonstrates—with the latter genre's explicit "racial consciousness," as Deborah Pacini Hernandez puts it, "replaced by the lush orchestral arrangements and insipid lyrical concerns of its stylistic successor, *salsa romántica*"—the "nationalization" or public embrace of that which was initially cast as música negra in Puerto Rico can also lead to a co-optation (or at least a transformation) of such genres for commercial ventures.[68] Indeed, as Puerto Rico's transnationally forged rap-reggae hybrid moves from the *underground* to the "mainstream" around the turn of the millennium, one hears (and sees) some striking shifts in sonic, visual, and textual articulations of community, especially as artists and producers seek more explicitly to market the genre, especially outside Puerto Rico, as the sound of an emergent, pan-Latino community.

FROM MÚSICA NEGRA TO REGGAETON LATINO: MIGRATION AND THE MAINSTREAM

As *underground* became more commercially lucrative over the late '90s and especially in the first half of the present decade, it also became, inevitably, less underground—both in aesthetic and economic terms. The advent of accessible digital tools for producing and distributing recordings radically changed the sound and reach of the genre, and vocalists and producers alike began to target new markets and audiences, often redrawing the lines of community in the process. No longer bound by Puerto Rico's shores or even by Nuyorican and wider diasporic circuits, reggaeton artists and record labels began to address a new and increasingly diverse listenership in the expanded contexts of national and international mediaspheres. Infusing the music first with the propulsive and suggestive sounds of techno (or *tecno*, as sometimes localized) and later with such "tropical" sources (again, to use the industry term) as bachata and salsa, the contemporary sound of reggaeton as a slickly produced club music—

indeed, as the world came to know it via the galloping synths of "Gasolina"—cohered around the turn of the millennium and quickly assumed the sort of stylistic orthodoxy one might expect from commercial ventures.

Despite subtle sonic reminders of the genre's roots and routes, such as the persistent presence of the *dembow* rhythm, familiar percussion samples, and certain vocal styles or flows, what had formerly been ubiquitous and obvious nods to hip-hop and reggae—and which seemed quite essential to the genre and its cultural politics in the mid-1990s—grew further submerged with reggaeton's burgeoning commercial success. Perhaps in part in order to avoid copyright litigation given newfound prominence (and profits), reggaeton producers increasingly favored synthesized backings, with the only remaining samples being the snares, kicks, and other bits of resonant percussion cut-and-pasted from the genre's foundational dancehall riddims (and, more and more, circulating as sample banks via e-mail and CD-RS). Reggaeton, as it came to be called during this time, began to throb with the heavy, bombastic sounds of club and dance anthems (i.e., house- and techno-infused pop). Grafted onto the genre's *dembow* template, the music was increasingly produced and promoted as the soundtrack of "perreo" and "bellaqueo" (i.e., doggy-style dance and horniness), of highly sexualized dancing and highly sexualized objects of the male gaze.

Mirroring the commercialism and exaggerated sexual license associated with club culture, as well as continuing a longstanding preoccupation for the genre (and a common projection onto reggae), song themes turned more squarely to sex—which is to say, macho fantasies about sex—often bordering on the pornographic: see, e.g., DJ Blass's *Reggaeton Sex* series or albums such as *Triple Sexxx*. If perhaps publicly challenging middle-class mores and Christian values, reggaeton's emphasis on sex (and, more mildly, romance) should also be seen as consistent with mainstream commercial American culture, not to mention enduring stereotypes about "hot blooded" Latin lovers.[69] It is but a short jump from here to the video for N.O.R.E.'s crossover hit "Oye Mi Canto," featuring an array of bikini-clad women waving the flags of Latin American and Caribbean countries. Reggaeton producers and performers thus seemed to embrace, if not amplify, a number of stereotypes about race, gender, and nation as the music moved into the mainstream marketplace. Given such changes in context and content, the genre's cultural politics might be seen (and heard) as undergoing a major shift around the turn of the millennium, moving away from a sonically, textually, and visually encoded foregrounding of racial community and toward nationalist (and often sexist, or at least gendered)

Latin/pan-Latin signifiers—or, to put it in the words of reggaeton performers themselves, from "música negra" to "Reggaeton Latino," the latter phrase enshrined and projected by a Don Omar crossover hit in 2005.

And yet, as far as the genre may have drifted from hip-hop and reggae in some ways, the embrace by reggaeton producers, performers, and record labels of "bling-bling" style and hustler archetypes; aggressive cross-promotion and media savvy; and the timbres and textures of hip-hop's and reggae's own overlapping digital millennial aesthetics—all these features show how the genre has remained in close conversation with its influences. Moreover, reggaeton's rise to mainstream visibility, audibility, and marketability is tied not only to such stylistic synergy but also to a certain degree of fortuitous timing. In 2003, directly prior to breakthrough hits by N.O.R.E., Daddy Yankee, and Don Omar, a wave of crossover hits and high-profile collaborations by such Jamaican dancehall artists as Sean Paul, Wayne Wonder, and Elephant Man had served to prepare U.S. (and international) audiences for, if you will, relatively unintelligible, dance-centric pop.[70] (For the average monolingual English speaker, Jamaican creole might as well be Spanish.)[71] Further prepping the listening public for Spanish and Spanglish songs, Jamaican dancehall's own success in the U.S. mainstream was amplified (if also appropriated) by U.S.-based Latino/a performers who employed the latest reggae riddims to support their own chart incursions: e.g., Pitbull's "Culo" and Nina Sky's "Move Ya Body" were both recorded over the *Coolie Dance* riddim, while Lumidee recorded "Never Leave You (Uh-Oooh, Uh-Oooh)" on the *Diwali* riddim, which had already propelled U.S. chart hits by Sean Paul and Wayne Wonder. Thus, as dancehall reggae artists piggybacked their way to new levels of international success on hip-hop's national and global resonance, reggaeton artists did the same, with the added assistance of their brethren from Jamaica, who readied stateside audiences for a new wave of Caribbean-inflected, foreign-but-familiar, rap-infused dance music.

Other forms of audible commercialization consistent with the mainstreaming of reggaeton from the mid-1990s to today can be heard in the increasingly commonplace effects and affects of R&B and American pop more generally, as also heard in the often overwrought singing styles of Latin pop ballads. While the singsong melodies of dancehall reggae as well as hip-hop's more monotonic flows have continued to underpin reggaeton vocals, other kinds of approaches—in particular, *American Idol*–style melismatic histrionics—have become more prominent since the mid-1990s, along with the rise of romantic themes and crooner-and-rapper duos (e.g., Angel and Kris, Alexis and Fido, Hector and Tito, Wisin and Yandel, Rakim and Ken Y). Similarly, the appearance of group and solo albums and compilations of discrete songs, as opposed to dense, nonstop mixtapes, might be seen as another attempt to bring reggaeton into the aboveground commercial marketplace. A similar shift has occurred at the level of the song: whereas early and mid-1990s productions were marked by more fragmentary routines following the regular if whimsical shifts of their collagelike accompaniment, by the late 1990s and especially after the turn of the millennium, it became far more common to produce separate songs following a verse-chorus-verse form and without too many stark departures in musical texture. Such discrete units and familiar forms are, of course, far easier to promote and sell in the mainstream market. Related to this push toward a certain orthodoxy, reggaeton's defining feature, the *boom-ch-boom-chick* of the *dembow* pattern, has assumed a level of rhythmic hegemony, such that one hears far fewer breaks into hip-hop or contemporary dancehall style.[72]

At some point in the late 1990s, though the exact date and particular neologist remain in dispute, *underground* (or *dembow*, *melaza*, etc.) was recrowned *reggaeton*, a name perhaps befitting the genre's increasing commercialization as well as a sense that it had emerged as a distinctive fusion, as neither hip-hop nor reggae (though it was still frequently described using both terms by fans and practitioners).[73] DJ Nelson is frequently credited, and takes credit, for renaming the genre. "In 1995 I put the name 'Reggaeton' on one of my albums," he told a reporter for the *Fader* magazine, "I started thinking, Let me put like 'Reggae Maratón' or 'Maratón Reggae' on it. And from there I started, like, simplifying words, and then I came up with 'Reggaeton.' "[74] According to DJ El Niño, a Bronx-born, Connecticut-based DJ who plays reggaeton alongside house, hip-hop, salsa, and a host of other styles, some people began using the term *reggaeton* around this time to describe tracks employing "original beats" —that is, those that did not rely on the well-worn reggae riddims and hip-hop samples of the '90s but instead primarily employed synthesizers.[75] DJ Blass's popular *Reggaeton Sex* series no doubt was crucial in popularizing the term as well as tying it to the new production style emerging in step with digital music software (not to mention significations of the sexual). And, of course, more recent media attention and industry hype around the genre, especially from 2004 to the present, have served to cement the term's connection to the music and to consolidate its resonance for producers and audiences.

Around the same time the genre was becoming known by a new name, the music had begun to accrue several of the stylistic features that propel today's radio-friendly, club-ready confections. The advent of new music production technologies, in particular synthesizer and sequencer software, has a great deal to do with this shift in sound. Programs such as Fruity Loops, with telltale "preset" sounds and effects, served to expand and change the sonic palettes of reggaeton producers. In part because such programs were often initially developed as tools for techno producers, the genre started to move away from reggae and hip-hop samples and toward futuristic synths, cinematic strings, bombastic effects, and (especially just before a "big" downbeat) crescendoing kick drums, snare rolls, and cymbal splashes. The latter formal devices sound more derived from trance-style techno anthems than anything else, if also, notably, sometimes syncopated in a manner more reminiscent of breaks in salsa or merengue. Established producers such as DJ Playero, DJ Nelson, and DJ Joe, as well as relative newcomers such as DJ Blass, helped move the genre's primary sound sources from samples to synthesizers, introducing the use of heavier kick drums, ravey synth "stabs," and trancey arpeggios as well as cartoonish digital sound effects (wind blowing, explosions). Their productions were not uniform or mutually indistinguishable, however, and each offers an interesting look at the development of the genre during a crucial transition. A brief survey will allow us to listen in on some of these changes.

For all the new sounds and technologies informing reggaeton style in the late '90s, prior to a kind of commercial consolidation around 2002 many productions maintained audible links to the genre's sample-laden days, and thus, perhaps, to the audible cultural politics of mid-1990s melaza. A number of familiar sources from hip-hop and reggae, if often employed in a self-consciously nostalgic manner, can still be heard on, say, *Playero 41: Past, Present, and Future* (1998–99), including a track tellingly titled "Old School View" which offers up a classic collage in *underground* style, referencing an earful of resonant samples in under thirty seconds: among other bits, we hear fragments from Slick Rick's "Mona Lisa"; the familiar saxophone stab from 45 King's "900 Number"; rapper Rob Base saying "I wanna rock right now" (from "It Takes Two"); the well-worn breakbeat from Bob James's "Take Me to the Mardi Gras" (as used in countless hip-hop songs); Chuck D's heavily sampled shout "Bass! How low can you go" (from "Bring the Noise"); a measure from House of Pain's "Jump Around"; and the stuttered synth stab from the opening of Dirtsman's "Hot This Year." More subtle connections to the genre's past also remain audible in Playero's late 1990s productions, especially in the unremitting presence of Jamaican riddim staples, which nonetheless appear in more fragmentary form as short "chops" and "stabs" integrated into increasingly synthesized pistas.

Other tracks on releases such as *Playero 41* strongly embody the genre's new techno- and pop-oriented directions. Notty Man's "Dancing," for example, features various techno synths, evoking the distinctively "squelchy" sounds of the Roland TB-303 and employing the characteristic filtering, or frequency sweeps, of electronic dance music. Daddy's Yankee's "Todas las Yales" is another case in point. The track begins with a "detuned" synth riff evoking any number of trance or techno tracks. As a four-on-the-floor kick drum augments the riff, one could easily mistake it for a standard, if not cliché 1990s club anthem, at least before the *dembow* drums enter. Once the 3 + 3 + 2 snares come in, along with Yankee's voice, there is no mistaking the track for anything other than reggaeton; nonetheless, it offers a clear example of how synthesized (or sampled) techno references came increasingly to supplant the genre's affinity for hip-hop and dancehall sources. The track still moves somewhat starkly between a hip-hop groove and a *dembow* rhythm, however, and such alternation maintains connections to mid-1990s style. Moreover, at points Yankee propels his lyrics with a couple (characteristically "out-of-tune") melodies borrowed from Culture Club's "Karma Chameleon" (1984) and the Bangles' ballad "Eternal Flame" (1989).[76] Although these references to '80s pop hits might seem slightly odd here, not to mention rather far from the symbolic links which borrowed hooks from reggae or hip-hop songs might once have evoked, they are actually consistent with what has long been an ecumenical outlook for the genre—an approach derived in part from hip-hop's and reggae's own voracious practices. Finally, "Todas la Yales" also offers a window into the enduring presence of Jamaica via Panama: the term *yales*, which Yankee at times interchanges here with *mujeres* (i.e., women), comes from the Panamanian slang *guiales*, which itself adapts *gyal*, a Jamaican creole version of *girl* or *girls*.[77]

Productions by The Noise and DJ Joe during this period demonstrate similar trends. On *The Noise 9* (2000), for instance, one hears the telltale sounds of Fruity Loops presets and effects alongside other synthesized sounds, especially the pounding bass drums for which techno is known. One also hears, however, the same big bass synths, chopped-and-stabbed hip-hop references (e.g., squealing Cypress Hill samples), repeatedly triggered vocal lines, allusions to dancehall melodies (Ruben San crams several into a single song), and *Dem Bow* samples (especially the snares, but also the riddim's resonant bass drum) for which melaza had been known. The *Bam Bam*, *Fever Pitch*, and *Poco Man Jam* riddims also rear their heads in the mix. Although the pistas still shift in shape and feel at regular intervals, sometimes fairly radically, the music is less pastichelike than on earlier recordings, and the song forms more closely resemble standard pop fare. DJ Joe's millennial mixtapes also seem to confirm these directions. Whereas the producer's late 1990s mixes retain a great deal of melaza style, shortly after 2000 the influence of Fruity Loops and nods to techno become far more pronounced. With the exception of *Dem Bow* drum samples, by the release of *Fatal Fantassy 1* (2001), big, cheesy club synths, digital explosions, and melodramatic percussion crescendos dominate the tracks' textures, overshadowing any sample-based connections to earlier styles. Vocalists still employ dancehall-related melodies as well as various pop allusions (including the '50s hit "Mr. Sandman"), though one also hears a refinement of such a melodic approach: a distinctively Puerto Rican approach to melodic contour and vocal timbre—often evoking the nasal singing styles of many *soneros*—seems to emerge after a decade of recycling a handful of tunes. A connection between the sounds of techno and the sexual already appears rather reified by this point, underscored in DJ Joe's case by the suggestively (mis)spelled reference to a popular video game (*Final Fantasy*) on the *Fatal Fantassy* series.

Despite these parallel movements across the reggaeton scene, during the first few years of the new millennium DJ Blass might rightly be credited as most audibly promoting the *tecno* sound, conflating it with sexual license, and ushering in a good number of the elements which remain staples of the genre today and mark most of its mainstream hits. Blass's *Reggaeton Sex* series employs the futuristic, tactile synths and bombast of rave-era techno and contemporary trance to great effect, creating physically and psychologically compelling music over which (male) vocalists and (female) "phone-sex" samples repeatedly invoke the body and the bawdy. Over saw-tooth synths and ping-pong arpeggios, crescendoing kicks and snares and cymbal crashes, vocalists exhort (and/or order) women to "move it," *perreo*, and do a fair number of other, more explicitly sexual acts. Rather than the pliant, reggae-derived basslines of the mid-1990s, synthesized bass tones serve instead to accentuate the kick drums on each beat, often with a I-V ("oompah"-style) movement and sometimes tracing out simple chord progressions—a rudimentary rhythmic and harmonic role for the bass which has remained a feature in a great many commercial reggaeton productions.[78] Against these steady bass tones and heavy kicks on each beat, the snares—sampled from *Dem Bow*, *Bam Bam*, and other favorite reggae riddims—frequently come to the fore, pulling against the foursquare feel with their 3 + 3 + 2 accents and making quite prominent what is, at times, the only audible, timbral connection to the genre's *underground* roots. Gesturing to the regularly shifting forms of the mid-1990s, Blass often switches between different snare samples at 4-, 8-, or 16-measure intervals, creating a subtle sense of form against the otherwise rather static synth vamps.

One strong contrast to what seems like a creeping sameness among reggaeton producers around this time can be heard in the productions of DJ Nelson, even if, remarkably, he is also partly responsible for ushering in the most hegemonic force in recent reggaeton style, the duo known as Luny Tunes. Beginning with his production work for The Noise in 1992, Nelson's productions have consistently put forward an ecumenical orientation, as well as one that remains closely connected to contemporary movements in hip-hop and reggae. During an interview segment in the *Chosen Few* documentary, Nelson characterizes himself and his style as "adventurous": "I like to experiment," he says, "to fuse different genres, for example: salsa and reggaeton, electronic music and reggaeton. I always try to bring something new to the genre, to give people new rhythms." (Appropriately, while he is describing himself in this manner a bachata-reggaeton fusion plays in the background.) Most recently, Nelson has been at the forefront of salsa-reggaeton fusions and infusions, but his premillennial productions also demonstrate a great deal of variety. Nelson's album *The Flow* (1998) balances early synth explorations with a hefty number of samples and obvious references to other songs (e.g., Eurythmics' "Sweet Dreams"). Notably, as many tracks on the album employ hip-hop grooves (see figure 4) and dancehall's distinctive stomp (figure 2) as reggaeton's well-worn *boom-ch-boom-chick*; indeed, the second half of the album might best be described simply as Spanish-language hip-hop, suggesting that reggaeton could have gone in a rather different direction altogether. A series of popular productions by Nelson's former apprentices, Luny Tunes, however, seems to have pushed the genre most firmly into a kind of *dembow* orthodoxy.

The rise and runaway success of Luny Tunes and the defining role they played in shaping what is today known as reggaeton would seem to symbolize the central role that migration has played in the ongoing formation (and reformation) of the genre. Both Luny (Francisco Saldana) and Tunes (Victor Cabrera) were born in the Dominican Republic and moved to Massachusetts as teenagers. But rather than settling in Roxbury or Dorchester or Springfield —local areas known for their sizeable Spanish-speaking communities—the two found themselves (and found each other) living in Peabody, a relatively affluent, suburban town on the outskirts of Greater Boston. Although not far from the larger, more established Latino community in Lynn, the Spanish-speaking community in Peabody was fairly small and encouraged a kind of tight-knit fraternization. As Cabrera once framed it: "Since most of the Latin people there didn't speak English, and we were all together, we had to listen to our own thing."[79] In this case, "our own thing" primarily meant bootlegged reggaeton recordings circulating from Puerto Rico through familial and peer networks. The duo's deep, abiding engagements with reggaeton hence says a great deal about the longstanding transnational appeal and reach of the music. To some extent the emergence of such an important production team from such a seemingly marginal set of spaces (both the Dominican Republic and the Boston suburbs) suggests yet another decentralization of Spanish-language reggae-rap, a shift connected to migration and fueled by technology.[80] Of course, the fact that the duo eventually moved to Puerto Rico to set up shop speaks volumes about the enduring (industrial) center of the genre, new regional nodes of production notwithstanding.[81]

As can be heard on such Luny Tunes productions as "Gasolina" or any number of the pistas on *Mas Flow* (2003), *The Kings of the Beats* (2004), or *Mas Flow 2* (2005), the duo's penchant for synthesized textures, plucky melodic filigree, techno crescendos, and cinematic bombast builds on the prior innovations of Nelson, Blass, Joe, and others. Even so, Luny Tunes—and such cohorts as Nelly, Noriega, and Tainy—set themselves apart from their forebears through their facility with the latest generation of music production software and keyboards. (Scrutinizing Luny Tunes' sonic signatures as well as photos and videos of the duo at work, studio gear "trainspotters" have noted the presence of such keyboards as the Yamaha Motif 8 and software including Nuendo and Fruity Loops, especially the latter's brittle-sounding *Pluck!* synthesizer, as well as various VST plug-ins, or Virtual Studio Technology instruments and effects—e.g., SampleTank 2 XL, Sonik Synth 2, Hypersonic 2, and HyperCanvas.)[82] Using such synthesizers, Luny Tunes introduced and advanced a distinctive, pop-oriented melodic and harmonic language to the genre. Drawing on the latest technologies and employing musical devices more common to pop and R&B, the duo produced sleek, shiny tracks which seemed to embody in sonic form the flashy style of *blin-blineo* (or "bling-bling"), an aesthetic borrowed from commercial hip-hop and thus resonant with the predilections of the U.S. music industry and contemporary mainstream or urban radio. The duo's use (and recycling) of 2, 3, and 4 chord vamps, accentuating their simple but moving chord progressions with melodic lines and arpeggios that follow and bring out the underlying harmonic motion, has facilitated the kind of affective, often overwrought crooning which presumably appeals, *American Idol*–style, to a cherished market demographic: teenyboppers.

Maintaining audible connections to contemporary pop and hip-hop while eschewing reggaeton's well-worn sample sources—save for the indispensable percussion of the *Dem Bow* and *Bam Bam* riddims—Luny Tunes also proved crucial in moving the genre more squarely into the realm of "Latin" or "tropical" music by invoking the distinctive piano riffs of salsa and merengue and, especially, the trebly, swirling guitars of bachata. Imbuing their productions with a crossover appeal which had eluded more hardcore recordings, and tapping into a growing Latin-urban music market in the United States, the duo's productions served as significant sonic symbols, accelerating the genre's move from *música negra* to "Reggaeton Latino," from a principally Afro–Puerto Rican or Puerto Rican audience to a pan-Latino and mainstream U.S. consumer base. Their heavy use of the *dembow*-derived *boom-ch-boom-chick*, moreover—which has come to stand as another important signifier of the genre's Latinness, despite its foundations in Jamaican reggae—seems to have played a major role, especially via their most successful singles, in establishing what many hear today as reggaeton's rhythmic conservatism (or its monotony, to put it more pejoratively, as many detractors do). It is important to note, however, that despite their formidable influence on the "tropicalization" of the genre, Luny Tunes were not the first to infuse reggaeton with "tropical" sources. DJ Joe's *Fatal Fantasy 3* (2002), for example, offers some relatively early attempts to incorporate salsa into the mix: on Ranking Stone's "Todas las Mujeres" a salsa-style piano figure, as played on a chintzy digital synthesizer, dovetails with *dembow* drums; Noemi's "Voy Caminando Reggae Lento Mix" finds propulsion in a sampled salsa riff; and Negrito Truman's "El Phillie" employs a replayed version of the opening ostinato from El Gran Combo's "Ojos Chinos" (notably, a year or so before DJ Nelson would reanimate the same piano riff for Tego Calderón's "Dominicana").

In some ways, the timing was fortuitous for such sonic shifts, especially toward bachata, a Dominican genre originally confined to the slums of Santo Domingo which, like reggaeton, had been gaining prominence among urban, U.S.-based, Spanish-speaking audiences since the turn of the millennium or so.[83] The integration of bachata into reggaeton (and, it is worth noting, vice versa), fueled in part by producers of Dominican heritage with a love for both genres, again speaks to the role migration has played in reggaeton's formation. With increasing numbers of Dominicans living in San Juan and New York alike, bachata's unmistakable, shimmery guitar timbres became an increasingly common feature of these cities' soundscapes. According to DJ El Niño, the embrace of bachata by reggaeton producers was a marriage of convenience: "People who were into reggaeton hated bachata," he recounted via e-mail, "it even got dissed on some early reggaeton tracks . . . as things became more mainstream (including bachata) and not so underground it becameok and then u see watt happens now they all have at least 2 'bachata' tracks per cd . . . lol!!"[84] Indeed, based on my own daily listening while commuting from Hum-

boldt Park to Hyde Park in Chicago during the 2006–7 school year, contemporary Hispanic-urban, or "hurban," radio appears increasingly drawn
to reggaeton-bachata hybrids (sometimes referred to as *bachaton*). Crooning
R&B-style over *dembow*-propelled bachata guitars, "Dominican York" boy-
bands such as Aventura and Xtreme seem to be contributing in their own way
to this broader shift in reggaeton's cultural profile that is pop oriented and
pan-Latin.[85]

This is not to say that reggaeton is not still heard and projected as "black
music" by performers and audiences alike, or that genres such as salsa, bachata,
or merengue are not (or perhaps, *were* not) themselves cast as música negra.
For all its mainstream, pan-Latin strivings, reggaeton continues to be racialized
as black in the same way that Dominicans and Dominican music and culture
are racialized as black in Puerto Rico and, indeed, as Dominicans and Puerto
Ricans are, in such places as New York, together racialized as black according to
the binary racial logic of the United States. Especially due to the genre's enduring articulations—musically, sartorially, and discursively—with hip-hop and
reggae, reggaeton remains, for many, a "morenos" thing (i.e., African American, not Afro-Latin), as Tempo calls it while explaining in the *Chosen Few*
documentary that he "based [him]self on the hip-hop culture." A quick glance
through *In the House* magazine or at any reggaeton video reveals a plethora of
visual markers of hip-hop generation, African American culture: braids and
dreadlocks, chains and jewelry, oversized clothing, and symbols of "thug"
glamour more generally. (Notably, these same culturally charged markers of
visual style, prompted a Puerto Rican percussion teacher with whom I was
studying to give voice to enduring prejudices, remarking that Daddy Yankee
should dress in a manner more consistent with his fair complexion, taken as an
index of his assumed [high] class position in the same manner as he took Tego
Calderón's and Don Omar's phenotypical features to be signs, if misleading
ones, of their lower-class background.[86]) Moreover, the implicit and explicit
racialization of women as sexual objects in song texts and videos plays on and
reanimates longstanding myths about *negra* and *mulata* sexuality. Demonstrating the genre's strong significations of race and raciness as it finds favor among
audiences in Central and South America, recent debates and viral video phenomena on what we might call the Latin American YouTubosphere have consistently portrayed reggaeton artists and devotees as sexually licentious, morally depraved, and racialized Others.[87]

For all its audibility, then, the increasingly projected pan-Latino character of
reggaeton is also inextricable from visual and textual cues. It is telling that a
number of the genre's biggest crossover hits, especially N.O.R.E.'s "Oye Mi

Canto" and Don Omar's "Reggaeton Latino," offer explicit attempts to represent reggaeton as the music of a wider community (and market). Both songs address a "Latino" audience in the lyrics, and yet they do so, interestingly, without invoking musical signs of the "tropical," tending instead toward *dembow*-driven R&B. Instead of sonic signifiers, the songs attach themselves to iconic images of "Latin pride" via their videos, employing grainy footage of political figures, artists, and athletes in "Reggaeton Latino" and (light-)brown-skinned, bikini-clad women dancing under giant flags in "Oye Mi Canto." The pan-Latino, multinational flag-waving in "Oye Mi Canto" finds correspondence in the song's chorus, which invokes a now well-worn litany of Spanish-speaking identifications: "*boricua, morena, dominicana, colombiana*," sing Nina Sky, a Puerto Rican–born, New York–based duo, at times substituting *cubana* and *mexicana* to round things out. Notably, both songs were produced by Boy Wonder, a New York–born producer with family ties to the Dominican Republic and Puerto Rico who has been among the genre's biggest boosters—especially via his *Chosen Few* franchise. A revealing moment in the *Chosen Few* documentary portrays Boy Wonder in the studio coaching Nina Sky to add "mexicana" to the refrain. The young producer has proven himself rather savvy in promoting reggaeton (and his own efforts in the genre), at times embracing the for-hire, your-ad-here, self-commodification that commercial hip-hop has so successfully leveraged toward cultural and market dominance. "Every kind of message can be said with this music," he says at one point during the documentary, "and you can put a face on any product."

As somewhat cynically expressed in Boy Wonder's aspirations and productions, the genre's shift from música negra to "Reggaeton Latino" seems connected to, even as it informs (especially with reggaeton's growing visibility, audibility, and marketability), such broader phenomena as mass media marketing in the United States. Take, for example, the programming and on-air practices of Spanish-language media giant Univision's La Kalle radio franchise, which broadcasts on two signals in the Chicago area and which has sister stations in New York, Miami, San Francisco, Las Vegas, and San Antonio, to name a few. Seeking out the so-called hurban market and offering what they bill as "reggaeton y más" (but not too much *más*), La Kalle's DJs and promotional materials, presumably in an attempt to reach a wider audience, tend to downplay invocations of particular nationalities, addressing instead a general, Spanish- and Spanglish-speaking audience united under an implicitly racialized, urban American "street" identity (*kalle* is a misspelling of *calle*, or "street" in Spanish). Callers-in, for instance, are now prompted simply to say their name and the catch-phrase, "Yo soy *La Kalle*," rather than, as was previously the practice, representing themselves as both belonging to a national group and to the wider Hispanic community.[88] Reggaeton's success on such radio stations as La Kalle suggests that the genre's own marketing strategies—as advanced by artists, producers, and music industry executives—dovetail quite well with corporate media's initiatives to entice a prized demographic, the substantial and growing numbers of Spanish speakers in the United States.

At the same time, reggaeton's aesthetic shift toward *latinidad* and away from (explicit) negritude seems also to play into current debates in the United States about immigration, citizenship, and civil rights—debates which often erupt into a host of xenophobic, racist, and nationalist arguments on all sides. In this context reggaeton often emerges in the words of detractors as parasitic (on hip-hop and reggae in particular), and it is revealing that discussions (or dismissals) of reggaeton's musical value tend to come to the fore in such discourse, with allegations of monotony and lack of originality as the most common epithets. In the most provocative examples of such discourse, critics accuse reggaeton of horning in on hip-hop's and reggae's market share in the same way Latino immigrants are accused of stealing American jobs.[89] Thus one might infer that despite the repeated, inclusion of "morenas" in reggaeton's established litany of community relationships (which still serves to draw lines even as it connects dots), such an articulation with blackness functions rather differently in the broader context of U.S. and Latin American race relations than it did in the specific context of mid-1990s Puerto Rico. Similar to hip-hop and reggae, but with its own particular points of provocation, reggaeton has thus served in recent years to animate intense public conversations about race, nation, gender, and generation across the Americas. Given what can seem a tumultuous redefinition of social relationships in the wake of new migrations amidst competing projects of national and transnational (not to mention local) unity, it is hardly surprising that so much heated debate rages over the past and future of reggaeton.

TO WHERE FROM HERE? (WHERE'S "HERE"?)

As this essay has attempted to trace across time and space, reggaeton can be claimed and located as Jamaican, Panamanian, Puerto Rican, Latin, and/or black music. Depending on the particular sociocultural context and historical moment, reggaeton may be heard, embraced, and projected as representing any or all of these people and places, with significant implications for local cultural politics. Despite the genre's history of movement and shifting centers, with its recent rise to mainstream American and global prominence reggaeton today may stand as even further decentered, diversified, and subject to re-articulation in various sites of production and reception. The music is now crafted and consumed across the Americas and the wider world. That a number of the biggest hits of the genre have been pan-national, flag-waving affairs has further cemented a growing perception—a perception resented by some Puerto Rican cultural nationalists—that reggaeton is yet another genre in the global/Latin pop pantheon. This is a perception from which Puerto Rican artists still benefit a great deal, for they remain the major players in the scene and comprise the vast majority of international stars. But as the genre continues to grow and new regional centers develop, Puerto Rico may find itself as decentered in the reggaeton universe as is New York in global hip-hop's sphere of influence—an inevitable outcome of various artists and labels rushing headlong toward mainstream visibility, audibility, and profitability.

Lest my narrative come across as overly cynical in describing reggaeton's shift toward a pan-Latin profile, I should emphasize that the changes in musical style I have described emerge not simply out of Puerto Rican artists', managers', and labels' calculations about how to reach a wider market, but from the genre's increasingly and genuinely pan-Latino, grassroots popularity. Aspiring producers and performers from across the Latin Caribbean, Latin American, and Spanish-speaking communities in the United States have embraced the music as the sound of their generation, as a style that embodies signifiers of their Latino or national heritage as well as dimensions of the global, the modern, the urban and urbane. For all its core connotations, mainstream success has allowed the sound and style of reggaeton to escape local control; the genre is but the latest Latin dance style to find favor in popular U.S. culture. As such, it appeals to producers and consumers of all kinds. The advent of *reggaeton cristiano*, or Christian reggaeton, and the appearance of such compilations as *Reggaeton Niños* serve as telling confirmations of the genre's new status and significations. In some sense, this move from the margins to the mainstream—complete with a radical shift in the genre's perception and reception in Puerto Rico, moving from a target of censorship to a cause for celebration (if with an enduring ambivalence and anxiety)—follows a familiar arc for a lot of popular, and eventually national, music. Writing about the mbira in Zimbabwe, Thomas Turino observes: "As with the tango, the rumba, steelband, and merengue in the Caribbean and Latin America, it is often foreign interest in a local tradition that causes it to be selected and popularised as a paramount national musical idiom at home."[90] At this juncture we might rightly add reggaeton to the list.

As time goes on, the term *reggaeton* may come to describe a far wider, or narrower, field of musical activity. As the genre's influence sinks deeper into Latin, U.S., and global pop, it could simply be seen as an umbrella term for a range of styles—as, say, *rock* functions today, or perhaps even *hip-hop* at this point (which, according to some, including Vico C, would contain reggaeton). However, such diffusion might completely obscure the genre's presence, per-haps leading devotees (and no doubt marketers) to restrict the meaning of reggaeton to a more specific sense of style. Indeed, this may already be true: for many, reggaeton is simply the sound of synthy, *dembow*-driven Puerto Rican pop from the Luny Tunes era. Yet while such synth-driven, snare-shifting compositions remain at the heart of the genre (at least according to the radio, the media, and record sales), already such hybrid offshoots as *salsaton, bacha-ton, cumbiaton, chutney-ton, raï-ggaeton,* and *bhangraton,* among other novel-ties, point to further localizations and new possibilities for the genre's distinc-tive sonic footprint to propel the politics of culture (not to mention offering fresh opportunities to cash in on the latest global pop trend).[91] At the same time, a growing number of major pop acts—from Shakira to Britney Spears to R. Kelly to Ricky Martin—have employed reggaeton's telltale *boom-ch-boom-chick* in order to imbue their tracks with resonant, club-ready beats. And reggaeton's *dembow* drums, especially the use of snares to mark out a 3 + 3 + 2 polyrhythm, have also turned up increasingly as new rhythmic accents in rock en español as well as bachata, merengue, norteño, and so on.

Finally, although most mainstream reggaeton hits to date display some-thing of a stylistic orthodoxy, a number of prominent acts from Puerto Rico have also infused their music with a great deal of variety, expanding the sonic palette of the genre with the help of adventurous producers such as DJ Nelson, Danny Fornaris, and Visitante. In some sense, then, reggaeton could be de-scribed as fairly heterodox today, displaying at least as ecumenical an outlook as in the days of the sample-dense melaza collage (which, interestingly, has been rearing its head of late as a nostalgic, "retro" signifier for "old school" style). Tego Calderón has done a great deal of stylistic stretching in this regard, incorporating many of the Puerto Rican genres journalists so often take for granted as part of reggaeton's DNA (e.g., bomba, salsa), not to mention experi-menting with dancehall and roots reggae, hip-hop, and blues. For their part, Calle 13 (a.k.a. Residente and Visitante) have brought an art-school/class-clown attitude to the genre, expressed musically in their irreverence for any sort of stylistic purity. While referencing the *Dem Bow* and *Bam Bam* enough to convince the reggaeton faithful of their belonging, the group also nods to klezmer, cumbia, tango, and contemporary electronic pop, to name a few. Such eclectic, idiosyncratic musical approaches—in these cases combined with both Tego's and Residente's combination of reflexivity, earthy humor, and incisive social commentary—seem to suggest that the genre maintains a healthy degree of insurgent creativity. Similarly, we can trust that with bedroom producers from Minneapolis to Medellín seeking to put themselves on the map, reggaeton will not be "running out of gasolina" anytime soon, contrary to premature predictions of its demise.[92] Where the next fuel injection comes from, however, and how the music's future will embody where it has been, where it resides, and where it is going, are things that remain to be seen. And heard. (I'm going to keep my ears on the snares.)

I hope that in attempting to construct a metanarrative about reggaeton—a story about the stories people tell about the music, as well as a story I hear the music tell—that I have not proposed too overbearing (or overdetermining) a master narrative of my own. Part of what compels me to listen so closely to reggaeton is that it seems, especially in its mainstream manifestations, to challenge a number of master narratives about American culture and society. For all the conflicts and debates around the music, it also holds the promise—or perhaps gives voice to the postcolonial dream—of a convivial, cosmopolitan multiculture, as Paul Gilroy might put it, suggesting that our cities already sound so and that musical communities might as well act as political communities.[93] Whether reggaeton has the potential to change the status quo is deeply unclear to me, for it appears at this point to be co-opted by (and/or willingly "pimping" itself to) a system that thrives on, sells, and sows difference, distinction, and division. I do think, however, that I hear a different America in reggaeton, a different kind of mainstream—or perhaps the disappearance of the mainstream altogether. With regard to the emergence of an increasingly diverse, global, public archive of videos and other media, Jace Clayton has observed, "I enjoy watching the notion of a mainstream dissolve into a trillion scattered data-bites."[94] I feel similarly when I listen to today's digital *dembow* tracks and Spanglish raps. Can't we all just dance along?

NOTES

Thanks to Deborah Pacini Hernandez and Raquel Z. Rivera for their indispensable feedback, as well as to the many interlocutors who engaged with earlier versions of these ideas via various blog posts, e.g.: http://wayneandwax.blogspot.com/2005/08/we -use-so-many-snares.html; and http://wayneandwax.blogspot.com/2006/06/cabron- que-reggaeton.html.

1. For criticisms of the song (and the genre) as sexist, see, e.g., http://blogging.la/ archives/2005/09/latino_963_more_la_radio_sucki.phtml, and http://www.lacocte

lera.com/eme/post/2005/09/16/-no-al-reggaeton-perfil-del-fan-del-reggaeton#comen
tarios (accessed January 6, 2007).

2. By "breakdowns" I refer to the sections in the song when most or all of the percussive elements drop out (in the case of "Gasolina," e.g., from 1:10 to 1:20 or 2:12 to 2:22), thus creating anticipation for their return—an expectation typically intensified, in reggaeton and trance/techno alike, via the (re)entry of the drums, especially in rapidly subdividing form. Like a crescendo (or hypermeter) in classical music, these dense percussive passages highlight the return of the regular meter, or groove—or the beginning of a new section—by creating what is felt as a "big downbeat," sometimes further emphasized by a crash/splash cymbal or an explosion, etc. With regard to "tropical" music, I am referring to a category used by the music industry (e.g., Billboard) which tends to lump together various Latin Caribbean (dance) genres (e.g., salsa, merengue), distinguishing them from other Spanish-language music such as Mexican *banda* or *norteño*.

3. Daddy Yankee, a.k.a. Raymond Ayala, happens to have direct family ties to a number of bomba performers, e.g., Los Hermanos Ayala, which included his late father (Ramon "El Negro" Ayala) and his cousins. Hence, I would argue that the bomba connection I make here is not as perfunctory an observation as most invocations of the genre in writings about reggaeton, which tend to rehearse such connections (as I will discuss in this and later sections) despite the actual rarity of audible bomba references in reggaeton recordings. (Tego Calderón and La Sista, both of whom have explicitly incorporated bomba into their albums, stand as exceptional in this regard.)

4. From a description at cduniverse.com, an online vendor: "As one of the most popular musical styles of the mid-2000s, reggaeton gained favor across racial, ethnic, and even age boundaries. It was only a matter of time, then, until a 'reggaeton for kids' disc found its way to shelves, and REGGAETON NINOS VOL. 1 is just that. While many reggaeton raps concern themselves with sexual themes or the hard-knock thug life, the tracks on REGGAETON NINOS have been edited for content and language, so concerned parents can at last feel safe letting their young ones groove out to these infectious songs. The album includes several singalong tracks (identified as such) that feature a chorus of children singing the hook, adding to the charm and youth-accessible appeal of the set": http://www.cduniverse.com/search/xx/music/pid/6996932/a/Reggaeton
+Ninos+Vol.+1.htm (accessed October 20, 2006).

5. Spencer Ackerman, e.g., describes the ironic resonance and popularity of "Gasolina" among Kurdish "gas-hustlers" in early 2006 in an article hosted at openDemocracy.net: http://www.opendemocracy.net/conflict-iraq/kurdistan_3369.jsp (accessed October 20, 2006). Moreover, for listeners in Panama, where reggae has long been associated with "oil" and "petróleo" because of their metonymic connotations of blackness, "Gasolina" might have seemed like yet another familiar derivation of *reggae en español* (about which, more in the next section).

6. Moreover, as will be discussed in greater detail below, the track frequently features

a "timbal" figure also associated with the *Dem Bow* riddim in Puerto Rico, thus creating additional sonic links to Afro-Latin styles. Also, allow me to clarify here my various spelling choices: when I write "Dem Bow," I refer to the Shabba Ranks song; when I write *Dem Bow*, I refer to the riddim produced by Bobby Digital; when I write *dembow*, I refer to the abstracted rhythmic pattern derived from the *Dem Bow* as well as the genre in Puerto Rico named after the ubiquitous rhythm, which was/is sometimes also rendered, in local discourse, as *dembo* or *denbo* (and which is synonymous with "underground," "under," *melaza*, etc.).

7. The story of reggaeton's Panamanian origins has become such a commonplace in journalistic coverage that it seems almost a perfunctory gesture. Online message-board discussions, on the other hand, tend toward fairly heated disputes over which place truly lays claim to the genre. See, e.g., http://www.futureproducers.com/forums/show thread.php?t=64392&page=3 (accessed October 11, 2006); http://www.reggaetonline.net/ forums/threadnav805–1–10.html (accessed June 25, 2006).

8. At times throughout this essay I employ the construction "reggae/ton" when referring both to reggae and reggaeton, especially in cases where I am discussing reggae in Puerto Rico or Panama prior to the advent of the term *reggaeton* or seeking to describe the genre across historical periods. For examples of some rather contentious debates around reggaeton's geographical and cultural provenance, see, e.g., http://foro .univision.com/univision/board/message?board.id=reggaeton&message.id=91580; and http://www.bacanalnica.com/foros/viewtopic.php?t=11646, http://abstractdynam ics.org/2004/08/reggaeton.php (accessed January 6, 2007).

9. Among a great deal of other scholarship, the writings of John Storm Roberts—see *The Latin Tinge: The Impact of Latin American Music on the United States* (New York: Oxford University Press, 1999 [1979]), or *Black Music of Two Worlds: African, Caribbean, Latin, and African-American Traditions* (New York: Schirmer Books, 1998 [1972])—and of Ned Sublette—*Cuba and Its Music: From the First Drums to the Mambo* (Chicago: Chicago Review Press, 2004)—stand as persuasive efforts toward advancing and elaborating such a theory. The work of Ken Bilby, such as his essay "The Caribbean as a Musical Region," in *Caribbean Contours*, ed. Sidney W. Mintz and Sally Price, 181–218 (London: Johns Hopkins University Press, 1985), also offers a compelling narrative lens into these connections.

10. Audio samples illustrating the examples discussed in this essay are available at the following URL: http://wayneandwax.com/?page_id=139.

11. The differences in emphasis and arrangement between these genres are not inconsequential, however. One can thus get into vociferous disagreements about whether reggaeton and, say, salsa indeed share a similar rhythmic orientation or "feel." See, e.g., the "2005 Rolling Reggaeton Thread" at http://ilx.p3r.net/thread.php?msgid=5625584 (accessed January 6, 2007), which features such opinions as the following (made in response to a comment of mine): "There is a world of difference between the quarter note pulse existing (which yeah, of course it does) and being explicitly stated. It's not

stated in most dancehall, Afro-Cuban, New Orleans, etc. music. There's also a big difference between stating it on top with a cowbell or cymbal than on the bottom with the bass drum."

12. I should note that in my own experience taking bomba lessons in Chicago during the fall of 2006, however, such connections between these traditional genres and reggaeton were never elaborated by the instructor, and, indeed, reggaeton was at times denigrated—more because of its lyrics than musical style—as a dangerous, corrupting influence on Puerto Rican youth. The connections I make here, then, are largely my own attempts to provide a generous reading of what are perhaps, more often than not, tenuous attempts to connect reggaeton to traditions other than its most direct forebears, hip-hop and reggae (though I would like to acknowledge the expertise of Anton Kociolek in helping me to articulate these connections). Finally, I hasten to distinguish such structural rhythmic similarities from more specious assertions that particular elements in reggaeton were borrowed directly from bomba or plena, e.g., "While reggaeton is very similar to reggae, a notable difference are the extra claps and high hats derived from Bomba and Plena": http://xpress.sfsu.edu/archives/life/003326.html (accessed January 6, 2007).

13. Linton Kwesi Johnson, "Introduction," in *Tougher than Tough: The Story of Jamaican Music*, CD liner notes (London: Island Records Ltd., 1993), 5. It is significant that the DJs and producers Johnson names here are among the major touchstones for Puerto Rican producers and vocalists in the early and mid-1990s: Shabba Ranks's "Dem Bow," as discussed in the previous and following sections, became reggaeton's bedrock riddim; Buju Banton's gruff tone inspired a good many Puerto Rican DJs/MCs; and several riddims played and produced by Steely and Clevie, such as *Poco Man Jam* (1990) and indeed the *Dem Bow* itself, became staple samples for "underground" producers.

14. See, e.g., various essays in Tony Mitchell, ed., *Global Noise: Rap and Hip-Hop outside the USA* (Middletown, Conn.: Wesleyan University Press, 2001), a good number of which bear witness to a conflation of dancehall (often glossed as "raggamuffin") and hip-hop style in various contexts outside the United States.

15. There is a rich and growing literature on Jamaican (and West Indian/Caribbean) migration to New York in the late twentieth century: see, e.g., Mary C. Waters, *Black Identities: West Indian Immigrant Dreams and American Realities* (New York: Russell Sage Foundation, 1999); Philip Kasinitz, *Caribbean New York: Black Immigrants and the Politics of Race* (Ithaca, N.Y.: Cornell University Press, 1992); Nancy Foner, *Islands in the City: West Indian Migration to New York* (Berkeley: University of California Press, 2001); and, for a volume focusing on music, Ray Allen and Lois Wilcken, eds., *Island Sounds in the Global City: Caribbean Popular Music and Identity in New York* (Urbana: University of Illinois Press, 2001). As for musical texts, Boogie Down Productions' *Criminal Minded*, CD (B-Boy Records, 1987) is perhaps the best example of the currency that Jamaican style had come to assume in New York by this point. Full of direct references (as sampled, as replayed, and as rapped/sung) to contemporary dancehall, the album nonetheless allowed BDP to advance their claims to interborough dominance (as in the

battle with the Queens-based Juice Crew). That a "hardcore" New York rap group could represent the Bronx so convincingly with the sounds of Jamaica at this time speaks volumes. For similar, more widespread, and perhaps more pernicious representations of Jamaica as the locus of an exotic source of hardcore violence, see, for example, such Hollywood films as *Marked for Death* (1990) or *Predator 2* (1990), both of which feature fearsome, dreadlocked villains.

16. *Chosen Few: El Documental*, CD/DVDs (Chosen Few Emerald Entertainment / Urban Box Office, 82520110152, 2004).

17. The documentary's subtitles, which occasionally offer slightly odd interpretations of the interview texts, translate Master Joe's "en americano" to "in English" in order to distinguish from Spanish-language rappers. In the other cases here, unless noted, I directly quote the subtitles (after reviewing for serious discrepancies).

18. The Mean Machine, Ruby Dee and Whipper Whip, and Charlie Chase are among the earliest, New York–based "Latin rappers." For further discussion of the phenomenon, as well as the implications of its marginalization in the hip-hop narrative, see, e.g., Juan Flores, *From Bomba to Hip-Hop: Puerto Rican Culture and Latino Identity* (New York: Columbia University Press, 2000); and Raquel Z. Rivera, *New York Ricans from the Hip Hop Zone* (New York: Palgrave Macmillan, 2003).

19. See, e.g., a tribute to the late Big Pun in *XXL*, which begins with the lede "Four years ago, we lost Big Pun, a legendary lyricist who changed the game with his furious flow. In tribute, we examine his jump-off—Capital Punishment, the classic LP that proved Latin MCs could rhyme and go platinum": http://xxlmag.com/Features/2004/0204.BigPun/index.html (accessed February 1, 2007).

20. See, for instance, Victor M. Rodríguez, "The Racialization of Puerto Rican Ethnicity in the United States," in *Ethnicity, Race and Nationality in the Caribbean*, ed. J. M. Carrion (Río Piedras: University of Puerto Rico, Institute of Caribbean Studies, 1998), 233–73.

21. Big Punisher, "The Dream Shatterer," *Capital Punishment*, CD (Relativity, 1998).

22. For more on the tensions between hip-hop and reggaeton in Puerto Rico, see MC Welmo's essay in this volume. See also, Jesús Triviño, "Spanish Fly," *The Source*, March 2004, 99–101.

23. The segment in question can be found in chap. 8 of the *Chosen Few* DVDs, "Hip-Hop Latino vs. Reggaeton." Interestingly, Vico C's examples also differ in terms of tempo, as he performs the reggaeton rhythm noticeably faster than the hip-hop beat. Although hip-hop and reggaeton tracks alike can range fairly widely in terms of bpm (beats per minute), it is not altogether inaccurate to represent reggaeton as, on the main, generally faster than hip-hop. This, in part, relates to reggaeton's dance-centric character.

24. Not insignificantly, Vico C and El General are often discussed, and even marketed, together. For example, BMG issued a joint greatest hits CD for the two, despite that it simply offers alternating solo tracks from each: See El General/Vico C, *Juntos* (BMG 74321 92210–2, 2002). Also, it is worth noting that El General's influence on the Puerto

Rican hip-hop/reggae scene is perhaps as pervasive as Vico C's. El Comandante's *Asi Asi* (1991), for instance, in addition to a song written by Vico C ("She Likes My Reggae"), includes covers of El General's "Tu Pun Pun" *and* "Te Ves Buena."

25. An online search turns up a number of references in this vein, some asserting that reggae was brought to Panama in the early twentieth century, others alleging that Jamaicans came to work on the canal in the 1970s. See, e.g., http://www.reggaetonfever .com/reggaeton_history.php; http://www.rhapsody.com/latin/latinraphiphop/reggae ton/more.html; and http://www.hispanicscene.com/html/reggaeton.html (all accessed on January 6, 2007).

26. For examples in which reggae connoisseurs dismiss (as well as defend) reggaeton, see, e.g., http://www.bloodandfire.co.uk/db/viewtopic.php?t=2282&highlight=reggae ton, and http://www.bloodandfire.co.uk/db/viewtopic.php?t=3425&highlight=reggae ton (both accessed January 7, 2007); or http://www.dancehall reggae.com/forum/ showthread.php?s=5a0ba209bcd27a57513564dee20f2f27&t=99529 (accessed January 29, 2007).

27. Rex Nettleford, *Mirror Mirror: Identity, Race and Protest in Jamaica* (Kingston, Jamaica: LMH Publishing, 1970 [2001]), 20.

28. Ibid.

29. Deborah Thomas, *Modern Blackness: Nationalism, Globalization, and the Politics of Culture in Jamaica* (Durham, N.C.: Duke University Press, 2004), 43.

30. Panama Canal Authority, "Panama Canal Gallery": http://www.bbc.co.uk/ his tory/british/victorians/panama_gallery_04.shtml (accessed January 25, 2007).

31. The local interplay between these styles, not to mention what was referred to as *haitiano* music as well as Latin Caribbean and Central American genres, has yet to be analyzed in depth. (El General, for instance, in the interview with Christoph Twickel published in this volume, mentions the popularity of Haitian music in Panama at the same time reggae was catching on.) As the work of Carla Guerrón-Montero suggests, the ways these genres articulate with Panamanian cultural politics is a complex, interesting, and understudied story. In particular, it would be useful to know how and why reggae eventually came to such cultural prominence among Afro-Antilleans in Panama. See Carla María Guerrón-Montero, "Can't Beat Me Own Drum in Me Own Native Land: Calypso Music and Tourism in the Panamanian Atlantic Coast," *Anthropological Quarterly* 79, no. 4 (fall 2006): 633–63.

32. One well-circulated account also names an immigrant called "Guyana" as having "introduced" reggae to Panama, though this story sounds somewhat apocryphal given the already longstanding musicocultural links between Panama and Jamaica. See, e.g., http://es.wikipedia.org/wiki/Plena_(Panam%C3%A1) (accessed January 29, 2007).

33. Thanks to Mario Luis Small for telling me about *petróleo* (via e-mail, January 2007). For a colorful discussion of the differences between plena, bultrón, and reggaeton in Panama, see the following message-board discussions: http://foros.latinol .com/cgi-bin/ultimatebb.cgi?ubb=get_topic&f=47&t=000683; and http://foros.latinol

.com/cgi-bin/ultimatebb.cgi?ubb=get_topic&f=38&t=000051&p=3 (both accessed February 20, 2008).

34. Surveying some of the latest songs produced in Panama, one finds the practice continuing: hence, in 2006, one could hear the Panamanian DJ Principal proclaiming himself "El Rey del Dancehall" with the same cadences and over the same riddim that Jamaica's Beenie Man used to crown himself "King of the Dancehall" a few months earlier, or Panama's Aspirante employing for "Las Cenizas Dijeron Goodbye" (The Ashes Said Goodbye) the melody from Jamaican singer Gyptian's "Serious Times" over a reverent re-lick of the strikingly acoustic *Spiritual War* riddim that propels the original (though Aspirante changes the text from a meditation on the state of the world to a failed relationship). For elaboration on Jamaica's "riddim system" and the practice of re-licks, covers, and other kinds of versions—as well as a discussion of vocal or melodic approaches—see Peter Manuel and Wayne Marshall, "The Riddim Method: Aesthetics, Practice, and Ownership in Jamaican Dancehall," *Popular Music* 25, no. 3 (2006): 447–70.

35. Raquel Cepeda, "Riddims by the Reggaetón," *Village Voice*, March 28, 2005, http://www.villagevoice.com/music/0513,cepeda,62467,22.html (accessed February 1, 2007). Moreover, for all their commitments to upholding and engaging with reggae tradition, Panamanian artists have also transformed and left their own mark on reggae as the world knows it—and not simply by adapting the form for Spanish, which would eventually spur the reggaeton revolution in Puerto Rico. Here again Tego seems to hit the mark: "In Panama, there's more soca influences. It's faster," he told Raquel Cepeda (ibid.). And though that observation is not true across the board, it is consistent with El General's memory, as recounted in the *Chosen Few* documentary, of performing over sped-up reggae riddims during the formative days of Panama's plena scene, playing the instrumental sides of 33 rpm records at 45 rpm. In addition, although one finds a wide range of tempos across Panamanian reggae recordings, there is also an entire subgenre called "110," which directly refers to the number of beats per minute—an above-average bpm for most dancehall (or recent reggaeton, for that matter). And yet, in other ways, the Panamanian reggae scene has long been in conversation with developments in Puerto Rico, though the global rise of reggaeton and the more recent advent of new communication and information technologies have accelerated this exchange. Panamanian producer El Chombo, whose very nickname signifies "piel morena" (dark skin) in Panama, collaborated with Puerto Rico's DJ Negro in the late '90s for the first of his *Los Cuentos de la Cripta* (Tales from the Crypt) series, e.g., while a disc from another series, "Spanish Oil"—a reference to *petróleo* reinforced by the name of Chombo's label imprint Oilers Music—apparently carried the subtitle "From the underground with class," which clearly makes reference to the mid-'90s discourse around Puerto Rico's hybrid of reggae and hip-hop. (This bit of information surfaced in an online discussion about Panamanian reggae, as left in a comment by "cristo," May 31, 2005: http://www.fly.co .uk/fly/archives/2005/04/reggaeton_the_story_so_far.html [accessed January 28,

2007].) More recent Panamanian artists—such as El Roockie, Kafu Banton, Dicky Ranking, Aldo Ranks, Danger Man, and others—differ in the degree to which they engage directly with Jamaican dancehall or with a reggaeton-inflected style.

36. Notably, the compilation also includes contributions by both Afro-Honduran reggae singers such as La Diva and Arzu, as well as the Puerto Rican rapper Lisa M, demonstrating the rapid spread of Spanish-language dancehall reggae across cosmopolitan New York and its postcolonial networks.

37. For discographical information on these releases, as well as photos of the labels, see http://www.discogs.com/release/366596 and http://www.discogs.com/release/3666 00 (accessed February 2, 2007).

38. Orlando Patterson, "Ecumenical America: Global Culture and the American Cosmos," *World Policy Journal* 11, no. 2 (1994): 103–17.

39. *Dancehall Reggaespañol*, liner notes (Columbia Records, 1991), 3.

40. See, e.g., the message board debate at http://www.bacanalnica.com/foros/view topic.php?t=11646&postdays=0&postorder=asc&start=32&sid=d94a213b33a0169fa191c 301c8a09565 (accessed January 28, 2007). As with all of my Internet sources, I have preserved the ("incorrect") orthographical renderings here, despite that "puertoriqueña" would not be capitalized in Spanish, etc. For more on Panamanian perceptions of reggae, see Ifeoma Nwankwo's interview with Renato elsewhere in this volume.

41. See Deborah Pacini Hernandez's essay elsewhere in this volume for a detailed description of Oquendo's project, as well as its implications for understanding reggaeton's interplay with Dominican music.

42. Although many of these terms will be familiar to readers, I realize that for others this shorthand may appear esoteric. Briefly then, by "breakbeat" I refer to the sampled, looped, funk-derived drum tracks (also called "breaks") used in countless hip-hop tracks; and when I refer to a "dubby" bassline, I mean that it features a lot of repeated notes (at the level of the 16th note), a signature approach for reggae bass players.

43. A group such as Proyecto Uno, who emerged from the New York merengue, merenhouse, "Latin house" and hip-house scenes with a similar fusion around the same time (i.e., the early '90s) and sustained a career throughout the decade (and, to some extent, into the present), stands as an exception to meren-rap's brief bubble of popularity. It is noteworthy that such groups, however, as well as individual members such as Magic Juan, have in recent years incorporated the sounds and styles of reggaeton into their merengue-centered pop (see, for instance, Magic Juan's 2003 hit "Meniando La Pera"), not unlike the similar incorporation of reggaeton into contemporary bachata and salsa, among other popular, "Latin" genres.

44. "Flip-tongue" is a term I learned in Jamaica by which dancehall DJs refer to the double-time style of rapping for which they have become known and which served as a touchstone for many early *underground* MCs in Puerto Rico. This vocal approach, which usually involves an alternation between virtuosic double-time passages (often at the level of the 32nd note) and slower, regular cadences, can also be found on a great number of reggae-influenced hip-hop recordings from the early and mid-1990s.

45. Other notable producers of the period include DJ Eric, DJ Adam, DJ Goldy, Mister G, DJ Joe, and, later in the decade, DJ Blass and DJ Dicky. The forms such recordings took, of course, were directly tied to the media on which they circulated: thus, typically a mixtape contained two 20–30 minute continuous mixes (one for each side of the cassette).

46. As discussed in the opening of this essay, the alternating snares in contemporary productions such as "Gasolina" can thus be heard as subtly embodying a connection to this earlier pastichelike practice of alternating between recognizable, resonant samples from hip-hop and reggae. Moreover, recent songs such as "Reggaeton Latino" by Don Omar or "Sola" by Hector "El Father," continue, for all their commitment to the bedrock *boom-ch-boom-chick*, to employ contrasting grooves in order to propel the songs forward and, perhaps, to appeal to different audiences.

47. Again, just to be clear here, when I refer to hip-hop/underground "MCs" and reggae "DJs" in this context, I describe an essentially equal function—that of the rapper (rather than turntablist/selector). The terminology may differ depending on local parlance, but both MCs and DJs (in hip-hop and reggae, respectively) are descended from the radio and "talkover" DJs of the '50s and '60s who inspired early hip-hop and dancehall vocalists. For more on this nomenclature, as well as an explanation of the recycling of certain melodic contours in dancehall, see Manuel and Marshall, "The Riddim Method."

48. For extensive accounts of Puerto Rico's (and the Caribbean's) increasingly circular migration patterns and the social and cultural implications thereof, see Francisco L. Rivera-Batiz and Carlos Santiago, *Island Paradox: Puerto Rico in the 1990s* (New York: Russell Sage Foundation, 1996); Carlos Antonio Torre, Hugo Rodríguez Vecchini, and William Burgos, eds., *The Commuter Nation: Perspectives on Puerto Rican Migration* (Río Piedras: University of Puerto Rico Press, 1994); Patricia Pessar, *Caribbean Circuits: New Directions in the Study of Caribbean Migration* (New York: Center for Migration Studies of New York, 1996); and Jorge Duany, *The Puerto Rican Nation on the Move: Identities on the Island and in the United States* (Chapel Hill: University of North Carolina Press, 2002).

49. One of the most salient examples of such an invocation of *melaza* can be found in Ismael Rivera's version of Catalino "Tite" Curet Alonso's "Las caras lindas de mi gente negra": "Somos la melaza que ríe/la melaza que llora/la melaza que ama . . ." (We are the molasses that laughs/the molasses that cries/we are the molasses that loves . . .). Linked to ideologies of *mestizaje*, or race mixing, *blanqueamiento* refers to the processes, practices, and ideologies of social "whitening" in the Latin Caribbean and Latin America. Often linked to individuals' desire for social mobility or to elite and middle-class nationalisms (with all the exclusions and internal colonialisms of such projects), *blanqueamiento* has been explored by a great many observers and analysts of the region. See, e.g., Peter Wade, *Race and Ethnicity in Latin America* (London: Pluto Press, 1997), 84–87.

50. Raquel Z. Rivera, "Del underground a la superficie," *Claridad*, February 10–16, 1995, 29.

51. The following website, prepared in 2002 but referring to the debates of 1995, offers a series of talking points for those who oppose the morality expressed in "rap y reggae obsceno": http://www.moralidad.com/alertas/alerta1.htm (accessed February 7, 2007).

52. Raquel Z. Rivera, "Del underground a la superficie," 29.

53. See the *Chosen Few* documentary for DJ Coyote's testimony about putting reggaeton on the radio as well as a segment on *In the House* magazine.

54. For an extended discussion of the movements and meanings of "Dem Bow," see Wayne Marshall, "Dem Bow, Dembow, Dembo: Translation and Transnation in Reggaeton," *Lied und populäre Kultur/Song and Popular Culture: Jahrbuch des Deutschen Volksliedarchivs* 53 (2008): 131–51.

55. Significantly, it appears (to my ears) that the most common versions of the *Dem Bow* riddim circulating in Puerto Rico may in fact be sampled from Nando Boom's "Ellos Benia," produced by Dennis "the Menace" Thompson, rather than directly from Shabba Ranks's "Dem Bow" (though elements from the Bobby Digital version crop up as well).

56. I should confess that although I am able to identify a good number of the references in such recordings thanks to my acquaintance with the hip-hop and reggae repertories from that period, I am no doubt missing many others, especially, perhaps, references to Puerto Rican (pop and folk) songs—a testament to the sort of listening competency expected, rewarded, and engendered by these *underground* productions.

57. See, e.g., a message-board discussion at reggaetonline.com from November 2006, which offers the following opinion: "The use of the dembow beat came in *Playero 38* first, with the song 'La Musica Negra-Hispana' by Blanco. That song, in its pure and simple self, including the timing of the start of the song after Daddy Yankee's 'Me Quieren Ver Muerto En Mi Funeral', dropping the beat like that, is the essence of Reggaeton right there. If that doesnt make you get up and perrear and dance, I don't know what will." The same author, gsus25th, continues by contending "You can safely say that Playero popularized the dembow beat with *Playero 38*": http://www.reggaeton line.net/forums/threadnav15418–1–10.html. I am not sure why *Playero 37*, however, which features pistas that also employ *dembow*-style rhythms and *Dem Bow* samples, would not be given consideration in this respect, unless it was simply less popular. Appearing to affirm (or perhaps inform) this account, as of the date of access, the Wikipedia entry for DJ Playero describes *Playero 38* as having "established the dembow as the official rhythm of reggaeton": http://en.wikipedia.org/wiki/DJ_Playero (both accessed February 14, 2007).

58. Affirming this connection between "la raza" and blackness in mid-1990s Puerto Rico—as opposed to, say, the Mexican-accented meaning of "la raza," which signifies that country's particular, mixed racial heritage—Mayra Santos writes: "If before, 'Cocolos' (salsa fans) were the ones looked upon as the biggest delinquents in the community, and the ones to develop the discourse of a 'Latino' and 'black' identity, now

they're the rappers, the ones who, through their songs, create a new identity designated with the epithet of 'the race'. " "Puerto Rican Underground," *Centro* 8, nos. 1 and 2 (1996): 229.

59. Although I have not been able to find sufficient documentation, it is alleged that DJ Black and DJ Manuel were also involved in the production of *Playero 38*. It should be noted that most of these mixtapes were quite the collaborative endeavors, though many of these stories have yet to come to light.

60. See Joseph G. Schloss, *Making Beats: The Art of Sample-Based Hip-Hop* (Middletown, Conn.: Wesleyan University Press, 2004), 114–19.

61. For examples of (reggae) songs that employ these riddims, one can browse any number of online databases, e.g., http://www.dancehallmusic.de/riddimbase.php (accessed February 28, 2007).

62. For more on the use or reuse of such melodic contours and on unconventional relationships to key in the dancehall tradition, see Manuel and Marshall, "The Riddim Method," esp. 459–60.

63. Juan Flores, "Creolité in the 'Hood: Diaspora as Source and Challenge," *Centro Journal* 16, no. 2 (fall 2004): 289.

64. Ibid., 285.

65. Frank Moya Pons, "Dominican National Identity in Historical Perspective," *Punto 7 Review* (1996): 23–25 (quoted in Flores, "Creolité in the 'Hood," 289).

66. Flores, "Creolité in the 'Hood," 288, 283.

67. See, e.g., Peter Manuel, "Puerto Rican Music and Cultural Identity: Creative Appropriation of Cuban Sources from Danza to Salsa," *Ethnomusicology* 38, no. 2 (spring/summer 1994): 249–80.

68. Deborah Pacini Hernandez, "Dancing with the Enemy: Cuban Popular Music, Race, Authenticity, and the World-Music Landscape," *Latin American Perspectives* 25, no. 3 (May 1998): 113–14.

69. Carolyn Cooper, e.g., has argued that dancehall reggae's so-called moral slackness often served as a kind of class- and race-based critique of bourgeois values in Jamaica. See, e.g., *Noises in the Blood: Orality, Gender, and the "Vulgar" Body of Jamaican Popular Culture* (London: Macmillan, 1993). Although reggaeton's increasing emphasis on sex may seem an insignificant shift for a genre that had long represented itself, if perhaps wishfully, as "para la chica que le gusta el sex" (for the girl that likes sex; a sound bite from *The Noise 1* [ca. 1992]), it is worth noting that this turn also represents a commitment to commercializing the hardcore rather than cleaning it up for the mass market. Such a strategy stands in contrast, for instance, to the attempts at commercialization via romantic themes and "clean lyrics" during the mid-1990s in response to calls for censorship and seizures of cassettes. See, e.g., *The Noise 3* (ca. 1993), which bills itself as "temas románticos al estilo de reggae" (romantic songs in a reggae style) in the faux-radio intro, or *The Noise 4* (ca. 1995), which advertises "Clean Lyrics" on the cover.

70. It is worth noting as well that especially for audiences in Europe and Latin

America, the Panamanian artist Lorna's 2003 hit "Papi Chulo (Te Traigo El Mmmm)," produced by El Chombo, exposed international audiences to reggaeton style prior to Daddy Yankee's breakthrough.

71. My assertion here is supported only by anecdotal evidence, but various informal polls I have taken of students, friends, and colleagues have affirmed that few English monolinguals in the United States understand any significant portion of dancehall reggae lyrics, even by artists such as Sean Paul who strive for a certain level of "mainstream" accessibility.

72. See figures 1, 2, and 4 above for examples of such rhythmic patterns.

73. Well into the new millennium, I still routinely heard people refer to the genre simply as reggae. While working as a substitute teacher at Cambridge Rindge and Latin School and as a digital music instructor in Roxbury, Mass., from 2002 to 2003, I heard students discussing, or asking how to produce, "reggae," only to discover eventually that they referred not to Jamaican-style reggae but to the distinct timbres and rhythms of "Spanish reggae" or reggaeton.

74. Francis Jargon, "DJ Nelson," *Fader* 40 (September 2006): 158.

75. E-mail correspondence, September 28, 2006.

76. For a discussion of unconventional key relationships or "out-of-tune" singing in reggae (from which reggaeton seems to derive its own similar vocal practices), see Manuel and Marshall, "The Riddim Method," esp. 459–60.

77. Thanks to Mario Small for bringing this connection to my attention, as well as for offering other examples of localized Jamaican terms in Panamanian discourse, such as *liquiyu* (from *likkle youth*).

78. Given the "oompah" feel created by such bass patterns and a pronounced four-on-the-floor, it may be of little surprise that, according to an attuned observer in Chicago, some Jamaicans refer to reggaeton, presumably pejoratively, as "polka reggae." See http://www.gearslutz.com/board/rap-hip-hop-engineering-production/39561-where-does-reggaeton-fit-all.html (accessed April 14, 2007).

79. Jon Caramanica, "The Conquest of America (North and South)," *New York Times*, December 4, 2005.

80. See Deborah Pacini Hernandez's essay in this volume for a more detailed account of the role that Dominicans have played in reggaeton.

81. It is worth noting, however, that Saldana (a.k.a. Luny) also grew up in Puerto Rico, living with his mother and sisters before moving to Massachusetts to finish high school. Hence, his move to San Juan also represents a return, further complicating (or perhaps remaining consistent with) reggaeton's circuitous geography.

82. See, e.g., http://www.futureproducers.com/forums/showthread.php?t=130753 &page=2 (accessed May 8, 2007).

83. Of course, the mainstreaming of bachata in the United States and in Puerto Rico was preceded by the genre's rise to the mainstream in the Dominican Republic via such middle-class mediators as Juan Luis Guerra. For more on the historical development

and social status of bachata, see Deborah Pacini Hernandez, *Bachata: A Social History of a Dominican Popular Music* (Philadelphia: Temple University Press, 1995).

84. E-mail correspondence, September 28, 2006. I have left the spelling and punctuation, fairly typical of the informality of Internet discourse, largely unchanged here in order to preserve the tone of the exchange.

85. Adding to this impression is some additional, admittedly anecdotal, evidence. I have noticed since I began writing online about reggaeton and bachata that such search strings as "bachata guitar sample loops"—presumably, by aspiring reggaeton producers—bring people to my site fairly frequently; similarly, I have gathered a fair amount of informal evidence about the popularity of certain techniques and technologies used to produce reggaeton. Countless strings with some variation on the phrase "reggaeton samples para fruity loops," e.g., have led search engine sleuths to my blog. See, e.g., http://www.flickr.com/photos/wayneandwax/366562442 (accessed January 22, 2007).

86. For a provocative discussion of race and class stereotypes as projected onto reggaeton artists, see Raquel Z. Rivera's August 2006 blog post "Will the Real Blanquitos Please Stand Up?: Class, Race, and Reggaeton," http://reggaetonica.blogspot.com/2006/08/will-real-blanquitos-pleas_115637030500548739.html (accessed May 10, 2007).

87. I am thinking here of such examples as "Yasuri Yamileth," "Chacarron," and "Perreo Chacalonero," all of which inspired countless "karaoke" versions posted to YouTube. These responses to the original videos, and to other responses, frequently feature blatant performances of race and class stereotypes by the transnational, Latin American "digerati" who have access to such tools and technologies. I have written about these videos and their social and cultural implications in the following blog posts: http://wayneandwax.blogspot.com/2006/07/jajaja.html; http://wayneandwax.blogspot.com/2006/07/mas-chacarron.html; http://wayneandwax.blogspot.com/2006/07/chaca-riggity-ron.html; http://wayneandwax.blogspot.com/2006/10/we-are-all-yasuri-yamileth.html; http://wayneandwax.blogspot.com/2006/10/pooh-bear-yo-le-conozco-apenas.html; http://wayneandwax.blogspot.com/2006/10/ni-chicha-ni-limonada.html (all accessed May 10, 2007).

88. I'd like to thank a student at the University of Chicago, Diana Lester, for calling my attention to these changes in on-air practice.

89. For some fairly provocative, if perhaps tongue-in-cheek, examples of this sort of rhetoric, see a number of contentious posts by prominent hip-hop blogger Byron Crawford: e.g., "Ban reggaeton" http://xxlmag.com/online/?p=767, and "Rap against fence jumpers" http://xxlmag.com/online/?p=961 (both accessed May 10, 2007). A similar set of tensions can be read into Jon Caramanica's early 2006 article on reggaeton for the *Village Voice*, which concludes by speculating that Eminem is the least of hip-hop's worries: "Fuck a Slim Shady," writes Caramanica, "Hip-hop's race war begins here" ("Grow Dem Bow," *Village Voice*, January 10, 2006).

90. Thomas Turino, "The Mbira, Worldbeat, and the International Imagination," *World of Music* 40, no. 2 (1998): 86.

91. While fusions with salsa and bachata might be expected, more far-flung attempts to mix reggaeton with *raï* (by Spain's DOSHERMANOS) and bhangra (by such groups as Tigerstyle and Panjabi Hit Squad in the United Kingdom) suggest, again, an interesting loosing of reggaeton from its Latin/American moors. At this point, however, *desiton/bhangraton* tracks have yet to go beyond reggaeton remixes of bhangra or Bollywood tracks (and vice-versa), while raï-ggaeton appears to be little more than a one-song experiment. There may yet be a future for such fusions, however, especially considering hip-hop's and reggae's longtime Orientalist leanings. For example, calling herself Deevani, Luny's sister has taken a couple stabs at a Puerto Rican version of Hindi-esque vocals. (Thanks to Ana Patricia Silva for calling my attention to these phenomena.)

92. For a detailed description of the reggaeton scene in Minneapolis, see Peter Scholtes, "Reggaeton Animal," *City Pages*, November 22, 2006, http://citypages.com/databank/27/1355/article14906.asp (accessed May 12, 2007). Although I've yet to see a sustained study of the scene in Medellín, a U.S. blogger describes speaking with some young people there, noting, significantly, that "they were avid fans of reggaeton music above all else": http://www.katherinehouse.com/bendan/archives/2006/03/this_is_why_i_t.html (accessed May 12, 2007). And ethnomusicologist Michael Birenbaum Quintero has detailed the thriving reggaeton scene in Tumaco, Colombia, on his blog http://laguayabita.blogspot.com/2007/04/baila-negra-del-trasero-grande.html (accessed May 29, 2007). Finally, to read an early account of reggaeton's fall, see, e.g., Agustin Gurza, "When the Fad Goes Fizzle," *Los Angeles Times*, April 16, 2006.

93. Paul Gilroy, *Postcolonial Melancholia* (New York: Columbia University Press, 2005).

94. Jace Clayton, "ATLAS IMPRESSIONISTIK," http://www.negrophonic.com/2007/atlas-impressionistik (accessed May 14, 2007).

PART II
THE
PANAMANIAN
CONNECTION

Placing Panama in the Reggaeton Narrative

Editor's Notes

Although Puerto Rico would seem to have a rather strong claim on reggaeton, Panama has long occupied a special place in the story of the genre. As the birthplace of Spanish reggae, or *reggae en español*, the Central American country stands as an important link—New York notwithstanding—between Puerto Rico and Jamaica, which sent thousands of laborers there in the late nineteenth century and early twentieth, fostering the creation of Afro-Antillean communities where reggae, calypso, and other Caribbean genres would later take hold. While histories of reggaeton often pay lip service to the construction of the Panama Canal as establishing a sociocultural milieu for reggae en español, the story of how reggae became popular and was localized in Panama remains murky. Similarly, while reggaeton artists and aficionados frequently cite Panamanian DJ/rapper El General (a.k.a. Edgardo Franco) as a founding figure of the genre, the strange circuits he traveled to success have not become as enshrined in public memory, despite the important ways they bear witness to the role of migration in the story of the genre. El General's early singles "Pu Tun Tun" (1990), "Te Ves Buena" (1990), and "Muévelo" (1992) provided inspiration for a generation of aspiring vocalists across the Spanish-speaking world. Although these hit records were recorded in New York, calling attention again to the transnational dimensions of reggaeton, El General cut his teeth as a performer in Panama, notably as a member of the pioneering Panamanian reggae group, Renato y las 4 Estrellas.

Despite an acknowledgment of Panama's place in the reggaeton narrative, detailed accounts of reggae's presence and resonance in Panama have yet to come to light. Part II in this volume attempts to remedy this absence by presenting an overview of reggae in Panama alongside interviews with El

General and Renato (a.k.a. Leonardo Renato Aulder), allowing these seminal artists to tell their stories in their own words. Christoph Twickel's "Reggae in Panama: *Bien* Tough" was originally published in the German reggae magazine, *Riddim*. Translated into English for this volume, it offers a wide lens perspective on the social history of Panama's reggae scene. Importantly, the essay also portrays reggae in Panama today as a living, vibrant thing, in dialogue with Puerto Rican reggaeton but still closely linked to contemporary movements in Jamaica. Following the overview, Ifeoma Nwankwo's interview with Renato places the advent of Panamanian reggae in much needed historical and cultural context, and Twickel's conversation with El General fills out the picture further, giving a firsthand account of reggae in Panama and reggae en español in New York. Providing heretofore undocumented details of these foundational figures' careers; discussing the myriad connections between Panama, Jamaica, the United States, and Puerto Rico; and offering a lens into the cultural politics of reggae and Rastafari in Panama—among other contributions—these three pieces begin to flesh out an important but largely unexamined chapter in the story of reggaeton.

CHRISTOPH TWICKEL

TRANSLATED FROM THE GERMAN BY NOAH DAUBER

Reggae in Panama

Bien Tough

While reggaeton booms in Puerto Rico and the Dominican Republic, the only Latin American country in which there is a real tradition of reggae is Panama. It is there that the pioneers of *reggae en español* live, there that the most serious reggae radio stations are found, there that reggae is improvised on rickety buses, and there that Marcus Garvey found enlightenment on the canal. In short, Panama is the forgotten republic of reggae.

For a small country, there are many singers. Just 2.8 million people live in Panama, not counting the Colombian immigrants. But it sure doesn't lack artists. La Fabulosa, La Mega, Wao, Super Q . . . during the reggae boom at the end of the nineties almost a dozen DJs played the sound in the narrow stretch of land between Panama City and Colón, between the Pacific Ocean and the Caribbean, just eighty kilometers from each other. Twenty-four hours *full power*. The Panamanian dancehall compilations were called *El Imperio, Zona de Guerra, The Squad,* or *Cuentos de la Cripta* (Stories from the Grave). Every few weeks there was a new one, packed with cranked-up, technoid riddims, machine-gun fire, sirens wailing, battle rhymes, male and female choirs which hurl vulgarities at the other sex; they call it *la plena.*

What Panama was missing was record presses to cheaply produce singles and a sound system culture to play them. Thus a reggae scene which always lived "hand to mouth" but managed somehow to keep going. The record labels never really existed. The producers such as the legendary Pucho Bustamante or Rodney Clark, otherwise known as El Chombo, brought a few singers for 200 to 400 dollars a song into the studio, and mixed a compilation with 20 to 30 tracks; and the DJs pushed the CD on the market. Cheaply produced and heavily promoted, they used to sell a few thousand. But meanwhile Panama is also full of CD burners. Artists, radio DJs, producers—no matter whom you ask on the Panamanian isthmus—they all give the same answer: the market is dead. "The DJs on the radio promote albums differently because of the piracy," explained Rolando Guillén, one of the first radio DJs in the country and now at WAO 97.5 FM. "During rush hour, cars with speakers drive around and sell CDs for $5 at the intersection. This makes them more than if they sold them in the record stores. So they are competing directly with the pirates."

There is a sense of crisis in the motherland of reggae en español. And this just at the time when reggaeton—"Jump-up-Dancehall" with many hooklines and hardly any lyrics—conquered the dance charts of the Spanish-speaking world. Everything is produced in Miami, New York, and Puerto Rico. Panama Music Corp. is the only label in the country which can profit from the boom and produce reggaeton for export. In Mexico, Colombia, and Spain it has done well. The Panamanian teen sensation La Factoria is touring worldwide.

Every kid in Panama knows the story of Edgardo Franco, a.k.a. El General, the singer who has achieved the greatest international fame. In 1985 he ended up in New York, not so much hoping to become famous, but rather hoping to leave his teenage years as Dread in the outskirts of Panama City behind him and to study accounting.[1] A year later, his old friend Nando Boom visited him and told him that in Panama everyone was now singing in Spanish. He had already noticed that Spanish was better received on the occasions when he played parties with his Bachelor Sound System. In 1990 a producer brought him into the studio to give him a try. The result was "Tu Pun Pun,"[2] a beatbox, bassline and the squawking DJ style of El General. "Tu pun pun, mami, no me va a matar"—"Your boom-boom, mamma, doesn't kill me." It was the first Spanish dancehall song to make it onto the radio in the United States. Hits such as "Te Ves Buena," "Muévelo," "El Caramelo," "Las Chicas," or the "Borin-quen Anthem" with C&C Music Factory followed.

El General sits in his apartment in a skyscraper in the posh district of Paitilla, high above the bay of Panama City, and he recalls how it all began back in 1978. One of El General's friends was cleaning in a disco where they could pick up the B-sides of Jamaican singles on tape from the DJ stand—always higher pitched (i.e., sped-up) for greater effect. They forced the tapes on bus drivers and improvised live over them during the ride: Reggae Sam, Renato, Nando Boom, Mauricio, Chicho Man, and others. "You have to be able to improvise, and I was so good, that they called me 'El General,' because General Torrijos had the highest command." At that time it was still in Patois, and with dreadlocks that were as long as possible given that the police under the military dictatorship—first under Torrijos and then under General Noriega—would

1. From left to right: Rasta Nini and a friend in Colón, Panama. Photo by Christoph Twickel.

routinely cut them off. "Everyone thought we were crazy because of our hair. People didn't want to sit next to us on the bus." In 1979 in the Teatro Río there was the first battle between singers from Panama City and Colón. "The people from Colón bussed in their people. And they won. But not because of the singing, but because they had longer dreads. One of them, Rasta Nini, had hair to his butt."

Today Rasta Nini's dreadlocks reach his ankles (figure 1). He is the first Rastafarian of Panama; he is wearing a Bob Marley T-shirt, and above his beat-up sofa hangs a giant Lion of Judah made of glitter paper. "Today Spanish reggae is popular all over the world, everyone knows the Dominicans and the Puerto Ricans, but people don't know that the pioneers came from Panama," says Nini. "Kafu Banton, Aldo Ranks, Junior Ranks, Killa Ranks, Nes y Los Sensacionales, Tony Bull . . . Colón is the cradle of champions."

Here in his apartment in Calle 9 in Colón, they took up Spanish Reggae for the first time. The group was called Cheb, and Supa Nandy was the singer. In 1985 they put out an LP, one side in English, the other in Spanish.

Nini lives in a condemned house. A couple of years ago his balcony fell, and last year the ceiling of his living room caved in. But in this city at the Caribbean end of the Canal, 95 percent of the residents live in condemned houses. These are old houses built in the colonial style with wooden verandas, where one imagines that the higher-up employees of the U.S.-American Panama Canal Company lived in the beginning of the twentieth century. At that time around 100,000 Afro-Antilleans came to the country, to work on the canal. Around

30,000 of them died between 1881 and 1914 of malaria, yellow fever, or consumption. Most of them came from Barbados, Trinidad, Tobago, or Jamaica. Rasta Nini also found in the story of the West Indian martyrdom on the isthmus the beginnings of his religion. Panama should be considered the "Motherland of Rasta, the Rastafarian movement and black culture," he explains, and further states:

> Rastafarianism was born in the republic of Panama, in the province of Colón.
>
> Marcus Garvey worked during the building of the canal as a journalist, and he fought for better wages as a trade unionist. At that time wages were set according to the so-called Silver Roll for the blacks and the Gold Roll for the whites. It was here that he met prophets like Freddie Douglas. They foretold that a black king would come from the East who would free the black race from its suffering. And this emperor would be called Haile Selassie I. All that happened here. Then Garvey returned to Jamaica and preached what Freddie Douglas and the others had taught him.

In the year 2000 Rastafarianism was recognized as an official religion in Panama, not the least because of Rasta Nini's work in raising awareness. He also fought unstintingly for "roots and culture" in the Reggae scene, that is, for the turn to social and spiritual themes. One of the converted sits on Nini's sofa and argues about music and responsibility. "When you have a lot of twenty-something *muchachos* in front of you," says Kafu Banton, "you can't just sing culture, they want to jump around as well. But one has to begin to form them, to teach them, even if they don't accept it right away, they must swallow it." Kafu won a prize in 2003 with the song "Vivo en el Ghetto" (I live in the Ghetto), though it did not play very often on the radio. Banton continues:

> Before there was the censorship of the junta, but now it is the DJs, who do not bring up conscious things, because they are worried that people will turn to another station. But the DJs also have the responsibility not to play ten gunfight songs in a row. Here it's easy to get any kind of weapon; you bump into a twelve-year-old on the street and he shows you a 9-millimeter. And they use them too. Calle 2 has problems with Calle 5 over nothing, no one knows why they are fighting, but if you walk along the wrong street, they shoot you. The idea of One Love is opposed to all that.

Rasta Nini estimates that there are a couple hundred Rastafarians in Panama. In the eighties everyone wanted to go around like a Rasta, not because of the religion, but because it was cool. Today Jah has competition in the battle for lost souls in the ghetto. Many singers who were evangelized through the widespread Pentecostal churches of Central America promote the Christian God. "I made a mistake, I worshipped a foreign god," explains El Roockie, for instance, the most successful singer of the young generation. "I was just very influenced by Sizzla, and so I mentioned Selassie I in a song." His manager stands next to him, clearly a brother in the faith, and nods energetically. El Roockie, just twenty, grew up in San Miguel, one of the *barrios populares* of Panama City, the slums. "We had a kind of another reality in music," he says.

> I grew up with one of the worst gangs in the neighborhood Los Topa y Muere, but I had learned already that the lives of these people lead either to prison or death. When I became famous, I founded a crew with six of seven of my brothers, La Nueva Amenaza (The New Threat). I made money from our shows and could buy guns, I was their arms dealer. In time, I learned that we can't protect our lives with weapons; I had friends who died though they were carrying pistols. I needed to find something else to help me feel strong and safe and that could only be God. From then on I began to fill my songs with positive content and with what I have come to know of the lives of other people.

El Roockie is currently the number one star among teens in Panama. At the big free concert for the hundredth anniversary of the founding of the Central American minirepublic, he stood alone on the open-air stage and lip-synched his songs. One is called "Grave Error": "They believe they have the power of my God—what a grave error." Another is called "Falta Otro en el Barrio" (Another Is Missing from the Barrio) about a *compañero* who was caught. A good 50,000 kids sing along with him on the waterfront in Panama City. And once El Roockie begins to sing his romantic songs, they really lose it. "I'll go to the ends of the earth for your love," he sings, as the girls storm the stage, holding banners and swinging their hips. His debut album, signed to Sony for the international market, is three-quarters full of such love songs, and they are tolerably, tastefully produced by El Roockie.

"Before, everything was *bien tough*. But today those who are singing about the hard life are not as successful as those who are dealing with romantic themes," according to radio DJ Rolando Guillén. "Today you rarely hear a vulgar song on the radio any more." The new Panamanian compilations are full of "románticos," Latin pop ballads which try to sound like reggae. This has little to do with "lovers rock," but rather with the long tradition of bolero in Latin American countries. El Roockie relates that he played the bolero records of his mother, who kept them after she split up with his father.

In the classic bolero, which appeared in the forties and fifties, the male singer bemoans the false love of a woman—a sentimental symptom of the changing relationship between the sexes: With the movement from the country to the large cities of Latin America and the United States, women began to work outside the family and to escape the control of the men. Boleros were the pop-culture, macho, social reaction to the erosion of male dominance.

Naturally, Panama's reggae scene is dominated by men—the guys on stage, the ladies in the audience. But for over a decade now the Panamanian female singers have been busting in. Lady Ann (figure 2) launched one of the first female reggae offerings in 1993, when she was a dancer for Renato, with "Quiero Sentir un Hombre." "I want to feel a man," runs the title somewhat misleadingly, since the lyrics say: "Papi, you should behave yourself, because I know the law against sexual harassment."

"Men always want to one-up me, but I dominate." Lady Ann, alias Anina, twenty-eight years old and already a veteran of the genre, sits in her beauty salon in a shopping mall in La Chorrera, one and a half hours by bus from Panama City. "I want to be a sexy woman on stage, but I'm tough with them. If a man comes on the stage, I see to it that he stands there like an idiot." Lorna, Demphra, Kathy, Caterine . . . while there are some female singers in Panama, it is definitely Lady Ann who most insistently makes the battle of the sexes her theme. "Déjalo Que Aprenda, Mama" (Leave Him Alone, So He Learns It, Mama) is the name of one song, a message to the generation of mothers: The mammas should stop cleaning up after their men. "If you want to eat, go to a restaurant or learn to cook." Her specialty is *trabalenguas*, tongue twisters: "A-pa-ni-pi-na-pa" is the name of her anthem, which the Panamanian girls in preschool already have figured out: "Apa-nipi-napa-espe-mipi-nopom-brepe," which decoded means "Anina es mi nombre" (My Name Is Anina) and even this is not lacking a message: "You have to understand that the woman has the say here."

On a hill above the shanties of Chorrillo the government has given permission for a kind of Panamanian mini-Disneyland to be built. It's called Mi Pueblito, and for a dollar one can see all the folk cultures which are to be found in the "rainbow of races" of Panama: in the camps of the Kuna Yala they sell real indigenous jewelry; in a village square in the style of the Chiriquí municipality, a *típico* band is entertaining a wedding party; and in an Afro-Antillean-style wooden house, there is a screening. Professor Gerardo Maloney, who runs an Afro-Caribbean library here, shows his documentary about calypso in Panama. The sleepy Caribbean town of Bocas del Toro at the border with Costa Rica is the birthplace of national calypso. Old men, descendants of the canal

2. Lady Ann poses in front of her beauty salon in La Chorrera, Panama. Photo by Christoph Twickel.

or banana plantation workers from Trinidad, show what they can do: Lord Wimba, Sir Valentino, Black Majesty, Two Gun Smokey, Lord Delicious, and Lord Kontiki. At the top is, naturally, Lord Cobra, "King of Calypso," ever since he outsung Mighty Sparrow in the Club Nacional in the '50s, blowing him off the stage. "Sparrow will never come back to Panama," Cobra sings in a hoarse voice.

El General is also there. "Calypso was really big here," he says. "Actually it was through it that we learned what it meant to improvise. Because these guys had unbelievable skills." Professor Maloney is proud that the man who has brought the Afro-Caribbean culture of Panama to the world has come to the screening. At that time, at the end of the '70s, the professor was the only one who had the desired stuff which El General and the other teenagers needed. Besides books on Rasta culture, Maloney brought back reggae singles from his trips to Jamaica. "Thus we always came to him, borrowed the records, and made our tapes with them. He was the only one who had them."

NOTES

A version of this essay was first printed in *Riddim* magazine in May/June 2004.

1. Editors' Note: *Dread* is used here as a synonym of *Rasta* and points both to El General's adherence to the Rastafarian religion as well as to wearing his hair in "dreadlocks."

2. Editors' Note: Although El General refers to the song as "Tu Pun Pun," which is what he sings as well, the record was released under the title "Pu Tun Tun," presumably to avoid censorship.

The Panamanian Origins of *Reggae en Español*

Seeing History through "Los Ojos Café" of Renato

Reggaetón, as most people outside Latin America know it today, and as many within Latin America represent it, is associated with Puerto Rico above all. This essay complicates conventional histories of reggaetón by focusing on Panama, and on the genre's roots in the black West Indian descended communities of the Isthmian nation. Especially foregrounded here is Renato (Leonardo Renato Aulder), an individual widely recognized throughout Latin America as a key founding father of *reggae en español*, the broad genre of which Puerto Rican reggaetón is one manifestation. Renato and his fellow pioneers blended Jamaican beats, U.S.-American style, and Panamanian language and culture to produce the first reggae-based songs in Spanish. Renato's career was launched in 1984 with "The D.E.N.I.," which became a hit thanks to DJ Héctor Tuñón. In 1985, Renato created the song "La Chica de los Ojos Café," the first reggae en español song to become an international hit. In the first few years after he first made the song, it was so popular that other Latin American musicians began to do covers of it. For instance, Dominican artists such as Wilfrido Vargas and Richie Ricardo did merengue versions. Renato was pleasantly surprised by his and the song's continued popularity during a trip to Ecuador in 1994, almost ten years after he first recorded it. Here he provides significant insight into the cultural milieu and context out of which the song and the genre arose, as well as into his own development as an artist and as a Panamanian man of West Indian descent. From Renato's "American" childhood on the Canal Zone; to the birth and growth of the "sound systems" and their role in the creation of the genre; to the formative influence of Jamaican reggae and U.S. R&B on him and on the genre; to the similarities, differences, and connections between the Panamanian and Puerto Rican manifestations of

1. Renato at the studio. Photo by Rose Cromwell.

the genre; to the future of both—this piece allows us to gain a more developed sense of the man, the history of the genre, and the interactions between the nations and cultures that met and meet "inside the heart of Panama."[1]

As Renato reveals, the Jamaican connection was especially crucial to the formation of the genre, from the *Pounder* or *Dem Bow* rhythms that are still the base of virtually all reggaetón, to the ways the music was made and spread (sound systems), to the content, phrasing, and delivery of the songs. Even the names of a substantial number of Panamanian reggae artists then and now are Hispanicized reworkings of typical Jamaican reggae musicians' names or key phrases (El General, Nando Boom; Kafu Banton; Raíces y Cultura [Roots and Culture]). According to radio DJs Fussa and Rudy (from Panama's "Fabulosa Stereo" 100.5 FM radio station), "Panama has always had the influence of Jamaican reggae, the Jamaican rhythm."[2] As both DJs have noted, Sizzla and other Jamaican artists are still quite popular on the isthmus. Panama was actually the first Latin American country to produce and popularize Jamaican reggae rhythms with Spanish lyrics, a new musical form that drew Puerto Rican artists such as Vico C and Ivy Queen to visit Panama repeatedly during the genre's Panamanian early heyday. Renato himself has succinctly noted: "we are [the Jamaicans'] sons and the Puerto Ricans are our kids."[3] The impact of U.S.-produced R&B and, more recently, hip-hop should also not be ignored: "Many of us come from the R&B music because it's what we knew." Gladys Knight and the Pips were among Renato's favorites. Out of this All-American (in the continental sense) stew came Renato the man, and reggae en español, the genre.

AN AMERICAN CHILDHOOD

I'm from Pedro Miguel in the Canal Zone. My father and mother were moving when I was in the womb. They were moving to a place in Río Abajo called Parque Lefevre. When it was time for me to be born, there was a problem in Panama between Americans and Panamanians. It was 1961, and they were trying to cross to Gorgas Hospital . . . There were students from the National Institute fighting with the soldiers in the Canal Zone. They decided to take me to Saint Thomas Hospital. I was born there, and the day after they took me to Gorgas Hospital because my father was a worker in the Canal Zone, in the dredging division. My mother also worked in the zone in Amador. My grandfather was a security guard at the Gamboa prison. Now they call it "El Renacer."

. . . My upbringing was completely American. I didn't know I was Panamanian. I spoke English. I didn't know how to speak Spanish.[4] I played American football. Then we had problems, like always happens in families, my grandfather with my grandmother. In '72 my mother went to the United States, and when she went, it was hard for us, because we were kids. I was eight years old . . . We were all just kids. So I grew up with my grandmother. My grandmother raised me, and my grandmother was a little superstrict. I was in Saint Mary's School, a private school with English nuns, Sister Bonaventure and all them. [Later, when] Attending the Panama school, I learned Spanish. I can't complain about my childhood. My grandparents loved me. They gave me everything I wanted: Tonka trucks, a pool table, American football. I played basketball. I played baseball. I played tennis, hockey on skates. I had a childhood full of sports. I was an athlete, and I liked to dance, because at that time, all kids liked the Jackson 5. It was what we were hooked on. At that time, it was all about the Jackson 5.

(All Panamanians like R&B. I got into Whitney Houston, the Manhattans. We listened to the Manhattans, Whitney Houston, the O'Jays, Marvin Gaye. I liked their music. All Panama was listening to Kool and the Gang, Lionel Ritchie, the Commodores. This was the music that came into Panama. All adults, whether white, black, whatever color, knew their music. Everyone danced to it. They still dance to it.)

When I moved to Panama [from the Canal Zone in 1978], I found a bunch of friends who danced in groups. I thought I was going to be a dancer, because I danced.[5] I did choreography for *quinceañeras* [celebration of a young woman's fifteenth birthday], weddings, and I started to put together a group. I met Rául, known as Pánchez, Frankito, known as El General. I met Everett. (Also Reggae Sam.) I also met Mario, who is in the United States and is a teacher, who was also part of the group. Gregorio Bellamy who is a pastor of the Tabernacle of Faith. There was another boy. We were a group. At first, everything started in Río Abajo as a game. I made songs for the public buses, because the buses in Panama had music. At that time, there was a man named Mauricio who had a recording studio called 6A, and another who had [a sound system called] Dracula Sound . . . When I was in the Zone, I listened to the American Top 10, Casey Kasem. I knew what was happening, what was new, what was coming up. (I knew about music of Bob Marley, and the music of Haiti—Tabou Combo, DP Express. Here they listened a lot to Bob Marley, Steel Pulse, Gregory Isaacs and other singers from Jamaica, like Yellow Man, who was [the one] who caused us to make our type of dancehall in Spanish. Yellow Man sang fast, more animated. We could get that feeling . . . Also Peter Metro . . . those were the artists we heard and attempted to imitate, but with our own style.)

We started to do songs for politicians [in 1980]. . . . We used to rap for the politicians. This was like a game. People liked it, because it was another way to say something political. In the buses, there was a time when the bus drivers . . . would ask us, "I want you to make me a song that says, I'm the hottest, the best looking, that my ride is the best, that all the people want to get on my bus, that I have the best music." They wanted their fame. We got instrumentals, the versions that came from Jamaica on the 12-inch record, and we sang on top of that. One person who changed it up was Wassabanga, who was popular in all the discos in Río Abajo at night. I had this desire to learn . . . at 2:00, 3:00, 4:00 in the morning. I was a kid, sixteen, seventeen years old. Well, he came here, played, went out with women, was very famous, and I liked him for his music. All the people followed him for his music, and that's how I learned. He told me, "Look, you have to learn how to move a crowd." He said to the people "Alright mamita, move you batty, man, lift up you han'." He said it all in English because it was a West Indian thing and I know it in English. There came a time when the club [Brooklyn 54] was filling up so much. . . . He would get the crowd hyped in Spanish, "Todo el mundo con una mano arriba. Yes,

mam . . . Mueve tu bam bam, mami" [Everybody put your hands in the air . . .
Yes, man. Shake your booty, mami]. I started to listen and learn from him.

When I was working in the most famous sound system in Panama [starting in 1983], which had the "electro disco" sound, I had recorded several songs on cassette. I had one that was called, "Me Voy a Viajar" (I'm Going to Travel), [another was a version of Yellow Man's] "Zungu Zungu" [but] in Spanish, and these were played in buses. There was a time when there was a sound system contest, and at that time, Revelation Viekito from Colón had made [the song] "Babylon Boops" hot. [They announced] "We're the ones who made this record hot, we are the Revelation." The people screamed. The other sound systems (like one named Sony Tape) . . . said no, we're the ones who make things hot—[with our record] "Don't Bend Down.". . . It was about making the people know that they were the ones making this hot record. (Both "Don't Bend Down" and "Babylon Boops" were songs by Jamaican artist Lovindeer.)

. . . [My song "The D.E.N.I." 1985] was a Spanish version of "Babylon Boops,"[6] but since I didn't know much Spanish, I couldn't translate it, so I started to create a story similar to the melody of "Babylon Boops." That was what I could do. "The D.E.N.I." was at that time like the police, but they were more rude than the police. They were like the CIA here, so I said in the song what D.E.N.I. could do, what they can do, like saying what the policeman can do. We had the song on cassette, and we distributed it to the buses. We charged three dollars for a cassette. The bus drivers liked that song more than any other, so there came a time when the song was so popular that a man named Héctor Tuñón took the song and put it on the radio, and it was played over and over, and it was requested and was in the top ten on BB radio. My boss said, "Hey, I'm getting calls in the office about your latest record. They want a hundred 45s of your record. Others want 200 of the record."

Well, there came a time when they had a sound system competition. I was thinking about what I should do. I said, "Look, we're going to make a record and put out a 45." He ordered a thousand 45s and had orders for 2,000. He came and said, "They asked me for 2,000 45s of your record." I didn't believe that man, but 500 arrived, and they sold out in one day, so I ordered 3,000, and "D.E.N.I." sold 10,000 copies, so much that my first payment as a recording artist was almost $800. Eight hundred dollars in '85 was like a million dollars. I didn't know what to do, because I was working as a DJ, and as a DJ at that time, I earned $100 something for two weeks, according to how much I worked, and it wasn't bad. My mom sent money from the United States, and I didn't know what to do with the money. I knew I was going to buy what I wanted. In Panama everything was expensive, my Nike shoes and everything else. [. . .]

The record was so popular. I started to get sponsors. The Harari family got me the Nike sponsorship. We did the "La Chica de los Ojos Café" (The Girl with the Coffee-Colored Eyes). "La Chica de los Ojos Café," for me, was a protest, because at this time there were too many soap operas. Soap opera fever was starting, and one was [*La Muchacha de los Ojos Café*], so I took the names of all the soap operas. I changed the verses. I wrote three verses and did the song called "La Chica de los Ojos Café" [and kept adding and changing verses as it became more popular and as I performed it more, making it more melodious]. In Panama there was a Jamaican group called Digital West or something like that, and they did a loop of a song called "Don't Run Him Down." We did it on piano and played it almost the same, [and used it as the base for "La Chica de los Ojos Café"] but you can tell it's not the "Don't Run Him Down" track. It doesn't have the same sync. It sounds the same, but it's not the same sync. They played it the way it sounds on the record. There's a part were they [turntable DJ scratching noise] so it would sound like the record. I liked that record . . . It was the longest song in the world, more than six minutes [once all the new verses were added in]. We made a cassette first to see if the song would be popular, and we made a 12-inch record, and my boss made, if I'm not mistaken, like 5[,000] or 6,000. They were all sold. The record caught on so much that it reached Colombia. After Colombia, then it went to Venezuela. It went to Ecuador. The record caught on in all of Latin America and in countries where I didn't know it had caught on. I didn't know anything about author's rights or copyrighting lyrics. I didn't know any of that. The record went to Puerto Rico, Chile, Peru, Argentina and many places, and it became so popular that I said I have to follow up. (The song stayed especially hot for at least eight years because as the soap opera moved from country to country, the audience for the song in that country increased.)

Eloy Pincay made a hit—"Xiomara la Pipona." I still hadn't conquered the art of translating. I had a friend named Xiomara who had a problem with her parents. She got pregnant, and they kicked her out of the house. I did this for her. It was a record that caught on so much that they censored it, and afterward they stop censoring it, because it was a record that talked about how I trusted in you. As your father, I'm not going to abandon you. Very cool, right? The song caught on. There I became more of a singer. More people started becoming singers.

I was going to record with Reggae Sam. I was going to record "La Chica de los Ojos Café" with a group and then with a guy from Colón, but they cheated us, as we say. They didn't call us so they could record an LP. They made an LP at the same time that I did "The D.E.N.I.," but the difference is they did it in

Spanish and English. Mine was just Spanish. It was a 45, and the people bought it. The LP they recorded didn't catch on . . . "The D.E.N.I." caught on. "La Chica de los Ojos Café" caught on. "Xiomara" caught on, and I started making records, and there started to be more singers, like Coco Man, then Nando Boom . . . Many came, like Dominique. Later came Nes y Los Sensacionales. Chicho Man came. More guys started to sing, and they started to get more ratings, more fame for the genre reggae en español.

PANAMA TO PUERTO RICO AND BACK

It became popular in all countries. In Puerto Rico, Vico C rose up, but he had the rap influence. Vico C used the footsteps of rap. He didn't do reggae, but really rap in Spanish. For me the first to do rap in Spanish was Vico C of Puerto Rico. In the revolutionizing of reggae in Spanish, the Puerto Ricans had the rap style. They started to adopt the style pretty fast. Their records started to come out and arrived in Panama. We listened to their records because they were short records. They were short records . . . One was "Para las Chicas Que Le Gusta el Sex" [Sings] They were repetitive records so that the people could learn them rapidly. Ivy Queen, started to catch on. Alberto Stylee, Baby Rasta y Gringo, OG Black, Mexicano, Don Chezina. They were the ones catching on. Ivy Queen came along (in the 1990s) . . . and she hit big here in Panama. She got "Reggae Respect"[7] [Sings] . . .

. . . From there, there was another change. El Chombo entered. Other Panamanian producers (like Gumy and Celia Torres, and later Elian Davis) got into doing Spanish reggae, making records quickly. That's when *La Cripta* came on.[8] This rhythm caught on in Colombia and many other places. That rhythm was real hot, and then Mr. Pucho Bustamante came back from New York. He knew Dennis Halliburton, who did a record called "Pounder" that really caught on, and also was big in Panama. The base of the record was [Shabba Ranks's] "Dem Bow." When [Halliburton] was in Panama, he did a CD that caught on because it had the same rhythm as "Dem Bow." This is what was called "Dem Bow." This "Dem Bow" got really popular in Panama, but in Panama things are always advancing and changing. We started to look for a new rhythm, and "Dem Bow" was not completely the base.

Some boys from Puerto Rico came. And they saw that in Panama there were ballad singers in reggae en español, "animadores" [hype men or crowd movers] in reggae en español, rappers in reggae en español. We didn't have one genre like them. Here there were a lot of romantic singers. The only one from Puerto Rico who sang like the Panamanians was Alberto Stylee, and for that reason he caught on. . . . He had a melody. The others shouted, but his was "pretty." . . . They were records that really caught on. But here in Panama, we had everything in sectors. Nando Boom was a rapper . . . Nes and I sang. We were different. We weren't all the same. We all had a different style, and the time came when the Puerto Ricans started arriving, little by little. They started to come in. Ivy Queen started coming in again . . . from 2000. Daddy Yankee started to show up. . . . Records by various artists started to arrive in the hood in Panama. Nicky Jam arrived. . . . Nicky Jam had been in Panama, had sold records when he was younger, but now he was catching on. Daddy Yankee started to catch on. Ivy Queen. Wisín and Yandel's "Dem Bow" started to hit hard. . . . They came to Panama, charging $5,000 for the first tour four years ago.[9]

Then a person arrived who, for me, really opened things up. It [happened through] Hector and Tito, the Bambino [who had a really popular television show called *Jams*]. It was Don Omar. He started to sing records like "Pobre Diabla," and the record that hit was ["Otra Noche," 2004]. This was the song that took him to a higher level. After Don Omar arrived, it opened up the market, and television . . . had the Puerto Ricans in heavy rotation. More singers from Puerto Rico started to show up. Now they were no longer just rappers, all about rapping. You could see there were more singers. And singers are accepted by the women because of the things they sing about. So, then came the first rapper who attracted the young people and the older people. It was Tego Calderón. This is what was hot here in Panama, Daddy Yankee, Don Omar, Tego Calderón, Ivy Queen. . . .When reggaetón was really blowing up big, Daddy Yankee came and put "Gasolina" on the fire. Boom. With the "Gasolina," he did all the work. Many say—I believe the Puerto Rican guys did a good job at commercializing reggae. To not give such a long name as reggae en español, they said, "el reggaetón of Puerto Rico," "this is the reggaetón of Puerto Rico." Saying Puerto Rican reggaetón is localizing it, but in reality, many people believe that the Puerto Rican reggaetón is the reggaetón of Panama. It was born in Panama. . . . (Reggaetón was made first in Panama and then Puerto Rico, and commercialized in Puerto Rico and the U.S. We created it, but did not promote ourselves enough. The record companies did not have faith in us or in the music.) [The Puerto Ricans] changed the flow, [because of the influence of] the Dominicans who came in and mixed the music. It was introduced by DJ Nelson [for example]. We're talking about Luny Tunes and Noriega. They changed the form of the melody to what Puerto Ricans were singing, because it sounded like the melody was missing. And there it was. Panama doesn't just sing reggae [though]. Panama sings soca. Panama sings salsa. The reggae singers in Panama, we are very versatile. We're not just rap, rap, rap completely. No. We're not completely rap. We sing rap, but we're more singers than rappers, so now there is Mach & Daddy, that have caught on internationally, Aldo Ranks. There is La Factoria. I'm still hot in certain countries in Latin America. There is Eddie Lover; El Roockie, who has a contract with Luny Tunes; Latin Fresh, who also has a Puerto Rican style; and there are many more. There are many more singers than those the Puerto Ricans have already seen and said they're worth looking at . . . .

(In Panama there are different divisions, in the "Culture" music, there's Kafu Banton, Raíces y Cultura. There are people who are dedicated just to "Culture." There is dancehall. There is Renato. There is . . . Comando Tiburón, Aldo Ranks . . . Junior Ranks . . . There's the dancehall clan. There is La Factoria. Now in romance, there is Aspirante, Eddie Lover, Roockie. Roockie is "culture" and dance. He does both. Rappers: Latin Fresh, Japanese, Gone Business, Danger Man. If you talk about the barrio, 50 Cent here is Danger Man. We have different genres. They are not all the same, and they all have their style.)

(. . . Lady Ann was the first [female reggae en español artist] to hit here in Panama. Lady Ann was a singer. She caught on, and Ivy Queen caught on . . . There was Mami K, and then Denfra, and then Wila Rose, and at this time, they were the only ones who caught on. Ivy Queen had problems. Everybody knows that. Lady Ann got married. Mami K got into religion. Rose stopped singing . . . but they played a very, very principal role . . . You have to have women in reggaetón, reggae en español . . . I listened to others who weren't so popular, but they are getting into it . . . The women also have their participation.

Kathy [Phillips] was a [very young] girl who was with us, who had a lot of potential . . . She was a child but she got into this. She was the daughter of the boss and she liked this [music thing]. Kathy was a child, six or seven years old, and she was singing like [us] . . . I gave her chocolate to sing with me, and she started to make records, and I don't remember the name of the record. She recorded three or four records after that. She had a promo CD that caught on last year. She has evolved, and now she is a TV personality. She has a program . . . on Telemetro called *Reggae Mania* . . . She is finishing a new CD that she gave me. She is going to move ahead, and I hope she continues . . . All the girls should come on. The more people we have, the better it is for all of us.)

. . .

The history is written. It's a genre that isn't going to die. It's going to continue. What one always asks for is respect for the veterans . . . Vico C . . . Renato . . . Nando Boom . . . Chicho Man, Ivy Queen . . . We are the people who suffered the discrimination. "Don't turn black. These are thugs. They sing for the thugs." We suffered all this discrimination. After we did all this work, now the youth has arrived, and they are reaping the economic benefit and publicity benefits. Because many people don't know how to use what they're given. They should use it, and maybe because of their age, some continue to sing, but if it weren't for the veterans, there would be no genre called reggaetón. If it weren't for the producers who suffered and struggled like a Louis Philip (Wicho), a DJ Nelson, a DJ Negro, a Luny Tunes and Noriega, a Chombo or a Nayo, or a DJ Greg. If it wasn't for all them, the things they did, there wouldn't be this genre now. Now they have worldwide respect. Before, we didn't have it, and now we do.

NOTES

Extra special thanks to Cleveland Cooper/iCliff, without whom this contribution would surely not exist. Parentheses—( )—mark text from the interviews positioned "out of order" to facilitate the flow of this piece. Square brackets—[ ]—indicate text inserted by this collector/editor to clarify or contextualize statements made during the interviews. This interview was translated from the Spanish by Premier Transcription Service.

1. Ruben Blades, "West Indian Man," *Amor y Control*, CD (Sony Records, 1992).

2. Personal interview, February 2007.

3. Personal interview, March 30, 2007.

4. The upbringing Renato describes was common. British West Indians were brought to Panama by the United States to build and staff the canal, and the descendants of these workers, known as "los zonians" (the Zonians) developed a distinctive (some in Panama would say insular) culture that blended Anglophone West Indian and U.S. culture, and were, in many ways, more culturally U.S. American than Panamanian, but at the same time not really fully U.S. American. As another respondent put it in a conversation with this collector/editor "[you were] born under the flag (but) you were not American; living in Panama but you weren't considered Panamanian." Interview with Ruthibel Livingston, February 2007.

5. Renato and his group did, among other things, R&B "flow shows" in which they re-created the shows of the Manhattans and other U.S. African American soul groups.

6. This song was a complaint about the police, called Babylon in the Jamaican songs.

7. "Reggae Respect" is a song by Ivy Queen. It is included on her 2005 compilation album *Flashback* (Univision Music Group).

8. *Cuentos de la Cripta* is a series of mixtapes/CDs (like Playero's or *The Noise*) released by El Chombo.

9. Panamanian singers were being paid $500.

INTERVIEW BY CHRISTOPH TWICKEL

TRANSLATION BY RAQUEL Z. RIVERA

Muévelo (Move It!)

From Panama to New York and Back Again,

the Story of El General

Considering that the genre has roots in Panamanian reggae as well as Puerto Rican hip-hop, Panamanian Edgardo Franco—a.k.a. El General—is frequently cited as one of the founding figures of reggaeton. When El General began his career in New York in the 1980s, he was coming from an underground movement born in Panama City and Colón barrios. From his apartment in the prestigious Paitilla neighborhood of Panama's capital, Edgardo speaks about the history of reggae in the isthmus.

_____

Reggae in Panama started when and how?

Basically, this began in the early seventies in the Río Abajo barrio where I come from. That was where the majority of the people that came to build the Panama Canal went to live. Many of them were from Jamaica, Trinidad, Barbados. And one of the things they brought was their music and some seeds of the food they ate. There was a professor, Gerardo Maloney, a professor of communications. He always traveled to Jamaica. He made documentaries and he always brought back records. We would go to his house to get the records. We had a DJ friend who worked at a discothèque. In the morning, when people were cleaning the discothèque, we would go in and record. Then we would take the recordings to the buses. We would sell them to bus drivers. That was the biggest way to promote yourself here in Panama.

When was that?

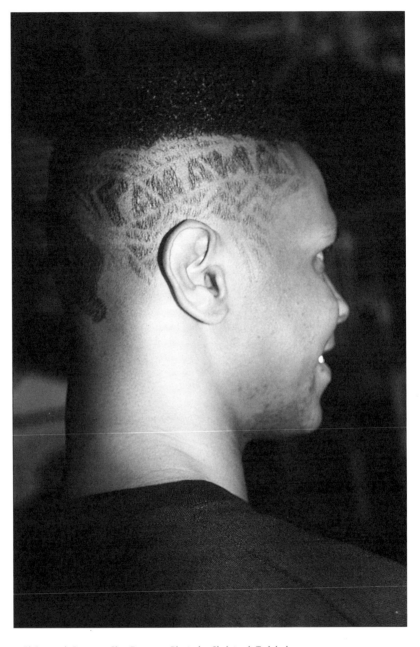

1. El General, Panama City, Panama. Photo by Christoph Twickel.

We're talking 1978–79. Buses here in Panama are peculiar; back then they were like a moving discothèque. The school kids always waited for the bus that had the latest cassette—the newest *plenas*,[1] the latest songs. That's how we started to make a name for ourselves.

Back then there were sound systems?[2]

There were some. There was one called Sound Power Disco. That was where I started. Nando Boom, Renato, Mauricio all started there . . . and also a man called Guasabanga. Guasabanga was one of the best-known DJs at that time because every time there was an instrumental section, he would start making things up. He would grab the microphone and get everybody to dance. It was really him who started this whole thing.

And always in Spanish?

No at the beginning we sang in English, in Jamaican patois.

You speak patois . . .

Yes. Both languages. We saw people liked it—but the only obstacle was that they didn't understand, so we translated the songs to Spanish.

What year are we talking about?

I'd say that was around '82, '83. Renato was the best-known DJ back then. Every time he played at a party, he invited us. He would give us the microphone and then we would pass the hat. We would go to girls' *quinceaños* parties [celebration of a young woman's fifteenth birthday]. We would go everywhere. And we really did it with passion. We loved it. We never saw it as a way of making a living, like a business or something like that. Those were really great moments, really beautiful. If there was the opportunity to get on a microphone—we would be there singing.

Was it a movement accepted by the "mainstream"?

No, in the beginning they said we were crazy. That all started in the bus. Not only reggae but also Haitian music, because those two things were really fused together. There was a place called El Garbutt, and there they waited for the bus of a driver called Calixto because he really liked reggae. So everybody waited for that bus and danced there . . . .

Reggae was not in the discothèques?

No, they still weren't playing reggae unless it was in Río Abajo or in Colón. I remember the first time I told my father I was going to sing reggae, he said: "Reggae? What's that? I'll give you a bucket of lemonade so you'll go out and sell it. You're not going to sell anything with your voice!"

And the first recordings that were made on vinyl?

A group came—I can't remember if that group was from Jamaica or Costa Rica—and they were looking for artists to record. That day I got there late, Reggae Sam got there late, but they recorded Renato and also a group from Guyana that were from Colón; they were all Rastafarian.[3] And then I had to go to the United States in 1985. And the music here was growing and growing and growing. It was incredible. If you didn't put reggae music at a dance, people would get mad and stop dancing.

And how did you get the name El General?

One of the things that dominated in this music was improvisation. You had to know how to improvise. Somebody could come up on stage when you were singing, start improvising and steal your audience. So we always had to be really sharp at improvising. I loved to improvise so much they named me El General because I was always improvising, and the maximum authority here in Panama was a general—General Torrijos.[4]

And that didn't cause problems for you? I imagine that the military didn't like that an Afro-Panamanian young man proclaimed himself a "general."

Well, our movement was really underground. It was small parties. At that time we had Rastas—dreadlocks—and when we went to the parties, the police would go after us. They would say, "Oh, so you call yourself El General, huh?" And they would cut our hair. It was a very difficult moment for us because that was a part of our religion, our music . . . .

So religion was an important part of that movement?

Yes, yes.

And is it still an important part?

Well, I'm not Rasta like in the beginning. I am in my heart but not in . . . certain things. That was one of the things that gave us more strength, because we read the papers that came from outside the country and we would see there were

Rastas that were doctors, that were lawyers. And we would ask: "Why do they treat Rastas like that here?" They wouldn't let people have their hair like that in school. Those were hard times and we expressed everything through music, everything that was happening. And people liked that.

And then you left for New York?

In '85 I went to New York to be with my mother. There I finished my degree in business administration. There was no time for music. In New York, life was a lot faster. Until a friend of mine, Nando Boom, came to New York one time. He had stayed in Panama doing music. He recorded and everything. He was a hit. He told me: "What happened, man? You have to sing. You're the one who put me on to this." Nando Boom's sister and my brother have kids together, so I always went to visit my nephews and would take Nando with me to sing. So I said: "OK, I'm going to start recording again."

You recorded in New York?

Yes. I met a Jamaican producer,[5] and that was where I recorded my first hit that was called "Tu Pun Pun."[6] And that's when my career started, three years after I left Panama.

Had you recorded anything before you left Panama?

Cassette. Everything in cassettes. I worked as a business manager in New York. I recorded the song to do something, so I wouldn't have that in my mind later when I got older: "Oh, I could have been . . ." So I said: "No. I'm going to do it to see if it works. If it doesn't work, then at least I won't have that bothering me like a thorn, because I already tried it." I was surprised when the producer called me: "That song is number five in American radio!" He was Jamaican so he didn't know anything about Latino radio stations, so he was trying to promote the song in American radio. So he says: "Listen, I have a place called Red Zone. How much will you charge them?" So I tell him: "Well, in Panama I would charge around a hundred dollars, fifty dollars. How much do you think I should charge here?" And he says: "No. You should charge them more. Charge them around a thousand!" I say: "OK, then let's do it for a thousand." But the guy said: "No. Seven hundred." So I sang. When I got to the place a lot of people were outside, and the firemen were closing up the place because there were too many people. So I got there and I said: "Hey, I'm here to sing tonight." So the guy says: "Who are you?" I say: "I'm El General." Then the guy said: "Sure. I'm Prince!" He didn't believe I was El General. So I called the other guy:

"Listen, I'm here outside the discothèque. How am I going to get in to sing?" And the guy says: "What? I'm coming to get you."

"Tun pun pun" was the only song I had recorded, but I had a lot of songs I had done in Panama. That night I saw how people reacted. I saw that there was a hunger for that music. So I decided to leave my job and dedicate myself to music.

Reggae in New York was really strong at that time, but there was no reggae in Spanish. Did you have the option of singing in Spanish or in patois?

Yes, I had to make that decision. But since I had been working when I went to the United States, I bought my sound system. I had my sound system in New York that was called Bachelor Sound. So I did parties, just like I had done in Panama. When I would do it in Spanish, I would see a stronger reaction. That was why I decided to record in Spanish instead of patois.

Latinos were your audience back then?

No, basically the audience was American, Anglo-Saxon. Like I told you before, that producer didn't know how to reach Latinos. So I sang for an American audience. Imagine, I used to sing with Cold Crush [Brothers], C&C Music Factory. When I was starting I used to sing with them on the same bill, with Martha Walsh, with all those people from back then. They would put me there like a bonus track. Little by little the audience started getting into me. I started opening up shows for Shabba Ranks, but then the guy said: "No. I don't want him to open for my show any more." It was because a lot of Latinos started coming. Latinos were starting to identify with me.

So he didn't want that competition?

He didn't want the competition.

Did you still have contact with the movement in Panama?

Everything was through the telephone because when I got there [to the United States] I was undocumented. I had a hit everywhere and couldn't travel because I didn't have my visa, didn't have a green card. I traveled as a student but when it was time to come back [to Panama] after I graduated, I stayed over there. Then in Latin America the news that El General had died started spreading. People were saying he had thrown himself off the fifteenth floor of a building in Puerto Rico, the same hotel where this guy had jumped off. This guy . . .

Héctor Lavoe?

. . . Héctor Lavoe. I had gone to Puerto Rico and I stayed in that room, so everybody started saying that I had jumped off like Héctor. Because of that many groups came out like El General y los Gatos, El General and this, El General and that. They were interpreting songs and taking advantage of the fact that I couldn't travel. Later they finally gave me a visa for extraordinary talent, and I was able to travel. The first tour was "La resurrección del General" (El General's Resurrection). It was hard getting people to go because everyone knew El General had died. I had to go on TV and invite people.

What year are we talking about?

This was like 1990–91. I already had a whole bunch of hits like "Tu Pun Pun," "Te Ves Buena," "Muévelo," but I couldn't travel. In 1992 I performed again in Panama, but like a star from outside, from the United States. The show was at Atlapa. It was an amazing show. I was reunited with my friends. It was a very emotional show because there in the audience were all those people that I had sung for at a dance, or at a Christening. They had become my fans. It was a very exciting moment—and I could only come for two days. Then the tour kept going to Ecuador, Salvador, Chile.

Then I get to Chile and this crazy situation happens. Pinochet didn't want me to come into the country, or that I call myself El General, or that I wear the uniform. He was saying he was the only general. That no other general can go there. So when we get to the airport in Chile, we had to stay like for three hours. They inspected our bags, then closed them, then inspected them again. They confiscated all of El General's uniforms. Everything having to do with El General they confiscated. And they made me sign a document saying that if I sang I couldn't say I was El General. I had to say I was Edgardo Franco. I did that concert with regular clothes and as Edgardo Franco.

What do you think of today's movement, those CDs with titles like Sin Censura, *Panamanian plena with violent and explicit lyrics?*

It's a totally different spirit. Before, we didn't do it for the money. Now there are a lot of rivalries. We . . . Renato, Sam, myself . . . Every time I had a show and they didn't hire Sam and Renato, they would come up on stage. But now I see these CDs made by different producers; they try to put the artists "you against this one," "you against this other one." They manipulate artists a lot. Back then we didn't let ourselves be manipulated because for us the music was sacred. No one could tell us: "Sing this" or "Don't sing that." Actually, we got into a lot of trouble because we sang things the government didn't want to hear.

For example?

There were a lot of protest songs against racism during that time. The racism that existed was impressive. We would protest about our hair being cut. We would ask if they would like it if we just grabbed one of their family members and cut off their hair.

Has the situation in Panama changed with regards to racism?

Yes, it has changed a lot. Not only in Panama. You can see it in many places. Now people camouflage it—in other words, racism is a thing of the past, now it's about money.

In the 1980s racism was very visible in Panama . . .

When we would get on the bus with our long hair, people would get up. No one wanted to sit next to us. They'd say: "Nah, those guys are crazy." They saw it as a crazy thing because here it's so normal that people cut their hair and keep it neat. Then suddenly you see a guy with dreads. Sometimes buses would pass by and not stop for us, taxis too.

You mentioned the rivalry between Colón and Panama.[7] How did that play out?

There was always a competition between Panama and Colón because those were the strongest groups in this movement. There was a lot of migration to Colón, even people from Guyana, Rastas that came to live here in Colón. In those days someone gave me a flyer for the first competition between Panama and Colón, in 1979, around there. First they did it here at the Teatro Río. It was one of those famous theaters that don't exist anymore. People would come in buses from Colón to support the folks from Colón. And the Panamanians would come to support Panama. But the folks from Colón won here in Panama! Everyone was mad because they hadn't done it[8] because of the singers, or their careers. They did it because it was the first time that they saw Rastas with their hair down to here in the capital! For them it was very impressive. Rasta Nini—he was part of one of the groups because he was always the president of the Rasta Association. His hair drags on the floor now. Back then that was a novelty. Sam that day put on fake Rastafarian hair, and it fell off. So Panama lost.

Later we went over there to Colón. And the day before we got to Colón, the police got us and shaved off our hair. Many of us were minors. At thirteen, fourteen we were singing in these places and talking about strong topics, so people would say: "What's going on with those kids, someone has to do something about them."

None of you had visited Jamaica?

No, it was all through books. The only one that traveled was Professor Maloney. He would bring Rastafarian books about religion, about how they lived and everything, their food. He is still a communications professor here at the university.

Was calypso also an influence here?

Yes. Calypso was very strong. That's where we really learned what improvisation was. Those guys had an impressive gift of improvisation. There was a rivalry between the calypso singers from here against the ones from Trinidad. Every time a singer from Trinidad would come here, there was this thing against them. One of the greatest, Mighty Sparrow, came here and had a competition with a singer called Lord Cobra. Cobra won so they made a song that said, "Sparrow will never come back to Panama."

Have you been to Jamaica at some point in your career?

Yes. I've gone on a few occasions. I've recorded a few things over there. And, in New York, almost all Jamaicans went to a studio called ACNF. That's where they all recorded, Shabba Ranks, all of the Jamaican artists recorded in that studio and it was like you were in Jamaica.

NOTES

This interview was conducted in Spanish, November 2003. Many thanks to George Priestley, Larnies Bowen, and Yvette Modestin for their assistance in translating Panamanian vernacular terms.

1. Editors' Note: Reggae in Panama is also known as *plena*.
2. Editors' Note: Sound systems are mobile discothèques, typically comprising not only the sound-playing and amplification equipment (e.g., turntables and speakers), but a crew of personnel to set the system up, run it, protect it, etc. Sound systems became a common feature of public musical practice in Jamaica in the 1950s and have been a staple of reggae scenes worldwide ever since.
3. He is probably referring to the group Cheb.
4. Omar Efraín Torrijos Herrera (1929–81) was leader of the military junta between 1968 and 1981. He died in an accident under unclear circumstances after General Manuel Noriega took over the position.

5. Editors' Note: The producer is, most probably, Karl Miller.

6. Editors' Note: Although El General refers to the song as "Tu Pun Pun," which is what he sings as well, the record was released under the title "Pu Tun Tun," presumably to avoid censorship.

7. Editors' Note: Here, *Panamanian* and *Panama* refer, not to the whole country, but only to Panama City and its residents.

8. Editors' Note: "They hadn't done it" refers to the judges awarding the prize to the artists from Colón.

PART III

(TRANS)LOCAL STUDIES AND ETHNOGRA-PHIES

Policing Morality, *Mano Dura Stylee*

The Case of Underground Rap and Reggae in Puerto
Rico in the Mid-1990s

In February 1995, the Drugs and Vice Control Bureau of the Police Department of Puerto Rico raided six record stores in the San Juan area. Hundreds of cassettes and compact discs of *underground* rap and reggae music—a genre known in the Island simply as *underground* and which later developed into reggaeton[1]—were confiscated. These recordings were said by the police to violate local obscenity laws through their crude references to sex and their "incitement" to violence and drug use.[2] The high-profile raids brought *underground* music to the forefront of public discourse and triggered a fierce debate regarding morality, censorship, and artistic freedom.

Underground was indeed often vulgar and violent. Sex, marijuana, and guns figured prominently in many of its lyrics. This led to the conclusion that *underground* was part of a "subculture of violence, drug use, sexual libertines and a lack of respect for others"—to quote the conservative media-monitoring group Morality in Media[3]—that incited young people to engage in "illicit" sex, violence, and drug use. It was statements like these that dominated and shaped the public discussion of *underground*.

This simplistic relation drawn between music and youth behavior constituted one of the pillars of the moral panic unleashed by the music's growing popularity and the widespread public support for state censorship.[4] Art and reality were taken to be one and the same. The declared state of national moral emergency precluded an analysis of greater complexity which could acknowledge that though art may influence reality and vice versa, there is no plain and direct causal relationship between artistic representation and lived relations.

It was partly because of this assumed causal relationship that *underground* triggered such an enormous moral panic—which reached a high point in 1995 but which has had lasting influence over the public imagination. But then again, there were other crucial factors fueling the panic directed at this genre.

First, the youthfulness of *underground* audiences exalted public apprehensions. Young people, much more so than adults, are thought to model their behavior after the lyrics they listen to. Furthermore, since the principal contradiction in our society has been most often portrayed as one of values (and not as one of structures of oppression), a key battle for social order and safety was imagined to be taking place in *underground*: the forces of good and evil (or morality and immorality) were confronting each other through youth in the *underground* arena. Whereas one youth sector was seen as the susceptible target of wayward influences, another sector was imagined to be the main agent of social disorder. Youth were being perceived as inhabiting the fragile juncture where order and compliance met disorder and transgression.

Second, the evil image of *underground* was inflated by the fear that a cultural form developed by "marginal" youth was becoming popularized among the wider population. As a music primarily developed by and identified with youth of the laboring-impoverished classes, *underground* spoke the voice of those demonized in the public imagination.[5] The youngsters accused of spreading mayhem through *underground* were branded by the presumed markings of the ghetto. Barrios, *barriadas* (slums), and *caseríos* (public housing projects) were taken to be the epicenters from which *underground*, as a cultural malaise, was radiating. The "periphery" was thus perceived as threatening the "core" with cultural contagion.

Third, rap and dancehall reggae have been accused by many of being "foreign" forms of musical expression which threaten the integrity of Puerto Rican national culture.[6] Thus, *underground* music was further debased for being a cultural product of United States' ghetto culture, which was pronounced as the original source of contagion for local youth.

Underground was monitored and repressed in the name of public morality; that morality was policed in the name of social order. This essay illustrates through the case of *underground* how the policing of public morality serves to strengthen social consensus and demonize transgressors, as well as cement power relations, social prejudices, and structures of oppression. It also discusses how issues of power influence the definition, enforcement, and contestation of morality and social order.

Rap and reggae music have been a vital part of youth culture in Puerto Rico since the early 1980s. Grouped under the term *underground* in the early 1990s, its most direct musical sources have been U.S. rap, and Jamaican and Panamanian dancehall reggae.[7] Its lyrics have been either rapped or sung (dancehall style), and its underlying rhythm tracks have typically been either funk heavy in the U.S. rap tradition or have followed the Caribbean-influenced hip-shaking aesthetic of dancehall grooves.

Tricia Rose's proposition that rap "is a complex fusion of folk orality and post-modern technology" also rings true in the case of Puerto Rican *underground* music.[8] Rap, dancehall reggae and, by extension, *underground*, are part of a continuum of longstanding African American and Afro-Caribbean (including Puerto Rican) musical practices.[9] Cheryl Keyes describes rap, along with other hip-hop art forms, as an example of "cultural versioning—the foregrounding (both consciously and unconsciously) of African-centered concepts in response to cultural takeovers, ruptures, and appropriations."[10]

The term *underground*, as it has been used in Puerto Rico, is somewhat elusive. It has been the name of a music genre that existed from the early to late 1990s. But it has also been used as a more general term to differentiate mainstream commercial rap and reggae from that produced and distributed in the informal economy. And it has also been used to describe a music that is perceived as "hard" and "raw." Underground has been usually boisterous, vulgar, violent, or otherwise hard edged. It has been identified by its participants with a street-oriented, vernacular, spontaneous, and uncensored mode of expression, as opposed to the studio-oriented, glossy, sanitized aesthetic of the mainstream market. DJ Playero has described it as music that is faithful to the "underground ghetto aesthetic," even if it has had mainstream commercial success.[11]

DJs were originally the business people at the core of the production and distribution network of underground recordings. In the early 1980s, DJ Playero, DJ Negro, and other DJs like them began making a modest and erratic number of copies of recordings (typically close to twenty) and then selling them at clubs, at work, and around their neighborhoods. Those copies were then quickly bootlegged and distributed all over Puerto Rico. Given the constant migratory flow of people between the island and the continent, these tapes soon reached Puerto Rican communities in the United States. Despite the simplicity of its production, promotion and distribution, the early underground market still covered extensive ground.

In Puerto Rico, underground rap (reggae came a bit later) had been a popular music—albeit outside the scope of the mainstream media—for close to a decade when it began catching the general public's eye in 1994. It was then that underground recordings began to circulate within the formal economy. Wiso G.'s *Sin Parar*, released in 1994, was the first underground production by an "aboveground" record label and sold in stores. Later in the year, *Playero #38*, already enormously popular through informal channels, made its appearance in stores and became one of the biggest-selling underground productions.

Whereas commercial rap and reggae had been tailored to fit media requirements regarding language and themes, *underground* music—until the release of Wiso G.'s *Sin Parar*—developed and thrived with a great measure of independence from the prospect of media policing and censorship. Thus, *underground* had not been forced to rid itself of language considered to be too crude, vulgar, or violent for mass media exposure. While the language of mainstream productions was closely monitored, underground artists[12] prided themselves on being faithful to their everyday language.

Vico C's "De la Calle" was a rap song that became wildly popular in the mid-1980s, strictly through informal channels.[13] It is remembered as one of Vico's "classics," partly for its lyrical deftness, but also for its embodiment of the ultraviolent early underground aesthetic. "De la Calle" is today a nostalgia-filled symbol of a pre-mass-media, pre-state censorship age of (raw) innocence. Vico introduces the track by establishing that his "dirty language" is justified, "valuable," and necessary. Then he goes on to warn a rival:

> *Sí, soy de la calle, no me tengas miedo*
> *No quiero problemas, no quiero pelear*
> *Pero pendejito, si te pones guapo*
> *Te llevo a La Perla y te mando a picar*
> *Te rajo, te castro, te rompo el pescuezo*
> *Te parto la cara y el culo también*
> *Y si sigues vivo, canto de hijoeputa*
> *Te pego tres tiros y te llevo a Lloréns*[14]

Yes, I'm from the street
I don't want trouble, I don't wanna fight
But asshole, if you act tough
I'll take you to La Perla and have you cut up
I'll tear you, I'll cut your balls off, I'll snap your neck
I'll break your face and your ass as well
And if you're still alive, motherfucker
I'll shoot you and take you to Lloréns

"De la calle" is a good early example of how the underground aesthetic was constructed by its participants. *Underground*, as an expressive form, was developed as hypermasculine, violent, foul-mouthed, hard, street savvy, ghetto identified, and lawless—the very same adjectives that in the public discourse define urban marginality.

Underground's self-identification with ghetto hardness and lawlessness was an attempt at vindicating urban marginality. At the same time, *underground*'s self-construction can also be argued to be a defeatist celebration of the stereotypes associated with poor urban populations. Given the scope of this essay, I am unable to elaborate on these issues for now.

The increasing popularity, visibility, and mass availability of *underground* eventually began generating concern among parents, educators, activists, and government authorities regarding the possible effects of this music on its largely youthful audience. However, the urgency of the problem was not so much related to *underground*'s existence. After all, it developed without major interference until 1995. *Underground* became a public safety issue once it was no longer confined to "marginal" spaces. Its power resided in threatening "the center" with contagion.

Milton Picón, leader of the conservative media-monitoring group Morality in Media, explained how the group became aware of *underground* music and why they began campaigning against it. In doing so, he also illustrated how the music was constructed as a menace only after it was no longer contained in "marginality."

> Teachers and social workers began calling our attention to this type of music, which we were completely unaware of. When we began interviewing school children and realizing the crudeness of this type of material, and when we realized that this material was *no longer really in the underground* but was being openly sold in stores, we alerted the police, who then undertook an investigation.[15]

To Morality in Media's satisfaction—and in no small manner thanks to Picón having previously worked in the Police Department—the investigation undertaken by the police soon led to the 1995 raids, the confiscation of *underground* recordings, and charges being filed against some commercial establishments that sold them.

The raids conducted during the first week of February 1995 were nothing less than spectacular. They were a high-profile affair that garnered prominent media coverage and captured the public's attention. Six record stores were targeted; three of them were located in Plaza Las Américas—one of the most prestigious shopping malls in San Juan. Four hundred and one cassettes and compact discs were confiscated. Six store employees were issued court citations.[16]

Media time and space were dominated by arguments condoning state censorship on moral grounds. *Underground* was obscene and pornographic, thus immoral, thus dangerous; thus it should be censored. It was that simple. *Underground* was seen as filth and degeneration posing as art.[17] It was portrayed as a cultural expression eroding the fiber of morality and decency upon which social order rests. The mainstream media's "discovery" of *underground* and its irreverent lyrics came as a great shock and created a sense of national alarm. Numerous TV and radio shows, as well as newspapers and magazines, took up the topic of *underground* and censorship. It was open season on *underground*.

The way in which the media coverage proceeded and the public debate unfolded put in evidence an intense public fascination with new *cucos* (bogeymen) and scapegoats that can explain social fear and disorder. It was also a display of a morbid public fascination with an issue that included the core components of both yellow journalism and the social imaginary of fear: crime, violence, and sex. The shock and alarm with which the news was received included a dimension of voyeuristic pleasure through indulgence in scandal, in dirt, in immorality.

A few days before the raids, Carmen Teresa Figueroa moderated a TV special which promised to "uncover the 'secrets' of *underground*."[18] The show was aimed at parents who wanted to know how this "noxious" music was affecting their children. Several days later, TV show host Luis Francisco Ojeda joined the *underground* bashing crusade. His star guest was Waldemar Quiles, president of the Puerto Rican House of Representative's Commission on Education and Culture. The legislator expressed that his objective was to amend the Puerto Rican Penal Code in order to typify the production of *underground* rap as a serious crime. In both TV shows, the "noxious" character of *underground* was treated as a proven fact.

Yolanda Rosaly, media critic for *El Nuevo Día*, one of the most prestigious and powerful daily newspapers, wrote an impassioned column five days after the raids alerting parents against the dangers of this "submundo" (underworld) music. Rosaly's word choices were quite telling of the classist hysteria fueling the attack on *underground*. She deemed *underground* to be equivalent to the music of a sinister "underworld," that is, the criminal underworld of the poor and young. For her, the lyrics were "simply horrendous and revolting" and reflected the perverse attitudes and beliefs of criminals; therefore, the Police Department had acted in the defense of social order and the public well being by censoring them.

In the process of constructing *underground* as a criminal subculture, critics circulated ample distortions and misconceptions regarding this genre. A common charge was that lyrics advocated the use of "all types of controlled substances."[19] Some went as far as claiming that "underground is a front for the drug trade, by stimulating the use of drugs and the creation of new clients, new addicts."[20] However, in reality, the only controlled substance ever mentioned in *underground* was marijuana. In the frenzy to indict this music, wild myths were circulated.

The fact that media time was monopolized by procensorship views does in no way mean that there were no voices being raised against state censorship. Dissenting voices were still heard over the airwaves and made their way to the pages of several newspapers such as the *San Juan Star*, *Diálogo*, and *Claridad*.[21] The token rappers present in radio and TV shows also argued strongly against censorship and the myths being propagated about underground. One of the principal myths they had to debunk was the equation of the off-stage lives of underground artists with their performative personae; in other words, the assumption that there was no separation between the off-stage person and the performer, or between artists and their texts.

The charges brought against the commercial establishments that sold *underground* were eventually dismissed by the Superior Court of San Juan. This court decision prompted the following reaction from Police Chief Pedro Toledo: "We will investigate where it was that we failed. We will continue our struggle. . . . If the courts want to permit the sale of this type of pornographic material, we have to figure out a way to fight this evil."[22]

The court decision was greeted with relief by all of us who treasure tolerance and artistic freedom. However, the paranoia unleashed by the state's dramatic censorship actions could not be overturned by a court order. The most profound effect of the raids and the public discussion that ensued was that the hysterical misconceptions and prejudices circulated about *under-

ground lingered on. Furthermore, the attempt to criminalize *underground* solidified the public legitimization of state efforts to control the youths most closely engaged with this genre. I will return to this topic in a later section.

The raids also prompted a visible change in *underground* lyrics. The threat of state censorship and public scandals resulted in a vastly different lyrical content. This is not to say that artists completely turned away from the raw lyrics of the preraid heyday, but that overall rawness dropped considerably. The content of recordings and videos was the aspect of the music most clearly affected, whereas live shows continued to provide a safer space for uncensored material.

REALITY AND REPRESENTATION: "NO ES LO MISMO NI SE ESCRIBE IGUAL" (IT IS NEITHER THE SAME NOR IS IT WRITTEN THE SAME WAY)

The primary accusation directed toward *underground* was that it had a dangerous influence on youth. For censorship advocates such as Reverend Milton Picón, the columnist Yolanda Rosaly, and Police Chief Pedro Toledo, the alleged fact constituted sufficient grounds for censoring this music. In contrast, for more moderate critics such as José Luis Ramos Escobar, a professor of theater arts at the University of Puerto Rico, nothing productive is accomplished by censorship.

> To censor is to refuse to debate, confront, educate. The greatest risk of censorship is that there will always be a reason to censor: today it is underground music, yesterday it was the pro-independence struggle, tomorrow it will be whatever doesn't please the authorities or those that proclaim themselves the keepers of the dominant values of a society. Censorship is the impotence of those in power: since they can't convince, they repress.[23]

Nevertheless, despite their disagreement on the issue of censorship, conservative and moderate critics agreed that underground had indisputable harmful effects on society, particularly children and adolescents.

A frequently unchallenged assumption shared by the procensorship as well as the anticensorship positions was thus the question of meaning and effect, or representation and consumption. Much of the moral panic ensuing from the disclosure and "decoding" of *underground* lyrics was based on the assumption of a simplistic connection between lived relations and artistic representation.

Art and reality were conflated as most critics refused to acknowledge that there might be a distance between rappers and their texts. The difference between art and reality was also ignored when audiences were assumed to consume passively and mimic obediently. For example, Ramos Escobar stated in an article in *Diálogo*, the University of Puerto Rico's monthly newspaper, that "there is no doubt that underground is an element of incitement and stimulus to certain types of conduct that frequently threaten human dignity and the common good, defined in communal and not institutional terms."[24]

Underground music was accused of promoting and inciting certain types of behavior. However, it is difficult, if not impossible, to assess effect. Two U.S. legislative commissions on pornography and dozens of scientific research teams have not been able to settle the issue of how violent art influences reality.[25] So even though many claim that common sense is proof enough that there is a direct correlation between artistic representation and action, there is no conclusive evidence to support this.

Carmen Oquendo and Lilliana Ramos, in the following month's *Diálogo*, questioned Ramos Escobar's assumption that *underground* lured children into depraved behavior. For Oquendo and Ramos

> it is innocent to think of a neat causal relationship between rap and violence without scientifically examining how much teen violence stems from rap and how much from violent homes and divorces, parents' alcohol abuse, incest, neglect and abandonment.[26]

The act of art consumption is not uniform across individuals, groups, or contexts. Theorists such as Stuart Hall and Michel de Certeau assert that consumption is such a complex process that it should be considered another act of production.[27] In order to understand consumption, the possibility of multiple interpretations needs to be taken into account. John Fiske argues that texts must be understood as "producerly texts,"[28] allowing the consumer room for interpretation. I agree. Some people who take the Bible as their spiritual guide are respectful and tolerant people; others are intolerant, rabid homophobes. Similarly, some people who read the Bible are sex offenders; other sex offenders prefer porno magazines. The Bible and porno magazines, like *underground* lyrics, are texts. The impact that they might have on people's beliefs and actions varies widely. They cannot be said to "make" anybody do anything.

But how about the relationship between *underground* artists and their lyrics? Once again, we can rely on Fiske's notion of "producerly texts," where meanings are not fixed, sober, intelligible, but often tightly linked to fun and the carnivalesque. Lyrics cannot be taken as windows to artists' souls. Some rappers express their deepest feelings in their lyrics; others step up to the microphone as actors playing whatever character they please.

There is no denying the violent misogyny in a popular Guanábanas Podrías rhyme:

> *Malditas putas, malditas bellacas*
> *Se pasan toda la vida saboreando matraca*
> *Chingan en los paris, chingan en los montes*
> *Chingan en tu carro y donde quiera que se monten*
> *Méale la chocha, escúpele la cara*
> *A esa jodía perra que no vale nada*[29]

> Damn whores, damn horny bitches
> They spend all day sucking dick
> They fuck at parties, they fuck on the hills
> They fuck in your car and wherever else they go
> Piss on her face, spit on her cunt
> 'Cause that fucking bitch, is not worth much

However, this does not necessarily mean that the members of the Guanábanas do (in real life and outside the sphere of artistic representation) engage in such behavior.

The Guanábanas Podrías could, in fact, be gang rapists who go around spitting and urinating on their victims. But they could also be disgruntled young males who would never spit on a woman but seek to assert their masculine power through their lyrics; they could be constructing their superiority at the level of artistic representation, since in real life that power is constantly being questioned. Furthermore, they could also be purposefully writing outlandish lyrics just to laugh at the mainstream outrage and shock. Another possibility is that they are expressing a deep-seated violent sexism in half-joking, hyperbolic terms. Yet another possibility is that the artists are writing their lyrics according to what they think their audience likes; if images of violent sex are popular (and they are), then violently sexual lyrics will sell. Finally, all or some of the above statements could simultaneously be true.

The Guanábanas indictment of "loose" women should come as no surprise. Our society constantly punishes and stigmatizes sexually aggressive or promiscuous women. These lyrics have been taken by critics of *underground* as proof of the aberrational low regard that these rappers have for women. But, really, are they any different from the venerable Sonero Mayor of salsa, Ismael Rivera, telling "his" woman in the song "Si Te Cojo" (If I Catch You) that if he comes home and his potatoes aren't ready, she will catch a beating? How much do they differ from Marvin Santiago in "La Pela" (The Beating)—another salsa classic—promising to beat his lover for deceiving him? Perhaps the great big difference only resides in *underground*'s use of vulgar and explicit language.

Though the crass language of *underground* intensified the danger attributed to it, this music was not merely targeted for censorship because of its raw language and violent imagery. The issue was not only about rhymes and images, but about who was rhyming and constructing those images.

"MARGINALITY" AND CONTAGION

The public discussion of *underground* was invested in separating "the margins" —where immorality and chaos are presumed to breed—from "the center"— where order is maintained. *Underground* artists were imagined as infectious elements, posing the threat of cultural contagion. These artists were most often construed as pathological agents (nature makes them do it), though at times they were portrayed as victims of circumstance (nurture made them do it). But let's leave aside the issue of causality. What remains is that they were considered "marginal," which in the public discourse was synonymous with "deviant."

"Marginality" and "deviancy," though used as self-explanatory and obvious categories are anything but. Marginal from what? Deviant from what? Where and who are the core against which marginality is defined? What is the norm against which deviancy is defined?

Marginality and deviancy are purported to be defined by behavior—lest our society's democratic "innocent until proven guilty" axiom is breached—not by living conditions. Thus, ghetto living or poverty, in and of themselves, are not supposed to be the crucial markers of marginality. However, "deviant" or criminal behavior is in actuality not sufficient to classify someone as marginal. Marginality has both a behavioral and a class or racial component. Never will white-collar criminals, for example, be defined as marginal. The very definition and construction of crime are implicated in class and racially based hierarchies and structures of oppression.[30] In short, you are marginal if you break the social contract of order, but you must also belong to the lower, phenotypically "darker" classes.

The reason why *underground* was a target for censorship had as much to do with structures of economic and racial oppression as with moral concerns. As in the United States, hip-hop culture and dancehall music in Puerto

Rico have become commercialized and popularized among mainstream audiences; however, in both cases they are still very much ghetto-identified artistic expressions.[31]

One of the reasons *underground* was a target for censorship was that within the social climate in Puerto Rico, youth from poor communities were being seen as the main perpetrators of crime and social disorder.[32] Policing and restricting *underground* could, therefore, be easily portrayed by government authorities as a logical extension of anticrime state policies. The "Mano Dura Contra el Crimen" (Tough Hand against Crime) policy that went into effect during Governor Pedro Rosselló's first term in 1992–96 featured the National Guard takeovers of public housing projects, increased surveillance and harassment of citizens, a failed attempt at restricting the right to bail, along with numerous other tactics. Under the Mano Dura, while the military occupation of housing projects was about control of movement and places in order to reimpose "order," the censoring of *underground* was an attempt to control a much more abstract or elusive aspect of "disorder"—ideas and cultural expression.

In such a climate of apprehension, where crime and social decay were virtually synonymous with youth of the (racialized) laboring-impoverished classes, *underground* destabilized the prevailing social structures by speaking the voice of marginality.[33] Regardless of whether the lyrics were innocuous, randomly violent, or insightfully indicting state violence against poor communities, they provided this youth sector with a voice and a platform that the general public had problems grappling with. The predominant public perception of *underground* as morally reprehensible was closely related to these youths' position as the scapegoats of the government's rhetoric and policies.

A month before the raids, Ranking Stone—a popular rapper among both underground and mainstream audiences—described how ghetto youth were stigmatized as criminals.[34] The outward markings of social marginality, according to him, were "being black" and "dressing like a *rapero*."[35] Ranking Stone charged that "black," "poor," "criminal," and "rap fan" were perceived as virtually interchangeable categories.

Puerto Rico is a racially mixed society organized according to a hierarchy in which people of darker hues are disproportionately at the base of the socioeconomic pyramid.[36] Race, poverty, and unemployment operate as categories that are "synchronized."[37] Furthermore, since poverty is constructed with respect to race, and poverty is associated with criminality, crime is also racialized.[38]

Underground was identified (from within this realm of musical expression, as well as from its outskirts) as the music of the poor, "black," and young. Since this was precisely the same sector demonized in social discourse as the embodiment of criminality, it was no surprise that this music was portrayed as the musical expression of a sinister, incomprehensible, marginal, and criminal subculture.

The construction of behavior or a segment of the population as "marginal" serves as a way to cement and enforce group cohesiveness and compliance with the social order. Equating marginality with danger enforces obedience in one sector of the population and legitimizes surveillance and repression over another. As Mary Douglas has stated: "Attributing danger is one way of putting a subject above dispute."[39] So as *underground* participants were demonized, the general public found comfort in understanding the source of evil and disorder. This demonization also served to assure public approval of state repressive measures.

Rap was derisively described by renowned poet Edwin Reyes as a "primitive form of musical expression" hailing from the ghetto, which transmits "the most elementary forms of emotion" through its "brutalizing and aggressive monotony."[40] His insidious description is an example of how rap was perceived as the cultural expression of that most primitive, dark, and dangerous sector of the population. Rappers were the feared "techno-aborigines,"[41] disdained for being part of a marginal population allegedly unable to express itself in an intelligent, sublime, or profound manner.

The state censorship of underground and the public debate that ensued highlighted the perceived looming threat of a sector of the population labeled as criminal brutes. In other words: Not only will these guys carjack you, and not only will they come into your home and rob you, but they will corrupt your family from the inside, targeting your children through their so-called music! Underground participants were deemed a fear-inspiring marginal population whose primitive art forms merely transmitted their pathological culture and behavior to other segments of the population.

There was yet another element contributing to the powers of contagion attributed to *underground* music: its perceived "foreignness" to Puerto Rican culture. Given that rap and dancehall have their origins in New York and Jamaican ghettoes, *underground* was posed as an "alien" cultural element which threatened the integrity of "truly" Puerto Rican forms of expression via local marginal youth.

Fernando Clemente asked from the pages of the leftist weekly *Claridad*:

And who benefits from the "rapper look" and—even worse—the "rapper conduct"? Puerto Rican culture? Definitely not! Where it leads us to is, whether we like it or not, to our colonial condition and the vulgar dominance of the United States' economic power.[42]

Clemente wrote as if rap were not already an integral part of Puerto Rican culture, as if rap were not already the most cultivated musical genre among Puerto Rican youth, and as if Puerto Rican culture were not the one that is lived but the one that he would like to see.

From the pages of the same newspaper, Edwin Reyes expressed a similar sentiment when he posed "la tontería del rap" (the silliness of rap) as a counterpoint to "our music, learned and popular, multiple, beautiful, irreducible, the one that Juan Antonio Corretjer always exalted: the sublime music of Puerto Rican–ness."[43] Rafael Bernabe, in an article entitled "Rap: Soy boricua, pa' que tú lo sepas" (Rap: I'm Puerto Rican, Just so You Know), criticized Reyes's position for "dripping with classist prejudice" and attempting to pose itself as "the arbiter of national identity" by seeking to uplift rap enthusiasts from "tuserías" (lowliness) to Puerto Rican–ness.[44]

These accusations of *underground* music as a lowly, aesthetically worthless, and pathological cultural expression of a marginal sector of the local population, and also as a foreign destabilizing menace for Puerto Rican culture, were certainly not unprecedented phenomena. Similar pronunciations against other musical forms have previously consumed the public imagination and been the subject of heated national debate.

Bomba and *plena*, today largely considered either harmless or vital components of the national culture, have faced similarly virulent racial and class prejudices. Bomba, for example, was at one point characterized by certain "folklorists" as possessing "grotesque rhythms" and being an "expression of primitive frenzy" where "the dancers gesticulate and scream songs of naive contents, some of them unintelligible."[45] Regarding plena, Juan Flores notes how "the epithets 'vulgar' and 'lumpen' accompanied [it] for the first three decades of its existence, and here they are once again, in 1988, in the assessment of Cortijo."[46]

Various popular genres of the first half of the twentieth century—among them rumba, *guaracha*, *son*, bolero, jazz, and tango—were accused of being degenerative outside influences for Puerto Rican culture.[47] Mareia Quintero Rivera describes these accusations as an attempt to "whiten the nation's image" by drawing imaginary boundaries around "true" Puerto Rican national culture. Furthermore, she sees in those earlier charges of racialized "foreign" musical genres that corrupt the national culture a similar impetus to the one present in the more recent debates surrounding *underground* music, for they all "manifest at the discursive level an attempt to characterize marginality as an 'other,' in opposition to what is defined as 'authentic' culture."[48]

As Edgardo Díaz Díaz remarks of the musical debates during the early decades of the twentieth century, the contentions regarding *underground* music must be understood as "neither purely moral nor merely racial, but also a political matter, especially after the U.S. invasion in 1898."[49] *Underground* was viewed as a threat to Puerto Rican culture not only for being deemed the low-quality and morally reprehensible music of a racially and socially marginal sector of the local population, but also because it was imagined to be an outside force corrupting what is truly Puerto Rican.

NEUTRALIZING CONTAGION

It has been a longstanding historical trend that material and structural issues get displaced to the realm of culture and values. Given the complexity of addressing "social problems" in political-economic terms, the realm of culture provides a more manageable target.[50] The socioeconomic crisis of the mid-1990s in Puerto Rico was thus frequently explained away in terms of an alleged erosion of traditional moral values that had provided fertile ground for criminal activity.

Underground, with its violent topics and aesthetics, was taken as a concrete manifestation of the immoral or amoral behavior that was, supposedly, at the bottom of the social crisis. Censoring a music genre is, of course, a much more manageable task than reducing unemployment, improving the quality of public education, providing healthcare, or lowering the murder rate. It was also a concrete action that could be taken against intangible moral infractions.

It was only after *underground* became identified as a source of cultural contagion that the authorities moved against it. It was the threat against "good" kids that drove the authorities to action. *Underground*, as a tangible manifestation of a "deviant" value-system, was threatening to "poison young minds," in the words of TV talk show host Pedro Zervigón. This music was deemed a "poison," a source of contagion, a soiling agent, a polluting element.

Mary Douglas's notion of symbolic pollution proves a useful concept in illuminating this situation. She proposes that notions of symbolic pollution provide the possibility of redemption, through the physicalization of moral infractions. If immorality is represented physically as dirt or disease, then redemption is only a matter of cleaning up or purifying.[51] As Carol Smith-Rosenberg has noted in relationship to the same phenomenon, there is in the notion of symbolic pollution a fusion of the moral and the physical.[52]

In the case of *underground*, this genre and its participants were identified as embodying a deviant morality. Once identified as a concrete agent threatening to pollute the rest of society, the stage was set for condemnation and censorship as methods for scrubbing out the polluting element.

Julia Kristeva brings to our attention the connection between social structures and notions of pollution: "Pollution is a type of danger which is not likely to occur except where the lines of structure, cosmic or social, are clearly defined."[53] Or as Mary Douglas puts it: "The potency of pollution is therefore not an inherent one; it is proportional to the potency of the prohibition that founds it."[54]

In the case of *underground* in Puerto Rico, class and racial boundaries were being strictly policed given a discourse that assigned blame and polluting qualities along class and racial lines and reinforced a sharp "us vs. them" attitude. The force of the crackdown on *underground* was thus related to the strength of class and racial divisions, and hierarchy. After all, this music became a public safety issue once it was perceived to pose a threat to those social structures by having spilled over ghetto boundaries and by threatening middle- and upper-class kids with "infection."

POWER AND PLEASURE

Michel Foucault describes the social surveillance and control of sexuality as not only an extension of domination but also "a sensualization of power and a gain of pleasure."[55] This concept aids in the understanding of the simultaneous indignation, horror, and pleasure with which *underground* was monitored and suppressed. The censure and censorship of *underground* were as much about the pleasure of domination, as they were about preserving social order.

The tone of secrecy and confession that pervaded mass media coverage was an integral component of the perverse public pleasure which peeked from behind a veneer of apocalyptic worry and self-righteous indignation. The general public, the government authorities, and the mass media were partly invested in their roles of surveyors, classifiers, and censors because of the pleasure derived from these activities.

These perverse (partially) hidden pleasures stemming from the policing of *underground* do not negate the serious concern for social stability and public morality that also prompted the action and provided its rationale. On the contrary, these seemingly disparate experiences coexisted and reinforced each other. Similarly, the indignation against prejudice and censorship with which *underground* artists and audiences reacted was accompanied by a mischievous delight in their transgression. Those doing the policing relished the pleasures of exercising power and enforcing social norms; those being policed got off on evading power and social norms.

In explaining the connection between pleasure, and enforcing and subverting power, Foucault mentions some of the agents involved. Not coincidentally, many of these agents were central participants in the game of "capture and seduction" that enveloped *underground*: parents and children, adults and adolescents, educators and students.

Power, however, does not only reside within the agents engaged in policing morality. An explanation that only visualizes those who claim to be preserving social order through their suppressive activities as the sole wielders of power provides an incomplete picture of the existing power plays. Of course, if we limit our understanding of power to the capability of suppression and enforcement of social norms, then the morality police is the one with the power. It was government agents, "responsible" public figures, and other "respectable" adults who had the power of confiscating recording material and monopolizing the media with justifications of censorship. *Underground* artists and audiences could never reproduce such actions and public reactions even if they tried.

The alleged agents of social disorder had no power of enforcement or suppression. They were not the ones enforcing public policies and making economic decisions. They had little to no economic power. However, at the symbolic level, they had the power of the threat. Their marginal status linked them with danger, which invested them with the symbolic power of disruption and corruption. This was a power that, ultimately, served as justification for the repressive actions taken against them and which cemented even further their marginality from social structures and discourses.

The threat posed by *underground* participants resided not only in their presumed marginality (whether this status is held to describe class position or "deviant" behavior), but also in their "liminality." Carol Smith-Rosenberg explains that a liminal person "is in movement between two states and consequently possess[es] the roles and responsibilities of neither." Adolescent youth are the quintessential liminal beings.[56] They are perceived as having left behind the innocence of childhood, but not having yet acquired the responsibility and mature sensibility of adulthood. As youth, *underground* participants were liminal; as racialized and criminalized youth from poor communities, they were marginal.

Whereas order is associated with the center, disorder is related to the margins and transitional states. Disorder is a threat to existing patterns; it is related to both danger and power. The so-called underworld of *underground* was, thus, a powerful, marginal, and liminal space capable of instigating dangerous transformations.

During the eighteenth century in the United States, pubescent males were seen as both marginal and liminal. The bulk of Victorian sexual discourse was aimed at them. As apprenticeship as a sociosexual institution disappeared and young men started going to boarding schools and moving into cities, a fear began developing of a youth culture that could thrive independently of adult and institutional supervision. The situation that Smith-Rosenberg describes in the United States during the eighteenth century is oddly similar to that of 1990s Puerto Rico.[57] A marginal and liminal population—defined in one case as young males and in the other as young males of a certain social class—is identified in the dominant social discourse as a primary agent of disorder. Both cases evidence a fixation on youth sexuality as an important sphere that functions as both source and manifestation of disorder.

The attack on *underground* was informed by a profoundly conservative ideology that lumps together violence and drug use with youth extramarital sex as the evils eroding social order. Youth sexuality is deemed, by definition, precocious, libertine, and illicit. Knowledge or discussion of sexual matters is thought to lead to promiscuity. Promiscuity is a big, bad, horrible thing. Young people should not know about sex, let alone talk about it, rap about it, or engage in it.[58] The problem is that youth do. *Underground* music allegedly incited them to do it more.

Underground was bashed for being "obscene" and "pornographic." The proverbial "community standards" according to which obscenity laws are defined went largely unquestioned.[59] The charge that pornography is inherently harmful went unrefuted, for the most part. The issue, therefore, reached beyond the repression of youth sexualities to seeking a wider sort of sexual repression. Around the same time that the *underground* raids took place, Condomanía—an adult novelty shop and bookstore—was raided. The Police Vice Squad also raided Cups, a lesbian bar of the San Juan area. The target was, thus, not only youth sexuality, but sexualities that were deemed "illicit" or "peripheral." Nonheterosexuals and the libidinous were also considered threats.

A discussion of power, pleasure, and *underground* would be incomplete without acknowledging how *underground* was an agent of power in terms of enforcing patriarchal structures of oppression. *Underground* was, with precious few exceptions, wholeheartedly implicated in reproducing our society's sexist and homophobic norms.[60] Though challenging class and racial structures of oppression, *underground* was in strict compliance with sexism and homophobia.

Misogyny in *underground* ranged from excluding women from active participation in the genre, to lyrics where female domesticity was exalted and reinforced, to the uninvited groping of women's bodies at clubs, to lines about violently punishing a woman for being "loose," to rhymes about rape.

Many censorship advocates took up the issue of misogynous lyrics in *underground* as one of their central arguments. *Underground* indeed had a role in the perpetuation of a sexist and violent culture. However, this music was merely one aspect of a fundamentally misogynous culture. So why just target *underground*? The answer goes back to the scapegoating of a youth art form mostly cultivated by a stigmatized sector of the population.

The youths engaged in *underground* were portrayed as misogynous deviants who took part in a pathological criminal culture. What was seldom mentioned was that they were mimicking the dominant cultural values learned through passive and acritical consumption.[61] *Underground* lyrics took part in the reproduction of the dominant sexist ideology that perpetuated the myths, stereotypes, repressions, and double standards that cement patriarchy. The crucial difference between the misogyny that passed largely uncommented and that which triggered a vociferous public reaction is that the latter—in this case *underground*—expressed vulgarly and without the least bit of decorum the same sexist ideas prevalent in the rest of society.

CONCLUSION

Underground was partly a target for censorship because of its crude, outlaw, and violent themes and aesthetics. In this manner, *underground* challenged notions of proper moral behavior and law-abiding citizenship that are held by the dominant public perception, as well as in governmental and ecclesiastical rhetoric, to insure social order. But had *underground* not been so tightly linked to young males of the local laboring-impoverished classes, we can question whether its aesthetics would have triggered the repressive measures and moral panic that it did.

The public discourse surrounding *underground* was firmly grounded in the "Mano Dura" scapegoating of this youth sector. *Underground* was perceived as the physicalization of their moral infractions; it was also invested with powers of moral contagion. Censorship was framed as the way to scrub out the infractions and neutralize the contagion.

Ironically enough, as the general public viewed *underground* with increasing horror and paranoia, the delight in transgression augmented for its audience. The demonization and suppression of *underground* actually boosted its transgressive mystique.

The construction of *underground* as a public threat gave further legitimacy to state repression and surveillance. It fostered a climate of fear and paranoia where civil liberties were set up to be relinquished in exchange for the state's soothing surveillance and control. Ultimately, the persecution of *underground* cemented the class and racial divisions, inequalities and frictions that fuel unhappiness, instability, and rage.

AFTERWORD

The debates and moral panic that greeted the rising popularity of *underground* music during the mid-1990s in Puerto Rico were quite different from the relatively more measured arguments brandished against its later incarnation as *música del perreo* at the time of the 2002 legislative hearings spearheaded by Senator Velda González. As chair of the Puerto Rican Senate's Special Commission for the Study of Violence and Sexual Content in Puerto Rican Radio and Television Programming, Senator González became the leader of a much-publicized campaign that, in theory, sought to address all sources of "offensive" and "indecent" material in the media but that, in reality, focused on the video images, song lyrics, and brazen style of dancing of the music genre that was still not uniformly referred to as reggaeton.[62]

While in 1995 the logic of extreme censorship ruled the public discussions surrounding *underground*, in 2002 the state-led actions and the positions advanced in the Puerto Rican media tended to favor a more moderate regulation over outright banning of perreo. In both cases, the public debates over these music genres were prime-time news fodder and generated much public scrutiny, debate, and anxiety. Back in 1995, and still in 2002, it would have been hard to imagine that the much-maligned and marginalized genres known then as *underground* and *música del perreo* would only two years later rise to international prominence as reggaeton—the prime musical export of Puerto Rico, the "reggaeton nation."[63]

NOTES

This paper (save for the afterword) was presented in 1998 at the Puerto Rican Studies Association Conference and served as the basis for various journalistic articles, but, as an academic paper, remained unpublished. Though some of my views have changed, I have resisted the urge to update the essay substantively, so that it can fully serve its purpose as a historical document. Translations of Spanish-language quotations are my own. "Stylee" is a term borrowed from Jamaican dancehall reggae slang and often used during the 1990s in the rap and reggae scene in Puerto Rico to mean "style."

1. See Wayne Marshall's essay in this volume for a discussion of the porous boundaries between the genres known as *underground* and reggaeton.

2. John Marino, "Police Seize Recordings, Say Content Is Obscene," *San Juan Star*, February 3, 1995; *San Juan Star*, "Court Dismisses Charges against Music Stores," February 24, 1995.

3. Jorge Luis Medina, "Rappers Rap Bum Rap and Hypocrisy," *San Juan Star*, February 19, 1995.

4. On moral panics, see Stanley Cohen, *Folk Devils and Moral Panics* (London: Mac Gibbon and Kee, 1972); Stuart Hall et al., *Policing the Crisis: Mugging, the State and Law and Order* (London: Macmillan Press, 1978); and Madeline Román, "El Girlie Show: Madonna, las polémicas nacionales y los pánicos morales," *bordes* 1 (1995): 14–21.

5. See Pedro T. Berríos Lara, "Underground: ¿Obscenidad o realidad?" *La Iupi*, January–February, 1995; Raquel Z. Rivera, "Rapping Two Versions of the Same Requiem," in *Puerto Rican Jam: Rethinking Colonialism and Nationalism*, ed. Frances Negrón-Muntaner and Ramón Grosfoguel (Minneapolis: University of Minnesota Press, 1997), 243–56; and Mayra Santos, "Puerto Rican Underground," *Centro* 8, nos. 1 and 2 (1996): 218–31.

6. Rafael Bernabe, "Rap: Soy boricua, pa' que tú lo sepas," *Claridad*, January 19–25, 1996; Raquel Z. Rivera, "Cultura y poder en el rap puertorriqueño," *Revista de Ciencias Sociales* 4 (1998): 124–46.

7. Santos, "Puerto Rican Underground."

8. Tricia Rose, "Orality and Technology: Rap Music and Afro-American Cultural Resistance," *Popular Music and Society* 13, no. 4 (1989): 38.

9. Juan Flores, "Rappin', Writin' & Breakin'," *Centro de Estudios Puertorriqueños Bulletin* 2, no. 3 (1988): 34–41; Dick Hebdige, *Cut 'N' Mix: Culture, Identity and Caribbean Music* (New York: Methuen, 1987); Peter Manuel, *Caribbean Currents: Caribbean Music from Rumba to Reggae* (Philadelphia: Temple University Press, 1995); Tricia Rose, *Black Noise: Rap Music and Black Culture in Contemporary America* (Hanover, N.H.: University Press of New England, 1994); and David Toop, *Rap Attack 2: African Rap to Global Hip Hop* (London: Serpent's Tail, 1991).

10. Cheryl L. Keyes, "At the Crossroads: Rap Music and Its African Nexus," *Ethnomusicology* 40, no. 2 (1996): 224.

11. DJ Playero, interview with author, January 25, 1995.

12. There was no absolute separation between mainstream and underground artists. Many artists did both mainstream and underground productions.

13. This song was never released "aboveground." To listen to this and other early songs by Vico C see http://www.myspace.com/elfilosofodelrap (accessed June 1, 2008).

14. Residencial Luis Lloréns Torres is a public housing project in San Juan.

15. Milton Picón made this statement in a TV show hosted by Pedro Zervigón called *Al Grano*, February 5, 1995.

16. Marino, "Police Seize Recordings."

17. See Pedro Sandín Fremaint, "Los cuentos no son todos iguales," *Diálogo*, May 1995: "Rap, with the help of some academics has proclaimed itself art." See also Yolanda Molina, "Un llamado contra el rap," *Diálogo*, March 1995: "They dare classify underground lyrics as art and attribute an aesthetic dimension to it." See also Lilliana García Arroyo, " 'Rap underground': ¿Nueva alternativa o pornografía?" *Claridad*, March 24, 1995.

18. The TV show was known as *Hablando con Carmen Teresa*. This episode aired January 30, 1995.

19. Yolanda Rosaly, "¡Alto a la música 'underground'!" *El Nuevo Día*, February 7, 1995.

20. Statement made during Pedro Zervigón's *Al Grano* TV show, February 5, 1995.

21. See Carmen Luisa Oquendo and Raquel Z. Rivera, "Rap: ¿Censura o represión?" *Diálogo*, February 2005; José Luis Ramos Escobar, "Rap underground: Entre la censura y la ingenuidad," *Diálogo*, March 1995; Rafael Bernabe and Nancy Herzig, "Sobre sexo, sexismo y censura," *Claridad*, April 7–13, 1995; Raquel Z. Rivera, "Two Guanábanas and a Little Mayhem," *San Juan Star*, September 10, 1995.

22. *El Nuevo Día*, February 17, 1995.

23. Ramos Escobar, "Rap underground." The subtitle of this section, "No es lo mismo ni se escribe igual," is from a saying in Spanish that literally means "it is neither the same, nor is it writen the same way."

24. Ibid.

25. See Edward Donnerstein et al., *The Question of Pornography: Research Findings and Policy Implications* (New York: Free Press, 1987); Neil M. Malamuth and Edward Donnerstein, *Pornography and Sexual Aggression* (Orlando: Academic Press, 1984); Linda Williams, "Second Thoughts on Hard Core: American Obscenity Law and the Scapegoating of Deviance," in *Dirty Looks: Women, Pornography, Power*, ed. Pamela Church Gibson and Roma Gibson (London: British Film Institute Publishing, 1993), 46–61; United States, Commission on Obscenity and Pornography, *The Report of the Commission on Obscenity and Pornography* (New York: Random House, 1970); United States, Attorney General's Commission on Pornography, *Attorney General's Commission on Pornography: Final Report* (Washington, D.C.: U.S. Department of Justice, 1986); United States, Department of Justice, *Beyond the Pornography Commission: The Federal Response* (Washington, D.C.: National Obscenity Enforcement Unit, Criminal Division, U.S. Department of Justice, 1988).

26. Carmen Luisa Oquendo and Lilliana Ramos, "Censura docta, censura pastoral," *Diálogo*, April 1995.

27. Michel de Certeau, *The Practice of Everyday Life* (Berkeley: University of California Press, 1984); Stuart Hall, "Encoding, Decoding," in *The Cultural Studies Reader*, ed. Simon During (New York: Routledge, 1993), 90–103.

28. John Fiske, *Understanding Popular Culture* (New York: Unwin Hyman, 1989).

29. *The Noise 1* (ca. 1992).

30. James W. Messerschmidt, *Capitalism, Patriarchy and Crime: Toward a Socialist Feminist Criminology* (Totowa, N.J.: Rowman and Littlefield, 1986); Kelvin Santiago-Valles, "Policing the Crisis in the 'Whitest' of the Antilles," *Centro* 8, nos. 1 and 2 (1996): 43–55.

31. Kevin Arlyck, "By All Means Necessary: Rapping and Resisting in Urban Black America," in *Globalization and Survival in the Black Diaspora: The New Urban Challenge*, ed. Charles Green (Albany: SUNY Press, 1997), 269–87; Peter McLaren, "Gangsta Pedagogy and Ghettoethnicity: The Hip Hop Nation as Counterpublic Sphere," *Socialist Review* 25, no. 2 (1995); Rose, *Black Noise*; Santos, "Puerto Rican Underground."

32. See Carlos Fortuño Candelas, *El auge de la actividad criminal en Puerto Rico* (Levittown: Ediciones Bandera Roja, 1993); and Santiago-Valles, "Policing the Crisis in the 'Whitest' of the Antilles." Though I speak here of a specific time period in Puerto Rico, this phenomenon of criminalizing youth of the most impoverished classes is neither exclusive to Puerto Rico nor limited to that time period, but is a more generalized phenomenon.

33. I use *marginal* to describe a position with respect to social discourses and structures, not to impute any kind of "deviancy."

34. Patricia Vargas, "Entrevista con Ranking Stone," *TeVe Guía*, January 14–20, 1995, 65.

35. *Rapero*, in Puerto Rico, has been used to name both rap artists and audiences; whereas in the United States, *rapper* has been a noun restricted to those who rap.

36. Samuel Betances, "The Prejudice of Having No Prejudice in Puerto Rico," *Rican* 2 (1972): 41–54; Santiago-Valles, "Policing the Crisis in the 'Whitest' of the Antilles."

37. Hall et al., *Policing the Crisis*.

38. Ibid.; Santiago-Valles, "Policing the Crisis in the 'Whitest' of the Antilles."

39. Mary Douglas, *Purity and Danger: An Analysis of Concepts of Pollution and Taboo* (New York: Praeger Publishers, 1969), 40.

40. Edwin Reyes, "Rapeo sobre el rap en Ciales," *Claridad*, December 28–January 3, 1995–96.

41. Santos, "Puerto Rican Underground."

42. Fernando Clemente, "Entrando por la salida," *Claridad*, February 18–24, 1994. My first publication ever was a response to Clemente's article, which I titled "¿Que el rap no es cultura?" *Claridad*, March 4–10, 1994.

43. Reyes, "Rapeo sobre el rap en Ciales."

44. Bernabe, "Rap."

45. Isabelo Zenón Cruz, *Narciso descubre su trasero, Tomo I (El negro en la cultura puertorriqueña)* (Humacao, P.R.: Editorial Furidi, 1974), 290.

46. Juan Flores, *Divided Borders: Essays on Puerto Rican Identity* (Houston: Arte Público Press, 1993), 95. Rafael Cortijo was a famed Puerto Rican musician, composer and bandleader.

47. Edgardo Díaz Díaz, "Puerto Rican Affirmation and Denial of Musical National-ism: The Cases of Campos Parsi and Aponte Ledée," *Latin American Music Review* 17, no. 1 (1996): 1–20; Mareia Quintero Rivera, "Música 'inmoral' de las Antillas," *Diálogo*, September 1995.

48. Quintero Rivera, "Música 'inmoral' de las Antillas."

49. Díaz Díaz, "Puerto Rican Affirmation and Denial of Musical Nationalism," 5.

50. George Yúdice, "Postmodernity and Transnational Capitalism," in *On Edge: The Crisis of Contemporary Latin American Culture*, ed. George Yúdice, Jean Franco, and Juan Flores (Minneapolis: University of Minnesota Press, 1992), 1–28.

51. Mary Douglas, *Purity and Danger*.

52. Carol Smith-Rosenberg, "Sex as Symbol in Victorian Purity," in *Culture and Society: Contemporary Debates*, ed. Jeffrey Alexander and Steven Seidman (Cambridge: Cambridge University Press, 1990).

53. Julia Kristeva, *Powers of Horror: An Essay on Abjection* (New York: Columbia University Press, 1982), 69.

54. Mary Douglas, *Purity and Danger*, 113.

55. Michel Foucault, *The History of Sexuality: Volume 1*, trans. Robert Hurley (New York: Pantheon Books, 1978).

56. Ibid.; Smith-Rosenberg, "Sex as Symbol in Victorian Purity."

57. Smith-Rosenberg, "Sex as Symbol in Victorian Purity," 166.

58. Around the same time that the *underground* debate was raging, there was a huge uproar when the secretary of public health, Carmen Feliciano, dared suggest that mas-turbation should be presented to young people as a safer sex alternative. See Rafael Bernabe and Nancy Herzig, "Sobre sexo, sexismo y censura."

59. See the Penal Code of Puerto Rico, articles 112–17.

60. The same can be said of *underground*'s direct heir: reggaeton.

61. Santos, "Puerto Rican Underground"; bell hooks, *Outlaw Culture: Resisting Rep-resentations* (New York: Routledge, 1994), 173–82.

62. The newspaper and magazine articles devoted to the controversy boasted head-lines such as "Perreo Has Constitutional Guarantees," "Perreo Videos before the Sen-ate," "Agencies Set to Attack the 'Perreo,'" and "In Its Final Phases the Anti-'Perreo' Bills." See Leonor Mulero, "Garantía constitucional al perreo," *El Nuevo Día*, May 16, 2002; Israel Rodríguez Sánchez, "Ante el Senado los vídeos del perreo," *El Nuevo Día*, May 30, 2002; Carmen Millán, "A atacar las agencias el 'perreo,'" *El Nuevo Día*, June 11, 2002; and Sandra Morales Blanes, "En su fase final los proyectos anti 'perreo,'" *El Nuevo Día*, June 12, 2002.

63. See Frances Negrón-Muntaner and Raquel Z. Rivera, "Reggaeton Nation," NACLA *Report on the Americas* 40, no. 6 (November/December 2007): 35–39.

DEBORAH PACINI HERNANDEZ

Dominicans in the Mix

Reflections on Dominican Identity, Race, and Reggaeton

I have been writing about Dominican communities and their music since the early 1980s, and have followed the trajectories of merengue and then *bachata* as their popularity spread beyond the Dominican Republic to New York and sub-sequently to other parts of the northeastern United States with large Dominican communities (e.g., Lawrence, Massachusetts, and Providence, Rhode Island). Since 1960, more than 1 million Dominicans have migrated to the U.S. main-land. Another 100,000 have settled in Puerto Rico, largely in metropolitan San Juan's most poverty-stricken neighborhoods alongside similarly poor Puerto Ricans. I became curious about the musical implications of this island-to-island migration and the nature of musical exchanges between these two Spanish Caribbean populations with long histories of musical exchanges, particularly in the wake of the international explosion of reggaeton, whose epicenter was precisely the sort of inner-city neighborhoods (such as Villa Palmeras in San-turce) where Dominicans were likely to have settled. As I examined the bur-geoning number of narratives regarding the emergence of reggaeton, I was struck by how little was being said about Dominican participation beyond the obvious contributions of the Dominican production team Luny Tunes, which seemed strange given that Dominicans were occupying the same marginalized urban spaces from which reggaeton was said to emerge. Indeed, Puerto Rican and Dominican artists regularly collaborate, merengue and bachata influences permeate reggaeton, and reggaeton lyrics are peppered with references to the Dominican Republic and its culture. Moreover, many of reggaeton's most important artists have at least some Dominican ancestry—although they are seldom represented as such. Why, then, have Dominicans been so invisible in most reggaeton's "birth stories"?[1] One can also ask why it matters, especially since the circumstances of musical genesis are usually unverifiable, especially in the context of the constant musical exchanges that have characterized musical developments in the Americas for centuries. Nevertheless, it is important to analyze how competing narratives of musical origins and ownership are constructed, because of what they tell us about Dominican–Puerto Rican relations and, more broadly, about the formation of Spanish Caribbean racial and ethnic identities on the island and in New York.

DOMINICANS IN PUERTO RICO: SOCIOECONOMIC CONTEXT

On first glance, the geographic and cultural proximity between the Dominican Republic and Puerto Rico might make musical interactions between the two groups seem easy and natural. Nevertheless, relations between the two populations have historically been vexed, alternating between solidarity and collaboration, and conflict and mutual hostility, which have influenced their musical interactions in profound ways. I begin, therefore, with some brief observations on the sociocultural contexts in which these musical interactions have been taking place over the past decades, in order to construct a broader framework for thinking about reggaeton history and development.

Large-scale Dominican migration to the United States and Puerto Rico began largely as a result of two events: first, the fall of the dictator Rafael Trujillo, who had restricted emigration for decades, in 1961; and the institution of the Family Reunification Act, which gave U.S. visa preferences to immigrants' family members, in 1965. The first Dominicans to arrive in U.S. territory—primarily New York but also Puerto Rico—were in large part middle class and educated; after the 1965 coup and subsequent occupation of the Dominican Republic by U.S. troops, they were joined by political activists who had been given visas in order to reduce political pressure on the island. These pioneer Dominican immigrants established anchor communities in both New York and San Juan, which provided later arrivals, whose socioeconomic levels fell with each succeeding decade, with assistance in finding housing and jobs as well as social and cultural resources.[2] The majority of Dominican migrants headed to New York, where they settled primarily in Manhattan's Washington Heights and Inwood neighborhoods; another 12 percent of them entered Puerto Rico. Many of those who entered Puerto Rico believed the island was only a stepping stone on their journey to the U.S. mainland, but they ended up settling in Puerto Rico, which offered the advantage of being Spanish speaking and culturally similar, as well as an economy and social service sector directly linked to the United States. Furthermore, living in Puerto Rico allowed Dominicans to acquire permanent U.S. residence and citizenship, since the island is considered a U.S. territory for immigration and naturalization purposes. Currently, the total number of Dominicans in Puerto Rico is estimated to be approximately 100,000, of whom about one-third are believed to be undocumented.[3] Dominicans are thus the island's biggest ethnic minority, accounting for 56 percent of the island's foreign-born population.[4]

Some Dominicans have arrived in Puerto Rico on tourist visas and overstayed, but the majority of undocumented immigrants cross the dangerous forty-mile Mona Straits between the eastern end of the Dominican Republic and the western coast of Puerto Rico in flimsy open boats called *yolas*, because it is easier and cheaper to take a yola than trying to enter by airplane, where the INS presents a much higher obstacle. Thus, much like the Mexicans who risk their lives crossing into the United States on foot, the Dominicans who enter Puerto Rico by yola have been, in sociocultural terms, the sending nations' poorest, most uneducated citizens. Moreover, coming from a nation where class correlates closely to race, they are also, in general, the nation's darker-skinned citizens.[5] The Dominicans who arrived in Puerto Rico, itself beset by significant socioeconomic problems, such as high unemployment rates and widespread poverty, have thus had more trouble integrating economically there than their generally better-educated counterparts who have taken up residence alongside Puerto Ricans in New York.[6]

The presence of so many Dominicans in Puerto Rico created the same sort of resentments as those generated by poor immigrants in the United States (or Haitians in the Dominican Republic, for that matter): that they fray the social safety net, they take jobs away from locals, they lower wages, they are responsible for an increase in crime, they refuse to assimilate, and so on. These fears have been compounded, however, by racial anxieties. As other authors in this volume, such as Raquel Z. Rivera and Tego Calderón, note, Puerto Ricans have long denied, ignored, or rejected people and culture considered "too black." Dominicans, arriving by the thousands, threaten to "blacken" a population that considers itself to be much whiter than the Dominican Republic's—indeed, in 2000 80.5 percent of Puerto Ricans identified as white.[7] (Note the relatively high percentage of self-identified black Dominicans in Puerto Rico—37.8 percent, according to the 2000 census.) As Jorge Duany notes, "The social construction of race and ethnicity in contemporary Puerto Rico increasingly conflates black with Dominican,"[8] and he concludes, "Anti-Dominican sentiment has proven to be a . . . formidable barrier to interethnic relations. Many Puerto Rican residents harbor strong resentments against foreign newcomers to the island, especially Dominicans. . . . An ever expanding repertoire of ethnic jokes and folk stories perpetuates the myth of the dumb, ignorant country bumpkin from the Cibao."[9]

In San Juan, Dominicans settled in the city's poorest and most undesirable neighborhoods, such as Barrio Obrero and Barrio Gandul in Santurce and Barrio Capetillo in Río Piedras. Unlike in New York, however, where Dominicans in Washington Heights are ethnically dominant, in Puerto Rico Dominicans are much more likely to live side by side with Puerto Ricans who are similarly poor, poorly educated, and dark skinned: 52 percent of the black population in Duany's Barrio Gandul study were Dominican, while the other 48 percent were Puerto Rican; in contrast, 87 percent of Barrio Gandul's white population were Puerto Rican.[10] This breakdown corresponds to 2000 census data, which show that only 36.2 percent of Dominicans in Puerto Rico classified themselves as white, while the remaining 63.8 percent said they were black or "other" (mostly meaning mulatto).[11] Duany goes on to observe, "Whether or not they liked it, Puerto Ricans lived side by side with Dominicans in most residential areas of Santurce."[12]

Duany's 1998 essay on Dominicans concluded that "despite their physical proximity [to Puerto Ricans in poor neighborhoods] Dominican immigrants tend to be culturally isolated and socially distant from Puerto Rican residents . . . [and] . . . many immigrants are reasserting their own cultural background. This move may be taken as an example of what has been called an oppositional or reactive identity."[13] His 2005 study, however, includes information suggesting that Dominican isolation may be more characteristic of the first generation than of the second: demographic data demonstrate that the majority of immigrants—60 percent—have been women, and most of these have arrived young and single.[14] Census data also indicate a high rate of intermarriage with Puerto Ricans: in 1990, 5,558 persons were born in Puerto Rico of two Dominican parents, but a far larger number—13,944—had only one Dominican parent.[15] Thus, while first-generation Dominican immigrants may have tended to maintain their cultural practices and identities, their Puerto Rican–born children, many of whom have a Puerto Rican parent, have grown up attending public schools alongside Puerto Ricans and absorbing whatever music is being listened to by their counterparts—and throughout the 1990s that music consisted of the (often overlapping) genres known as rap, reggae, and *underground*. The influences have not been unidirectional, however: as Duany notes, "The growing Dominican presence in Santurce and Río Piedras has visibly transformed the physical and cultural landscape of several neighborhoods . . . [and] is most evident in popular language, music, religion, and food preferences"—more about which will be said in later sections.[16]

Musical—and more broadly, cultural—exchanges in the Caribbean have been longstanding and extensive,[17] but they have been particularly active between the two neighboring islands of Puerto Rico and the Dominican Republic, indeed, going back to the nineteenth century.[18] Puerto Rican *jíbaro* music, for example, was a major influence on the development of Dominican bachata in the 1960s, and in the 1970s Dominicans joined much of Latin America in embracing salsa (including Johnny Pacheco, the Dominican-born salsa musician and founder of the seminal salsa record label Fania Records).[19] In the other direction, merengue has long been familiar to Puerto Ricans on both the island and in New York. The 1980s, however, witnessed a confluence of musical influences swirling through Puerto Rico as well as through the Dominican Republic and Spanish Caribbean New York. In New York City, the coexistence of multiple Latin American and Caribbean musics associated with various immigrant groups has always been a characteristic feature of the city's soundscape, and working musicians have been expected to be familiar with all of them.[20] In Puerto Rico, by contrast, the presence of non–Puerto Rican musics has generated public controversies regarding their impact on the island's national culture and identity.[21] In the 1980s, for example, young *roqueros* (rockers), were seen by cultural nationalists as cultural traitors for embracing the music of the colonizers, and compared unfavorably to *cocolos*, the vernacular term for those who preferred the more "authentic" salsa. These debates also had class and racial undertones, as many of salsa's most passionate fans were working class and dark skinned, while rock fans were more likely to be whiter and more affluent.[22]

Below the surface of the public controversies between salsa and rock during the 1980s, Puerto Rican youth living in the island's poorest barrios were actually gravitating toward rap—which was clearly not a native Puerto Rican music. Rap generated similar objections from cultural nationalists, but it nevertheless seeped into poor neighborhoods, brought to the island by New York–based Puerto Ricans who had grown up listening to and performing rap alongside their African American neighbors in the South Bronx and East Harlem. By the end of the 1980s, rap had been indigenized by rappers such as Vico C, whose Spanish lyrics and vernacular language assertively articulated oppositional working-class sensibilities. Some *rap en español* was released commercially by artists such as Vico C, Lisa M, Brewley, and Francheska in the early 1990s, but most Puerto Rican rap en español artists at the time had little access to the media or commercial distribution because of their explicitly sexual and violent lyrics—hence the term *underground* applied to the style.

Concurrently, another non–Puerto Rican music was making inroads on the island (as well as in Latino New York): merengue. In the 1980s a number of Dominican merengue bands such as Conjunto Quisqueya and Jossie Esteban y La Patrulla 15—and, later in the decade, Toño Rosario—took up residence in Puerto Rico because the economically better-off island offered more performance opportunities. In spite of its Spanish Caribbean roots, merengue also generated controversy, although the concerns were more economic than cultural: Puerto Rican musicians accused Dominican bands, who were willing to work for less, of taking work away from salsa musicians; Dominicans countered that they were simply providing fresh sounds to fans losing interest in salsa's trajectory toward increasingly formulaic arrangements and romantic balladlike lyrics.[23] Both Puerto Ricans and Dominicans were, of course, aware that merengue's dominance over salsa represented a turning of tables, as salsa had previously overshadowed merengue in popularity in the Dominican Republic in the 1970s. By the 1990s merengue was so entrenched in Puerto Rico that Puerto Ricans themselves began forming merengue groups, and some of them, such as Olga Tañón and Elvis Crespo, even began winning Grammys for their merengues.[24]

One Puerto Rican entrepreneur, Jorge Oquendo, took advantage of these popular but nonintersecting musical trends, and by doing so participated in laying the foundations for what was later to become reggaeton. Oquendo was born in the United States but raised on the island by his well-off Puerto Rican father and Spanish mother. In the mid-1980s he lived in Harlem while attending Columbia University, and became immersed in hip-hop. When he returned to Puerto Rico in 1987, he noticed that young working-class Puerto Ricans were listening to the same music. Oquendo recalls that around 1990, when he and his partner Miguel Correa started producing concerts of American hip-hop, "Vico C comes along asking to do an opening act, I think it was for Public Enemy. I asked him what he sang, because I didn't know anything about Vico C. He brings me a demo, and we decided to let him open the concert and then to record a record."[25] Oquendo's record label, Prime Records, went on to successfully market Vico C and then recorded Vico C's dancer Lisa M (whose mother was Dominican); her similarly successful recordings opened doors for Francheska and other women rappers. In the late 1980s, when Dominican *merenguero* Toño Rosario separated from his group Los Hermanos Rosario and moved to Puerto Rico to develop his own career, he was signed by Prime Records and went on to become one of the island's most successful merengue performers.

Oquendo then conceived the idea of combining the two genres—rap and merengue—by encouraging collaborations between his most popular rap artists—Vico C, Lisa M, Francheska—and his most popular merengue artists—Toño Rosario and Jossie Esteban. Oquendo recalls that it was not easy to convince any of the artists to participate, because no one had previously tried to mix the two genres, but his Dominican arranger Israel Casado agreed to the project and did the arrangements. The resulting fusion, called merenrap, was primarily driven by merengue's signature 2/4 rhythm accented by the genre's indispensable *tambora* drum and *güira* scraper as well as its prominent horn sections and saxophone arpeggios, but the fusion with rap was expressed in lyrics that were rapped rather than sung, and synthesized drums that occasionally augmented the more traditional rhythm section. These experimental sounds sold well in Puerto Rico as well as in the United States, and stimulated musicians who had originally held back to try their hand at merenrap. In 1991 Prime Records released a compilation entitled *Merenrap*, containing merenrap songs that had appeared on individual artists' previous recordings. Another version was released in the United States (and beyond) that same year by BMG, which was followed by another similarly titled compilation in 1993.[26]

Around 1990, within months of Prime Records' first merenrap experiments, Oquendo accompanied Toño Rosario on a tour to New York, and was approached by a young Panamanian musician who said, as quoted in an interview on July 23, 2006, " 'I hear you are making rap in Spanish. I do reggae in Spanish.' And so we signed El General. . . . [who] was established in New York and had 2 songs ['Tu Pun Pun' and 'Te Ves Buena']. We produced four more, on a record with six songs." The profound impact of Prime Records' 1990 release of El General's "Te Ves Buena," with its catchy Spanish lyrics over Jamaican dancehall rhythms, is documented in Wayne Marshall's essay in this volume. It is noteworthy that a remix of "Te Ves Buena" was also included in the 1991 BMG version of *Merenrap*; since it did not appear on Prime Records' version released earlier that year, its inclusion on the BMG version appears to be opportunistic. Even the original Prime version of the 1991 compilation, however, already contained songs fusing *reggae en español* with rap and merengue: Lisa M and Santi y Sus Duendes' version of El General's wildly popular "Tu Pun Pun" (listed as "El Pum Pum"[27]), and Brewley M.C.'s "Nena Sexy." The sounds of reggae en español in this widely heard CD even further confused the already blurred distinctions between rap, reggae en español, and merenrap. As Lisa M recalled in an interview, "El ambiente y la industria nos confundían a nosotros mismos los artistas porque, por ejemplo, acababa mi disco y en vez de ponerme en rap o en hip hop, me ponían en tropical o en pop, porque acuérdate que antes no existía el género. Entonces, para entrar al mercado, claro está, teníamos una variedad de ritmos y de fusiones. Pero nunca dejó de ser rap, yo nunca dejé de ser rapera." (We artists were confused by the general public as well as the industry, because, for example, I finished my record and instead of putting me in rap or hip-hop, they put me in tropical or pop, because remember that the genre [reggaeton] didn't exist before that. In those days, to enter the market, of course, we had a variety of rhythms and fusions. But it never stopped being rap, I never stopped being a rapper.)[29]

It is important to note that meren-rap was a studio experiment rather than a grassroots cultural phenomenon like Puerto Rican *underground*, and it was short lived. As musicians adopted reggae en español's dancehall beats, the style all but eclipsed meren-rap in Puerto Rico. Nevertheless, as Oquendo notes, it was a milestone at the time: "At first people didn't see that [fusions could work], because merengue and rap existed before, and both were strong for years, but they hadn't been fused. They marked the precedent of fusing popular rhythms, with the result also being popular."[30]

The role of meren-rap in the evolution of reggaeton is subject to interpretation: for some it was a parallel development that had no direct influence on reggaeton, while others, including Oquendo, see it as part of the musical stew from which reggaeton emerged. Oquendo, of course, has a vested interest in promoting a history of reggaeton in which his record label plays a central role, but his thoughts are nonetheless worth reproducing: "Remember reggaeton was an evolution, it didn't emerge from one day to the next. First rap and merengue, then rap and reggaeton, then the three of them mix. . . . Meren-rap is the foundation of reggaeton, the essence, reggaeton comes out of it. On one hand, its all rap, because that's the form of interpreting it. Then there's merengue and there's reggae. The fusion of the three is called reggaeton."[31]

If fusions of rap and merengue were no longer being produced in Puerto Rico, they continued to develop in New York City throughout the 1990s, with the music of Proyecto Uno and DLG (who also fused salsa and rap); both groups were composed of New York–based Dominican and Puerto Rican musicians. The Dominican group Fulanito, in contrast, fused rap and the more folkloric *merengue típico*. Successful as these recordings were, such fusions of rap and merengue and bachata did not coalesce into a new genre, nor were they in dialogue with developments taking place in Puerto Rico's *underground* scene, where, as Marshall points out in this volume, fusions of rap and dancehall reggae predominated. It was not until a decade later, after reggaeton had emerged as a distinct style, that the sounds of merengue, and the relative newcomer, bachata, appeared (or reappeared).

The appearance of Dominican styles in reggaeton coincided with the arrival in Puerto Rico of the Dominican-born production team Luny Tunes—although they are not solely responsible for this development. Luny (Francisco Saldana[32]) moved to Puerto Rico from the Dominican Republic with his mother and sisters as a child, where he "[grew] up listening to underground Puerto Rican rap";[33] as a teen his family moved to Peabody, Massachusetts, just outside of Boston. Luny met Tunes (Victor Cabrera) in Peabody, where both of them attended high school (Tunes' family had immigrated directly from the Dominican Republic). The two friends listened constantly to reggaeton tapes brought from Puerto Rico, and began working together as producers, with Luny producing the drum patterns and sound engineering while Tunes provided melodies. In 2000 Luny received an opportunity to work in the studio of the reggaeton producer DJ Nelson in Puerto Rico, and Tunes accompanied him.[34] They began producing a string of successful releases for reggaeton artists from Ivy Queen to Tego Calderón to Daddy Yankee. Luny Tunes collaborated with Tego Calderón on his influential 2002–3 recording *El Abayarde*,[35] considered to be a milestone in reggaeton development, not only because his lyrics explicitly addressed the issue of racism, but also because of his extensive use of live and sampled instruments, and the extraordinary diversity of the rhythms he engages with, from Puerto Rican bomba and salsa, to hip-hop, to Jamaican reggae/dancehall.[36] Another song, "Pa' Que Retozen [*sic*]," features the unmistakable guitar sounds of Dominican bachata—although it was produced not by Luny Tunes but by DJ Joe. (In a video of a live performance of this song, a guitarist sits behind the rapping Calderón, playing bachata's characteristic arpeggios.) Luny Tunes' own 2003 hit compilation, *Mas Flow*, also included a Tego Calderón song, "Métele Sazón," which exhibits bachata's signature guitar arpeggios as well as merengue's characteristic piano riffs.[37]

In the wake of the success of these songs, other musicians began incorporating merengue and bachata into reggaeton.[38] Of these two Dominican genres, the guitar-based bachata has been incorporated into reggaeton more frequently than merengue, although it is important to note that bachata can also be played in merengue rhythm; in other words, a reggaeton song can simultaneously have bachata's guitar-based sound and merengue's rhythm. A smaller number of reggaeton songs incorporate merengue aesthetics—particularly its repeating piano patterns—without references to bachata. Ivy Queen's "Te He Querido, Te He Llorado" and "La Mala," for example, contain bachata's signature guitar sound and slower, more romantic rhythm; in "La Mala" Ivy Queen also adopts bachata's exaggerated emotional singing style. Don Omar's "Dile," in contrast, incorporates the bachata-merengue style—bachata's characteristic guitar sound over a merengue rhythm. Daddy Yankee's "Brugal" (whose song title refers to the popular Dominican rum of that name) incorporates only merengue's characteristic keyboard riffs.

Noted Puerto Rican hip-hop DJ, MC, and radio host Velcro (the Puerto Rico–born child of a Dominican mother and Mexican father) noted, "In the same way you can mark reggaeton before and after Tego, there's a before and after Luny Tunes. . . . Luny Tunes contributed something very positive, because they solidified the marriage between bachata and reggaeton. It made it what it is, a tropical music, in that way it distinguished it from hip-hop."[39] Today, as producer Boy Wonder (himself of Dominican descent, born and raised in New York) notes, "Bachata and merengue is hot, it's been a major success . . . and now every album has to have some Latin influence."[40]

These changes have transformed reggaeton, as Wayne Marshall has noted in this volume: "the genre's cultural politics might be seen (and heard) as undergoing a major shift around the turn of the millennium, moving away from a sonically, textually, and visually encoded foregrounding of racial community and toward nationalist . . . Latin/pan-Latin signifiers—or, to put it in the words of reggaeton performers themselves, from 'música negra' to 'Reggaeton Latino.'" Not everyone has appreciated these developments, particularly hip-hop artists, who felt that the new style—more melodic and party-oriented, and far more commercial—was distancing reggaeton from its original role as "the primary voice of the street."[41]

A further development in the use of bachata occurred in 2005, when producers began remixing existing reggaeton hits with bachata's characteristic guitar sounds and marketing them as *bachatón*, defining it as "bachata a lo boricua" (bachata, Puerto Rican style). In addition to the infusion of Dominican musical aesthetics, textual and visual references to the Dominican Republic and Dominican culture abound in reggaeton songs and videos. The video for Angel y Khris's hit song "Ven Báilalo," for example, was filmed in the Dominican Republic's resort town Boca Chica, and features stereotypically tropicalized images of the Dominican Republic (e.g., black women carrying large pans of fruit on their heads, multicolored parrots, straw hats, painted buses) and scenes of the artists dancing with light-skinned Dominican women. Similarly, the multiple references to Dominican places, beers, and rums (and women) in Daddy Yankee's song "Brugal" clearly locate the singer as a visitor in the Dominican Republic, as Tego Calderón similarly does in his song "Dominicana."[42] Tego Calderón and Don Omar have also performed duets with the New York–based bachata stars Aventura.

Such amicable references to Dominican culture are not altogether surprising, given the longstanding popularity of Dominican musics (if not Dominican people) among Puerto Ricans, and the fact that the Dominican Republic is a popular vacation destination for Puerto Ricans.[43] More important, Dominicans represent reggaeton's primary non–Puerto Rican fan base, so such references also have economic benefits:[44] as Jorge Oquendo notes, "Everyone has the same goal, to sell records, so the Puerto Rican producer will use Dominican elements that he knows about, and the Dominican producer will use the Puerto Rican elements, and mix them as well as he can."[45] Even though the Dominican Republic is not a lucrative market for record sales—it is poorer than Puerto Rico, and piracy there is rampant—reggaeton artists routinely travel to the Dominican Republic to perform, as salsa and merengue singers did before them. Commenting on the frequency of these tours, the Dominican journalist Máximo Jiménez argued that the Dominican Republic has become an important stepping stone for Puerto Rican artists wanting to make headway in the United States, because there are more radio and television stations playing Spanish Caribbean popular music in the Dominican Republic than in Puerto Rico, thus offering Puerto Rican musicians easier access to the media. Miami-based radio stations, he goes on to claim, routinely monitor what is popular in the Dominican Republic in order to identify upcoming hits.[46] (He did not mention, however, that radio stations in Puerto Rico are monitored as well.)

Unlike in New York, where reggaeton's popularity is relatively new, reggaeton has been circulating in the Dominican Republic since its inception in the 1990s. Indeed, the concurrent presence of rap en español and reggae en español (including the experimental meren-rap) that characterized the *underground* music scene in Puerto Rico was virtually paralleled in the Dominican Republic —as were the fuzzy boundaries between these genres. Orquídea Negra, the twenty-seven-year-old female rapper in the New York–based reggaeton duo L.D.A., was born in the Dominican Republic and lived there until she was seventeen; she recalls that as an adolescent in the early 1990s, she and her friends listened to rap en español and reggae en español—and meren-rap. "It was initially reggaeton, not only from P.R. but also from Panama. But mostly from P.R., the tapes that were famous at the time were the Playero tapes. There were some beginnings of Dominicans rapping and singing Spanish hip-hop and reggaeton. I recall the first [Dominican] group that I knew back then was MC Connection, they used to do Spanish reggae and hip-hop."[47] Enough of it was Puerto Rican, however, that the common term for *underground* artists in the Dominican Republic was *playeros*, a reference to the seminal Puerto Rican DJ Playero.[48]

Orquídea Negra also remembers listening to fused merengue and rap by a group called Sandy y Papo, which she distinguishes from the Puerto Rican productions, which were collaborations between merengue and rap artists, while Sandy y Papo were rappers rapping to a merengue beat: "This was not a collaboration; it was not a merengue featuring rap artists. The real meren-rap was rappers doing merengue."[49] Sandy y Papo released their first recording in 1996,[50] but the Dominican fusions did not flourish as well as the contemporaneous productions of their Puerto Rican counterparts. One reason was that the then more authoritarian Dominican government subjected young rappers to even greater levels of censorship than in Puerto Rico, hindering Dominican rappers and *reggaetoneros* in their ability to access the media and develop a mass public fan base.[51] Orquídea Negra, who listened to rap as an adolescent in the early 1990s in Santo Domingo, recalled:

> When it first started making a lot of noise it was perceived as a very negative music and a lot of people didn't support it. My father was one of the first individuals to do parties that would play that type of music. The neighbors would send narcotics [agents] there; they would send the police, because it was different. . . . People used to dress very baggy, wear their clothes backwards, their hair style was wild, so most people in the Dominican Republic, adults, they were not so fond of the music. When the music started I saw it as a rebellion type of thing for youth to express themselves. The topics were very raw: there were sexual topics, about the government, the police, about parents, and it wasn't accepted at all when it came out.[52]

In addition to experiencing greater levels of censorship, Dominican artists also lacked the advantage of access to the resources—capital, technology, media— afforded by the United States that were available to Puerto Rican musicians. Puerto Ricans' success, however, opened doors to their Dominican counterparts, and as reggaeton's international popularity spread in the wake of recordings such as Daddy Yankee's 2004 *Barrio Fino* (much of which, including the mega-hit "Gasolina," was produced by Luny Tunes), reggaeton from the Dominican Republic began finding more outlets. Among them were Don Miguelo, whose 2006 "Cola de Motora" was the first Dominican reggaeton to become a hit in Puerto Rico and New York,[53] and Papi Sanchez, who has released two recordings with Sony since 2004.[54] Another Dominican group,

Aguakate, distinguished itself by mixing reggaeton with the accordion-based sounds of merengue típico.[55]

In New York City, on the other hand, where young Dominicans and Puerto Ricans born or raised in the United States were more attached to hip-hop, reggaeton didn't really take hold until a few years ago. Orquídea Negra, who moved to the United States in 1996, suggests some of the reasons why this may have been so:

> It started the same way—not during the same time—but the same influence: first we were doing more Spanish hip-hop and then evolved more towards the reggaeton side. Our influences are more hip-hop, *moreno* [black] hip-hop, so our styles are different because the way of living is more different; we are more hip-hop, you know? Like I'm hearing Busta Rhymes, Method Man; we listen more to that type of music, and so I think it influences our style to be a little more different. Now, ever since reggaeton became so mainstream—you see every artist whether they are from Dominican Republic, Puerto Rico, or from here—they dress like from the hip-hop culture from the United States. It was not like that before. Two, three years ago if you look at the CD covers they used to dress more like with slacks; they look more preppy, but artists from United States who do hip-hop and Spanish reggaeton, we always dress baggy.[56]

While reggaeton had been quietly circulating on tapes in New York (as it had in Boston when members of the Luny Tunes production team were living in Peabody), its public arrival in New York was marked by the sold-out August 2003 Reggaeton Summerfest concert at Madison Square Garden. Another subsequent milestone was the December 2004 release of the first reggaeton documentary, *The Chosen Few*, a DVD with interviews and live performances by the likes of Vico C, El General, Daddy Yankee, Don Omar, Tego Calderón, Luny Tunes, and many more. The DVD documentary was packaged with a CD containing recordings by the featured musicians. *The Chosen Few*'s producer was Manuel Alejandro Ruiz, a.k.a. Boy Wonder, born and raised in New York by his Dominican mother. Around 2003 Boy Wonder went to visit his mother's family in the Dominican Republic, where he discovered a music scene immersed in both hip-hop and reggaeton: "It was crazy, here were Latinos making new sounds, not just imitating what had come before, or ripping beats. I had seen the future!"[57] After returning to New York, Boy Wonder was determined to make a documentary about reggaeton, notwithstanding his lack of any experience with filmmaking. Fortunately his maternal uncle July Ruiz was able to open doors to key music industry personnel: July Ruiz was one of the Dominican Republic's most important sound engineers, who had won a Grammy credit for his work on Juan Luis Guerra's 2000 *No Es Lo Mismo Ni Es Igual*.[58] *The Chosen Few* CD and DVD set, which sold over 500,000 copies, ranked on *Billboard* charts for months, many of them in the top five. Indeed, *The Chosen Few*'s success in disseminating this new music—as well as its associated images, spaces, fashions, and cultural ideologies—did for reggaeton what the films *Wild Style* accomplished for hip-hop in 1983 and *Our Latin Thing* for salsa in 1972.

Today, a few years after reggaeton triumphed in New York, the economic potential of the city's powerful Latin music and hip-hop media and hundreds of thousands of Latinos of all nationalities have helped transform New York into an important center of reggaeton production. As Orquídea Negra responded when asked if she had encountered any resistance within a rapidly exploding music scene dominated by Puerto Rican artists:

> The music was considered only a particular race could do this type of music; I've heard that mentality. . . . When we were not at the level we are at now, it was more difficult to go to a record label and say "hey this is mine"; they would be like "you are an outsider." Because you are an outsider, before they would even listen to the music it would influence the way they see the music that you present to them.

Orquídea Negra went on to say, however, that things have changed, and indeed, in New York the collaborations between Puerto Rican and Dominican artists—and African American artists—have been extensive and significant, one well-known example being N.O.R.E.'s "Oye Mi Canto," which features U.S.-Dominican artists Gem Star, Big Mato, and L.D.A. Another of N.O.R.E.'s collaborations with New York Puerto Ricans and Dominicans is his song "Más Maíz," a version of a Dominican merengue originally performed by Raúl Acosta of the popular merengue group Oro Sólido (which was censored in the Dominican Republic because of its lyrics).[59]

Boy Wonder's label Chosen Few has been particularly active in supporting New York–based talent of Dominican descent, such as L.D.A. Scores of other Dominican reggaeton groups are beginning to emerge. Some, such as Jhosy & Baby Q and Noztra, have been signed by record labels and are releasing recordings that identify the musicians as Dominican via their use of Dominican vernacular and references to Dominican merengue and bachata; other hopeful Dominican newcomers promote themselves on the Internet.

In summary, on the U.S. mainland, where both Puerto Ricans and Domini-

cans are both marginalized ethnoracial minorities, relations have been generally more cooperative than on the island—reggaeton's "home base"—where
the differences in status and power between native Puerto Ricans and immigrant Dominicans has been more pronounced. On the mainland, constructions of reggaeton as a solely Puerto Rican creation have also been challenged
by notions of reggaeton as an Afrodiasporic and/or a pan-Latin genre characterized precisely by its hybridity. Indeed, reggaeton's hybridity has been credited with enhancing its appeal to young Latinos throughout the hemisphere.
Opinions about reggaeton's origins and ownership have thus become more
dependent on locality. As Boy Wonder observed, "Somebody from here [New
York] who knows reggaeton who's never been to Puerto Rico would probably
see it from that angle, but someone who knows reggaeton who's only lived in
Puerto Rico and saw reggaeton start and sees how big it is now would judge it
as music from the island. I see it both ways."[60]

REGGAETON AND THE NEGOTIATION OF DOMINICAN
AND PUERTO RICAN IDENTITY

Reggaeton's explosion into the international music arena, and the concomitant
growth of its economic value, has stimulated cultural observers (including
those contributing to this anthology) to propose historical narratives of reggaeton's origins, which now abound in the press and on the Internet. Reggaeton's Jamaican, Panamanian, and African American antecedents are widely
acknowledged; with the exception of the incontestably influential Luny Tunes,
the contributions of Dominican musicians and Dominican styles have been far
less visible. Additionally, there has been little recognition that among the
residents of the poor, black, marginalized neighborhoods in Puerto Rico from
which reggaeton emerged and whose voice reggaeton is assumed to represent,
are thousands of poor, black, ethnically Dominican, and thus triply marginalized, youths. Both the Puerto Rican Don Omar and hip-hop artist SieteNueve,
of Dominican ancestry, for example, were raised in Villa Palmeras, a San Juan
barrio with a rapidly growing population of Dominican immigrants. The
Dominican-origin O.G. Black and his Puerto Rican collaborator Master Joe
came together in San Juan in just such a location: "We united in Puerto Rico
Cazerillo [sic; caserío is the slang Spanish term meaning "public housing projects" or " 'hood"] and that's when the first CD was born, 'Playero 37,' which
featured artist [sic] such as Daddy Yankee. It was just made for all the local kids
in the hoods and just to have something to play in the stereo during parties."[61]

In short, if reggaeton, like other grassroots forms of popular music, is the expression of a community that shares a particular kind of social context—which most reggaeton observers and critics indeed claim—the Dominicans who shared the same spaces and the same experiences of class- and race-based discrimination must be taken into consideration as part of the cultural matrix from which reggaeton emerged. Moreover, second-generation Dominicans born and/or raised in Puerto Rico have also been producing and consuming reggaeton since its inception. Francisco Saldana (Luny), whose immersion in Puerto Rican *underground* took place in the San Juan barrio where he spent his early adolescence,[62] is the best-known example, but many of Puerto Rican reggaeton's biggest stars appear to have one or both Dominican parents, including Eddie Dee,[63] Baby Ranks (both parents Dominican), Nicky Jam (Puerto Rican father, Dominican mother, born in Dominican Republic), O.G. Black,[64] and Javia.[65] Interestingly, while their Dominican parents are acknowledged on fan websites, these artists are seldom represented as Dominican. Indeed, the island's slippery ethnoracial terrain seems to be producing fewer Dominican-identified groups than in New York. MC Welmo E. Romero Joseph (born in Puerto Rico of Dominican and Haitian parents) notes that a reggaeton artist of Dominican ancestry but born and/or raised in Puerto Rico who identifies as Dominican has not emerged: "It's strange that after fifteen years of reggaeton there hasn't been a Dominican identified artist. . . . It's interesting; [it's like] I can take your music and I can use your music, but in the production space. But as MC then they can't participate."[66]

Some of the individuals I interviewed ventured that one reason Dominicans are not more visible in Puerto Rico's reggaeton scene is because the Puerto Rican–born children of Dominicans assume a Puerto Rican identity. There is nothing new about this process: during the early twentieth century, when the direction of migration was reversed as Puerto Ricans migrated to the Dominican Republic and Cuba to take advantage of the neighboring islands' more robust economies, Puerto Rican children born abroad tended to assume the identity of their parents' adopted nations. Similarly, the children of Cuban exiles who settled in Puerto Rico after the revolution tended to identify as Puerto Ricans—all of this suggesting that the similarities between these Spanish Caribbean cultures facilitates this reidentification.[67]

Moreover, unlike multiethnic locations such as New York, where children of immigrants are more likely to maintain some degree of ethnic identity (whether as a proactive political stance or as a defensive response to their marginalization), Puerto Rico's more ethnically homogenous population may discourage such "hyphenated" identities. Puerto Ricans' intense preoccupation with cultural identity in the context of its colonial status might further push island-born youth to assume a Puerto Rican identity rather than to assume a mixed identity. The example of mainland-based Puerto Ricans, whose Puerto Rican–ness is constantly challenged by their island counterparts because of their biculturality, surely serves as an additional deterrent. Nevertheless, the preference for assuming a Puerto Rican rather than a hyphenated identity may also be the product of pervasive anti-Dominican sentiments, which would not encourage public displays of ethnic affiliation and pride. Raquel Z. Rivera raises this very issue when she interprets a song called "Ji-baro-jop" by Siete-Nueve, in which he openly celebrates both of his national heritages: "Considering the rampant discrimination and ill feelings existing towards Dominicans in Puerto Rico, it is doubly significant that SieteNueve actually opts for flaunting his Dominicanness. To add even more complexity to the matter, SieteNueve is not explaining that he is Puerto Rican even though his parents are Dominican. He is proudly celebrating that he is Puerto Rican and Dominican."[68]

Under such circumstances, the efforts of second-generation youth to negotiate a mixed Puerto Rican and Dominican identity is perilous indeed, as a blog by a young man of mixed Puerto Rican and Dominican heritage, but raised in New York, painfully conveys. The young man's anxieties about his identity are generated not only by his location in New York, which makes his Puerto Rican–ness vulnerable to challenge by island Puerto Ricans, but also because in New York, unlike in Puerto Rico—where Puerto Rican–born Dominicans are expected to assume a Puerto Rican identity—he is expected to embrace both of his heritages, even though his Dominican heritage renders him vulnerable to Puerto Ricans' anti-Dominican discrimination.

> If Puerto Rican identity wasn't difficult enough to define and maintain, try being half-Puerto Rican. Try having the other half being *Dominican*— the *unwanted* immigrant class of Puerto Rico. I am not one to deny my ancestrial [*sic*] bloodline, which 50% is Dominican, but I really did not grow-up loving D.R. (Even though I seek new knowledge on that nation all the time) I grew-up loving (and still to this day love) Puerto Rico. Sadly, it is inferred by many Boricuas that because I am half-Dominican then therefore I am less than a "true" Boricua, or whatever that means. Whenever I disagree with a fellow Boricua's point of view on a particular island theme, my Dominican heritage is thrown into my face. I am also tired of people thinking, especially Boricuas that believe because I look like a mulatto, that I *must* be Dominican.[69]

There are many gestures of collaboration in spaces occupied by hip-hop and reggaeton musicians and fans, but the longstanding tensions between the two nationalities simmer just below the surface and can easily flare up, especially around questions of musical ownership and participation. Raquel Z. Rivera, for example, noticed equal numbers of Puerto Rican and Dominican flags at the 2003 Reggaeton Summerfest concert at Madison Square Garden, and that the artists' "shout outs" to Puerto Ricans and Dominicans provoked equally enthusiastic responses. But she contrasts this scene of ethnic solidarity with fan behavior at a Tego Calderón performance she witnessed in a New York club the evening of the annual Puerto Rican day parade, when nationalist sentiments were running high. A young man mimicking Calderón's every word and gesture was invited up on stage and given appreciative applause, but when the song was over and Calderón asked the young man his name, the audience became noticeably disgruntled when he identified himself as Dominican. "Having violated the public's nationalist presumptions, the mini-Tego's declarations of love and respect for Puerto Ricans did him no good at all."[70]

Similar tensions underpin an online discussion between Puerto Rican and Dominican participants about Dominican participation in reggaeton. The following selections from a long discussion began with a simple question, but quickly heated up when questions of musical ownership fanned out to encompass other points of conflict, including the impact of racism and the economic and political disparities between the islands. (Note: I deduced nationalities from references contained in the longer thread.)

ANTILLANO

07–17–2005, 09:11 AM

Do any of you know of any popular Dominican Reggaetón stars? I've noticed that as Reggaetón has hit the mainland U.S. mainstream, most of the genre's fomented stars have been Puerto Rican, but there must be some Dominican Reggaetón artists, since it is P.R.'s closest neighbor and Boricua Reggaetón artists routinely perform there.

YARI [PUERTO RICAN]

08–26–2005, 10:01 PM

Yes some BACHATA & MERENGUE ARTIST are jumping on the wagon which I think is rediculous because it is not their genre, they are just wanting to go with what's popular . . . . PLUS this music been on the scene, underground that is, for forever.

DADDY1 [DOMINICAN]
08–27–2005, 07:02 AM

in another year or so . . . that same beat duplicated for every song will tire out, and all of you know que Puerto Ricans saturate everything, just like they did with there bomba style merengue[71] . . . that music can only survive for so long . . . before it sticks badly between your ears and makes you sick to your stomach after seeing one hundred artist from P.R. do the same thing and play the same damm beat over and over again.

MAMI_TE_LA_COMO [PUERTO RICAN]
08–27–2005, 08:01 PM

I know that the merengue bomba us Puerto Ricans took it and made it look like it was all the same and maybe people got bored with it, but at the same time we made merengue more popular than any other merengue players have. We won a bunch of premio lo nuestro, latin gramys and not only that but if u put attention to the words of the puertorican merengue bomba is more about love, gurls beauty, and stuff like that not like LA VACA or LA POPOLA u see the difference?[72]

About reaeggeton . . . its a combination of Jamaican reaegge and puerto rican flava ;) . . . Same here we are the best at it . . . . we invented reaggeton and we have take it to every corner of the world inch by inch u cant say no about it . . . . This is for daddy1

DRAGONFLY32837 [DOMINICAN]
08–27–2005, 09:00 PM

Please don't say that all Dominican merengues talk about popolas and vacas. And please don't say that Puerto Rican merengue is better than Dominican merengue. Please! And it is not that you made it popular. Ever heard of payola? It happens with most American radio stations that play Hispanic music. Especially La Mega.

LESLEY D [DOMINICAN]
08–27–2005, 09:34 PM

I so agree with Dragonfly's post. I wasn't going comment but I just want to remind Puerto Ricans (who I think have great music in their own right don't get me wrong) if it weren't for Toño Rosario who moved to P.R. when he formed his own band in the early 90's there would be nothing to boast about when it comes to merengue from P.R. Merengue began to have renewed popularity in P.R. thanks to Toño.

YARI [DOMINICAN]

08–28–2005, 04:30 AM

YOU cannot even seriously believe that pr put merengue on the map . . .
not so missy!! Es algo muy dominicano y no lo puedes negar [It's something that's very Dominican and you can't deny it]. but on the other hand,
maybe the elvis crespo or the olga tanon music TO YOU sounds better
than some of our music. para los gustos se hicieron los colores [different
strokes for different folks], your ears, your choice.

You guys have salsa (for the most part cuz we have some dope salseros
too as well as colombia, venezuela etc . . .) please dont try to claim
merengue too. JUST NOT ACCURATE. whats next, gonna take credit for
putting bachata on the map?? :lick:

ASOPAO [DOMINICAN]

08–28–2005, 02:48 PM

PS: this is for the PR guy or girl (cant fig it out) who made the original
comment. . . no one country is better than the other.

Puerto Rico is not a country, it is a COLONY. They can call it so called
"Estado Libre Asociado", but it is just a cover up name for colony.

They don't have their own passports

They don't have their own currency

They don't have their own military

They can't make diplomatic decisions withouth Washington's approval

So, Please, don't call Puerto Rico a " country" ever again. P.R. never has
been a " country".

MAMI_TE_LA_COMO [PUERTO RICAN]

08–28–2005, 03:05 PM

No we r not going to claim bachata and we r not claiming merengue either
we just help out merengue when it was in this time where merengue were
not winning anything or when people in Europe or other parts of the
world were not listening to it . . . . Merengue is very very dominican and
yea i cant denied that but u cant denied that we helped merengue when it
was in a crissis. OOHHH and one more thing . . . . If bachata get in a crissis
then why not us taking it and help it out and put it back on the road, we
know how to do that ;)

The thing is that we r not trying to keep merengue we just gave it a
boost when it was dead, thats all.

MAMI_TE_LA_COMO [PUERTO RICAN]
08–28–2005, 03:22 PM

jajaja asopao, u dont even know what ur saying about PR I dont answer u the way im sopposed to because i respect DR and most of my friends r dominicans and not only that but my gurl is dominican and i have a daughter and another baby comming that r half dominicans so if u want to know who rule this world even tho u r disque "independent" thats U.S.A. yup u read rigth U.S.A. every country if they make a bad decision in something theres U.S.A. a little war or something there goes U.S.A. So study more watch the news and then talk ok. I dont even know why u change the subject anyways we r talking about merengue or regaeton not Politics.

ASOPAO [DOMINICAN]
08–28–2005, 07:14 PM

you're right, USA is the richest country on Earth and the boss/police of the world and Puerto Ricans are smart in keeping the colonial status. Otherwise they would be the ones taking up the yolas and going to DR instead of viceversa. I don't think a single Dominican would take a yola to PR if it were an indepentent country instead of a U.S. Colony. D.R. is mad poor but we are very proud of our independece and our history (didn't have to wait for uncle sam to liberate us from Spain as far as 1898!). Anyways, this is not political thread, you're right

On the music topic, where do you get the idea that P.R. "rescued" merengue? hahaha, merengue was in a crisis?? you got to be joking? Wilfrido Vargas alone with his baile del perrito took merengue even to Mars! what you say about Juan Luis Guerra? please, I respect Puerto Rican talent, you can say that they help to " pump it", but to " rescue it from a crisis"?? that is ludricous ! haha, talking bunch of babosadas. D.R. merengue has always been the best and most prominent merengue,and always will be.

MAMI_TE_LA_COMO [PUERTO RICAN]
08–28–2005, 08:10 PM

Going back to the music, I agree with u that talents like Wilfrido and Juan Luis have put the merengue up there but u have to give props tu us that we have done it and is not our music not only that but our musicians are as good as dominicans u can ask all those merengueros that lived in PR that u guys mentioned before like Toño or Jossie Esteban, Sandy Reyes, Angelito Villalona, Wilfrido, they played with puertorican musicians . . . hows that? ;)

LESLEY D [DOMINICAN]
08–28–2005, 08:18 PM

Asopao,

I think you should leave the political piece out of this thread that is flowing nicely. There is no correlation between the thread topic and politics so I think we should respect the O.P. and not disrespect Puerto Rico in the process.

In my opinion P.R. has its own version of merengue not to be confused with Dominican merengue. Personally, I think D.R. merengue bands have the edge but their marketability has been lost to the P.R. market. That's the problem!

YARI [DOMINICAN]
08–28–2005, 11:24 PM

since you adamantly proclaim that merengue was put on the radar by P.R. . . . I'll tell ya what, maybe you might think this because on tv or on American radios you heard more pr merengue. you may be right, u may be wrong. im not going to argue that. but if you are right, it is because of RACISM that pr artists like elvis crespo are being marketed better or portrayed more in mainstream America. on these award shows, why would they pick an artist of the mostly black populated dr when they can choose one from pr? countries populated by dark skinned people are always scapegoated. look at the many countries of Africa that are in turmoil, or even our neighboring Haiti.

sorry guys, I know I got heavy here, but I think that the cause of many trivial injustices such as this, is racism. call me bitter, I don't really care. :lick:[73]

REGGAETON: BRIDGE OVER TROUBLED BORDERS?

It is in the context of such complex, highly flammable interethnic relationships that narratives of reggaeton's history and development are being constructed; therefore, they must be interpreted with these tensions in mind.[74] A longer historical view underscores the importance of approaching controversies regarding musical ownership with a critical eye, especially in the case of quintessentially hybrid musics that coalesce in a particular location during a crucial period of their development. The debates about "who owns salsa" are a case in point: The Cubans, because of the foundational importance of Cuban *son* as the aesthetic backbone of salsa? Or Puerto Ricans, because the style that emerged in New York was the expression of the city's working-class Puerto Rican community? Attempts to untangle the exact origins and definition of salsa have been greatly complicated by the long history of intertwined relationships between Puerto Ricans and Cubans sharing the same social spaces in New York.[75] Yet, even as Cuban genres overshadowed Puerto Rican styles in the Latin music boom in the 1940s and '50s, when Puerto Rican musicians were numerically dominant as performers as well as fans in New York, the relations between immigrants of these two nationalities were less precarious than those that developed between native Puerto Ricans and Dominican immigrants to the island in the 1980s.

It is instructive to compare the Puerto Rican/Dominican equation in reggaeton's development to the similarly close but unequal relationships characterizing African Americans and Puerto Ricans in New York during the early years of the development of hip-hop, because it illuminates the importance of both demographics and economics in shaping public perceptions of musical ownership. In New York, where Puerto Ricans were in the numerical minority relative to their African American counterparts in overall population, contributions of the former were largely erased as rap became commercially successful and the economic stakes involved in issues of cultural ownership became higher—leading to widespread perceptions that hip-hop was an exclusively African American creation. It wasn't until the 1980s, when Juan Flores and in the 1990s, Raquel Z. Rivera, revisited and reinterpreted the cultural matrix from which hip-hop emerged, foregrounding the impact of shared social context rather than focusing on narrowly defined racial identities, that Puerto Ricans' participation in the development of hip-hop could be appreciated.[76] At the same time, as the purchasing power of Latinos increased alongside rising levels of immigration, Afrocentric narratives of rap's origins became, as Raquel Z. Rivera noted, more "ghettocentric," a more inclusive narrative space in which both historical and contemporary participation by Puerto Rican musicians and fans could be acknowledged.[77]

In summary, if it is unassailable that reggaeton emerged as a popular commercialized genre in Puerto Rico during the 1990s and that to date, the majority of the genre's most successful artists are Puerto Rican, it is also true that Dominicans have been part of the mix since its inception. The historic tensions between the two groups have muted the visibility of Dominicans in public discourse about reggaeton, but the future may be brighter, since contemporary reggaeton in New York as well as Puerto Rico (and in the Dominican Republic itself) seems to be providing and nourishing a common ground for creative and productive cultural interactions between the two groups. As Orquídea

Negra observes, "We have come a long way to prove that it doesn't matter where you are from. You can still have the same passion for the music and do it as well."[78]

NOTES

I want to acknowledge my debt of gratitude to Raquel Z. Rivera, Jorge Duany, and Wayne Marshall, whose thoughtful comments made major contributions to this essay. Translations of Spanish-language quotations are my own.

1. One exception is Irmary Reyes-Santos's Ph.D. dissertation "Racial Geopolitics: Interrogating Caribbean Cultural Discourse in the Era of Globalization" (University of California, San Diego, June 2007), in which she notes "Though reggaetón has been widely recognized as a Puerto Rican genre, Dominicans have participated in its production in the island and abroad since its beginnings." As an unpublished manuscript, however, it has not yet affected the discourse about reggaeton's origins.

2. For more detail on the causes of Dominican migration, see Ramona Hernández, *The Mobility of Workers under Advanced Capitalism: Dominican Migration to the United States* (New York: Columbia University Press, 2002).

3. The statistics on the Dominican population in Puerto Rico are often confusing because they are sometimes based on the number of visas issued (some of these people then proceed to the U.S. mainland) while others estimate the actual numbers residing on the island. I asked Jorge Duany, whose work I cite in this essay, to clarify: "The 2000 Census found 61,455 residents of Dominican birth in Puerto Rico, clearly an undercount. In addition, my fieldwork and other studies have suggested that roughly one third of all Dominicans in Puerto Rico are undocumented. Plus, the INS estimated that 34,000 undocumented immigrants were living on the Island in 1996. So, one could guesstimate that at least 100,000 Dominicans are living in Puerto Rico as of 2006." E-mail message to author, August 10, 2006. The 2005 Puerto Rico Community Survey, administered by the U.S. Census Bureau, estimated that there were 66,117 persons of Dominican origin in Puerto Rico.

4. Jorge Duany, "Dominican Migration to Puerto Rico: A Transnational Perspective," *Centro Journal* 17, no. 1 (2005): 247.

5. Jorge Duany, "Reconstructing Racial Identity: Ethnicity, Color and Class among Dominicans in the United States and Puerto Rico," *Latin American Perspectives* 25, no. 3 (1998): 147–72. In the Dominican Republic darker-skinned people are referred to as *indios*; the term *black* is reserved for Haitians.

6. Duany, "Dominican Migration to Puerto Rico," 248. Jorge Duany draws these conclusions about the relative success of Dominican immigrants in Puerto Rico and New York based on the percentage of Dominicans engaged as managers and professionals and in retail trade and light manufacturing in New York compared to their counterparts on the island, who are more likely to work as domestics and in construction.

7. Jorge Duany, *The Puerto Rican Nation on the Move: Identities on the Island and in the United States* (Chapel Hill: University of North Carolina Press, 2002), 248.

8. Duany, "Reconstructing Racial Identity," 166.

9. Ibid., 163.

10. Because race was a topic of "considerable unease" among both Puerto Ricans and Dominicans, Duany's investigators classified their subjects by observation as white, black, and mulatto; in New York they also added another category, mestizo.

11. Francisco Rivera-Batiz, "Color in the Caribbean: Race and Economic Outcomes in the Island of Puerto Rico" (paper presented at the conference "Puerto Ricans on the Island and in the Mainland: New Directions in Social Research," Russell Sage Foundation, New York, May 21–22, 2004).

12. Duany, "Reconstructing Racial Identity," 161.

13. Ibid., 164.

14. Duany, "Dominican Migration to Puerto Rico," 258.

15. Ibid., 260.

16. Ibid., 263.

17. Kenneth Bilby, "The Caribbean as a Musical Region," in *Caribbean Contours*, ed. Sidney W. Mintz and Sally Price (Baltimore: Johns Hopkins University Press, 1985).

18. Paul Austerlitz, *Merengue: Dominican Music and Dominican Identity* (Philadelphia: Temple University Press, 1997). Nineteenth-century musical exchanges between the islands produced variations on the European contredanse that developed into the *danzón* in Cuba, *danza* in Puerto Rico, and merengue in the Dominican Republic. For more on cultural exchanges between Dominicans and Puerto Ricans, see Rita de Maeseneer, "Sobre dominicanos y puertorriqueños: ¿Movimiento perpetuo?" *Centro Journal* 14, no. 1 (spring 2002): 53–66.

19. Deborah Pacini Hernandez, *Bachata: A Social History of a Dominican Popular Music* (Philadelphia: Temple University Press, 1994).

20. Ruth Glasser, *My Music Is My Flag: Puerto Rican Musicians and Their New York Communities* (Berkeley: University of California Press, 1995).

21. Raquel Z. Rivera, "Will the 'Real' Puerto Rican Culture Please Stand Up?: Thoughts on Cultural Nationalism," in *None of the Above: Puerto Ricans in the Global Era*, ed. Frances Negrón-Muntaner (New York: Palgrave Macmillan, 2007).

22. Jorge Duany, "Popular Music in Puerto Rico: Toward an Anthropology of Salsa," *Latin American Music Review* 5, no. 2 (1984): 186–216; Frances Aparicio, *Listening to Salsa: Gender, Latin Popular Music and Puerto Rican Cultures* (Hanover, N.H.: University Press of New England, 1998), 69–82; *Cocolos y Rockeros*, film recording, directed by Ana María García (Pandora Films, 1992).

23. Regarding competition between Dominican and Puerto Rican *merengueros*, Welmo E. Romero Joseph (whose essay is included in this volume) recalled that in the 1990s Puerto Rican merengue groups were publicly criticized for paying "counterpayola," or payola to radio stations *not* to play Dominican merengue groups. Interview

by author, May 10, 2006. For more on the competition between Puerto Rican *salseros* and Dominican merengueros in the 1980s, see Pacini Hernandez, *Bachata*, 108–10.

24. On the rise of merengue singers in Puerto Rico, see Jorge Duany's essay " 'Lo tengo dominao': El *boom* de las merengueras en Puerto Rico," reprinted in *La Canción Popular* 14 (1999): 21–24.

25. Jorge Oquendo, telephone interview by author, July 23, 2006.

26. The 1991 compilation is *Meren-rap* (Ariola, 3277–2-RL); the 1993 compilation is *Merenrap II* (Prime/RCA, 3469–2-RL).

27. Oquendo, interview, July 23, 2006.

28. As Wayne Marshall notes in this volume, the title of this song, originally released as "Pu Tun Tun," has appeared in many versions; the name changes may have been an attempt to get past censors.

29. Mariela Fullana Acosta, "Lisa M llega a recuperar su lugar en el reggaetón," *Primera Hora*, February 14, 2006, http://www.puertadetierra.com/figuras/artistas/lisa %20m/Lisa__M.htm (accessed August 2006).

30. Oquendo, interview, July 23, 2006.

31. Ibid.

32. The Spanish surname Saldaña is very common, while Saldana is not, so Spanish speakers assume the *n* rather than an *ñ* is a typographical error; however, I use it here because it is the version used in the artist's own website, http://www.masflowinc.net/ (accessed April 2007).

33. EMI Music Publishing, "Luny Tunes," http://www.emimusicpub.com/world wide/artist__profile/luny-tunes__profile.html (accessed August 2006).

34. Ibid.; Jon Caramanica, "The Conquest of America (North and South)," *New York Times*, December 4, 2005.

35. According to Raquel Z. Rivera, the album was originally released in 2002 by White Lion, but then more widely rereleased (and re-pressed) by BMG in 2003. Personal communication with the author, September 7, 2006.

36. Jorge Oquendo, interview, July 23, 2006. Jorge Oquendo was a pioneer of sorts in fusing bachata and rap as well. After he signed bachata musician Zacarías Ferreira to Prime Records, he tried, unsuccessfully, to convince Ferreira to experiment with a fusion of rap and bachata. Oquendo produced some mixtapes for radio and disco-thèques, including a 2002 version of *bachatero* Joey's song "Paloma" by a DJ called Chiclín, but he never released any of it commercially.

37. In terms of musical structure, merengue piano riffs resemble the repeating piano patterns in Cuban music called *guajeos* or *montunos*.

38. Sometimes bachatas played in merengue rhythm are called bachata-merengues or merengue-bachatas—but not always. If bachata is characterized by its guitar-based sound, "classic" merengues—i.e., the styles that predated guitar-based merengues—are characterized by their reed-driven sounds produced either by the accordion (in merengue típico) or the saxophone (in *típico moderno* and *merengue de orquesta*).

39. MC Velcro, interview by author, May 10, 2006.

40. Boy Wonder, telephone interview by author, July 22, 2006.

41. MC Velcro, interview, May 10, 2006.

42. Tego borrowed the tune of "Dominicana" from a song by El Gran Combo called "Ojos Chinos," but he added his own (highly erotic) lyrics.

43. In addition to air travel, Puerto Ricans can easily visit the Dominican Republic via a car ferry from Mayagüez, and with their U.S. passports (and until recently, government-issued ID cards) they have no difficulty obtaining short-term tourist visas. Dominicans can also avail themselves of the ferry, but they need U.S. visas to enter Puerto Rico—a much more difficult proposition even for tourist visas.

44. Puerto Rican reggaeton is also widely popular in Cuba, but since Cuba does not have a well-developed commercial music market, and thanks to the blockade, profit streams from that island to U.S.-based record companies are negligible.

45. Oquendo, interview, July 23, 2006.

46. "No es casual que Daddy Yankee considere a República Dominicana como su 'segunda patria'. Mucho antes de que el afamado intérprete de 'La gasolina' se convirtiera en la estrella de la música que es hoy, venía al país a principios de los 90, con el claro objetivo de conectar con el público dominicano, que es más exigente de lo que se considera. . . . En Miami hay varias emisoras muy pendientes de cuáles son los éxitos del momento en el país. . . . [T]ambién influye la proliferación de medios de televisión, radio, Internet y prensa escrita que tiene a su disposición el mercado local. En Puerto Rico son dos o tres emisoras que programan música tropical, mientras que en República Dominicana tenemos más de seis periódicos, más de 200 emisoras y un número considerable de canales de televisión" [It is not an accident that Daddy Yankee considers the Dominican Republic as his "second home." Long before the famous interpreter of "La gasolina" became the music star he is today, he used to come to the country in the early 90s, with the clear objective of connecting with the Dominican public which is more demanding than commonly thought. The proliferation of television, radio, Internet and print media that takes into consideration the local market is also influential. In Puerto Rico there are a few stations that program tropical music, but in the Dominican Republic we have more than six newspapers, more than two-hundred stations and a considerable number of television stations]. Máximo Jiménez, "Artistas de P.R. Usan," *El Caribe*, June 2, 2006, http://www.elcaribecdn.com/articulo_multimedios.aspx?id=87927&guid=5CAFA5A36B5741DB9EACBEDF3410B747&Seccion=66 (accessed August 2006).

47. Orquídea Negra, telephone interview by author, July 24, 2006.

48. Los Que he Oido, "DJ Playero," http://www.angelfire.com/ny2/munne/oido.htm (accessed August 2006). Orquídea Negra recalls that rappers and anybody wearing baggy clothes were also called "Joes"; rockers were called GQs. Orquídea Negra, interview, July 24, 2006.

49. Orquídea Negra, interview, July 24, 2006.

50. The entry from the *All Music Guide* by John Bush notes: "Meren-rap duo Sandy y Papo blend the rich rhythms of classic merengue with hard-hitting beats reminiscent of American club music, both house and hip-hop. Recording for Parcha Records, the

group debuted with the 1996 LP *Hora de Bailar*. *Otra Vez* followed one year later, and Sandy y Papo's *Remix Album* was released in July 1998." http://www.allmusic.com/ cg/amg.dll (accessed August 2006).

51. Puerto Rican reggaetoneros, including Tego Calderón and Daddy Yankee, have also been banned from performing in the Dominican Republic because of their lyrics, and the offending songs receive no radio play. See for example, "No reggaeton en D.R.," April 9, 2006, http://www.ahorre.com/reggaeton/musica/music_business/(accessed August 2006). It should be noted that censorship in the Dominican Republic has never been applied consistently, and class-based biases often determine what is considered too lewd for public dissemination; see Pacini Hernandez, *Bachata*, 176. More recently, the innocuous song "Camisa Negra" by the popular Colombian rocker Juanes was banned because of its "negative lyrics" and double-entendres, despite the fact that the Dominican Republic's popular music is known for far more erotic sexual double-entendres.

52. Orquídea Negra, interview, July 24, 2006.

53. "Cola de Motora," in *Contra el Tiempo*, CD (Sony International, B000FDFS1S, 2006). A highly controversial remix of Don Miguelo's "Cola de Motora" called "Cola de Camiona" transposes the original double-entendre story of a girl riding on the singer's motorcycle and urging him to go faster, to a dialogue between a policeman and an undocumented Haitian immigrant who refuses to get off the truck deporting him to Haiti.

54. *Yeah Baby*, CD (Sony International, B0002ZMILC, 2004); *Welcome to the Paradise*, CD (Sony International, B000BQ7JES, 2005).

55. *De Otra Galaxia*, CD (Universal Latino, B0002C4IMM, 2004).

56. Orquídea Negra, interview, July 24, 2006.

57. Karl Avanzini, the American Society of Composers, Authors and Publishers, "The Chosen One," http://www.ascap.com/playback/2006/winter/radar/boy_wonder .html (accessed July 2006).

58. Interestingly, in the 1980s, years before the (then) disreputable bachata was legitimated by Guerra's earlier Grammy-winning *Bachata Rosa* (1999), many struggling bachata musicians rented studio time from Santo Domingo's EMCA Studios where Ruiz worked at the time. Pacini Hernandez, *Bachata*, 186–87.

59. Miguel Cruz Tejada, "Alcaldía de Jersey City en N.J. reconoce a Raúl Acosta el 'Presidente del Merengue' y orquesta Oro Sólido," *Primicias*, April 6, 2007, http:// www.primicias.com.do/articu10,2378,html (accessed August 2006).

60. Boy Wonder, interview by author, July 22, 2006.

61. "Master Joe y O.G. Black," http://masreggaeton.com/masterjoeogblack.php (accessed July 2006).

62. EMI Music Publishing, "Luny Tunes," http://www.emimusicpub.com/worldwide /artist_profile/luny-tunes_profile.html.

63. The artists' bios posted on Internet sites are often unreliable because they are written by fans, but on the other hand, such sites are often the only source of information on artists whose record labels do not provide authorized biographies. In the case of

Eddie Dee, his Dominican background was mentioned by several of the individuals I interviewed, including no less of an authority as Boy Wonder—himself of Dominican extraction—but I could find no mention of Eddie Dee's Dominican heritage on the Internet.

64. "Master Joe y O.G. Black," http://masreggaeton.com/masterjoeogblack.php (accessed August 2006). O.G. Black is identified as Dominican on a reggaeton website, but it does not specify whether he is Dominican by birth or ancestry, or both.

65. Boy Wonder, interview, July 22, 2006. The information on Javia's Dominican ancestry was conveyed to me by Boy Wonder. As Raquel Z. Rivera notes, Javia is also spelled Jahvia and Javiah, personal communication with author, September 7, 2006.

66. MC Welmo E. Romero Joseph, interview by author, May 11, 2006.

67. See Jorge Duany and José A. Cobas, *Cubans in Puerto Rico: Ethnic Economy and Cultural Identity* (Gainesville: University Press of Florida, 1997); Yolanda Martínez–San Miguel, *Caribe Two Ways: Cultura de la migración en el Caribe insular hispánico* (San Juan: Callejón, 2003). For more on the identity of the children born to Puerto Rican migrants to the Dominican Republic, see Duany, "Dominican Migration to Puerto Rico," 246. Raquel Z. Rivera, who has Puerto Rican / Cuban relatives and who has also participated in the Center for Puerto Rican Studies' efforts to document the Puerto Rican diaspora in Cuba, notes that the children of Puerto Ricans living in Cuba have historically identified as Cuban—although some individuals have retained their claims to Puerto Rican ancestry for various reasons, including obtaining authorization to relocate in the United States. Personal communication with author, September 7, 2006. See also Raquel Z. Rivera, "Cubano-boricua busca historia de sus antepasados," *Siempre*, July 14, 2004, 3; and Sandra Mustelier, *Ecos boricuas en el oriente cubano* (San Juan, P.R.: Editorial Makarios, 2006).

68. Rivera, "Will the 'Real' Puerto Rican Culture Please Stand Up?," 230.

69. Xavier, "DominiRican?," Trescaminos Blog, entry posted July 21, 2005, http://trescaminos.blogspot.com/2005/07/ dominirican.html. The word *unwanted* was boldface in the original.

70. Raquel Z. Rivera, "De un pájaro las dos patas," *El Nuevo Día*, April 4, 2004.

71. For more on "bomba-style merengue," see Paul Austerlitz, *Merengue: Dominican Music and Dominican Identity* (Philadelphia: Temple University Press, 1997), 95. The writer's reference to "bomba style merengue" probably refers to a style of merengue originally popularized in a hit song called "Bomba" by Dominican merengue group Los Hermanos Rosario. The style, adopted by Puerto Rican merengue groups, is characterized by a particular beat called *maco*, which Paul Austerlitz defines "as a two-beat pulse evocative of disco music"; he continues, "recording engineer July Ruiz attributes the maco's popularity to its similarity to North American dance rhythms. Indeed, party goers often abandon the ballroom dance position and dance disco-style to maco arrangements."

72. The writer incorrectly identifies the song "La Popola" as Dominican, most likely because the song's musical aesthetics lean heavily toward merengue. The song is Puerto

Rican and made famous by reggaeton singer Glory (discussed in this volume by Félix Jiménez).

73. The preceding discussion was edited from the original: http://www.dr1.com/forums/general-stuff/41767-reggaeton-dominicano.html (accessed August 2006).

74. Thanks to my husband, Reebee Garofalo, for his apt rephrasing of Simon and Garfunkel's phrase.

75. Peter Manuel, "Puerto Rican Music and Cultural Identity: Creative Appropriation of Cuban Sources from Danza to Salsa," *Ethnomusicology* 38, no. 2 (1994): 249–80. I should note that some of the claims in this essay have been intensely contested by other salsa scholars; see, for example, Marisol Berrios-Miranda, "'*Con sabor a Puerto Rico*': The Reception and Influence of Puerto Rican Salsa in Venezuela," in *Musical Migrations: Transnationalism and Cultural Hybridity in Latin/o America*, ed. Frances R. Aparicio and Cándida F. Jáquez (New York: Palgrave Macmillan, 2003).

76. Both Juan Flores and Raquel Z. Rivera have published many articles on the subject of Puerto Ricans in hip-hop. See, for example, Juan Flores, "Wild Style and Filming Hip Hop," *Areito* 10, no. 37: 1984; Juan Flores, *From Bomba to Hip Hop: Puerto Rican Culture and Latino Identity* (New York: Columbia University Press, 2000), 115–39; and Raquel Z. Rivera, *New York Ricans from the Hip Hop Zone* (New York: Palgrave Macmillan, 2003).

77. Rivera, *New York Ricans from the Hip Hop Zone*, 97.

78. Orquídea Negra, interview, July 24, 2006.

The Politics of Dancing

Reggaetón and Rap in Havana, Cuba

This essay is not a brief history of Cuban reggaetón. Such a history should focus partly, or perhaps predominantly, on Santiago de Cuba, the country's second-largest city.[1] Rather, this is an introduction to the controversies stirred up by reggaetón in Havana, the Cuban capital. Havana is the center of Cuban cultural politics and intellectual debate, the media and the music industry, and is also the heart of the rap scene—a pertinent detail given that a number of leading *reguetoneros* are former rappers who have been, or still are, managed by the Havana-based Agencia Cubana de Rap (ACR). Reggaetón has ruffled feathers across the Caribbean and Latin America, but the arguments provoked in Havana, while overlapping in some respects with those in other contexts, also present distinctive features that reflect the marked differences between Cuba and other societies in the hemisphere. The verbal, musical, and corporeal styles of reggaetón have posed unprecedented challenges to dominant conceptions of Cuban national culture, and the resulting debates illuminate both recent developments in Cuban cultural politics and also, more broadly, the contradictory and conflicted relationships between socialism and capitalism, ideology and pleasure that are characteristic of Havana in the new millennium.

In 2003 I began observing Havana's rap scene, which has burgeoned since the early 1990s, but reggaetón has been a constant and growing presence during my research. The formation of Cubanito 20.02 by ex-members of pioneering underground rap group Primera Base was both a pivotal moment in the emergence of reggaetón in the capital and a watershed in Cuban rap. In the wake of this successful bid for a higher commercial profile, most rappers have followed one of two paths: dancing with the enemy and embracing reggaetón, or resisting the new genre vociferously. The resisters deride reggaetón for being trite and mindless, for promoting pointless diversion and dancing over social commitment and reflection: Los Aldeanos' song "Repartición de Bienes" begins with a parody of a reggaetón track by Cubanito 20.02, "Mátame," and is just one of many barbed critiques that have circulated within underground rap circles since 2004.

> *Repartición de bienes*
> *Reggaetón pa' mover el culo*
> *O rap pa' poner madura*
> *La mente del immaduro*

> Distribution of assets
> Reggaeton for shaking your ass
> Or rap for maturing
> The mind of the immature

The relationship between rap and reggaetón has been one of the most common (and contentious) topics of conversation within hip-hop circles in recent years. Despite resistance from some other artists, however, reguetoneros have emerged as clear winners; reggaetón has developed rapidly into the dominant form of popular music among young Cuban listeners, and this has provoked a significant widening of the debate.

Several articles critical of reggaetón have been published in the Cuban press since 2004, in particular in *Juventud Rebelde*, the newspaper of the Union of Young Communists (Unión de Jóvenes Comunistas). The most notable, entitled "¿Prohibido el regueton?," criticized the repetitive beats, suggestive lyrics, and licentious dance moves associated with the genre, which the author perceived not just as "banal, corny, trashy" but also as potentially inciting vulgarity, lust, vice, and drug abuse. While not actually proposing prohibition, the article suggested that something needed to be done.[2] Even a more balanced analysis by the cultural commentator Alberto Faya Montano centered on a lengthy critique of international reggaetón's supposed corruption by commercialism.[3] State figures have also pronounced on reggaetón, with Alpidio Alonso, president of the Asociación Hermanos Saíz, publicly declaring at the Eighth Congress of the Union of Young Communists in 2005. "Careful . . . with so much terrible reggaetón, with so many second- and third-rate groups."[4] Yet the anxieties provoked by reggaetón are much more widespread. Many professional musicians see it as damaging to the broader panorama of Cuban popular music, eroding traditional genres, and betraying their high professional standards with amateurish yet addictive musical creations.[5] One distinguished musician recently claimed that reggaetón had set the country back by fifty years in musical terms.[6] At times, it seems hard to find anyone over the age of thirty with a good word to say about reggaetón, a genre which appeals predominantly to those in their teens and early twenties in Havana and which leaves many older listeners cold (or worse).

The aura of negativity around reggaetón has rarely been countered by academic interventions on the subject. There has been a plethora of studies of Cuban rap in recent years, but these predate, ignore, or dismiss the boom of reggaetón. Alan West-Durán, in an otherwise valuable contribution to the rap literature, relegates reggaetón to a single footnote, as "often a bad equivalent of what might be considered Jamaican dancehall at its most frivolous."[7] Advocating one form of music over another is nothing new among those who study popular music, often occurring in the context of championing a supposedly "resistant" form over more commercialized genres. Rap has often been the beneficiary of such an approach in Cuba and other non-U.S. contexts in which "message rap" *à la* Public Enemy has been taken as the primary template for local production, whereas commercialized, dance-oriented genres such as reggaetón have tended to lose out within academic circles.[8]

To date, the only serious attempt to provide an academic analysis of reggaetón in Havana is an unpublished report produced by a team of researchers from the Centro de Investigación y Desarrollo de la Música Cubana (CIDMUC) in Havana in 2005.[9] This valuable study employs a wide range of analytical tools and is an important milestone in the investigation of the genre. Nevertheless, despite the principal researchers' efforts to remain evenhanded, their backgrounds in research on rap and *timba*—popular genres often regarded as counterposed to reggaetón—surface occasionally in concerns over reggaetón's supposed deficiencies in comparison with its longer-established cousins: negative perceptions include a poverty of ideas (in relation to rap) and discontinuity with Cuban popular traditions and artistic standards (in relation to timba). While keen to point out the positive aspects of reggaetón, they struggle to find many, regarding most Cuban reggaetón production as mediocre or worse in terms of both musical and lyrical content and describing the genre in terms such as "lexical violence," "impoverishment," and "loss of the most basic aesthetic standards"; the "simplistic" results, the report notes, "may retard the individual listener in the evolution of his/her aesthetic personality."[10] This report is a genuine and significant attempt to understand reggaetón, containing much valuable data, but it also reveals the depth of reggaetón's challenge to Cuban cultural and intellectual traditions.

The negative responses to reggaetón across artistic, critical, and institutional spheres suggest that some important issues are at stake. Susan McClary's discussion of the politics of music making is highly relevant in this respect: urging greater attention to body-centered genres (of which reggaetón is a prime example), rather than those which focus on politicized lyrics, she claims that "the musical power of the disenfranchised . . . more often resides in their ability to articulate different ways of construing the body, ways that bring along in their wake the potential for different experiential worlds. And the anxious reactions that so often greet new musics from such groups indicate that something crucially political is at issue."[11] I will take this as a call to move beyond the widespread dismissal of reggaetón as simply music "for shaking your ass" and ask: Is reggaetón's appeal to the body stimulating "different experiential worlds" among Havana's youth, and, if so, what is their significance? Why has reggaetón provoked such anxieties? And what are the social and political issues at stake?

"LINGUISTIC VIOLENCE," GLOBALIZED SOUNDS, AND THE PROBLEM OF NATIONAL CULTURE

Reggaetón in Havana has several faces. The sounds heard in the streets are often imported from Puerto Rico and the Dominican Republic. There are also three broad strands of locally produced reggaetón: music produced by officially sanctioned reguetoneros who receive airplay in the media and support from government institutions (e.g., Cubanito 20.02, Eddy-K, Gente de Zona), recordings produced by underground artists and circulated via informal distribution networks, and the reggaetón-timba fusions created by many leading timba groups in order to maintain their popularity in the face of this "new wave."

Even reggaetón's critics have often admitted the seductiveness of its beat, but the words are another matter: in his key press article, Osviel Castro Medel sums up the genre as "a very rhythmic music, but one with rather poor lyrics."[12] Critiques of Cuban reggaetón center on the banality of the ideas expressed—which focus on sex, dancing, and the singer himself, in various combinations—but also on the language in which these "non-ideas" are articulated. Locally produced reggaetón in Havana is not contentious in the same way as gangsta rap, or indeed reggaetón, in some other countries; references to weapons or drug use, for example, appear to be very infrequent. In an interview with a BBC reporter, Oneilys Hevora of the Havana group Los 3 Gatos claimed, with some justification, "I don't move anyone to violence with my music."[13] The authors of the CIDMUC report, however, disagree, though they locate the aggression at the level of language, describing reggaetón texts using terms like "lexical violence." Indeed, their highlighting of a perceived flow of slang from reggaetón lyrics to everyday popular speech suggests that their concern about reggaetón centers on the "violence" that it does to established conceptions of national linguistic culture.

In fact, the authors are careful to distinguish between three registers of language, corresponding broadly to the three strands of local reggaetón: the only one that they regard as seemly, however, is that used by professional timba groups in their fusions. The texts of "official" reggaetón groups are characterized as banal and generally mediocre, while those of "underground" groups are considered variously as vulgar, obscene, or even pornographic. The authors reveal a sense of regret that the Cuban popular linguistic tradition of *picardía* (puns, double-meaning, euphemism) has given way to blunt, obvious signification.[14] There is certainly some justification for these judgments, but it is also worth considering that these texts—with their directness, simplicity, and hedonistic focus—offer a particular challenge to a national culture framed by Marxist ideology, in which respect for and the dissemination of elaborated ideas are so fundamental.[15] The high profile of ideas is immediately apparent to the visitor to Havana: political slogans displayed prominently on large billboards include "Battle of ideas, a struggle for our times" and "Ideas are more powerful than weapons." Language, too, is prized. Gabriel García Márquez's recent portrait of Fidel Castro began, "His devotion is to the word."[16] In reggaetón, however, there appears to be a conscious refusal to engage at the level of ideas or lyrical discourse, coupled with a transgression of linguistic norms.

This marks a clear departure from most Cuban rap production. Cuban rap, after difficult early years in which it was associated with U.S. cultural imperialism and racial divisiveness, became gradually accepted as a part of a national culture conceived in terms of linguistic and intellectual excellence: rappers made a name for themselves both at home and around the world because of the elaboration and commitment of their lyrics, something which ultimately made their work comprehensible or even attractive to the state. Rap has been successfully assimilated in part because of the many points of coincidence between the philosophy of underground hip-hop and the revolutionary ideology of the Cuban state.[17] By focusing on the level of verbal discourse and ideological commitment, rap could be incorporated more easily into official visions of the nation and presented as a "revolution within the Revolution." But reggaetón shares little or no discursive space with the state: reggaetón artists tend to stand outside socialist principles altogether, refusing to engage with ideology on any level. Their perceived banality or vulgarity and yet extreme popularity among Cuban youth raises rather thornier issues about national culture and identity than rap, explaining the bewilderment or hostility of many cultural commentators who had come round to the idea of *rap cubano*.

Concerns over the relationship of reggaetón to a national culture traditionally focused on linguistic dexterity and ideological exchange are exacerbated by the musical aspects of reggaetón in Havana, which is dominated by Puerto Rican models: in contrast to more established Cuban dance musics such as timba, electronic sounds predominate and characteristic Cuban musical elements, such as instrumental timbres and rhythmic or melodic virtuosity, are notably scarce. This, too, has caused anxieties in intellectual circles. While Cuba has long absorbed external influences, a compromise between international musics and nationalist intellectual traditions has typically been brokered through a discourse of "Cubanization"—an adoption-adaptation model which stresses the transformative power of Cuban culture. This discourse eventually opened the gates of national culture to include rap cubano, the lyrics and music of which were slowly recognized as bearing distinctive national characteristics. Rap groups such as Anónimo Consejo and Obsesión—by incorporating traditional Cuban musical elements such as African-derived drums and Yoruba chants and by reflecting in a sophisticated, critical manner on Cuban realities—have been widely accepted as representing an organic development of Cuban musical and lyrical traditions. Reggaetón, however, has so far proved somewhat resistant to such indigenization. Not only are the musical "backgrounds" (the term used in Cuba for instrumentals) perceived as relying excessively on foreign models, but there is little sense as yet of a distinctive Cuban reggaetón vocal "flow." The CIDMUC report includes a critical description of a popular reggaetón song which imitates Puerto Rican slang and vocal intonation, while Cubanito 20.02 told me that although they did not see themselves as heavily influenced by Puerto Rican reggaetón, they felt a strong affinity with Jamaican ragga (something which is immediately audible in their vocals). Although a few artists, such as Eddy-K and Gente de Zona, have made moves toward "Cubanizing" their music, the general critical view is that this process still has a long way to go before reggaetón can be considered an "authentic" manifestation of national culture.

Indigenization may simply be a matter of time: most accounts of Cuban rap stress an initial "mimetic" phase followed later by adaptation and assimilation, and the recent growth of timba-reggaetón fusions suggests a move toward a certain kind of "nationalization."[18] Nevertheless, the range of reggaetón fusions is thus far somewhat narrower than those found in rap, and these fusions tend to be imitations of those created in other parts of the Caribbean (such as bachata-reggaetón) rather than mixtures with more obviously Cuban styles, though there have been a few notable exceptions. One factor currently working against indigenization is that of audience demand: consumers of reggaetón in Havana currently show a marked preference for Puerto Rican reggaetón and local imitations thereof, and enthusiasm for "Cubanized" reggaetón by critics and foreign record companies has not been matched by that of young *habaneros*. The reasons for this preference for foreign reggaetón are debatable: some regard it as simply reflecting the higher quality of overseas musical production, stemming from superior technological resources, though it could also be argued that the attractiveness of reggaetón to young Cubans, few of whom have left the island or have access to the Internet, may relate precisely to its transnational character. Whatever the causes, the pervasiveness and appeal of Puerto Rican reggaetón have had an undeniable effect on local production: the most audible reggaetón artist in the streets of Havana in 2007 was Elvis Manuel, an underground performer whose productions invariably combined *perreo* (Puerto Rican–derived) musical backgrounds with often hardcore lyrics. At the time of writing, Cubanized reggaetón certainly exists, but it is yet to emerge from the shadow of its Puerto Rican elder sibling.

Musical nonadaptation has thus proved persistent and, in the eyes of some observers, problematic: the journalist Osviel Castro Medel, while trying to be evenhanded about reggaetón, nevertheless refers to the genre in terms of "a possible aggression against national culture," suggesting again that reggaetón's refusal to conform to national cultural canons is partly responsible for its negative reception.[19] In contrast, though, to the early days of rock or rap on the island, there seems to be no suggestion that this aggression has an imperialist aspect or that reggaetón is politically suspect due to its association with the United States, in this case via Puerto Rico. The perceived threat seems to relate rather to the sheer dominance of reggaetón in Cuba, its overwhelming popularity among young listeners (to the exclusion of "national" genres), and its association with the transnational music industry, a frequent target of criticism; most observers suggest that this threat could be readily reduced by a greater effort toward local adaptation and production. In the articles and studies quoted in this essay, reggaetón is presented primarily as an "authentic" Caribbean genre which is unfortunately corrupted in many cases by the commercialism characteristic of nonsocialist societies and even by a lack of discernment on the part of the Cuban media, rather than as an inherently problematic cultural form, inescapably tinged by U.S. imperialism, as rock and rap were initially perceived by most cultural authorities.

The dependence on Puerto Rican models within Havana reggaetón is tied to the transgression of hegemonic notions of national culture in more ways than one: not just the dominance of foreign music, but also the irruption of amateur, often untrained musicians into the professionalized, highly skilled sphere of Cuban popular music. For all the anxious reactions (or nonreactions) to the emerging dance music of timba in the 1990s, this music was characterized by a high degree of musical complexity and its leading performers were musicians of formidable skill and training, many of them graduates of Havana's impressive music education establishments.[20] In many other countries, there has been much more of a DIY ("do it yourself") ethos within the sphere of popular music—best exemplified, perhaps, by the genre of punk—and it is quite normal for musicians to have had little or no formal training, but Cuban popular music has long been distinguished by its rigorous, hierarchical training programs and by the quality control imposed by state systems of musical employment. Rap and reggaetón, however, have shifted the goalposts over the last decade, as their central musical component consists of electronic backgrounds; knowledge of and access to computers and music technology have become more important than traditional musical training, posing a major challenge to established ideas of a professionalized popular music scene. These newer genres have opened a door for those without formal musical training, a democratic step, in many ways, but one which has caused anxiety among some professional musicians and cultural observers at the disturbance of the hierarchical structures of Cuban popular music. Such observers fear, quite simply, that amateur reguetoneros are lowering the high professional standards that made Cuban popular music a productive symbol of national identity during the twentieth century; practicing musicians in other genres are also clearly concerned that the rise of reggaetón threatens their position in the emerging musical marketplace in Havana.

It could be argued that the amateur status of many reggaetón producers feeds back into the widespread preference for Puerto Rican sounds. Such producers often lack both training in Cuban musical traditions and the kinds of connections necessary to open up the possibility of working with live musicians. Experimenting with fusions with Cuban music is a risky path for those without formal training, as Cuban audiences are likely to be much more discerning in their judgment of more familiar musical styles. There is a perception, then, that such fusions are best left to the professionals. With many reguetoneros falling into the amateur category, the nonadaptation of much local reggaetón production may be linked to the greater difficulties that such adaptation poses.[21] Given their experience and resources, it is much more practical for them to imitate Puerto Rican backgrounds and to adopt a more overtly electronic sound; this is also a solid commercial strategy, given the popularity of Puerto Rican artists in Cuba. Furthermore, a combination of the recent expansion of computer ownership and a relatively liberal cultural climate has resulted in regguetoneros becoming the first stratum of popular music producers in socialist Cuba to be freed from the pressure to fit in with dominant cultural norms. In the 1990s, the emergent hip-hop movement found that the quickest way to gain a space in the official cultural sphere, and thus access to scarce production and recording facilities, was to engage in a dialogue with cultural gatekeepers and move away from a "mimetic" approach toward one of Cubanization. Today's reggaetón producers have their own equipment and are therefore much more independent from the state; the wider availability of resources has freed up these amateur musicians to make their own rules.

The amateur/professional divide runs throughout the CIDMUC report, in which many of the perceived negative characteristics of the genre, such as musical and lexical poverty, are attributed primarily to amateur producers; the future "transcendence" of the genre is seen to be dependent on greater adoption by professional musicians, particularly by timba groups. This notion of transcendence—the idea that a new music emerges as a kind of rough diamond which can then be polished—is characteristically Cuban, for it encompasses not just the incorporation of "foreign" elements into national culture, which is encountered across Latin America, but also the unique structure of the music profession in Cuba and the equally distinctive idea of *superación*, or self-improvement. Transcendence in the case of Cuban popular music is not just a question of local adaptation: it specifically implies the elaboration by professionally trained musicians of musical styles developed by amateurs and/or the professionalization of the amateurs themselves through a structured, formalized process of superación.

This process is one toward which rappers have taken some steps. With the creation of the Agencia Cubana de Rap, a number of rap groups turned professional and some participated in *cursos de superación* at the Ignacio Cervantes "professional improvement school" in La Víbora, Havana, allowing them to deepen their formal music skills and knowledge of Cuban musical traditions, but also facilitating the incorporation of these artists and their music into hegemonic constructions of national culture.[22] The mere act of engaging with the process of superación, whatever the results, is a sign of assimilation of ideals of self-improvement and incorporation of national traditions. Thus while rap, too, was critiqued in the 1990s for its lack of professionalism, this view has been tempered as some groups have taken state-sponsored music courses and have gained experience and, more recently, the kudos associated with working within a formal agency, the ACR. Rap is today regarded by most cultural observers as having "transcended" to a new level—that of national culture. Most reggaetón production, however, currently stands outside this formalized, distinctively Cuban process; its homemade feel and simplicity, its preference for globalized electronic sounds and often scant regard for Cuban musical traditions, and its insistence on provoking pleasure without necessarily adhering to traditionally defined notions of "quality" (based on criteria such as rhythmic, melodic, and timbral virtuosity and variety) all suggest a lack of engagement with the striving and serious intent behind the concept of superación.

Reggaetón has shaken up Cuban popular culture in unprecedented ways. It has challenged the indirect, playful linguistic traditions of Cuban popular music with often vulgar straight-talking and has invaded its formerly professionalized musical world with the homemade, computer-generated creations of amateurs who have learned their skills through experimentation rather than the extended, state-supported education received by their peers in genres such as timba and jazz. The resulting music continues to rely heavily on foreign models and is thus somewhat resistant to incorporation within the canons of national culture via the discourse of "Cubanization." The disturbance of the rigid hierarchies of Cuban popular music has been seen as much more transgressive and threatening in the case of reggaetón than of rap, not least because of its unprecedented popularity across the island. Cuban rappers never received the level of exposure of leading regueestoneros today. While rap was initially perceived as more dangerous because of anxieties about U.S. cultural imperialism, those associated with the nascent "movement" perceived a way toward state acceptance in the social commitment of "message rap" and its association with U.S. black radicalism, long viewed in a positive light by the Cuban government. Reggaetón, however, currently offers no comparable route to ideological compatibility. With both music and texts attracting censure, it poses a rather more intractable problem for both its defenders and for the guardians of Cuban culture.

THE POLITICS OF DANCING

The challenges of reggaetón are not to be found solely in the fields of musical and lyrical production, but also in its audiences. One thing shared by all the variants of reggaetón in Cuba is a focus on dancing, often at the expense of lyrical elaboration. This has provoked the scorn of those rappers who have not been tempted over to the "other side." Cuban rap has been predominantly "conscious" since the mid- to late 1990s, and many rappers espouse the strict dichotomy—music for listening (positive) versus music for dancing (negative)—articulated by Los Aldeanos.[23] This hierarchical mind/body division is also constructed much more broadly within Cuban political and intellectual spheres: as Robin Moore notes, Cuban socialist thought prefers music that contains an ideological element and a politicized message, and the same could also be said of many who discuss and write about music, both in Cuba and around the world.[24]

Where rappers, intellectuals, and state officials may characterize body-centered music simply as an ideological vacuum and the negative pole of "music for the mind," it is also possible, following McClary, to discern something rather more active and challenging. It has been suggested by more than one writer on timba that dance music and its attendant pleasures and physicality may be an oppositional space in Cuba; in a highly politicized context, being apolitical or perhaps nonideological, may be an effective form of political statement. Vincenzo Perna claims that dance music has been at odds with officialdom for much of the revolution.[25] The only form to meet with official approval has been rumba, which was recuperated as a useful symbol of national identity shortly after the revolution. The white elite preferred serious styles such as *canción* and *nueva trova*, which focused on individual performers, were meant for listening and not for dancing, and lacked the carnivalesque nature of Cuban dance music. "Conscious" rap has numerous parallels with nueva trova, parallels that are emphasized by members of the rap community in order to boost acceptance of their music. Both genres were initially misunderstood but later supported by the state. Their shared distrust of dancing—expressed by leading underground rappers such as Los Paisanos, Papá Humbertico, and Los Aldeanos in song lyrics, interviews, and public discussions—is one similarity that is mentioned less often. Robin Moore, meanwhile, has talked about the resurgence of timba in terms of an "antisocialist" aesthetic of hedonism and materialism.[26] He discusses the opposition between pleasure and thinking in official ideology, with the former seen as working against efforts to persuade people to elevate themselves: as a result, politicians and cultural officials have promoted "serious" music with political or socially conscious lyrics.[27] The recent espousal of reggaetón and its ethos of personal gratification by Cuban youth may be interpreted as a rejection both of such politicized music and, more generally, of the state's enthusiasm for thought-provoking culture.

Moore regards the avoidance of seriousness and political correctness in timba and the emphasis on pleasure as a form of liberation from cultural norms. The idea of dance as liberation was evoked by many interviewees cited in the CIDMUC report, who perceived reggaetón dancing in terms of freedom from the social and choreographic conventions of Cuban couple dancing.[28] As with the *despelote*—the newer, solo style of timba dancing, performed by women—which emerged in the 1990s and came to overshadow the couple-dancing style known as *casino*, the traditional physical dominance of the male partner has been reversed in reggaetón: men play a subsidiary role while women are the main focus of attention and the principal driving force behind the dance. Unlike in couple dances, in the despelote and reggaetón the female does not need a partner and does not need to be "led"; during live shows, female dancers are often prominently placed on the stage, and in the audience, female dancers invariably dance alone or in front of their partner, to whom they have their back turned and who thus dances in their shadow, his role reduced from leader to follower or even observer. Reggaetón dancing is not only female centered but also transgressive in its open sexuality. Perna has argued, in the case of timba, that this reflects changing gender dynamics linked to the social and economic upheavals in Havana since the early 1990s, and these new dance styles may thus be seen as participating in renegotiations over gender roles and liberation from social conventions.[29]

Yet, more broadly, dancing and bodily pleasure can provide temporary freedom from hardships and pervasive ideology, whether the Marxist principles of Cuban society or the capitalist ideologies of productivity and exchange value found elsewhere. Reggaetón is a music of pleasure par excellence; pleasure is constantly referenced in both lyrics and movements. Cubans often consider sexuality to be an important aspect of life that lies outside government control, and the body may thus be perceived as a key site of freedom and self-expression. Yet it is also a site of contestation, for the phenomenon of *jineterismo* (literally "jockeying," covering a range of activities from mild hustling to prostitution), which has assumed a major role in Havana's social imaginary and informal economy, is periodically the target of efforts at state control. Since the early 1990s, with the explosion of jineterismo and consequent efforts at its policing, the bodies of young habaneros have been a nexus of struggle with the state for access to the benefits of tourism: hard currency, material goods, the possibility of travel, and so on. Bearing in mind McClary's comment that "the musical power of the disenfranchised . . . more often resides in their ability to articulate different ways of construing the body, ways that bring along in their wake the potential for different experiential worlds," the rise of an exhibitionist pleasure-centeredness in dance, specifically timba and reggaetón, may be interpreted as resistance to the reduction of the body to a productive machine and rejection of socialist values of hard work, in line with the shift from a socialist to a "sociocapitalist" economy.[30]

In the context of the profound crisis in Cuban society since the "Special Period" of the early 1990s, during which the body emerged as an important source of social and economic capital, the fact that reggaetón refers constantly to the body and sex in both lyrics and movements cannot be produced—as it is often by observers—as evidence of its inconsequentiality. A celebration of the body and sexuality, whilst not literally rebellious, can be read as a statement of liberation from social, political, and even economic constraints, as constructing a "different experiential world" and reinventing the body as a site of pleasure, personal gain, and social mobility rather than productive, collective labor. It is also a refusal to engage with the state on the state's preferred terms, at the level of ideology and articulated discourse. The government is able to exercise some control over the field of verbal discourse, for example through censorship and restrictions on media content, but dancing bodies are much harder to reign in. The body might be perceived as a prime articulator of free "speech" in a context in which ideas and verbal expression are subjected to regulation by the state. "Ideas are our weapons" proclaims a political sign in Havana; "bodies are our weapons" might be closer to the truth for many young Cubans today.

The body may thus be perceived as a creator of complex meanings rather than, as many rappers and critics would have it, simply the absence of mind, and this perspective can be brought to bear on the issue of reggaetón's problematic relationship to national culture. As noted above, the fact that Puerto Rican reggaetón is so popular in Havana and that local producers have tended to copy its models has caused anxieties for intellectuals whose prime model for analyzing the interaction of global and local is one of adoption and adaptation at the level of production. Yet it appears to be primarily in the sphere of reception—of dancers' bodies—that local and global, traditional and modern are mediated. Local reggaetón dance styles have evolved (to a greater extent than the music) from the Puerto Rican perreo to a more indigenous blend of reggaetón and breakdance moves with those derived from timba (*tembleque*), rumba, and various other Cuban dances of African descent, giving rise to distinctive movements known as *el reloj, el tranque, la onda retro*, and so on.[31] For all that reggaetón dance holds the power to scandalize and counterrevolutionize, it seems to be in the sphere of bodily movement that the transformative capacity of Cuban culture—Cubanization—is most in evidence.

Thus far the challenges of reggaetón have been located in its production and reception, but another key reason reggaetón has provoked concern at state level is its distribution and diffusion to an unprecedented extent via unofficial channels, independently of the state-run media. The drivers of bicycle-taxis played an important role in popularizing reggaetón in the capital in the first years of the new millennium, blasting out the suggestive songs of the Santiago-born Candyman and others from stereos mounted on their vehicles, and the music then spread via pirated CD sellers who set up temporary stalls on the street and through informal street parties known as *bonches*. Despite the existence of a few high-profile, officially sanctioned reguetoneros, Havana's reggaetón "scene" is one in which recordings predominate over live performances, informal distribution networks—dependent on the recent spread of CD copying technology—overshadow the official media, and public dances are often planned at short notice and therefore unsupervised and unregulated. All of these factors pose new challenges to the Cuban state, which has relied for the last half century on its control of the media and of performance spaces in order to filter the musical products reaching the ears of most Cubans. Reggaetón, however, is a "street" music that exists to a considerable extent under the radar in Havana: it is everywhere yet nowhere, heard on almost every corner despite its relatively insignificant (though growing) presence in concert venues or the media.[32] Even the pirated CD stalls that I visited in 2006 had little Cuban reggaetón, suggesting that most locally produced music is distributed privately. Copied CDs, passed from hand to hand, are impossible to control, and it is notable that underground reggaetón with hardcore lyrics is particularly popular among the capital's youth, despite its exclusion from official channels and spaces. Indeed, availability through the official media seems to lessen the appeal of many Cuban songs to dedicated reggaetón fans, while limitation to informal distribution is apparently little hindrance to popularity.[33]

Reggaetón has presented new challenges to the government: it is not just provocative in its production and reception, but also accessible to the general population to a degree that earlier musical "invasions" such as rock and rap never really were. While these earlier imports also circulated via unofficial channels, the conditions and musical products were very different. Rockers and rappers, in the early years of their respective "movements," had little possibility of acquiring the equipment necessary for recording and distributing their music, and the recordings that circulated were thus almost entirely of foreign origin, whereas Havana's reguetoneros have profited from recent technological advances and the resulting proliferation of bedroom "studios." It is only over the last few years that more than a handful of Cuban musicians have been able to produce, reproduce, and distribute their music without recourse to professional studios and other branches of the state-controlled music industry. Where Beatles records circulated in the 1960s and Public Enemy cassettes in the 1990s, today the CDs by Daddy Yankee and Don Omar appear alongside recordings by young habaneros keen to establish a foothold in the music industry. A young, aspiring reguetonero will create his (and they do appear to be entirely male) CD and distribute free copies to friends, acquaintances, DJs, and pirated CD sellers in the hope of creating a "buzz" that will lead to paid live performances and possibly an opening in the media. The nature and function of the circulating products are thus quite distinct from earlier periods.

Social, political, and economic changes have also played their part in reggaetón's unprecedented accessibility. Informal bonches are a phenomenon that emerged along with the rap scene in the early 1990s, but they have flourished much more visibly with the rise of reggaetón, due in part to the decline in the number of official spaces that resulted from the dollarization of many music venues during the tourism boom from the early 1990s onward. Above all, reggaetón has arisen at a time of comparative cultural freedom: while there has been some official concern about reggaetón, the general artistic climate is much more open than that of the 1960s and early 1970s, when rock struggled in a "gray period" of authoritarianism and restriction of expression that was probably the toughest phase of the revolution for artists and intellectuals. Some musicians and fans who showed open preferences for rock were jailed, sentenced to hard labor, or sent to "rehabilitation camps" or "reeducation sessions"; Silvio Rodríguez lost his radio job simply for mentioning the Beatles on air.[34] While pirated records were available, most people heard rock only at private gatherings and at low volume, and rock's early days in revolutionary Cuba were characterized by "a pervasive climate of apprehension and fear."[35]

Whereas rock and rap were at first acquired and circulated in a predominantly clandestine manner, for example, by picking up radio broadcasts from the United States on illicit aerials, reggaetón is distributed much more openly. Today, pirated reggaetón recordings are sold at stalls in public places, and it is by far the most commonly heard music in the streets of the capital. Havana now provides opportunities for small-scale yet visible and officially tolerated musical entrepreneurship based on the demand for pirated CDs: one seller even told me that he paid a monthly fee to the government for his "patch." Finally, reggaetón has achieved its unprecedented spread not just due to the availability of recording technology, but also because it has crossed linguistic and racial divides to a greater extent than its predecessors. Reggaetón is the only one of these genres to circulate entirely in Spanish, and it has achieved a popularity across all sections of Cuban youth that has never been matched by rock or rap, which took root predominantly among the white and black sectors of the population respectively.[36] Thus while informal circulation certainly occurred with earlier imported genres, it did not occur on the same scale, or with the same openness, as with reggaetón today.

"¿PROHIBIDO EL REGUETÓN?"

In the face of reggaetón's widespread and multilayered transgression—linguistic, musical, corporeal—how has the state responded? Reggaetón in Cuba has been described variously within official and intellectual circles as a problem that needs solving, an infection that needs curing, an invasion to be countered, a flood threatening to drown the island, and an avalanche. Andi Aquino, president of the Federation of University Students in Granma Province, memorably compared reggaetón to pork: "It's not very nutritious, but it's tasty. If you eat too much it can be bad for you, though you don't care about that while you're consuming it." He described his proposed solutions as "the best medicine" for this problem.[37]

It is notable that the CIDMUC report, an academic investigation, makes much of the need to define the positive and negative aspects of reggaetón in order to take remedial action, and it concludes with a series of policy recommendations.[38] These include

> Selecting the best examples for diffusion in the media
> Ensuring compliance with current regulations with regard to the music offered in recreational, commercial, and dining centers and in public events run by state organizations
> Increasing the number of spaces for live dance music, emphasizing variety and quality in order to attract the public
> Providing more state-sponsored dance venues as an alternative to street parties, which tend to be uncontrolled and to generate social conflicts.

While information about government measures is scarce, there is nevertheless patchy evidence of strategies of observation and control. A Cuban journalist, Alcides García, has talked of a "national crusade against reggaetón,"[39] and there is no doubt that the state-run media have been extremely selective in their choice of groups and songs to be aired on TV and the radio, with former and current ACR employees such as Cubanito 20.02 and Eddy-K and timba-reggaetón fusions by groups such as La Charanga Habanera, Los Van Van, and Haila appearing with greatest regularity. According to the CIDMUC report, an analysis of TV programming in 2003–4 revealed that Cuban rap and reggaetón made up just 6.2 percent of the content of music shows, with international artists in these genres comprising a further 2.2 percent. Reggaetón thus had little presence in the media, but the fact that young people aged sixteen to twenty-six interviewed as part of the investigation claimed that they listened to reggaetón primarily in informal spaces and via pirated CDs, rather than on the radio or TV, suggests that such limitation on media exposure was having little effect on listening habits.[40] A DJ told the BBC that the state was also limiting the diffusion of Cuban reggaetón in educational and cultural centers such as the community Casas de la Cultura because of its bad language;[41] however, in mid-2006 the Casa de la Cultura of Centro Habana had a weekly showcase for rap and reggaetón groups, suggesting a policy of selectivity, education, and surveillance rather than prohibition. Indeed, Cuban journalists revealed to a Reuters correspondent that the progressive minister of culture, Abel Prieto, had rejected the prohibition of reggaetón but had requested the promotion of the best examples in the media and recommended that the phenomenon be studied carefully.[42]

The preferred solution, as proposed by the report, seems to be to provide the Cuban public with more official spaces; a healthier, more varied musical diet; and better music education, rather than the more heavy-handed tactics that some feared in the wake of the article "¿Prohibido el regguetón?" in 2004. Given the impossibility of controlling the diffusion of reggaetón, thanks to modern technology, the state has apparently decided to take a rather different approach to the hard-line measures prompted by rock in the 1960s. Indeed, the CIDMUC report itself might be seen as part of this attempt by the government to study and understand rather than simply crack down on reggaetón. Bonches, or street parties, scene of the most "problematic" reggaetón, are considered a consequence of the decline in affordable live-music venues and thus a trend which could potentially be reversed by the state. Another, closely linked implication of the CIDMUC report is that good, live timba may be an important ally in the fight against bad, recorded reggaetón. Critics have complained about the saturation of music events by reggaetón, and the report's authors argue that more variety of styles and greater exposure to live dance music will lead to more catholic tastes among Cuban youth. They also urge professional musicians to create new fusions of reggaetón with local genres, though the authors note that "*unfortunately* this type of reggaetón is

1. "Reggaeton a lo cubano" concert poster, Havana, Cuba. Photo by Geoff Baker.

not currently the most widespread among the Cuban population."[43] The solution to the "problem" of reggaetón is thus seen to lie in the hands of *timberos* rather than the reguetoneros who currently enjoy greatest popularity. Cubanization and transcendence of reggaetón are still seen as achievable, but through its adoption by professional musicians who specialize in established Cuban styles—"diluting" reggaetón—rather than through the efforts of its own predominantly young, amateur practitioners. The current prevailing attitude to foreign culture is not that it should be banned but that it can and should be "nationalized," as Moore contends.[44]

Solutions have also been sought by a few Cuban cultural observers who have attempted to Cubanize reggaetón discursively, despite the difficulties discussed above. Alberto Faya Montano, for example, makes much of the idea of a Caribbean musical melting pot, invoking the godfather of *cubanía*, Don Fernando Ortiz. Emphasizing a history of mutual influences across the region, he draws out parallels with established Cuban genres in order to familiarize reggaetón and present it as neither as new as it seems nor as threatening.[45] The distinguished Cuban musicologist Danilo Orozco has claimed that the *dembow* rhythm, like its Cuban cousins the *tresillo* and the *habanera*, has its origins in the music of the Bantu and Dahomey cultures of Africa.[46] Even the scandals around reggaetón have been used to indigenize it, by drawing parallels with similar reactions to *son* in the early twentieth century.[47] Thus despite anxieties over reggaetón as unassimilated "foreign" music, it is perceived by some observers as overlapping with Cuban traditions. However, while reggaetón is not seen by such figures as fundamentally alien, the dominant discourse of Cubanization nevertheless requires a further, more active process of adaptation rather than the simple acknowledgment of shared roots in order for the genre to achieve more widespread acceptance as compatible with national culture. This view is also shared by foreign music producers, who have an interest in encouraging or creating a distinctive Cuban reggaetón for the international market. The group's core members of Cubanito 20.02 were encouraged by their label Lusafrica to work more with live musicians and Cuban musical traditions for their second album, *Tócame*. There has also been an attempt to nationalize reggaetón in Cuba by giving it a new name, "Cubatón" (see figure 1), though this label—created by the president of a Swedish production company—has never really caught on.[48] Thus while a number of strategies for filtering and assimilating reggaetón are in place, their effectiveness has so far been mixed.

"¡HIP HOP, REVOLUCIÓN!" TO "MUEVE LA CINTURA"

One of the most important features of the emergence of reggaetón in Havana since 2002 has been its fractious relationship with the rap scene. The boom of reggaetón in Havana is as much a story of a crisis in the world of Cuban rap as of the localization of a transnational genre. This relationship is worth examining in detail, for it tells us much about both musical genres and also, more generally, about the culture and society of which they are a feature.

Rap took root in Havana in the early 1990s. The first Havana rap festival was organized in 1995, and in 1997 the state began to support the festival through the Asociación Hermanos Saíz (AHS), the cultural wing of the Union of Young Communists.[49] By the turn of the millennium rap was booming in Havana: there were reportedly hundreds of groups in the city, the state provided performance spaces and festival funds, and there was considerable international interest in the rap movement. The leading groups started pushing the government for greater promotion and commercial opportunities; these negotiations led eventually to the creation of the Agencia Cubana de Rap in 2002, which also happened to be the year that reggaetón started to take off in the capital. The initial roster of the ACR included two reggaetón groups: Cubanito 20.02 and Cubanos en la Red, though the former, who signed to the French label Lusafrica, did not remain for long. By 2004, the total number of groups represented by the ACR had dropped from ten to eight, but four of the original rap groups (Eddy-K, Alto Voltaje, Primera Base, and Papo Record) were turning increasingly to reggaetón, leaving reguetoneros in the majority within the rap agency.

The creation of the ACR was already a controversial move: while it had been sought by a number of leading rappers, it instantly divided the scene into professional groups within the ACR and amateur groups tied to the AHS, leading to inevitable and bitter disputes over the legitimacy of the agency's selection procedures, the appropriateness of professionalizing rap, and so on. But the adoption of reggaetón by the majority of ACR groups within two years of its creation was the final straw for many observers, and the gap between the two institutions that supported rap became a chasm. It was not only among rappers and reguetoneros that the battle lines were drawn, with the former accusing the latter of betraying the rap movement and wasting an unparalleled opportunity to promote hip-hop in Cuba. While spokespeople for the newer ACR were carefully diplomatic, many employed by the AHS were as scornful of reggaetón as the rappers whom they represented: it was the president of the AHS, Alpidio Alonso, who publicly criticized reggaetón at the Eighth Congress of the Union of Young Communists in 2005. It is important to note also that the newspaper *Juventud Rebelde*, the source of Alonso's comments as well as most of the critical articles about reggaetón, is the official mouthpiece of the Union of Young Communists and therefore tied indirectly to the AHS; the debate about reggaetón in the pages of this paper appears to be part of a campaign against the genre by various branches of the Union of Young Communists.

Debates over the relationship between rap and reggaetón have thus been raging in Havana. Controversy has been stoked by the perceived gulf between the ideologies behind the genres in question and by the subsequent polarization of institutions and groups connected to this process, which has its roots in the considerable cultural and material investment in rap by the state since the late 1990s. There is a sense in which certain key rap artists, by switching styles, have undermined a unique and surprisingly productive pact between state, musicians, and critics. For at least the five years up to 2002, Cuban rap had been constructed by artists, state cultural officials, academics, journalists, and documentary makers as a socially committed, critical, yet constructive movement that exemplified the richness of Cuban culture in comparison with the poverty of dominant manifestations of rap in the United States. These various parties had found in committed rap a shared language and set of concerns, encapsulated in the phrase "¡Hip hop, Revolución!"—which was coined by the duo Anónimo Consejo but then widely adopted—and local rappers had gained international recognition (though little economic benefit) for their "conscious" stance.[50] The sudden boom of hedonistic reggaetón, therefore, and above all its adoption by a number of leading figures in the rap movement, was a great letdown for the many observers who had championed Cuban rappers as figureheads of social commitment. Underground legends of the mid- to late 1990s—such as Amenaza, Alto Voltaje, Papo Record, and Primera Base—whose dedication to revolutionizing Cuban society from within had been trumpeted not only by the artists themselves but also by many admirers of socially conscious music, underwent a remarkable conversion: the first three groups left the island and ended up performing predominantly reggaetón in Europe, while the fourth split into Cubanito 20.02 and Primera Base Megatón, the latter fronted by the former godfather of Cuban underground rap, Rubén Marín. Norlan of Alto Voltaje was reborn in Finland as "the missionary of reggaetón."

How might we interpret this seismic shift in the urban music scene from "message rap" to reggaetón? Is it a negative development, a move away from idealism and commitment toward banality and commercialism? Or can it be conceived more positively, as the displacement of an overly American import by a Caribbean genre that is closer to Cuban musical traditions and thus more easily assimilated by Cuban audiences? Both viewpoints have their adherents. While the ACR artists in question presented their change in direction as a logical artistic progression, some of their admirers were shocked by what they perceived as a U-turn and betrayal of ideals. On the one hand, the fact that reggaetón has achieved far greater popular success than rap might suggest that from the point of view of the general public, this shift simply consisted of the adoption of a more appealing style, one more suited to Cuban tastes. On the other hand, for all that it has seized the ears and bodies of young Cubans, reggaetón does not fit easily with dominant visions of national culture. Rap cubano, though never a commercial or popular success, is now well established among musical, critical, and institutional circles as a "national" genre, and the shift to reggaetón, with its obvious reliance on Jamaican and Puerto Rican styles and the implication of a certain denationalization of popular music, has been less welcomed by cultural commentators.

Viewed from the perspective of cultural studies, there is little doubt that the rise of reggaetón has posed some difficult questions about politicized music. Rap appeared to be a powerful social force when it was fashionable, but almost as soon as reggaetón appeared on the scene, rap began to fade quickly from view. Groups such as Primera Base and Alto Voltaje, which had been singing until recently about Malcolm X and Nelson Mandela, were now to be found urging their audience to move their waists (mueve la cintura) and shake their booty. This was a rather sudden conversion, considering that in contrast to the evolution of rap in the United States, Cuban rap became increasingly socially conscious during the 1990s and that the Havana hip-hop festival of 2002—with its defiantly controversial performances by Alto Voltaje, Papá Humbertico, and others—is widely considered to have marked a high point in the political commitment and outspokenness of the movement. Where had the engagement with black radicalism gone? There may be a lesson here about the risks of rushing to embrace ideologically charged music and overstating its social and political significance. For all that Cuban rap is a cultural movement with fascinating social and political resonances, it is also a reminder that politics embedded in popular culture is, to a large degree, at the whim of fashion. The heady critical celebration of Cuban hip-hop in the years around 2000 looks somewhat more problematic from today's perspective. Yet, as I have argued above, any attempt to dismiss reggaetón as politically insignificant because of its lack of ideological elaboration needs to be treated with considerable caution.

It could be argued that the features that made Cuban rap so attractive to intellectuals and foreign observers actually contributed to its decline. The seriousness, commitment, and anticommercialism of the rap scene made it a joy to behold for cultural critics, but its underground fundamentalism led to a gulf between truly popular culture and "conscious" culture, leaving the rap movement wide open to the "invasion" of good-time reggaetón from 2002 onward. A number of people, including rappers who had "converted" to reggaetón, told me that rap carried the risk of overloading people with information and "burning them out"; "conscious" rap has a strong appeal to the politically minded, especially those who live in consumerist societies, but in a highly politicized society such as Cuba, it may simply be too didactic for many, too much like "more of the same." The social commentary of reggaetón, limited though it may be, is more tongue-in-cheek and ambivalent, less lecturing or hectoring; with its humorous, risqué approach, reggaetón contrasts strongly with official rhetoric and speaks to more young people in contemporary Havana than the serious, committed music traditionally promoted by the state.

ACR VS. *AHS*: THE INSTITUTIONALIZATION OF URBAN POPULAR MUSIC

The division between rap and reggaetón that has been perceived (and constructed) over the last few years in Havana relates to a series of other dichotomies: underground versus commercial and amateur versus professional, but also Asociación Hermanos Saíz versus Agencia Cubana de Rap. The AHS— the main institutional support for amateur rappers—is an old-fashioned socialist cultural association linked to the Union of Young Communists, while many of the professional reguetoneros are or have been linked to the ACR, the new-style commercial agency created in 2002 with the aim of promoting and commercializing its groups. Of course, these categories are artificially neat: there are many amateur, underground reggaetón producers, while three of the professional ACR groups are focused on "conscious" rap. Nevertheless, debates in Havana revolve around such polarizations, for they represent two distinct and competing visions of Cuban culture and society in the new millennium.

Once again, the emergence of Cubanito 20.02 from Primera Base is instructive. The members of Cubanito 20.02 told me that concerts by Primera Base were occasional events, sometimes poorly attended and usually unpaid. In 2004, however, two years after their "conversion" to reggaetón, they had released a CD on the Lusafrica label with a second in the pipeline, their songs and videos had opened the doors for reggaetón on national radio and TV, and they were often performing several concerts a week around the country. They were soon to add lucrative foreign tours to this list of achievements. Because of the virtual nonexistence of a domestic CD market in Cuba, their 2003 release *Soy Cubanito*, while enormously popular across the island, had yet to bring them significant financial rewards—they told me that they would be millionaires if all the CDs that they had sold were originals—but they made a very good living from their live performances, and by undertaking foreign tours, they opened up the possibility of significant hard currency earnings. In 2005 and 2006, other reggaetón groups—such as the ACR artists Eddy-K and Gente de Zona, and the EGREM-signed Triángulo Oscuro—while yet to replicate the success of Cubanito 20.02, had regular, well-paid gigs at the two Casas de la Música in Havana as well as other venues around the capital, whereas no rap groups had this level of exposure.

The debates that have accompanied the high-profile emergence of such groups have tapped into broad questions over the relationship between art and commerce and the place of globalized, commercialized culture in this rapidly changing socialist society. While reguetoneros have seized their commercial opportunities, underground rappers are, in a sense, refusing to accept the commercialization of life in the capital since the economic crisis of the Special Period. Not only do they criticize this growing materialism in their lyrics, but they proclaim their amateur status as a badge of honor: it is a sign of refusing to take a commercial path, of maintaining their independent line.[51] While professionalism may mean high musical standards to many Cubans, it has quite different connotations to some artists, especially within the sphere of influence of the Union of Young Communists. It is significant that a number of reguetoneros were formerly struggling, if admired, rappers: their success led to the characterization of reggaetón as a "temptation" which had to be resisted or given in to. "Staying firm" with rap was a sign of strength and morality, while adopting reggaetón was portrayed as weakness in the face of the seduction of commerce.[52] Within artistic and intellectual circles, then, reggaetón is not just a new form of popular music: it is a symbol of the commercialization of Havana's culture and society, and one's position on rap and reggaetón is, arguably, a position on this process and on the contradictory realities of late socialism itself. A negative view of commercialization is a prominent feature of artistic, academic, and journalistic responses to reggaetón in Havana, and the blame for reggaetón's "corruption"—primarily in other parts Latin America, though also, to a degree, in Cuba itself—is laid firmly at the door of the media and the international music industry, which are portrayed as guilty of ignoring socially conscious reggaetón and promoting only shallow, banal, vulgar music.[53] Cuban rap, on the other hand, is seen as ideologically progressive and largely untainted by commerce. The polarization of debates around urban popular music thus reflects conflicting reactions to the uneasy marriage of socialism and capitalism in contemporary Havana, for discussions of rap and reggaetón are entwined with judgments about this controversial political and economic process.

A brief consideration of the Cuban Rap Agency is revealing with respect to changes in the capital's cultural scene over the last decade. There has been much muttering since the foundation of the ACR that it was created in order to control Cuban rap. While such a motivation may indeed have been present, the ACR works in many ways just like a music agency in any other country. Precisely of interest is that this kind of professional, commercial agency was created in socialist Cuba, and that it was the culmination of the burgeoning underground rap movement of the 1990s, which had been supported by the amateur, politicized AHS. In other words, the ACR is significant because of its contrast with the AHS, an old-style socialist institution which promotes amateur culture for culture's sake and was the standard-bearer of Cuban rap from 1997 to 2002. The disputes that emerged between the artists and functionaries of these two organizations are indicative of recent shifts in cultural policies and divisions between branches of the Cuban state, and betray the tensions between socialist and capitalist ideologies and practices that have grown in Havana since the mid-1990s.

There are useful parallels to be drawn here with Thomas Cushman's study of rock music in the last years of the Soviet Union and the early post-Soviet period, which puts forward the argument that instead of seeing free-market economics as the major driving force of cultural freedom, "the replacement of political control of culture by the commodification of culture represents the substitution of one form of constraint on human expression for another."[54] Cultural perestroika there (the restructuring of key organizations, in particular the state music company Melodiya) led to a new commercial focus in cultural production, which contributed in turn to "an emerging division in the rock community between those musicians who saw in music a viable means for the voicing of protest and opposition and those who considered music primarily as an aesthetic experience and form of entertainment."[55] Cuba went through its own "perestroika" in the 1990s as a direct result of the collapse of the Soviet Union; as the economy underwent wholesale transformations, the music scene became considerably more commercialized, with marketability and sales assuming an unprecedented importance.[56] This led eventually to the division of the Cuban rap scene described above, as senior figures, by switching to reggaetón, embraced music "as an aesthetic cultural commodity rather than an aesthetic means for the expression of dissent," as many Soviet rockers had done.[57] Despite its skirmishes with state censorship and incomprehension in the 1990s, rap's greatest challenge turned out to be the boom of reggaetón in the following decade. State control became less significant as the attractions of media exposure and commercial success entered the equation. Leading artists such as Primera Base/Cubanito 20.02, by switching from underground rap to reggaetón, from protest music to entertainment, were able to profit from this newly commercialized cultural environment and to gain access to the media, to much larger audiences, and to economic rewards. With such opportunities on the horizon, the numbers of young aspiring artists who were prepared to take the uncompromising (and, from an economic perspective, unrewarding) line of underground rap diminished sharply. If one interpretation sees the rise of reggaetón in terms of the decline of rap's idealism and political force, then, as with Soviet rock, it is not the state so much as the incursion of the market into Cuba which has been primarily responsible for the waning influence of this critical, socially committed musical movement.

AFTER THE CRISIS: MUSIC, SOCIAL CHANGE, AND THE "BATTLE OF IDEAS"

What broader lessons might we learn from the rise of reggaetón in Havana? What do the sounds, lyrics, and dances tell us about society in the Cuban capital today? Cuban researchers have analyzed reggaetón in terms of a "pendulum swing" away from timba; reggaetón is thus regarded as a simple response to the excessive complexity of timba music and dance, as freedom from the latter's choreographic constraints.[58] In the light of the discussion above, it might also be instructive to consider reggaetón as a swing away from rap, one linked to broader changes in Cuban society since the 1990s.

The relationship between the emergence of new body-centered musics and social upheavals has long been recognized, going back to Plato.[59] Angela Impey's analysis of kwaito is of particular interest in this respect, for she relates the rise of this genre, with its numerous parallels with reggaetón, to a major moment of political change in South Africa.[60] According to Impey, "kwaito's tendencies are towards materialistic, hedonistic, and flighty preoccupations, and groups such as Boom Shaka appeared to unleash amongst young black consumers an explosive desire to disengage from the long years of oppression and political protest of the apartheid era."[61] She goes on: "Kwaito represents the music, style and attitude of post-apartheid black urban youth; it represents a sub-cultural practice which liberates black urban youth from the culture of protest of the '80s."[62] David Coplan, also on the subject of kwaito, writes of urban youth's demand for a society that "accepts their pleasure principle as a valid replacement for the now painfully passé politicised ideology of social sacrifice." To these writers, then, the body-centered hedonism of kwaito is indicative of postpolitical music for a postideological moment.

Other commercialized dance genres widely criticized for their hedonism and overt sexuality ("slackness") have also been recuperated by perceptive scholars for their resistance to certain hegemonic trends and ideologies. If kwaito may be reclaimed from its critics as an expression of liberation from the relentless political focus of popular culture of the apartheid years, Brazilian funk, which evolved from U.S. models into a distinctive local style in Rio de Janeiro in the mid-1980s, might also be considered a reaction against the elaborately discursive, politicized music of the long years of military rule (1964–85). George Yúdice's analysis of funk in Rio reveals many parallels with reggaetón, in particular a resistance to engaging with established ideologies and identities (national, political, social) and an emphasis on individual freedom expressed through the pleasure of dance rather than adherence to notions of collective identity and action.[63] Carolyn Cooper, meanwhile, in her study of female slackness in Jamaican dancehall, claims: "It can be seen to represent in part a radical, underground confrontation with the patriarchal gender ideology and the pious morality of fundamentalist Jamaican society. In its invariant coupling with Culture, Slackness is potentially a politics of subversion. For Slackness is not mere sexual looseness—though it certainly is that. Slackness is a metaphorical revolt against law and order; an undermining of consensual standards of decency. It is the antithesis of Culture."[64]

It is worth considering these various body-centered genres in order to illuminate reggaetón's contestatory power in Havana. While there has been no political change in Cuba to match the end of apartheid or of Brazilian military rule, the collapse of the Soviet Union led to a period of social and economic crisis in early-1990s Cuba, the Special Period, which shook the country to its foundations. The 1990s was a decade of crisis and transition from a socialist to a "sociocapitalist" economy based on tourism, joint ventures with foreign companies, and limited private enterprise. By the turn of the millennium, the worst of the Special Period was over, and the new social and economic reality, however contradictory, had settled considerably. Both state and individuals had had to learn new ways of getting by, and more recently burgeoning alliances with the Venezuelan president, Hugo Chávez, and with China have lent greater stability to the Cuban economy and political establishment. If, as Perna claims, timba was the "sound of the Cuban crisis"—and I would suggest that rap could be characterized in the same way, given that it too flourished in the mid-1990s during the trials of the Special Period—then reggaetón may be considered the postcrisis sound.[65] I would argue that the shift in Cuba from protest music (rap) to postprotest music (reggaetón) relates to a broader swing, since the start of the Special Period, away from a politicized national culture of socialist ideology, collectivity, and self-sacrifice toward one increasingly centered on pleasure, the reassertion of individuality, and self-fulfillment.

Cubanito 20.02 explicitly linked their abandonment of Primera Base and their switch to reggaetón with social and economic changes: they told me that the circumstances which had spawned underground rap in Cuba no longer pertained and that the moment for rap had passed with the worst of the Special Period. In some ways, though, the boom of reggaetón could also be seen as revealing a subsequent, hidden, ideological crisis, more subtle yet just as pervasive as the earlier economic one. Reggaetón seems to be linked to a new phase in which state ideologies play a much reduced role in people's thinking, above all among young people, though older generations may adhere more to long-established ideas of national culture, ideological struggle, and so on. Reggaetón's core audience is teenagers, who are too young to remember Cuba before the Special Period; they have grown up with the contradictory realities of post-1990 Cuba and have never witnessed socialism properly in action. It is not surprising that many are apolitical—they are the first late socialist generation, which has known neither the "purer" socialism of their parents' childhood nor the capitalism of their grandparents' formative years. For this generation of Cuban youth, socialism is a concept as much as a reality. Tourism and foreign investment have brought huge changes to Havana: principles and ideas have given up much of their hold to images and display. When the state has abandoned key ideological tenets, in practice if not discursively, and capitalist wealth is visible daily on the streets of the city, then it may be unsurprising that many individual citizens, particularly the young, feel little connection to politicized ideologies.

Yet for all the creeping materialism of contemporary Havana, the state has not abandoned its ideological efforts. On the contrary, the *batalla de ideas* (battle of ideas), launched in 1999 as the economic turbulence of the Special Period started to abate, is a sweeping campaign—considered by some to be Castro's last major political initiative—to safeguard the revolution by revitalizing the ideological commitment of Cubans, especially the young, "reflecting the new impulse for participation and commitment and seeking to fortify ideological resolve against the pressure from individualization and social division, and against the corrosive effects of the dollar and tourism."[66] It is worth noting that the "commanders" of this battle are a group of loyalists drawn from the Union of Young Communists, the same organization behind much of the negative press directed at reggaetón, implying that the Union of Young Communists may have taken its stand against reggaetón because it is seen as antithetical to the central aim of the batalla de ideas: to reengage Cubans with the ideals of the revolution.

The enthusiastic adoption of reggaetón by Cuban youth may therefore reveal much about late socialism and the progress of the "battle of ideas" among young residents of the capital. Listening and dancing habits may speak eloquently about realities and attitudes that are still not officially admissible. Perhaps bodily expression is the best way to speak truth to power in Cuba. Reggaetón seems to encapsulate a rejection of ideas and ideology, of the discipline, blurring of individuality, and abnegation of self under socialism; its focus on self-indulgence and pleasure (often sexual) is implicitly a form of liberation from the official, politicized national culture. To draw a parallel with Cooper's analysis of Jamaican dancehall, in Cuban reggaetón it is arguably the moralizing, paternalistic discourses of socialism that are being rejected through slackness. For all the state's recent efforts, then, reggaetón's popularity suggests the existence of a postpolitical generation which came of age during the Special Period and which has remained largely immune to the consciousness-raising campaigns of the batalla de ideas. Any attempt to understand the significance of reggaetón in Havana must take into account the fact that the "Special Period generation"—the prime consumers of this defiantly apolitical musical genre—is also the key target of the battle of ideas.

When in Havana in 2006, I was interested to hear rap and reggaetón researchers talking about the "marginal" barrios in which these genres are supposedly rooted; the acknowledgment of marginality came as something of a surprise in a context long ruled by a principle of equality. Yet the appeal of rap to intellectuals and the state in Havana was that its producers, although from marginal neighborhoods, were actually producing a sophisticated critical discourse which seemed to illustrate that social, economic, or geographical marginality in Cuba did not carry implications of a parallel ideological stance. Rappers from tough, distant barrios—particularly those artists linked to the Union of Young Communists via its cultural wing, the AHS—could be seen as participating on some level in the batalla de ideas. Reggaetón, though, poses deeper problems: its vulgar, "banal" language seems to reveal a more fundamental marginality and to suggest that social commitment and ideological resolve do not spread evenly across society after all. Cuban critics are troubled by the question of why reggaetón lyrics are so popular among Cuban youth, despite their much vaunted educational advantages compared with those in other countries of the region, and so far they do not seem to have found many reassuring answers.[67] Contrary to the earlier evidence of rap, it seems that the battle of ideas is being lost on the urban margins after all—or perhaps young habaneros are simply refusing to fight.

The swing from rap to reggaetón is thus revealing. Rap was a music of the transitional period of the 1990s, expressing the pain and bewilderment of the shift from socialism to "sociocapitalism," but today, to many listeners, it sounds like the music of a former era, just as "music with a message" in South Africa soon came to sound very dated after the end of apartheid.[68] Reggaetón's insistence on pleasure has made rap's politicized ideology, with its noticeable overlap with the state's rhetoric of the batalla de ideas, look rather shopworn in

Havana. This depoliticization of culture is not limited to rap and reggaetón: timba, too, has seen a marked decline in the controversy of its lyrical topics since the late 1990s. Concern about this depoliticization explains the moves against reggaetón by various high-profile individuals associated with the Union of Young Communists. However, rap's combination of socially committed lyrics and state support was out of step with the times once the worst of the Special Period was over. Today, irreverence and independence are the hot tickets, not seriousness and state subsidy, and the conservatism of underground rap at a time of rapid changes made it quickly redundant to large sections of the younger population. This conservatism is manifested in resistance to the breakdown of values since the Special Period; reggaetón, however, celebrates this breakdown with bluntness and insistent repetition.[69] Reggaetón's consolidation of the "pleasure principle" and its eclipse of socially committed rap suggest that, to echo Coplan on kwaito, politicized ideologies such as the batalla de ideas are now dismissed as "painfully passé" by the majority of the capital's youth.

CONCLUSIONS

So what can be learned from comparing perceptions of reggaetón to those of rap, and how do controversies surrounding rap and reggaetón mirror and participate in larger debates about the direction of Cuban society in the twenty-first century? Preferences for rap over reggaetón in Cuba reveal both national and academic agendas: Cuban rap may be viewed as both resistant to and at the same time participating in national discourses, and can therefore be talked about productively by artists, state officials, and Cuban and foreign critics; whereas reggaetón is generally viewed as too debased by intellectuals and too problematic by the state to be the focus of much more than dismissal or "solutions." Unlike rap, reggaetón cannot be recuperated by Cuban observers in terms of "constructive criticism" and a "positive message," and the internationalism that it expresses is the "wrong" kind, painting Cuba predominantly as the passive recipient of secondhand commercialized culture from overseas, rather than as a regional or global leader in a "serious" field of music (as in the case of "conscious" rap). Both rap and timba, another "problem" music of the 1990s, ultimately showed enough continuities with official conceptions of national culture to be redeemable, but reggaetón has yet to be embraced by cultural policymakers and critics.

What might be regarded as a local spat between fans of two rival styles of popular music thus links in with broader questions about national ideology and identity, and hegemonic academic and political discourses. The dismissal of reggaetón as trashy, trite, almost beneath consideration, is prescriptive as well as descriptive. "Conscious" rap has been harnessed to bolster state rhetoric about the centrality of moralistic ideas to the Cuban Revolution; reggaetón, a problematic source of fun and pleasure, is disciplined as deviant, in language that recalls so many moral panics over popular music down the centuries.[70] Debates about reggaetón have provided a vehicle for discussing issues of fundamental importance in contemporary Cuban society, and much censure of reggaetón relates to attempts to defend hegemonic notions of national culture and identity in the face of the challenges posed by globalized, commercialized culture.

Robin Moore's enlightening book on music and the Cuban Revolution ends with the observation that "now more than ever, the arts represent a quasi-independent realm of commentary in dialogue with the state. These creations, representing varied reactions to a unique environment, help provide an insightful and nuanced view of the revolutionary experience."[71] While his comments provide an illuminating summary of the forty-odd years of musical production that he analyzes, they are strikingly out of kilter with the recent arrival of reggaetón on the scene. Most reguetoneros seem uninterested in any sort of dialogue with the state, and even their fans are unlikely to argue that their views are either "insightful" or "nuanced." It would seem that reggaetón offers an unprecedented challenge to Cuban revolutionary culture.

NOTES

The research on which this essay is based was made possible by financial support from the University of London Central Research Fund and the Music Department, Royal Holloway, University of London. I am very grateful to the director and staff of CIDMUC, Havana, for allowing me to consult their unpublished *Informe sobre el regueton*, which has been invaluable in the preparation of this essay. Thanks to all the usual suspects in Havana's rap scene for making my work possible. Translations of Spanish-language quotations are my own.

1. Santiago is widely considered to be the "home" of reggaetón in Cuba. The city's location at the eastern end of the island places it directly in the path of musical currents emanating from Jamaica, including the *dembow* dancehall rhythm that became an essential building-block of reggaetón. Residents of Santiago can pick up radio signals from Jamaica, whereas some in Havana may, with considerable effort, receive broadcasts from the United States, explaining in part the greater identification of the former city with reggaetón and of the latter with rap.

2. Osviel Castro Medel, "¿Prohibido el reguetón?," *Juventud Rebelde*, February 13, 2005.

3. Alberto Faya Montano, "Algunas notas sobre el reguetón," *Cubarte: El portal de la cultura cubana*, March 28, 2005, http://www.cubarte.cu/global/loader.php?cat=actuali dad&cont=showitem.php&tabla=entrevista_2005&id=2685 (accessed May 26, 2005).

4. Castro Medel, "¿Prohibido el reguetón?"

5. CIDMUC, *Informe sobre el reguetón* (unpublished report, 2005), 79; Osviel Castro Medel, "Se cruzan balas por el reguetón," *Juventud Rebelde*, March 6, 2005.

6. Castro Medel, "¿Prohibido el reguetón?"

7. Alan West-Durán, "Rap's Diasporic Dialogues: Cuba's Redefinition of Blackness," *Journal of Popular Music Studies* 16, no. 1 (2004): 4–39.

8. See also Coplan's comments about academic preferences for rap over *kwaito* in South Africa. David Coplan, "God Rock Africa: Thoughts on Politics in Popular Black Performance in South Africa," *African Studies* 64, no. 1 (2005): 9–27, 25. In contexts such as Cuba, South Africa, and Brazil, rap is generally perceived as logocentric and as contrasting with the body-centrism of dominant dance genres (reggaetón, *kwaito*, and funk respectively). In Havana, this dichotomy, though clearly far from absolute, is widely recognized and perpetuated by artists, critics, and audiences.

9. CIDMUC, *Informe*. Jan Fairley has also made a significant contribution to the debate in her article (published after this essay had been written) "Dancing Back to Front: *Regeton*, Sexuality, Gender and Transnationalism in Cuba," *Popular Music* 25, no. 3 (2006): 471–88. A revised version of that essay is included in the present volume.

10. CIDMUC, *Informe*, 19, 34.

11. Susan McClary, "Same as It Ever Was: Youth Culture and Music," in *Microphone Fiends: Youth Music and Youth Culture*, ed. Andrew Ross and Tricia Rose (London: Routledge, 1994), 34.

12. Castro Medel, "¿Prohibido el reguetón?"

13. Fernando Ravsberg, "Cuba: 'Peligroso' reguetón," BBC Mundo, March 15, 2005, http://news.bbc.co.uk/hi/spanish/misc/newsid_4350000/4350595.stm (accessed May 26, 2005).

14. CIDMUC, *Informe*, 16–17.

15. See Robin Moore, *Music and Revolution: Cultural Change in Socialist Cuba* (Berkeley: University of California Press, 2006), 7–9.

16. Gabriel García Márquez, "The Fidel I Think I Know," *Guardian*, August 12, 2006.

17. Geoffrey Baker, "¡Hip hop, Revolución! Nationalizing Rap in Cuba," *Ethnomusicology* 49, no. 3 (2005): 368–402.

18. Indigenization may also be a matter of place: Alexandrine Boudreault-Fournier's forthcoming work on reggaetón in Santiago suggests that the music produced there shows more evidence of "Cubanization" than that in the capital. "From Homemade Recording Studios to Alternative Narratives: Positioning the Reggaetón Stars in Cuba," *The Journal of Latin American and Caribbean Anthropology* (forthcoming 2008).

19. Castro Medel, "Se cruzan balas por el reguetón."

20. Vincenzo Perna, "Timba: The Sound of the Cuban Crisis. Black Dance Music in Havana during the *Período Especial*" (Ph.D. thesis, SOAS, University of London, 2001). A revised version of Perna's illuminating thesis has been published as *Timba: The Sound of the Cuban Crisis* (Aldershot, England: Ashgate, 2005).

21. There may also be mixed feelings about musical indigenization, as there are in the rap scene, though this would need to be confirmed by further research. While a positive view of rap fusions can be found among many cultural observers and some leading rappers, this issue has long been controversial within the Havana rap movement. Many "underground" groups are outspokenly antifusion, preferring to measure authenticity by proximity to rap's U.S. roots rather than to Cuban musical traditions.

22. Moore, *Music and Revolution*, 89.

23. One leading "underground" rapper, Randy Acosta, describes himself in a song as "enemigo del meneo, del mikeo, del perreo" (enemy of booty-shaking, trendiness and doggy-style dancing).

24. Moore, *Music and Revolution*, 15. Antipathy toward reggaetón is found in many other Latin American contexts, and similar dance genres provoke parallel reactions: see, for example, the dichotomy of "music for remembering" (rap) and "music for forgetting" (Rio funk, *kwaito*) constructed by Patrick Neate in his book *Where You're At: Notes from the Frontline of a Hip Hop Planet* (London: Bloomsbury, 2003). The perceived dichotomy of "political" music versus dance music extends far beyond Cuba and current preoccupations; see McClary, "Same as It Ever Was." Thus while the Cuban context described here may be unique, the negative reactions to commercialized dance music are not.

25. Perna, *Timba*, 53–55.

26. Robin Moore, "Revolution with Pachanga? Debates over the Place of 'Fun' in the Music of Socialist Cuba" (paper presented at "Caribbean Soundscapes" conference, Tulane University, March 12, 2004).

27. Moore, *Music and Revolution*, 111.

28. CIDMUC, *Informe*, 21.

29. For more on timba and the despelote, see Perna, *Timba*, 157–61; on reggaetón dancing and gender, see Fairley, "Dancing Back to Front." The issue of dominance and submission in reggaetón dance is complex and beyond the scope of this essay: nevertheless, it should be noted that the characteristic perreo dance style of international reggaetón, which might be regarded as placing women in a submissive role, has been largely superseded by other styles in Havana and that young dancers—both male and female—interviewed as part of the CIDMUC investigation perceived solo dancing in terms of liberation. Furthermore, as Perna notes, the emergence of the despelote in the 1990s was intimately linked to the rising influence of young women in the informal economy of the "Special Period," and the evolution of the man's role from leader to supporting cast or observer was a potent metaphor for the declining economic role of

young men. On the other hand, the development of the female role could be regarded as one from an object of male "leading," to an object of the male gaze and thus as a dubious form of emancipation.

30. See Celeste Fraser Delgado and José Esteban Muñoz, "Rebellions of Everynight Life," in *Everynight Life: Culture and Dance in Latin/o America*, ed. Celeste Fraser Delgado and José Esteban Muñoz (Durham, N.C.: Duke University Press, 1997), 18.

31. CIDMUC, *Informe*, 20.

32. On the pervasiveness of reggaetón in Havana at the time of writing, but also the unease that its music and, above all, lyrics trigger outside its young core audience, even among culturally sensitive and perspicacious observers, see Leonardo Padura's article "¿Reggaetón: Signo de nuestra época?," *Los que soñamos por la oreja* 23 (October 2006), http://oreja.trovacub.com/boletin.html (accessed June 25, 2007).

33. CIDMUC, *Informe*, 21.

34. Moore, *Music and Revolution*, 149–51; Deborah Pacini Hernandez and Reebee Garofalo, "Between Rock and a Hard place: Negotiating Rock in Revolutionary Cuba, 1960–1980," in *Rockin' Las Américas: The Global Politics of Rock in Latin/o America*, ed. Deborah Pacini Hernandez, Héctor Fernández L'Hoeste, and Eric Zolov (Pittsburg: University of Pittsburg Press, 2004), 43.

35. Pacini Hernandez and Garofalo, "Between Rock and a Hard Place," 50, 48.

36. Ibid., 65–66.

37. Castro Medel, "¿Prohibido el reguetón?" The author also quotes another journalist, Pedro de la Hoz, who described reggaetón (again in the pages of *Juventud Rebelde*) as "threatening to drown us" and who claimed that "no one can save us now."

38. CIDMUC, *Informe*, 39–40.

39. Ravsberg, "Cuba: 'Peligroso' reguetón."

40. CIDMUC, *Informe*, 26, 39.

41. Ravsberg, "Cuba: 'Peligroso' reguetón."

42. CIDMUC, *Informe*, 84.

43. My italics. Ibid., 34, 9.

44. Moore, *Music and Revolution*, 13.

45. Faya Montano, "Algunas notas sobre el reguetón."

46. CIDMUC, *Informe*, 13.

47. See Castro Medel, "Se cruzan balas por el reguetón."

48. *Cubaton: Reggaeton a lo Cubano*, CD (Topaz Records, B000CIXDZE, 2006); *Cubaton II: Reggaeton a lo Cubano*, CD (Topaz Records, B000V6I6DG, 2007); and *Cubaton—El Medico*, film recording, directed by Daniel Fridell (Röde Orm Film, 2008).

49. There is a growing literature on Cuban rap by scholars including Deborah Pacini Hernandez and Reebee Garofalo, Alan West-Durán, Sujatha Fernandes, and Marc Perry. For my analysis and full bibliographies, see Baker, "¡Hip hop, Revolución!" and Baker, "*La Habana que no conoces*: Cuban Rap and the Social Construction of Urban Space," *Ethnomusicology Forum* 15, no. 2 (2006): 215–46.

50. See Baker, "¡Hip hop, Revolución!"

51. This discursive distinction, maintained by rappers themselves, is in some cases rather blurred in practice: see Baker, "*La Habana que no conoces.*"

52. Moore notes a broader movement toward greater moralism and criticism in nondance music in recent years, perhaps because many musicians feel marginalized by the centrality of dance music in the new urban economy. Moore, *Music and Revolution*, 243. The rap-reggaetón debate is not, therefore, an isolated phenomenon.

53. E.g., CIDMUC, *Informe*, 12; Faya Montano, "Algunas notas sobre el reguetón."

54. Thomas Cushman, "Glasnost, Perestroika, and the Management of Oppositional Popular Culture in the Soviet Union, 1985–1991," *Current Perspectives in Social Theory* 13 (1993): 25–67, 27.

55. Ibid., 52.

56. Moore, *Music and Revolution*, 241.

57. Cushman, "Glasnost, Perestroika, and the Management of Oppositional Popular Culture in the Soviet Union," 58.

58. CIDMUC, *Informe*, 33, 36.

59. McClary, "Same as It Ever Was," 29.

60. Ibid., 29–30; Angela Impey, "Resurrecting the Flesh? Reflections on Women in *Kwaito*," *Agenda* 49 (2001): 44–50.

61. Impey, "Resurrecting the Flesh?," 45.

62. Ibid., 49.

63. George Yúdice, "The Funkification of Rio," in *Microphone Fiends: Youth Music and Youth Culture*, ed. Andrew Ross and Tricia Rose (London: Routledge, 1994), 193–217.

64. Carolyn Cooper, *Noises in the Blood: Orality, Gender, and the "Vulgar" Body of Jamaican Popular Culture* (London: Macmillan, 1993), 141.

65. Perna, *Timba*.

66. Antoni Kapcia, *Havana: The Making of Cuban Culture* (Oxford: Berg, 2005), 181–82.

67. CIDMUC, *Informe*, 5.

68. Impey, "Resurrecting the Flesh?"; Simon Stephens, "Kwaito," in *Senses of Culture: South African Culture Studies*, ed. Sarah Nuttall and Cheryl-Ann Michael (Oxford: Oxford University Press, 2000), 263.

69. For example, the meaning of the reggaetón hit "A Ti Te Gustan los Yumas" (You Like Foreigners) evolved from humorous critique to affirmation through constant repetition (CIDMUC, *Informe*, 19); this is in marked contrast to the serious, moralizing treatment of the same theme in "underground" rap songs (Baker, "*La Habana que no conoces*").

70. See McClary, "Same as It Ever Was," on historical precedents.

71. Moore, *Music and Revolution*, 263.

You Got Your Reggaetón in My Hip-Hop

Crunkiao and "Spanish Music" in the Miami Urban Scene

Forty years of steady Latin American immigration have transformed the southern American town of Miami into a Latino city. Spanish is the language that animates Miami; proficiency or at least some knowledge of the idiom is a required skill for those who aspire to thrive in this tropical American capital. Billboards advertise everything from the latest *telenovela* to the next salsa music festival. Among them is a colorful poster for the local Latin hip-hop artist known as Plátano. Promoting his single, "Helicoptero," the poster informs passers-by that "It's Getting Heavy . . . 305 Style" (figure 1).

To the majority of those living in Miami-Dade County, the numbers 305 represent the telephone area code. But to an urban musical subculture, the numbers have come to serve as the de facto symbol for a nascent musical movement known as El Crunkiao (or *crunkiao*). Songs such as Pitbull's "305 Till' I Die" and Sito's "La Calle" characterize the style, which is most marked by a lyrical blend of Spanglish, Spanish, and English. Much in the same way that reggaetón artists once created their own movement by freely incorporating aspects from Jamaican dancehall and American hip-hop, crunkiao musicians are mixing Latin elements with the sounds of southern hip-hop (especially Atlanta-based "crunk"), Miami bass or "booty music" (a local predecessor to crunk), and freestyle—an '8os pop style that drew heavily on electro funk as well as Latin elements—all of which mingle in the Miami soundscape. Aided by the enormous popularity of reggaetón, Miami-based Latin rappers such as Pitbull, Plátano, and Sito are attempting to launch their careers from the city, reaching out to national and international audiences while cultivating a home-grown sound.

Still in its infancy, the crunkiao movement found an unlikely ally in reggaetón. Crunkiao artists, who tend to rhyme over hip-hop beats stylistically different from the reggae derived *dembow* rhythms of reggaetón, regularly perform at national venues headlined by their more successful reggaetón brethren. Some crunkiao rappers such as Pitbull have gained national recognition in no small part by collaborating on remixes with reggaetón artists such as Daddy Yankee and Voltio. "Reggaetón has helped us massively," says Plátano. "If it weren't for the success of artists like Daddy Yankee and Don Omar, we probably would not be getting that much attention at all. I guess you can say that reggaetón has brought awareness of Latinos and the different breeds of hip-hop within our communities." But not all Miami crunkiao artists would use the term *crunkiao* to classify themselves. Among them is Pitbull, who has so far resisted coining a name for his hybrid music, preferring instead to collaborate with artists and producers from various genres, including crunk, reggaetón, dancehall reggae, and hip-hop.

THE ROOTS AND ROUTES OF CRUNKIAO

A young man in his mid-twenties, Plátano, born Iván Rodríguez, moved with his family to Miami when he was still in his teens. "I was born in the Dominican Republic," Plátano relates. "But when I was 12 my family moved to New York City. It was a different culture, and it took me a while to get used to it." Like many other Caribbean-born Latinos making that transition, Plátano found his new life to be a challenge: "I loved New York City, but coming from the Dominican Republic I was surprised by the lack of space," says Plátano. "But New York was also exciting: in my old barrio of Washington Heights there was something always going on. I remember that we used to skip school and go to house parties. There was never a minute that I wasn't doing something, and I loved it."

The excitement of life in New York was, however, tempered by financial pressures in the form of gentrifying rents and a lack of enthusiasm for education, common to the lives of immigrants in the city. The deciding factor for the family was Plátano's younger brother's education. "My family decided that it would be better to take us away from the City," says Plátano. "I guess they felt that Miami would be a new start, with better schools and with more of a Latino flavor." He continues, "What surprised me about Miami was how much space we had. I mean, my house was huge and the streets were clean. Back in Washington Heights, New York City, I couldn't walk anywhere without having someone offer me drugs. All of a sudden we were in Miami, and my

1. Promotional image for Plátano's single "Helicoptero." Image courtesy of Heavy Management.

new school was so big it even had a field where I could play sports. I never had anything like that in New York. So being in Miami made me change my outlook about school."

Miami's demographic environment confronted Plátano with a new ethnic perspective: unlike New York City, where the Latino population stands at 27 percent, in Miami Latinos account for a whopping 65 percent.[1] His high school, located in the working-class suburban neighborhood of Coral Park, in South Miami, was by all accounts a pivotal catalyst for the nascent Miami movement. It was there that Plátano would meet future figureheads of the Miami Latin hip-hop movement such as rapper Armando Perez, a.k.a. Pitbull, and producer Isai González, a.k.a. Jibba Jamz. For González, a former student of Cuban American parentage, the ethnic makeup of the school represented a mirror image of Miami's demographic layout. "At the time [1998], Latin students were mainly Cuban," asserts González. "But because of the bad economic situations throughout Latin America, we started to see a lot of new kids from countries like Venezuela, Colombia, and Argentina. It started to become more international."

Plátano grew impatient with the dearth of postschool activities offered in his new neighborhood, but music offered an outlet. "Compared to life in New York, life in Miami was very tame," he comments.

Musically there was very little or no music coming from Miami. Most of the music that people at school heard was New York hip-hop, so that made me kind of popular because people were impressed with the fact that I had lived in New York. My friends and I were looking for something to do, and that's when my buddy Tricks [Joel Prenza] and I decided to throw parties where we could all get together and listen to our music. We wanted to have a place were other classmates could come and dance and just have a good time; we decided to call the parties Baja Panties [*Panties Down*].

The Baja Panties parties started out as a loose collective of friends who were trying to promote and find a way to listen to their music. The risqué name offered or implied a night of mischief and illicit fun. Plátano's fiestas would prove a success with teenagers too young to be admitted at the clubs for those twenty-one and over in glamorous Miami Beach. "Back then, the radio wasn't playing our music," asserts Plátano. "So we started selling lollypops and candy around our school, and that's the way that we raised the money to rent banquet halls and support the scene."

The parties' musical selections would serve as a template for elements of the crunkiao music style. The fiestas offered a blend of New York hip-hop and Miami bass, with some reggaetón, freestyle, and Latin dance styles added to the mix. "We would mix it up with salsa, merengue and Miami booty, like Luke Campbell and *el* hip-hop," adds Plátano. "But it was my boy Tricks who introduced me to reggaetón. I had heard it before, but the music had evolved. It was better produced, and the reggaetón guys could really rap in Spanish. So it was really an eye opener." With Plátano acting as the event's host, the popularity of Baja Panties quickly spread by word of mouth, and the party soon outgrew its humble banquet hall beginnings, moving to the Millennium merengue club located near the Miami airport in a working-class enclave of South Miami. For Isai González, who attended many Baja Panty nights, it was a chance to see something new—and promising. "It was a great feeling—by the year 2001 a lot of the people that first attended those early parties were starting to make the inroads in the music business," affirms González.

Inspired by his friends, Plátano decided to make the transition from event host to rapper. The idea of making music evolved naturally in the course of attending Coral High and spending time with his classmates. "I used to rap all around the place with my friend at *la hora del lunch*, you feel me," discloses Plátano, and that friend was Pitbull. Even back then he was known as Pitbull, so I have never really called him by any other name. The whole *episodio* of Baja Panty helped me as much as it helped Pitbull, because back then no one wanted to put him on a stage. Actually a lot of people didn't believe in him, so he calls me and says, "Oye loco, ¿cómo me puedo montar en la tarima de Baja Panty?" [Listen man, how can I get on the Baja Panty stage?]. And I told him not to worry, and that was the first time that Pitbull was on a stage, and until this day he will tell you that we were the first ones *que le dimos la mano* [that gave him a hand].

The irony of the situation should be evident: an up-and-coming Plátano gave Pitbull his first chance at rapping, but as time went on Pitbull would be the one Miami Latin rapper to attain popularity at a national level, scoring hits with Daddy Yankee and the Ying Yang Twins, while Plátano still toils to find national acceptance.

Motivated by the success of his parties and the early achievements of his friend Pitbull, who at the time was signed to legendary Miami bass label, Luke Records, Plátano and his high school friend and manager Tricks decided in 2001 to form the company Heavy Management and work full time in the production and promotion of their new music. "I wanted to do something original," says Plátano.

> Here in Miami we talk *en español* and in English. We talk in Spanglish too, and that's how my music is: I add all the elements that have inspired me and that make me who I am. But don't get it twisted: I don't sit down and say, now I will write a Spanish lyric. No, I let it happen naturally. My songs talk about my life, like when the Latino parents of my ex-girlfriend didn't want her to date me because of my [darker] skin color. So I rap about what I know, the only way I know how.

At around the same time, other South Florida–based artists, such as Sito Oner Rock, Don V.A., and the Sofla Kings, began to hone in on what would soon be known as the Miami crunkiao sound. Miami born and Cuban American, Sito Oner Rock (figure 2), a.k.a. Benhur Barrero II, was a Latin hip-hop artist who started to garner local attention for his ability to mix hip-hop with Latin styles. "I always loved hip-hop and, like many of my school friends, thought that Latin music was something for the older Cuban-born generation," confesses the baby-faced Sito. He recalls from his home music studio in the south Florida neighborhood of Hollywood:

It wasn't until I was twelve years old and I was at a full moon beach party in Miami Beach that I understood the impact of the *tambores*. Back then, a lot of Cuban families would go to Miami Beach to gather around, have a few beers, and play the tambores. I remember my uncle was playing the congas, and everybody knew the words to the songs—the music was real. And I felt left out because I didn't know the lyrics but I knew it was some hometown island shit that had good energy. I learned then that this music was in my blood. From then on I knew that I needed to find a way to connect my Latino side with my hip-hop.

Being part of a musical family helped Sito to recognize the many Afro-Caribbean influences existing within hip-hop music. "I would listen to Africa Bambaataa and I could hear the use of clave and the use of bongos," says Sito. "And I would notice that they were really not playing it in [the] right key. I mean, my father would play the congas a lot better than that. At first I thought it was just a Hispanic thing, but as I got older I discovered that those sounds were part of Africa too. So that's when I thought, oh shit, this is universal, and there's no rules." Yet for all the Latin influences that permeated hip-hop music, there was a lack of acceptance for Latino rappers. As Sito was soon to find out, the local scene did not support or didn't know what to do about Latinos and their Spanglish lyrics. "When I started rapping in Spanglish I thought that people would readily accept my rhymes," admits Sito. "But the thing was, that for a lot people at that time hip-hop was something that belonged only to African Americans and should only be done in English. So yes, it was a struggle when I started to rap in Spanish and creating my own thing but I had to be true to myself. Who said that you only could rap in English?" Surprisingly, a bulk of the resistance or aversion to the Spanish lyrics in hip-hop was coming from Miami's very own Latino community. For Shulika Alonzo, a twenty-seven-year-old Miami-born Dominican Puerto Rican who attended South West Miami Senior High and who is now a registered nurse, "Spanish music" was something for an older generation to listen to: "Around 1998 when I attended high school, Spanish music was not heard a lot." According to Alonzo, the music that most teenagers were listening to in Miami was hip-hop and alternative rock. Mainstream favorites such as the Smashing Pumpkins and Tupac Shakur were among the artists popular among Latino kids.

At that point, reggaetón had not made a significant impact in Miami. In those days the music came to Miami as an import from Puerto Rico or the Dominican Republic, as Alonzo recalls: "The first time that I heard reggaetón

2. Sito Oner Rock. Photo by Time-Shift Studios.

was back in 1998 when I was eighteen years old. My cousin Tito brought it from Puerto Rico and it was the funniest thing. I couldn't believe that people were rapping in Spanish. It sounded funny to me. I guess because of the lack of exposure, it was foreign to my ears; it was comical."

Interestingly, that would be a common reaction among U.S.-born Latinos living in Miami. The main criticism aimed at all forms of Latin hip-hop was that it was somehow inauthentic and inferior because hip-hop should only be sung in the English language. Miami teenagers such as Shulika, saw hip-hop as an African American genre having little to do with Latino culture. "For me, hip-hop—and I could be wrong about this—is African American music," declares Shulika, a long time hip-hop fan. "The first Latinos that I remember doing hip-hop were Cypress Hill, but they weren't cheesy like reggaetón music."

REGGAETÓN HITS THE TOWN

Sito's promotions manager, David "Suppa" Duperón was one of the kids who emigrated from Puerto Rico to Miami, bringing his taste for reggaetón along with him. His experience in adjusting to his new life reveals some of the prejudices that are sometimes present within Latino communities. "It was kind of crazy; it was like a culture shock to me," explains Suppa about his new life in Miami's HML High School. "When I got to my school in 2000, I saw a lot of racism and the funny thing was that it came from other Latino kids. The Miami-born kids would call those who didn't speak English the *reffs*, as in refugees. I had the advantage that I knew English but it surprised me to learn that there would be divisions within people of the same background." Not only did the students at HML High School in Miami make fun of their non-English-speaking counterparts; they also shared a certain distaste for Latin music. In turn students like Suppa were responsible for bringing reggaetón to the attention of the English-dominant kids. "They didn't know what reggaetón was, but I did," says Suppa. "Being born in Puerto Rico I saw it all happen and when I came to my school I had my mixtapes and I remember that some people didn't like it, so yeah all that they would listen to was all hip-hop all the time."

The number of mixtapes coming from Puerto Rico continued to increase, and by 2002 reggaetón was gaining wider acceptance among the Miami Latino youth. "Back then in 2000, I had to explain to a lot people what reggaetón was all about," recalls Sandra Chalco, a Miami Dade Community College student and a reggaetón music fan. "Most people knew who Vico C was and they knew about El General, but that was it. Reggaetón was really underground and you only heard a little bit of it on the radio. Then Tego Calderón came out with *El Abayarde*, and all of a sudden the dembow was everywhere." The rising popularity of reggaetón acts such as Tego Calderón and Daddy Yankee came at a time when the stylized Latin pop of artists such as Alejandro Sanz and Enrique Iglesias was starting to wane. "Reggaetón, for me, it was a breath of fresh air," continues Sandra. "I was born and raised in Peru, so I didn't get a lot of the references that the reggaetón artists rapped about, like when Tego says *guasa guasa* (liar, liar) or Lito y Polaco talk about *yenga yenga*, I don't know what that means. But I still liked it because it seemed real, unlike the Spanish pop playing nonstop on the radio." Language may have played a large role in reggaetón's impact and rapid rise to popularity among the Miami public. Many listeners cite Spanish as a key factor for their love of reggaetón. "What did it for me and for a lot of my friends was the *español*," asserts Sandra. "It was something that we could call our own. Guys like Tego made it clear that you could sound cool rapping in Spanish. It didn't have to be 'wack.' Some of the reggaetón artists can actually rap better than a lot the English-speaking rappers out there. Then Pitbull came and started to rap in Spanglish, and we could all relate to him because that's the way we spoke."

Having noticed the rise of reggaetón, Miami artists such as Plátano started to incorporate dembow beats into their sets. For Plátano it seemed like a natural transition. "By late 2001 I had made the move from party host to rapper," Plátano reveals. "I do some songs in the style of reggaetón because I see it all as part of the same movement, which is *una cosa latina* [a Latino thing]. But reggaetón is something that comes from Puerto Rico. And I didn't want to just imitate what guys like Tego and Yankee were doing. I wanted to come up with my own stuff." In turn, the sound of Miami's crunkiao music would borrow heavily from the Miami bass, or booty music, made popular over a decade earlier by such artists as 2 Live Crew and Boys from the Bottom. The booty sound never completely faded from the Miami soundscape: local booty music followers such as Power 96 DJ Laz and the Latin fusion revivalist DJ Le Spam kept the music alive in the nightclubs, while the former 2 Live Crew producer and frontman, Luke Campbell, continued to run his independent record label, Luke Records, with some success.

Another Miami-based style that crunkiao artists borrow from, lifting memorable melodies for crunked-up beats, is "freestyle music." Sometimes known as Latin freestyle, the genre had strong roots in Miami during its '80s heyday, when artists such as Stevie B recorded keyboard-driven pop hits marked by nods to Latin music. Saul Alvarez, a veteran music producer and music studio owner, worked as a producer for freestyle pioneer Stevie B and ties the freestyle movement to the mixing of pop and Latin styles: "In the beginning it was called *Latin Style*," explains Saul from his Miami record studios.

> It was really born in New York and it had the R&B, plus a lot of tropical influences, like clave and *tumbao*. Freestyle would sample records from Tito Puente and Pérez Prado. When I came to Miami [in 1987], I loved it because it was so open to new ideas. At the time Miami freestyle had very marked Latin influences. I was working on Stevie B's 'Party Your Body' song and we added Latin elements to the mix like the horn arrangements, with deep bass sounds, which later became known as the Roland system 808s and 909s. It was something that came natural, it was born in me.[2]

Miami's urban music had always been characterized in one way or another by its Latin influences. For many crunkiao artists, Latin elements seem to emerge naturally in their music, an expression of their musical heritage. When asked about the tropical influences in songs such as "Como Duele," Plátano professes that the outcome was unconscious. "I don't set out to write a song that will have a certain style. It just happens that I grew up in the Dominican Republic with bachata and merengue, so my songs will always have some of that flavor. It's who I am." Other artists, Sito, for example, prefer to add subtle hints of Latin rhythms to their music. "My base for most of my music is hip-hop," he says. "When I add Latin elements to a song, like tumbao or clave, I make sure that they don't take over the hip-hop beats." According to Alvarez, the hip-hop community eventually absorbed the Latin influences that infused the freestyle movement. Considering that Miami bass was a major influence for Atlanta hip-hop/crunk, things had come full circle. "Crunk from Atlanta is basically the new Miami bass: the rhythms and patterns are similar, only the tempo has changed. Crunk is a lot slower," says Alvarez. "What happened with Pitbull was that he got an opportunity to sign with something that was similar to the sound here in Miami," he explains, referring to Pitbull's collaborations with Atlanta crunk luminary Lil' John.[3]

Pitbull would similarly profit from his collaboration with reggaetón artists. Following the initial round of success of his hit song "Gasolina," Daddy Yankee proceeded to do a remix of the song that featured Pitbull rapping in Spanish. The remix would prove successful in bringing attention to the Miami Latin hip-hop movement. The publicist Paulina Blanco works for Nevarez PR, the Miami-based agency responsible for Daddy Yankee's public relations in the United States. Blanco considers Pitbull's collaboration on the "Gasolina" remix as vital in bringing the Miami movement into the international spotlight. "People liked what Pitbull did on that remix, and I believe that a lot of people recognized that Pitbull's slang and beat were unique to Miami," states Blanco. Moreover, Pitbull's strategy is not unique; crunkiao artist Sito has also benefited from allying himself to the reggaetón movement's success. Recently Sito was invited to host the segment *Estrellas del Reggaetón* on the Univision television show *Sábado Gigante*. "They [the producers] needed someone who could rap in English and Spanish," explains Sito. "I consider myself a hip-hop artist, but reggaetón has helped me to establish a name for myself. I also did a show in California in front of 30,000 fans and that was thanks to Don Omar, who was the headlining act."

CRUNKIAO AND REGGAETÓN IN THE LATIN MUSIC PLAYGROUND

Yet for many in the Miami crunkiao/Latin hip-hop movement, the overwhelming success of reggaetón has produced some conflicts. Publicist Diana López is the founder of Be Heard Media, a PR agency that has helped many young Miami urban artists to participate in exclusive invitation-only media events. According to López, the success of reggaetón has caused some polarization within the Latino musical community. "The salsa and merengue bands are not getting the top billing anymore," explains López. "The reggaetoneros are demanding and getting top dollar for their performances, so in the end there's less money to go around. Now when you go to a Latino festival, it's mostly reggaetón and that is hurting the other musicians. The Miami urban acts have benefited because they have managed to open shows for the reggaetón headliners, but at the end of the day they are all competing for limited funds and money."

Living in a center for Latin culture in the United States also presents unique problems for local acts, as Miami artists face unrelenting international competition in a cutthroat media environment. "You have to understand that all the established Latino artists from around the world come to Miami to launch their records," adds López. "So Miami rappers like Plátano have to compete directly against the entire Latin music industry. And a lot of times the radio stations won't play their records the way they should. Miami artists in general have a hard time breaking into this city because the media is geared towards the international market and what people want now is the reggaetón." Dealing with indifferent local media has thus become a reality for most of the artists in the crunkiao movement.

Melanie Byron, editor in chief for *Source Latino* magazine and the former host of the Latin urban TV program *The Roof*, acknowledges that Miami's independent urban acts face strong competition from international artists. "Miami is the central place for all Latin media in the U.S.," she explains.

> All the Latin record labels and TV stations have their headquarters here, and the media tends to give special attention to the Latino events that take place in the city. When Daddy Yankee performed at the American Airlines Arena in downtown, he got all the media in the city to cover that event. On the other hand, when the Black Eyed Peas came down that same month, they hardly got any press coverage at all. The entertainment press in this city is all about Latino culture; that's why all the acts from Latin America and Spain come to Miami first, before going anywhere else in the U.S. and the local artists sometimes do get lost in the shuffle.

In the past, Byron has encouraged Miami's independent Latin hip-hop artists to develop a professional promotions team and to dedicate more attention to their publicity. "Miami artists like Sito are great," acknowledges Byron, "but they need to understand that in the same way that there's only one Eminem, there can only be one Pitbull. The problem is that as reggaetón, and to a lesser extent Latin hip-hop, become more popular, the copycats and lesser acts jump on the bandwagon and co-opt the movements. This means that good artists like Sito have to find a way to promote themselves and get themselves heard."

In Miami's competitive atmosphere, successful Latino rappers such as Pitbull are the exception; more often than not, local rappers struggle to compete with the celebrities that stay in the city. For Plátano, the visiting celebrities become yet another obstacle to overcome. "A lot of celebrities come to Miami to promote their music and even to record their music," says Plátano. "But most of them work in a closed environment, where they bring their own producers and collaborators. From my experience, they never invite local artists to team up in their projects, and that's just the way it is. Miami is like their playground."

Another source of friction for some in the Latin hip-hop community is what they believe to be reggaetón's dominance over the Latin airwaves. As a DJ for New York's WCAA La Kalle 105.9 radio station, DJ Kazzanova observes that radio's preference for reggaetón is only a natural reflection of the genre's strong sales. "The only music that's selling right now is reggaetón," says Kazzanova. "Latin hip-hop will keep on growing and evolving, but right know the main focus will stay on reggaetón. What people like Daddy Yankee and Tego did is that they gave Latino kids a role model to call their own. Before we wanted to be like Jay-Z; now we want to be like Tego." Still, artists such as Sito and Plátano remain united in their love for the reggaetón movement, conscious of the fact that reggaetón has opened doors for their own music. While hip-hop heavyweights like Jay-Z would not likely ask Sito to open a show for him, for instance, reggaetón stars like Tego will happily provide Sito and Plátano with a slot at his concerts.

Indeed, for most of the Latino artists that make up the crunkiao movement the boundaries between reggaetón and crunkiao are mainly superficial in nature. Sito and Plátano, for instance, feel a sense of unity, and opportunity, that transcends the lines between Latin urban movements. "The reggaetón that we listen to in the radio today comes from Puerto Rico, and it really belongs to the Boricuas that are making it," asserts Plátano. "We here in Miami are doing our own thing, but at the end of the day we are all Latinos and there's really no difference. The reggaetoneros' success is helping us, and in turn our successes will help other Latinos. When I go to the clubs they play both reggaetón and Latin hip-hop. It really doesn't matter to me; it's all coming from the same place."

"When I first came to Miami there was no music scene for Latino hip-hop," Plátano continues. "Now when you go out to any party the DJ will play music by Miami Latin hip-hop artists, and everyone puts their 305 signs up in the air."

NOTES

This essay draws from the following sources: Tego Calderón, interview by author, Miami, September 12, 2006; Lisa M., interview by author, August 7, 2006; Plátano, interview by author, Miami, May 6, 2006; Isai González (Jibba Jamz), interview by author, Miami, June 22, 2006; Diana López, interview by author, Miami, May 15, 2006; Saul Alvarez, interview by author, Miami, May 14, 2006; May 14, 2006; Sito Oner Rock and David Duperón, interview by author, Miami, May 6, 2006; Melanie Byron, interview by author, Miami, June 5, 2006; Shulika Alonzo, interview by author, Miami, June 15, 2006; Jean Rodríguez, interview by author, Miami, May 6, 2006; DJ Kazzanova, interview by author, Miami, June 17, 2006. Translations of Spanish-language quotations are my own.

1. U.S. Census Bureau, 2000. See, e.g., http://quickfacts.census.gov/qfd/states/12/1245000.html, and http://quickfacts.census.gov/qfd/states/36/3651000.html (accessed July 10, 2007).

2. The 808 and 909 to which Alvarez refers are drum machines that became popular in the mid-1980s among producers looking for resonant kick drums. Both the Roland TR-808 and TR-909 became closely identified with the Miami bass and Latin freestyle sound, and their sonic footprint lives on in the booming drums of Atlanta crunk.

3. It is worth noting as well, especially in the context of Miami's pan-Caribbean soundscape, that Pitbull's career received a significant boost when his track "Culo" found its way into urban radio playlists across the country. Produced by Lil' Jon, who added 808 drums to a contemporary dancehall reggae riddim, the *Coolie Dance* (produced by Cordel "Scatta" Burrell), the track featured Pitbull rapping in Spanish and English, propelling his choruses with the melody from Jamaican dancehall artist Mr. Vegas's "Pull Up" (also recorded on the *Coolie Dance* and a minor hit in its own right at the time).

PART IV

VISUALIZING REGGAETON

Visualizing Reggaeton

Editors' Notes

Reggaeton may be a musical style first and foremost, but it circulates and resonates via various visual texts as well, from the mix of high fashion and street wear in artists' and audiences' sartorial styles, to the gestures, postures, and movements depicted in videos and enacted from the club to the *calle*. Reading reggaeton visually offers another set of lenses through which to view the genre's articulations of race, nation, class, and gender. Featuring images that both depict and critique reggaeton's visual dimensions, the following section offers a number of interesting angles from which to view this vibrant, complex cultural phenomenon.

First are three provocative images from Miguel Luciano. Two of them, as well as the photograph gracing the cover of this book, come from a series called *Pure Plantainum*. For the project, Luciano took an actual green plantain and plated it with platinum, the precious metal associated with massive record sales and the "bling-bling" (or *blin-blineo*, as reggaeton translates hip-hop slang) of shiny jewelry. *Pure Plantainum* suggests some poignant readings of reggaeton style by juxtaposing charged cultural symbols, bringing the plantain's evocation of field labor, racial and class stigmas, and national and/or Caribbean pride together with the contemporary connotations of platinum as a glorification of conspicuous consumption. Luciano both estranges this object, making it a museum piece, and puts it into the familiar and fitting setting of the display window at Harlem's King of Platinum jewelry store on 125th Street. Critical and empathetic, cartoonish and complex, the images seem to shine a funhouse mirror back at reggaeton. Similarly, the third image shown here comes from Luciano's *Filiberto Ojeda Uptowns—Machetero Air Force Ones* project, which also combines, painfully and playfully, charged symbols of colonialism and materialism in order to pose vexing questions about cultural identity and resistance in the reggaeton era. Again, Luciano juxtaposes two starkly different cultural symbols: on the one hand, Filiberto Ojeda, an activist for independence sometimes referred to as "the Puerto Rican Che Guevara"; and on the other, Nike sneakers—particularly, the Air Force One model, a central, coveted consumer item in the urban fashion aesthetics of reggaeton and hip-hop. About the project Luciano reflects, "A pair of Nike sneakers become an unlikely vehicle of veneration for the fallen leader that both complicate and question how nationalism and resistance are embodied within today's colonial consumerist society. Nevertheless, they engage alternative strategies towards reconstructing symbols of resistance from the objects of material desire, while questioning the commodification of Revolution."[1]

Next we have a series of stills by Carolina Caycedo. Part of a larger project called *Gran Perretón*, the images mix documentary and art, taken during a *perreo* marathon held in Rincón, Puerto Rico, at Don Raul's Bar. The images not only illustrate some typical *perreo* poses, with all the attendant issues they raise about gender and power relations; they also offer a perspective on the perreo that might be consistent with, as Caycedo argues, "a new feminism, where women take advantage of their sexual attraction, beauty and body language to achieve their goals."[2] Given the more reactionary responses the dance has elicited, particularly in Puerto Rico and across Latin America, this is a reading worth taking into consideration. Caycedo's images are additionally provocative in their "low-fi," washed-out quality, their monochrome graininess suggesting night-goggle voyeurism and the discomfiting allure of amateur porn.

Our visual readings are rounded out by several photographs by Kacho López that document Tego Calderón's 2006 visit to Sierra Leone during the filming of the vh1 documentary *Bling'd: Blood, Diamonds, and Hip-Hop*—a chilling exposé of the connections between the diamond industry, war, poverty, human rights violations, and hip-hop's diamond fetishism.[3] The selection of Tego Calderón along with Raekwon and Paul Wall as the three artists featured in the documentary exemplifies the ways in which reggaeton styles and fashion are intricately connected to hip-hop's; it is also a nod to the importance of Latinos and Latin Americans as consumers and producers of hip-hop music and fashion. Upon his return to Puerto Rico, Calderón described his experiences in Africa as pivotal in his renewed commitment to combating social injustice; renouncing reggaeton's bling aesthetics was part of that commitment. The first photo of this series captures Calderón's interactions with local children. The next one is a testament to the atrocious working conditions of diamond miners, who are paid not in wages but with food—unless they find one of those ever elusive and highly coveted pieces of rock. The third photo was taken during one of the most touching sequences in the documentary, when the artists visit a camp for amputees. The man shown here with his prosthetic hands clasped behind his back explains and embodies in the documentary the widespread practice of torture and mutilations during Sierra Leone's civil war, which was driven by the diamond trade. The last photo in this series captures Calderón's out-of-focus profile, as the camera focuses on the hip-hop artist and fellow traveler Paul Wall; seated between the two artists is the author and Sierra Leonean former child soldier, Ishmael Beah.[4]

NOTES

1. Artist's statement. Miguel Luciano, *Filiberto Ojeda Uptowns—Machetero Air Force Ones* (2007).

2. Artist's statement. Carolina Caycedo, *Gran Perretón* (2004).

3. *Bling'd: Blood, Diamonds, and Hip Hop*, film recording directed by Raquel Cepeda (Article 19 Films and Djali Rancher Productions, 2007).

4. Ishmael Beah, *A Long Way Gone: Memoirs of a Boy Soldier* (New York: Farrar, Straus, and Giroux, 2007).

Miguel Luciano

1. *Pure Plantainum at King of Platinum, 125th Street*, Miguel Luciano (2006).

2. *Pure Plantainum*, Miguel Luciano (2006).

3. *Filiberto Ojeda Uptowns—Machetero Air Force Ones*, Miguel Luciano (2007).

Carolina Caycedo

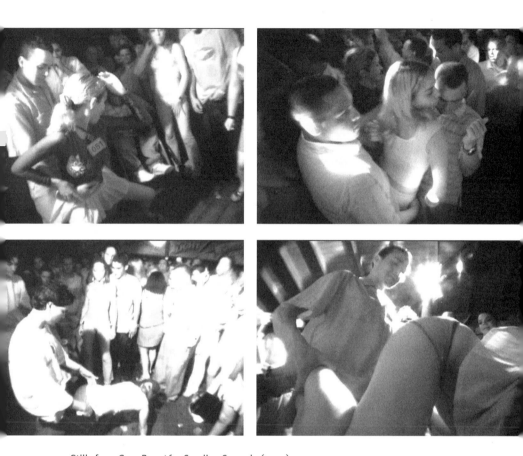

1–4. Stills from *Gran Perretón*, Carolina Caycedo (2004).

Kacho López

1. Tego Calderón and children, Sierra Leone. Photo by Kacho López (2006).

2. Diamond miners at work, Sierra Leone. Photo by Kacho López (2006).

3. Man with prosthetic hands, living testimony of a diamond trade driven civil war, Sierra Leone. Photo by Kacho López (2006).

4. From left to right: hip-hop artist Paul Wall, author Ishmael Beah, and Tego Calderón. Photo by Kacho López (2006).

PART V
GENDERING
REGGAETON

(W)rapped in Foil

Glory at Twelve Words a Minute

The spoken word is a bodily act at the same time that it forms a certain synecdoche of the body. The vocalizing larynx and mouth become part of the body that stages the drama of the whole; what the body gives and receives is not a touch, but the psychic contours of a bodily exchange, a psychic contour that engages the body that it represents.
—Judith Butler, *Undoing Gender*

ERASE YOURSELF: GLORY'S FEAT

For more than a decade, the reggaeton singer Glory has scripted herself into the aural canon of popular music by relentlessly, sultrily ohh-ing and ahh-ing reggaeton style as the kitten that would arouse the cats. In a preternatural whispery tone, Glory's vocals would become the go-to parts of superstars Daddy Yankee's and Don Omar's lyrics before either of them launched his first U.S. tour or sold a single disc in Japan. Ever the throaty object of desire, Glory was and is recognizable as the voice that foiled the dons and the dads record after hit record, yet retained her relative anonymity with a prepackaged, utilitarian, studied role that served the star singers' purposes—and the audiences' fantasies—as the woman the men loved to hear purring.

But belting one-line choruses as the male lead singer's foil also meant wrapping herself in that role, repeated and recast to fulfill the career demands of her more famous counterparts. Glory's glorious tenure as reggaeton's reigning underground performance queen had been predicated upon the auditory gendering of other people's songs. To extricate herself from the airtight persona of her twelve-year chorus career, Glory scripted a solo move with a 2005 album, *Glou*, that rearticulates gender and sexuality—her two chorus mainstays—as selling points, and even had one of its songs—"La Popola"— banned in the Dominican Republic on grounds of obscenity. But why has the golden chorus girl failed to unleash the magic glow and flow that have her recognized as the "Suelta como gabete" or "Dame más gasolina" sex-it-for-the-male-star "envoicement" of a woman? Why has she been outshined by Ivy Queen's shadow?

Those two particular choruses (for Don Omar's 2003 song "Dale, Don, Dale" and Daddy Yankee's 2004 breakout hit "Gasolina") catapulted Glory to the front of the cameras and the center of public notoriety, if only for a brief time, as a musical curiosity in search of a career. In the history of reggaeton in Puerto Rico, Glory stands as a paradigmatic case that reflects and generates the slowly evolving internal struggle of that musical genre, while at the same time attempting to reposition the boundaries established for female performers in the perceptual dynamics of Puerto Rican reggaeton.

The two well-placed lines (after many others without the same international commercial penetration) define and propel a career that had been developed in the pertinent obscurity of the call-and-response dynamics of reggaeton. Glory's oral acquiescence—of course—was the response to the call, in the strict biological "bow-coo" mating behavior of mate-ready singing birds. Glory's lines in chorus performances woven into the songs are the essential, yet parenthetical, asides to the male singer's "adjectivation"/objectification of women. On Don Omar's "Dale, Don, Dale," Glory succinctly proclaims her total surrender to the sexual shenanigans that the night may bring.

> Don Omar: *Me dicen, mami, que esta noche tú estás al garete*
> Glory: *(Dale, papi, que estoy suelta como gabete)*
> Don Omar: They tell me, baby, that tonight you are on the loose
> Glory: (C'mon, papi, I'm loose as a shoestring)

And on Daddy Yankee's "Gasolina", Glory simply asks for it:

> Daddy Yankee: *Le gusta la gasolina*
> Glory: *(Dame más gasolina)*
> Daddy Yankee: She likes gasoline
> Glory: (Gimme more gasoline)

So her lyrical career went—answering, and yielding, to men, within the narrow parameters of patriarchal condescension.[1] Glory's featured performances, and the standard abbreviated credits they garnered in male performers' recordings ("featuring Glory," or more commonly "feat. Glory"), had the twofold consequence of securing for her a place in reggaeton's tight family and, most of all, of *keeping her in her place.*

For the observer, Glory still is a cluster of convenient fictions who has not been able to live up to her name. Glorimar Montalvo Castro might well be the woman who "single-voicedly" provided the glue to a musical movement that at the outset was comprised of disparate parts. Born to lower-middle-class parents in Santurce, Puerto Rico, Glory is many things—a dancer, a singer, a college-educated health technician who once served as Don Omar's professor of medical technology at a technical college, a master's degree graduate from the University of Puerto Rico, and an avid follower of the musical scene. In the mid-1990s, Glory—encouraged and marshaled by her singer friends— undertook the formidable task of becoming the communal *It* voice, the sound that would homogenize the feminine in a hypermasculine world. Her voice, perfectly suited to the foxy and groany repetitive beat of the songs, framed the contrapuntal gender banters that defined the genre. As Glory the chorus girl, her persona perfectly fit the structures and strictures of the nascent under-ground reggaeton scene of the 1990s, perpetuating the familiar choruses, the customized-for-memory lines that translated songs into hits.

Sex, of course, was—and is—reggaeton's organizing register. And that regis-ter that reached its international climax with "Gasolina" and "Dale, Don, Dale" had in the mid-1990s the added bonus of a freedom that has since been curtailed—the shock of the new, the beat that was good, the curse words that flowed, the allure of the low, and the as-of-then freshness of a musical genre with untapped commercial possibilities. Glory's "central casting role" in the 1990s reggaeton revolution was to solidify the subservient female character, in acknowledged complicity with the genre's coherent—if flawed—gender front.

If, as Pierre Bourdieu states, "the denial of lower, coarse, vulgar, venal, servile—in a word, natural—enjoyment, which constitutes the sacred sphere of culture, implies an affirmation of the superiority of those who can be satisfied with the sublimated, refined, disinterested, gratuitous, distinguished pleasures forever closed to the profane," the aesthetics of reggaeton at first value would squarely be inscribed in the "lower, coarse, vulgar, venal" enjoyment rejected by many, an acoustic recasting of the Benjamin-Adorno debates on the "high versus low" dichotomy, on the banality of cultural creations.[2] Reggaeton's repertoire of cultural excesses—the violence it reflected or referred to, the real (and feigned) rivalries among performers, its homosociality and its hyper-sexuality—rearranged the collective Puerto Rican ear as well as the eye. If the natural comparative subjects for *reggaetoneros* were the male salsa singers of the 1960s and 1970s (Ismael Rivera, Héctor Lavoe)—whose macho posturing and edgy performances were inherited and expanded on—the main performative, aural, and visual differences between these two groups is the reggaetoneros' need for the constant representation of these excesses. The recording studio is where gender relations are established and regulated. For reggaeton performers, the structural dynamics of their act is predicated upon a visible subject, object, or both, in video and concert performances—in this case, a woman on the side. Not the dancing belle or the posing kind, but a veritable yet controllable counterpoint, a sonic intrusion of sorts that would engage the male singers' iterations of gender. Thus the Recording Reggaeton Woman was conceived, not as an afterthought, although clearly *thought after the fact.*

Moreover, the Recording Reggaeton Woman—as a creature of industry and commerce and its attendant titillations—was engineered in the sound studios as a flesh-made machine, a turn-of-the-century automated "yes-girl," resembling (in her condition of muted threat and axis of control and intimidation) the robotic woman of Fritz Lang's *Metropolis*, which Andreas Huyssen describes as a projection of both fear and desire.[3] The vamp and the machine in one—the gendered *Maschinenmensch*—also provided an opportunity to view mass culture as a woman gazed at and shaped constantly. As a technomusical hybrid construct, reggaeton proposes no frontal assault to gender conventions. Reggaetoneros, experts in repetition, created a generic woman that, in essence, could always be invisible and that in most reggaeton lyrics appears as a woman satisfied—as a verbal robot.

The robotics of "verbality" dissipates the perceived freedom of reggaeton's verbally aggressive woman by subsuming her into a constructed niche. If the existence of a let-it-all-out voice in the middle of a male-centered world promises a theoretical female guerilla-in-the-midst scenario, the male musical battlefield only yields lyrics that portray the female Recording Reggaeton Woman as a complicit comrade in arms in the *male* singers' struggle for market domination.

The generic reggaeton woman was paid to simulate her sensual bliss through her chorus singing, even if enjoying that simulation. Strategically, the built-in female response in reggaeton's choruses operates against the mythic femme fatale's freedom of action, thus assuring that the female intervention would not run counter to the songs' implicit goal of male sexual pleasure. Rather, the "dame más gasolina" and "suelta como gabete" responses are installed as anti-castrating devices, as vocalizations of perennial arousal.

Glory's choruses spelled satisfaction, and the magic of her spell was limited to guaranteeing that the reggaeton woman always could get it—that she could not *not get* satisfaction. The monotonous, monothematic iterations of a woman in lust served a threefold purpose in the underground reggaeton of the 1990s: to establish a formula that would be both recognizable and memorable; to conjure female availability; to bring listeners in. But the formula's spell brought listeners in to the *male* singers who gained top billing, while relegating the female choruses (sometimes only twelve or sixteen words per minute) to the sexy and passively aggressive vamp mode, with a perpetual willingness to accommodate to others. Career-wise, Glory's role as "the featured woman" in reggaeton recordings may have led to a financially lucrative dead-end street, without progression, a willing hostage to her collaborations. And indeed, she came close to that: as a result of her decade-long parenthetical "featuring," chorus-girl wannabes still turn to Glory for advice on how to succeed in the reggaeton business without really leaving the "Featuring [insert your name here]" formula.

In lending her voice to convey the psychic contours of the female reggaeton body, Glory was attributed the perceived characteristics of that verbal robot, and the "coarse, vulgar, servile" imagined disposition of reggaeton's hidden woman. When she responded with sexy defiance to Ranking Stone's taunts in "Castigo" ("Así que tira pa' lante / Que pa' luego es tarde" [So take action now / Later, it may be too late]) or with unabashed sexual comeuppances in Magnate and Valentino's "Fiera Callada" (Silent Beast), it was Glory who was "staging the drama," "engaging the body" that she represented by providing the transactional crux between the genders in song. In "Fiera Callada" Glory's *feat* is a confession of her silent desires—"la fiera callada pero no domada"— silent but never tamed.[4]

> Ya llegó tu fiera convertida en salvaje
> Quiero que en silencio me demuestres tu coraje
> Quiero que en la esquina de la cama me acorrales
> No hagas que te hale, y ven pégate suave
> y dale que llegó tu fiera, Glou
> La gata gángster, la bandolera
> La que consigue lo que quiere
> Cuando viene en ganas
> La que anoche junto a ti fue fiera callada

> Here is your beast gone wild
> I want you to show me your strength in silence
> I want you to corner me on the edge of the bed
> Don't make me get you, get close to me slowly
> C'mon, your wild one's here, Glou

The Gangster Kitten, the outlaw
The one who gets what she wants
Whenever she feels like it
The one who last night with you was fierce and silent

Negotiating the terrain of reggaeton's lyrics, awash with thugs and guns and sex and discos, Glory's first solo song—"Duro, Duro," included in DJ Anqueira's release *Innovando*—yielded no expressive truths, but rather a mirror image of the reggaeton men's wish list. In essence, her first solo song was nothing more than an exact tracing of the choruses she had sung and would later sing, complete with the "hurt me badly pose" and the call for unbridled sexuality.[5]

Y ahora las gatitas que se pongan sueltas
que bailen las casadas, que bailen las solteras
Agárrate un gato, hazlo tu pareja
Y cógelo, apriétalo, píllalo en la discoteca
Y dile . . .
Duro, duro Cheka bien duro
Duro, duro, duro
Papi, dame bien duro

And now kittens let's all get loose
Let the married ones dance, let the single ones dance
Get yourself a cat, make him your mate
and grab him, squeeze him, pin him down in the discothèque
And tell him . . .
Hard hard Cheka hard hard
Hard hard hard
Papi, give it to me really hard

In short, it signaled Glory-the-gendered-Maschinenmensch's graduation to another plane, the vocal robot's coming of age. It was, however, a lateral move: she now was one of the boys and wanted just what the boys wanted, individual fame included.

Since 2005, Glory's reconfiguration tactic has been relentless: attempting to obscure the transparency of her journeywoman years and her voluntary immersion in the rudimentary sexual politics of reggaeton. The slowly evolving public relations machine surrounding Glory in 2005 touted the recognizability of her voice and the relative anonymity of her countenance as a selling point for a market makeover. Her self-inflicted brand of fame—her robotic no-name, no-face, *invisible* success—was a stumbling block that could very well do away with her career mobility plans, and her range of possibilities. What's an invisible girl to do? Putting the body in motion, in ever-present display, seemed to be the answer. Glory was giving face now as a unity of body and voice, and recognizing the intricacies of a market that moves as rapidly as ever, instead of impersonating the sexually subservient role that her nickname La Gata Gángster so aptly describes. After a dozen years in the shadows, a solo album seemed to be the gateway to the recognition denied. But with the album, a new Glory surfaced, with more body than voice in mind, in an artistic breakout that would prove to be a fragile renaissance.

"My body is a tool of my trade" was Glory's new take on her solo effort, ironically acknowledging how obscuring the female as a face for so long can prove a hindrance when the time comes to attempt a career move and aim for the spotlight.[6] The problem is not how to leave a voice behind, but how to prime the most recognizable female voice in reggaeton for travel down the solo road. How to leave *yourself* behind. The perceived problem with Glory has been the quiet longevity of her particular brand of success. As an educated, strong woman she has been able to maneuver and traverse the male-dominated world of reggaeton, and negotiate her appearances in recordings by reggaeton's Who's Who—Eddie Dee, Yankee, Omar, Hector and Tito, and Magnate and Valentino. But her sporadic press coverage in Puerto Rico up to 2004 had more to do with the music men who made her career possible than with the woman who had made possible *their* careers as their nondescript foil.

When the chorus girl got the press to look her way, she was always surrounded by her reggaeton men or catering to their needs. In a 2004 interview, she talked about her leg accident—her left knee that was injured while visiting Don Omar, who was himself bedridden after suffering a motorcycle accident—and commented on the vital friendships and collaborations with the reggaeton men that nurtured her "career" with an endless gratitude that pays back.[7] In other instances, Glory described herself as "the woman in the middle," a mediator trying to help her two *main men*—Daddy Yankee and Don Omar—resume their fractured relationship after their much-publicized falling out.[8] They were the company she kept: the public men in Glory's life had been her colleagues. Never publicly attached to any partner, Glory also lacked the private, sometimes messy intimate imbroglios that adorn and spice up performers' media-based images, the dalliances and disasters that pay dividends and make them sellable. Thus, the sexy chorus voice was devoid of entourage, bodyguards, rumors virtuous or vicious; it was recorded musically yet without a verbal record of her private side, such as Ivy Queen's media-grabbing head-lines of her longstanding couplehood and, later, split from fellow reggaeton singer/producer and collaborator Gran Omar. Going it alone, Glory was coupled in the media with her chorus providers, with her reggaeton "posse," without a trace of a personal life, and without a personal *stance*, as if delaying every decision, public and private, waiting.

Glory's protracted entrance to the big leagues, after years of waiting for her breakthrough, would test if she could make it as a front-and-center woman, or if a front man was needed to keep her behind. In the process, she would rearticulate the verbal and visual cues necessary to enact her wishes, and confront individual and nationalist aesthetics in her attempts to leave behind her back-up years and establish herself as a front woman in a musical world so attuned (visually and lyrically) to the female backside. Ever a "throat for hire," her first solo offering, *Glou*, offered a newfound Glory, glowing out of the dark—shyly and slyly—making a run for reggaeton's female reign.

DISPOSABLE MATCHES

> Between the voice for the ear and the stridulation that rises through the throat, the abyss—like that between ego and the "I" without a self—proves impassable. Common sense protests that they are indeed the same voice. It's just that it speaks from the outside, confounding the relinquishment of hearing in the naked experience of existence with an interior dialogue. In this dialogue the ego splits in two and can hear itself arguing for and against itself: voice against voice, in narcissistic reflection.
>
> —Jean François Lyotard, *Soundproof Room: Malraux's Anti-Aesthetics*

The magic of a voice's touch in reggaeton is not a requisite for stardom or market appeal. Voices do not carry the weight of sales or concert dates as do the rhythm and the lyrics of the songs that have positioned reggaeton as the most marketable Latin musical genre in the first decade of the century. The fact that the internationalization of reggaeton was spearheaded by a white, lower-class, handsome Puerto Rican male—Daddy Yankee—underscores the intricate idiosyncrasies of a genre that has defied and conquered ominous judgments, countless protests, morality campaigns, government-sponsored hearings, and parental concerns.

Gender and sexuality ruled not only the content, but also the production of the genre. Aural promiscuity stands out as the benchmark of reggaeton, in which collaboration is the name of the game. The coupling of solo performers' images and intentions serve up collaborative market dishes (for example, duets featuring Voltio and Calle 13; Eddie Dee and Daddy Yankee; Tego Calderón and Voltio; Don Omar and Tego Calderón; Daddy Yankee, Wisin and Yandel; Eddie Dee and Tego Calderón; R.K.M. Ken-Y and Daddy Yankee) that have proven their indispensability by developing, sustaining, and nurturing new acts.[9] However narcissistic and overtly ego driven, testosterone dissolves into artistic collaborations and produces its own intimate "Six Degrees of Kevin Bacon"–type musical game. Thus, the reggaeton industry was able to serve as a breeding ground for its own, providing talent scouts with scores of male performers that were willing to record one song in a CD compilation, then later perhaps acquiesce to more collaborations when—and if—their careers took off. The quintessential "Woman in the Shadows" was Glory. As *the* voice that repeats itself in many male singers' records, Glory's chorus lyrics provided the subtext of desire, the aural ligament of Puerto Rican reggaeton. Her career was a permanent collaboration in which she would stand out as a self-contained circuit of availability and lust, an enticement for male ears. She was rendered as a concept and disguised as a package in songs that offered male collective representations of gender.

The unpacking of an invisible musical mirage such as Glory started with the unexpected marriage of politics, comedy, and reggaeton in 2004. The "suelta como gabete" chorus of Don Omar's international hit song launched and sustained Glory's public career for a brief period. The singer's circuitous entrance into popular consciousness was triggered not by a musical colleague but by, of all possible unintended allies, a female comedian. Noris Joffre appropriated the catchy phrase for her impersonation of Puerto Rican governor Sila Calderón, who with two divorces and two romances in a three-year span aroused and provoked public imagination. The politician's life, the comedian's ingenuity, and the singer's three-word phrase merged rather seamlessly. Joffre parlayed the catchy sexual innuendo of the phrase to countless TV, stage (and even cruise ship) appearances, including a made-for-TV comedic soap opera. In her impersonation of Calderón, the "suelta como gabete" chorus became the centerpiece.

Dressed as the governor, Joffre sang the chorus while dancing *perreo* style, in what was deemed an irreverent and highly controversial act for its overt criticism of Puerto Rico's first woman governor. The line served as a reminder of the widespread but unsubstantiated rumors regarding the governor's private life. As the island's first female governor, Calderón refused to comment, but many objected to the use—by a woman—of a line sung by a woman to injure another woman publicly. Yet free publicity, even if centered on controversy, has its rewards. Glory's countenance slowly began to be recognized as the "loose as a shoestring" woman, as the singer behind the comedian's skit, as an advertisement of her on-stage persona, and she was able to benefit from the music-politics-comedy triangulation. In an unusual co-opting of a potentially embarrassing situation, the State Elections Commission chose Glory to sing its official jingle to promote the youth vote in the 2004 elections.[10]

But the obvious sexual charge of a song turned comic relief also shortened the reach of Glory's verse. Glory's voiced chorus became synonymous with a governor's perceived libidinous persona through a comedian's opportunistic maneuvers. The triangulation of politics, music, and sex provided for a public reconceptualization of the singer. Glory no longer owned the phrase that she sang (she never did) but she owned the voice that sang it, and the "fame" acquired through its use. By January 2005, after the song's political life had been exhausted, Glory was in the background again, having provided a chorus for the comedian's performance and the politician's chagrin. Her television appearances again waned, and again she was left to conjure up a solo career on the basis of her chorus-member fame, detaching herself from the vocal pairings that had served her so well.

If she wanted to make it big, the question was simple: Where were the women of Puerto Rican reggaeton? When the hierarchical structure of the genre is examined, it yields a multitude of would-be genre kings (Daddy Yankee, Don Omar, Tego Calderón, Héctor "The Father") and only one undisputed queen. And after twelve years of birthing pains, the chorus singer seemed to be temper ready and glory bound.

     ¤   ¤   ¤   ¤   ¤

With a rendition of his hit song "Rompe," a pretaped romp through Miamian waters as visual fodder, and a live grand entrance to the Hard Rock Resort and Casino, Daddy Yankee tore into the core of the television audience of the Fourth Annual Billboard Latino Awards, a show that measures sales and airplay frequency in a no-nonsense statistical awards presentation in February 2005.[11] No juries, voters, or peer panels—you sell well, you win big. After three hours of hip-shaking Shakira, crooning Luis Fonsi, rocking La Secta and salsa-blasting Gilberto Santa Rosa, the show went off with a grand finale of sorts, the reggaeton triad of Tito El Bambino and Angel y Kris. Another awards show, another coup for reggaeton performers, and another "Viva Puerto Rico" grand finale.

"Viva Puerto Rico" sells, and it lives both as a mantra and as a market ploy that repeats itself incessantly. Reggaeton, thus, conjures up images of a visible Puerto Rican nation that can be paraded—and its new acoustic scaffolding. In that parade, a narcissistic misstep or ill-suited career shift may end a performer's chances, but no shift or self-serving comment has derailed the course of Ivy Queen, who early on in her career unsaddled herself from the Recording Reggaeton Woman template to which Glory adhered. In the Puerto Rican national acoustic scaffolding, only one reggaeton woman stands.

"It is up to Ivy Queen and me to be the spokeswomen for females in reggaeton," Glory declared when announcing the release of her solo album in May 2005.[12] The empowerment and ambition that her declaration carries are self-evident, but for the undercurrent of hostility or bitterness one must read between the lines. Two women with potentially the same fan base, the same musical friends, and the same years in the business, but different styles and physical presentations, had been placed in opposite sides of the tracks by their own colleagues: Glory as the dancer-turned-accompanist, Ivy as the songwriter-turned-singer; Glory viewed as the ever-present, trusted companion, Ivy Queen as a maverick, bold spirit possessing the lure of the unreachable. The Queen is the absolute standard of reference. It is clear that the overriding ambition of reggaeton's female performers is to be in "Ivy's League."

How long can Ivy Queen exist without another woman on the block? Long considered the strongest and best-selling voice in the genre, Ivy Queen could well be needing competition, but for the record there is no other female star so defined. Even *Time* magazine gave a nod to Ivy Queen in the article naming Daddy Yankee as one of the "100 Most Influential People" of 2006. "Other stars in the genre, such as Tego Calderón and Ivy Queen, have also attracted the attention of the major labels. Expect a lot more registers to be ringing."[13]

Ivy Queen made her imprint and started registering as the real female deal in reggaeton—La Diva, La Potra, La Caballota (the Diva, the Mare, the She-Horse)—and embracing her status as royalty since the release of her 1997 regally titled debut *En Mi Imperio* (In My Empire) and her 1999 follow-up *The Original Rude Girl*. Martha Ivelisse Pesante is the strongest of all female singers, a commercial success, and, in the face of reggaeton's male performers' cultivated ambiguities, perhaps the only performer to structure her career with a gender difference in mind. The force and fire of Ivy Queen's persona always has been public, publicized and subject to consumption, sporting her over-the-top manicured long nails as an emblem of danger that was not entirely sexual—as a possible weapon. Self-conscious to the core, she has never conceded a beat to her fellow singers and collaborators, which have included Wyclef Jean, Eddie Dee, Don Omar, Daddy Yankee—her peers in the gender equalized Ivy World. When she speaks about her representation of women, however, she acknowledges how women are tested against the fixity of the expected, and how she breaks the mold with her strength, which is the word, from which she derives her authority.

> I have to represent the females. Whether you're Latina or not. The main thing they think when you come into music and you are a woman is that you came here to shake your booty. Everything is about your body. For me, I break that barrier. It's all about the lyrics. It's all about fire.[14]

But in 2005, just as Glory was preparing her *Glou*, Ivy Queen was shifting gears, reinventing a more nuanced Ivy for corporate consumption. The cover for her *Flashback* album, in which she appears dressed in a low-cut, cleavage-showing little black dress, was a visual confirmation of what would follow. In a break with the carefree, untraditional image she had carefully constructed, Ivy Queen entered the realm of über-feminine trials and tribulations, feeding off the fashion-conscious press and the judgment of red-carpet fashion criticism. It was not all about the lyrics—there was some *shaking her booty* to be done publicly, too. Ivy Queen's appropriation of the accoutrements of "real" fashion came shortly after she was criticized for her dress choice at the 2005 *Lo Nuestro Awards*. To make up for her dubious fashion sense, she gladly surrendered herself to a *dress-me-in-femininity* makeover in Univision's *El Gordo y la Flaca* for the red-carpet of the 2006 *Lo Nuestro Awards* edition. Sans grittiness and with obvious glee, Ivy Queen shed the legendary physical prowess and freedom of the Caballota of her nickname and turned into a *mamisota*-for-hire in a day-to-day televised chronicle of her transition to femme. With the diva structure taking hold, complete with a revamping of her physical appearance, Ivy Queen confessed that the makeover stemmed from a "crisis" and "female vanity." From her resolutely tomboyish beginnings ("I was the flat girl, *la flaca esa*"), to the Colombia plastic surgeon who helped recontour her figure, to the divorce from her longtime husband and fellow singer Gran Omar, Ivy Queen's expansion of her physical reign found another cosmetic province. "When I started eleven years ago, I didn't look like this. I looked a little like a tomboy. People heard my tone of voice, and guys were like, 'Whoa.' Then they see me later and can't believe I'm the same girl."[15]

She had defined her career as predicated on the strength and directness of her words and her lyrics. As if sensing a backlash for her beautification, Ivy reiterated that her newfound attention to developing a fashion-conscious image did not imply a rejection of the songwriting skills that had paved the way for her construction as a reggaeton icon. "I have something to say, and it's always been that way," the redone, refashioned Diva reiterated.[16] To prove it, her songs in 2005's *Flashback* and 2004's *Diva Platinum*,[17] as exemplified by "Yo quiero bailar" (I want to dance), remained resolutely woman centered, retaining the power to reject all men, even if her body has been reengineered and clothed to entice even more.

> *Yo quiero bailar*
> *Tú quieres sudar*
> *Y pegarte a mí*
> *El cuerpo rozar*
> *Yo te digo sí*
> *Tú me puedes provocar*
> *Eso no quiere decir*
> *Que pa' la cama voy*

> I just wanna dance
> You just want to sweat
> And get close to me
> Feel our bodies merge
> I will tell you yes
> You can provoke me
> But that doesn't mean
> That in your bed I'll be

That *power of the word* that separates Glory and Ivy Queen surfaced as the reason for the disparity in their relative successes and degrees of recognition. Ivy Queen's public preemptive dismissal of Glory's bid for her throne, instead of focusing on the bodily battle with Glory (now more or less voluptuous equals) confronted Glory's possibility of articulation and her reliance on the patriarchal sexual comeuppance scheme of her solo album's lyrics. "Everyone is a slave of his words . . . If [Glory] wants to project herself with those lyrics, that's her problem."[18] Glory—Ivy Queen suggests—perhaps has nothing to say. As Judith Butler reminds us, "Spoken words are, strangely, bodily offerings: tentative or forceful, seductive or withholding, or both at once."[19] Ivy Queen's statements imply that Glory's bodily offerings are "tentative" and "seductive," while hers are "forceful" and "withholding." Words are the site of that lack for Glory, either because she is too much of a woman or not woman enough.

Ivy Queen's public statements regarding Glory's sexually charged lyrics were coupled with the Diva's self-definition as "a lady to the full extent of the word." "I am a woman from the *barrio* and very cultural . . . Now I'm both pretty and *recatada*, proper," the Queen decreed in a television interview, reclaiming her right to self-fashion herself both inside and outside what previously was her comfort zone, and redefining her gender performance.[20] The pretty, proper, and cultural Ivy Queen establishes a false distance from the tomboyish, ready-for-drag, no-curves starting point of her lower-class, Puerto Rican female body. Ivy Queen resurfaces as a palimpsest that acknowledges her "masculine" coded persona, a woman watermarked with her previous unglamorous self. She has left the traces of the old Ivy in her—her masculine strength is still legible. As Judith Halberstam states, "masculinity . . . becomes legible as masculinity when it leaves the white middle class body."[21]

Ironically, Ivy Queen's physical retooling is a remake in search of a rival, a partial shedding of her masculine disguise. As the only stand-alone female in Puerto Rican reggaeton, her body's refeminization stands in contrast to her perceived toughness. Only another woman perhaps could now challenge her, for she had beaten the men at their game: she had been declared an "equal" by her male peers, and even served as the unofficial spokesperson for the twelve singers who collaborated in Eddie Dee's *Los Doce Discípulos* (Twelve Disciples) disc. As the unruly woman redux, and the only female in that all-star group, Ivy Queen seemed to be enacting her need for career friction, for a rivalry that may be contested body to body, lyric to lyric, notwithstanding her charges that Glory has nothing to say, showing that the Queen is not impervious to what her competition (or noncompetition) is doing.

Ivy Queen criticized Glory's utterances, her presumed lack—Glory has had nothing to say, nothing that is really hers, buried as she was under the weight and whims of her collaborators/bosses. In the process, Ivy reinforced her own self-made woman persona, stressed her "genuine" and "original" qualities, and the fact that she has stood uncontested and resisted the normative, seemingly unyielding to any male, unwilling to make concessions: Glory's opposite.

The narcissistic reflection goes beyond a face-off between the writing/performing Ivy Queen and Glory the Recording Machine. It unites them as opposites. The two singers' careers are truly inseparable and feed off each other in codependent musical heaven. They grew artistically at the same time: Ivy before the public's eyes, Glory through the public's ears. Thus, Glory never was a specular option, but an *aural seduction*. Ivy stood alone as the go-to image; her drag persona, her "dragged-on" self, is a perennial favorite in Puerto Rico's drag scene, easy to imitate, with her dose of female masculinity, and a gruff voice to boot, always in key. In looking for gender authentication at the start of her career in 1994, Ivy Queen initially turned to her less-than-feminine image, something that Glory achieved through her imageless voice. You could have *owned* Glory's voice without buying her records, for her records always were *someone else's records*; you could have avoided her bodily existence.

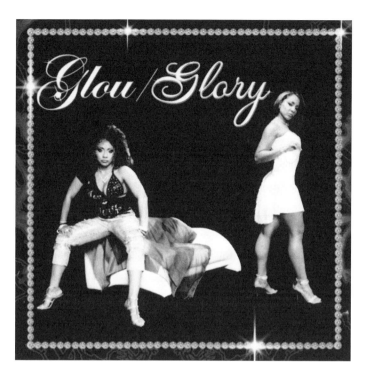

1. Detail of CD cover art, *Glou/Glory*, 2006. (First released in 2005.)

But when Glory and *Glou* decided to speak, her words contained the same gender-strict mechanics of her male counterparts. *Glou* erupted into the reggaeton world on June 28, 2005, as an appealing next step, a consolidation move. Solo, Glory was still her old self, although *Glou*'s cover and lyrics propose a double dose of Glory for image enhancement purposes. To remedy her image void and perceived lack of instant public recognition, the cover photographs split Glory into two distinct but complementary personas, severed doppelgängers. The cover is a body-double montage—the image on the left, Glory voluptuous, ready for the road; the image on the right, Glory a contrived, elegant, made-for-the-night vision (figure 1). The double fantasy—the *known* heavily made-up, wild-haired, wild-tongued Glory alongside the *unknown*, faux sophisticated, more self-assured woman—plays on the possibility of a rupture with a fixed image that, in a supreme irony, had not yet been totally formed in the public's eye. In a daring move, one of the CD's Internet ads boldly proclaimed in capital letters, "IVY QUEEN LOOK OUT, HERE COMES TROUBLE."[22]

But the disc did not stir up trouble for others, offering nothing more than standard-issue reggaeton lyrics in the singer's comfort zone. The publicity that preceded the record's reception established the erotic energy that Glory would stand for—a danceable spinoff of her choruses, with a higher sexual octane. Was it advisable for her to divest of all of her previous sexy chorus tricks, and turn that into a solo reggaeton act when the musical genre was at its commercial peak and moving to attract other publics? The melancholic remains of her willful chorus provocations (the "gimme" and "yes" and the "dale, papi") avoided risks, rendering the album an assembly-line concoction that ultimately suspends and erases any career rebirth that the solo debut may have signaled, an approximation that never reaches the exact boiling point, in spite of her sexed-up lyrics. The album stresses the singer's tried-and-true template as reggaeton's erotic interface, supersized and multiplied perhaps, but not retooled.

The uncalibrated banality of songs such as "Acelera" and "Perreo 101" did not resonate outside of her fan base as widely as the singer desired. The strategic positioning that her first solo disc followed backfired, proving that Glory is not a *raconteuse* on her own, but a fragment of reggaeton's male totality. And while assuming a more public role that again garnered her more press attention (attending education fairs, advising students to finish their college careers), La Gata Gangster only meekly undertook a slippery self-fashioning that toed the line, an act of self-fashioning that recast her sexuality as a declaration of *interdependence*.

Going solo did not bring a change in texture, for her lyrical line kept in line with her previous chorus performances in an unwarranted self-mimicry. "Perreo 101" ("Dale bien duro, papi / Papi, azótame / No pares, dale, papi / bésame, azótame") sounds and feels, in texture and lyric-by-lyric resemblance, like her song "Duro, Duro."[23]

> *Si quieres adivinar quién soy*
> *Sedúceme, sobetéame*
> *Soy conocida como Glory*
> *Otros me llaman Glou . . .*
> *Duro duro duro*
> *Papi, dame bien duro*
> *Duro duro duro*
> *Duro, duro, Papi, bien duro*
> *Duro duro duro*
> *Papi, dame bien duro*

If you want to find out who I am
Seduce me, caress me
They know me as Glory
Others call me Glou . . .
Hard hard hard
Papi, give it to me really hard
Hard hard hard
Hard, hard, Papi, really hard
Hard hard hard
Papi, give it to me really hard

For Glory, the essential tangible requirement for her songs seems to be the man's physical opposition and reaction to her body—the male body as organizing factor—whereas in Ivy Queen's case her lyrics and performance are not directly connected to her body (or the male body) as prize or punishment: flirting *does not mean that in your bed I'll be*. The singers' performative and verbal events, their public *executions of sexuality*, have them in opposite sides of reggaeton's diction of desire—Glory *unraveling* and surrendering to desire; Ivy Queen *dissecting* and directing it. Ivy Queen appropriating the male rhetoric; Glory making herself the example of that rhetoric.

One song stands as the litmus test of Glory's past-as-present existence and of the overtly commercial nature of her quest to queendom. "La Popola"—banned in the Dominican Republic on grounds of obscenity for its use of the title word, which in that country is a euphemism for the female sexual organ. Whether the use of that word for the song's title was an innocent mistake (as the singer contends) or a planned splash that would at least assure her a better platform for that Glory "brand" that had proven so elusive to manufacture, the first cut of her solo CD—a remix of an underground performance hit—was even more explicit than those of her male colleagues. Defending her song in the face of mounting criticism, the singer tried to explain in the press how well it was received in the United States, how it had become a "Tex-Mex Latino hymn" in the West and celebrated in music festivals in the East, how *relative to taste* the song was. "It all depends on what's inside each person's head. After it was done it became a hymn among Latinos, because even in Los Angeles there's a Tex-Mex version [of the song.]"[24] But while the *reaction* to the lyrics may have differed geographically, the lyrics themselves are not subject to "relativity of taste" or "what's inside each person's head" subjective tests, for they are the most sexually charged words of the singer's career, an unabashed tale of the use and abuse, pleasure and pain of female genitalia during the sexual act.[25]

> *Ay no me des más na'*
> *Que me duele la popola*
> *Ay no me des más na'*
> *Que me duele la popola*
> *Ay dale por allá*
> *Pa' que descanse la popola*
> *Ay dale por allá*
> *Pa' que descanse la popola*

> Oh, don't do it to me anymore
> 'Cause my popola's hurting
> Oh, don't do it to me anymore
> 'Cause my popola's hurting
> Oh, do it on the other side
> Let my popola rest
> Oh, do it on the other side
> Let my popola rest

Glory's public relations machine compounded the situation by comparing her single to Donna Summer's music, specifically her moans-included rendition of *Love to Love You Baby*—with a twist.[26] Yet, what transpires in her performance, recording, and defense of the song is the gap between performer and recording artist, the song and the singer, and her ambiguities toward the material. In her public statements regarding her solo career, it is possible to detect, in Lyotard's terms,[27] the conversation between her two inner voices sifting through, "arguing for and against itself: voice against voice, in narcissistic reflection," as if she has to deny the reality of her words and justify her "seductive" bodily offerings:

> I am even more meticulous now in my lyrics and in the way I dress, because little girls like to imitate me. I'm not pretending to forget myself, Glorimar, because I am flirtatious by nature, but I take great care in not making any mistakes. Sometimes I feel like Titi Chagua [a children's TV program presenter].[28]

The reference to her overcautious self stands in contrast to the lyrics, and situates Glory in the realm of the simultaneous personas that unsettle and that are the norm in the music industry. In previous interviews, she had stated that the responsibility for children's reception of her songs fell squarely on the shoulders of others (parents, guardians, teachers), but not on the performers'. Ironically, as the heated debate on her lyrics grew, she forgot she had made claims that she had "softened" her image, but it already was evident that her actions and words did not match. As Stuart Thompson observes, "popular music history became a wardrobe of provisional identities, song-personae that a performer could put on and then take off."[29]

While Ivy Queen was perfecting her domination through a more coherent, impermeable set of provisional identities not punctured by blatant ambiguities, Glory was prepping for submission again, in the totally different (and complementary) careers that define the parallel courses of women in reggaeton. Glory had allowed herself the injudicious luxury of maximizing and individualizing her sexocentric pitch in *Glou*. Although the solo album (recordings) did not imply that she was divorcing the all-star gang of reggaetoneros that had kept her in the background while bringing themselves to the fore, the fans constantly kept wanting her back in the background, where—ironically—her notoriety had *meaning*. The Recording Reggaeton Woman had unwrapped her whole package, and still remained wrapped in her past. Would it be fair to contend that entering the realm of profits, not as a contract player but as the main feature, would amount to taxing her "meaning" and "credibility?"

The strategy proved to be ambiguous. "La Popola" garnered scant airplay in Puerto Rico, none in the Dominican Republic and was not an add-on in her usual heavy-rotation reggaeton markets, for it was a song that could be performed but would not be broadcast by many station programmers. In choosing her material, Glory was left with tunes that mostly left her in the realm of live performance—ostensibly performable live, but not playable on radio or TV. Thus, *Glou*'s "Popola," the CD's *pièce de publicité*, had the dubious distinction of excluding Glory from what had been her bread-and-butter medium—radio—and blocking the solo ambitions of the original Recording Reggaeton Woman.

In the quest for unattainable queendom, and after starring alongside friend Daddy Yankee in his vehicle feature film *Talento de Barrio*, Glory turned her attention to a possible acting career, to further advancement by diversifying her perceived talents. Again, she recurred to the "body as a tool" philosophy, and her ability to enter a medium that would showcase her individual talents, this time through the combination of words and image. In a made-for-TV movie, *La última noche*, Glory lent her talent and her body to a tragic romantic story set in the reggaeton-centered culture of a Puerto Rican housing project, violence and death included.

"Glory is in her dying stage, only to be reborn again," confessed Glory herself, in one of those third-person self-references that celebrities assume when celebritydom is thought to be within reach.[30] Taking pride in her future resurrection, the post-*Glou* Glory finally acknowledges that it is her ultimate goal to leave no trace of the past (perhaps an impossibility), and point to the direction of a future reality, with crossover dreams and the lure of the English-speaking market on her mind.

GLORY, WHOLED

The abbreviating logic of reggaeton renders as simple the most complex chore-ographies of gender. Glory was a male-directed, male-created fantasy, a crea-ture of male subjectivity, and her overexposure as the female *companion* voice in the late 1990s and early 2000s later verified the nature of that male-bound synecdoche. Her early verbal robotics yielded all subsequent efforts tentative, lacking. In her commitment to find the right direction for her career, summed up by *Glou*, she miscalculated the import of her collaboration in her own lyrical subjugation, and the weight of that insurmountable chorus girl aura.

Then again, following convictions is a confusing, consuming enterprise. Stanley Fish examines the everlasting paradoxes that rule human conviction, probing the predicament faced by those utterly convinced of a direction. Con-viction, by Fish's definition, is not ultimately unidirectional. Fish states that "embracing your convictions . . . pushes you in no particular direction, but tells you that being in a particular direction is both the limitation (no tran-scendence available) and the glory (a field of opportunity is always opening up before you) of your situation."[31]

Glory embraced her convictions, convinced of a direction, and found that the direction was *both* limitation and (limited) glory. She patently materialized that conviction with the execution of sexuality in her *Glou*, but that risk would not fulfill her center-stage ambitions. In fact, it would bring her closer to a twin periphery—outside of the male-centered core in which she was a voice before, and outside of the circle of success she imagined was easily reachable through the invention of a new image. Glory was not left in the netherworld of the wannabes, nor would be left picking up the pieces, but her reality check after a dozen years at the center of reggaeton's recording world did not end with Glory's Hallelujah. Rather than pursuing the individuality denied by her lyrics, she now is confronted by the recognition accorded to her body—the admired ornament of flesh that now clings to her voice.

On July 13, 2006, Glory saw how her efforts to become visible landed her a modest triumph of sorts. In the Puerto Rican press, a Miss Universe 2006 contestant, Miss Northern Mariana, was hailed for her beautiful face and her eerie resemblance to Glory. Side-by-side, black-and-white photos of the beauty and the singer accompanied by the laudatory text "The 86 contestants could dance to the rhythm of reggaeton . . . if Northern Mariana's beauty queen, Shequita Deleon Guerrero Bennett, would only strut her stuff like Puerto Rican reggaeton singer Glory."[32] Glory finally had her face launching the thousand "psychic contours of the voice she represents"—but still compared to another queen. That same day, July 13, 2006, the Queen's synergy was brewing in Miami: Ivy Queen was surprised by her peers as she received a Career Achievement Award in Univision's *Premios Juventud* awards show, and was given the honor of performing the televised program's grand finale. Ivy Queen, glorious in her full-bloom splendor—the rude-to-glam route she had embarked on for the past two years now completed—performed as the *glam femme* in front of a certified television audience of 5 million Latinos in the United States. Truly glamorous—compared to none.

Two days later, Ivy Queen held court at her first concert, *The Diva Chronicles,* at the prestigious Fine Arts Center in Santurce, Puerto Rico, where she recounted her "sojourn from little Añasco, Puerto Rico to the Fine Arts Center stage";[33] kissed her new boyfriend onstage; sang with Glory's friend Don Omar, basking in her own glow; and announced she would soon be marketing her new Ivy Queen shoe collection, Ivy Queen clothing line, and Ivy Queen perfume.[34] For her effort, the critics hailed her as "the only female name that is always present in a genre dominated by men."[35] Her peers hailed her, too. "A historical marker in reggaeton's history," was Don Omar's take on the Queen's concert.[36]

As a voice that in her reggaeton beginnings was *only* a voice, Glory was boxed in. In imagining herself outside of her preassigned role as taunter/ seducer *for hire*—perhaps imagining herself as an *independent* taunter/ seducer—and not attempting to replicate Ivy Queen's strong woman persona, Glory La Gata Gangster undertook a slippery self-fashioning that toed the line. The cosmetic change did not bring a change in texture, for her lyrical line kept in line with her previous work, thus announcing devolution instead of evolution. The unwillingness or inability to transform seals her initial failure to step away from the untransferable, exclusive space she carved out in canonical subjugation to reggaeton's men. Her failure to repossess herself, or articulate a personal musical aesthetic, kept at a distance the career that eludes her, still a fabrication wrapped in her own past, foiled by the precariousness of a reinvention.

NOTES

Translations of Spanish-language quotations are my own.

1. Reggaeton's male performers have compiled a repertoire of terms designed to portray in their lyrics the sexual tension and subjugation of women. *Girlas, perras, yales, gatas* are part of the nominative cavalcade of terms that would substitute for the word *woman*, which rarely is used in reggaeton songs. Very early on in her career, Glory was tagged with the dangerous-sounding, sexually charged moniker of La Gata Gangster, "the Gangster Kitten."

2. Pierre Bourdieu, *Distinction: A Social Critique of the Judgment of Taste*, trans. Richard Nice (Cambridge, Mass.: Harvard University Press, 1984), 7.

3. Andreas Huyssen, *After the Great Divide: Modernism, Mass Culture, Postmodernism* (Bloomington: Indiana University Press, 1986), 68.

4. *Sin Límite*, CD (V.I. Music, B0000DG03B, 2004).

5. DJ Anqueira, *Innovando*, CD (Universal Latino, 1999).

6. Alfredo Nieves Moreno, "El flow de Glou," *La Revista*, El Nuevo Día, June 4, 2006, 16.

7. Rita Portela, "Glory," *El Vocero*, June 6, 2005.

8. Daddy Yankee's and Don Omar's private tug-of-war surfaced as a public disagreement in 2005, after both had established international careers, and spent less time in Puerto Rico, finally moving their musical headquarters to Miami. Their geographical displacement brought some distancing from but not a rift with Glory; both have collaborated with her since.

9. These collaborations also are common in U.S. rap, but not with such fervor and regularity. Also, from the outset, early reggaeton compilations had a communal flavor, as cassettes sold in the 1990s frequently featured the work of several performers.

10. Glory had become more politically active, although she has been careful not to identify herself with any political party in the island's politically charged environment. However, she had publicly stated that she was not supporting Calderón's party rival, former governor Pedro Rosselló, who was in his bid for a third gubernatorial term in 2004. Her government-related work continued after the "Calderón–Suelta como gabete" period, and in 2005 and 2006 she kept busy visiting schools to convince would-be dropouts to stay in school, attending education fairs, and advising students to finish their college careers.

11. In fact, *Billboard*'s press release for the event announced the grandiose plans for Daddy Yankee's splash: "Telemundo executives promise that Daddy Yankee's per-

formance—which will involve water—will be even more spectacular than those on previous awards shows, in which he has entered on a flying car, a caged tiger and through a wall."

12. Interview, May 2005.

13. Carolina Miranda, "Daddy Yankee, Reigning Champ of Reggaeton," *Time*, May 8, 2006, 157.

14. Nerissa Pacio, "Queen of Reggaeton," *Columbia Daily Tribune*, September 4, 2005, http://www.showmenews.com/2005/Sep/20050904vato11.asp (accessed June 5, 2007).

15. Ivy Queen, interview by Carmen Jovet, *Ahora podemos hablar*, Telemundo Puerto Rico, May 2006.

16. Ibid.

17. *Flashback*, CD (Univision Music Group, B000AA7HWY, 2005); *Diva Platinum*, CD (Universal Latino, B000184845, 2004).

18. Ivy Queen, *Ahora podemos hablar*.

19. Judith Butler, *Undoing Gender* (New York: Routledge, 2004), 172–73.

20. Ivy Queen, *Ahora podemos hablar*.

21. Judith Halberstam, *Female Masculinity* (Durham, N.C.: Duke University Press, 1998), 2.

22. Danza y Movimiento, product information for Glou/Glory CD. http://www.danzaymovimiento.com/shop/product_info.php?products_id=67771474702 (accessed June 5, 2007).

23. *Glou/Glory*, CD (Machete Music, B009JE5UI, 2005); DJ Anqueira, *Innovando*.

24. Frances Tirado, "Glory confía en el buen gusto de la popola," *Mundoreggaeton.com*, http://www.mundoreggaeton.com/noticias/359.htm (accessed November 27, 2005).

25. *Glou/Glory*, CD.

26. ArriveNet, "And Glory Was Her Name," June 6, 2005, http://press.arrivenet.com/entertainment/article.php/648483.html (accessed June 5, 2007).

27. Jean François Lyotard, *Soundproof Room: Malraux's Anti-Aesthetics*, trans. Robert Harvey (Stanford, Calif.: Stanford University Press, 2001), 88.

28. Frances Tirado, *Primera Hora*.

29. Quoted in Simon Reynolds, "Breaking the Wave," *Modern Painters* (July and August 2006): 75.

30. Nieves Moreno, "El flow de Glou," 18.

31. Stanley Fish, *The Trouble with Principle* (Cambridge, Mass.: Harvard University Press, 1999), 150.

32. "Lo curioso," *Primera Hora*, July 13, 2006, 41.

33. Ivy Queen, *Anda p'al cara*, Univision Puerto Rico, July 13, 2006.

34. Ivy Queen, *El gordo y la flaca*, Univision Puerto Rico, July 17, 2006.

35. José R. Pagán Sánchez, "La Reina hace vibrar a Bellas Artes," *El Nuevo Día*, July 16, 2006.

36. Don Omar, *Las Noticias*, Univision Puerto Rico, July 16, 2006.

ALFREDO NIEVES MORENO

TRANSLATED FROM THE SPANISH BY

HÉCTOR FERNÁNDEZ L'HOESTE

A Man Lives Here

Reggaeton's Hypermasculine Resident

> Gender cannot be understood as a *role* which either expresses or disguises an interior "self," whether that "self" is conceived as sexed or not. As performance which is performative, gender is an "act," broadly construed, which constructs the social fiction of its own psychological interiority.
>
> —Judith Butler, "Performative Acts and Gender Constitution:
> An Essay in Phenomenology and Feminist Theory," 279

In the early nineties, commercial Puerto Rican rap, as performed by such acts as Vico C, Brewley MC, Lisa M and Rubén DJ, among others, attained great popularity thanks in part to its socially minded, "clean" lyrics. By the mid-nineties, the genre declined as new sounds appeared.[1] A new musical genre emerged, eventually called reggaeton. This new kind of urban music—initially labeled *underground*—mixes Spanish reggae, dancehall, and hip-hop in a sound whose cadence, sexually charged lyrics, violence, and symbolic excess have granted access to widespread internationalization. Just like rap, reggaeton began circulating in the underground economy, recorded on tapes sold in a clandestine fashion. Producers such as Playero and DJ Negro were pioneers in this field, working with a number of young vocalists to produce what are considered the first recordings of the genre: *Playero 37* (ca. 1992) and *The Noise Uno: Así Comenzó el Ruido* (ca. 1994).[2]

Underground songs narrated the realities of the inhabitants of many neighborhoods and housing projects of Puerto Rico, drugs and their trade, the rivalries between street gangs, and the sexual parameters that energized young bodies, particularly in the place that would become the quintessential stage for reggaeton's narrative: the disco. Songs such as "Bien Guillao de Gangster" by

Don Chezina and "La Rubia" by Memo y Vale, which debuted in *The Noise Uno*, are clear examples of the formative attributes of reggaeton.

The success of *underground* music spurred production, and little by little new singers joined this emerging sphere of cultural, musical, and commercial production. Before long, underground mixtapes became available in regular stores. Nevertheless, their strong content soon sparked resistance from Puerto Rican authorities. According to Nieve Vázquez: "In February 1995, the vice squad of the [Puerto Rican] police launched an operation in establishments like La Gran Discoteca, Discomanía, Farmacias González, and Woolworths to confiscate all CDs and tapes with so-called *underground* music."[3] This operation was based on the premise that this music "promoted pornography and the use of drugs," according to Pedro Toledo, the Police commissioner, and Milton Picón, the leader of Morality in Media, a conservative Puerto Rican organization. The case against the stores for the distribution of "obscene" music did not advance, however, and they were simply required to use labels with the warnings "Parental Advisory: Explicit Lyrics" on the covers of the tapes.

The coauthors of "Más allá del perreo" contend that "the transcendence of the operation of the police department's vice squad went beyond the confiscation of recordings. It brought attention to a music listened to by a minority of the population."[4] This argument explains why at a general level, after this operation, underground—later called reggaeton on account of its new commercial character—gained an increased following. A new audience eagerly began to consume a music that, until then, was exclusively limited to marginal sectors. The increase in popularity of reggaeton and its signature dance, *perreo* (doggy style), soon encountered new objections. In 2002—with the support of Velda González, then a senator belonging to the Popular Democratic Party—the government of Puerto Rico approved legislation to censor perreo, judging it obscene and pornographic.[5] Reggaeton was attacked from many sides in Puerto Rico. This sparked growing interest from the audience, initially composed of people belonging to social groups that did not share the criteria for decorum that the state sought to impose.

Félix Jiménez describes the reasons for the 2002 controversy when he points out that primordially it emerged from the hypermasculine content and the dancing evident in music videos, directed for the most part by Héctor "El Flaco" Figueroa. Nonetheless, the stars of reggaeton contributed to the "solution" of the controversy, not only through a "softening" of the imagery in music videos, but also through a shift in the nature of lyrics. This latter aspect could be considered an act of self-regulation that did not necessarily respond to official demands and which hushed their cultural expression.[6]

In his defense of the imagery of hypermasculine rap, Figueroa has expressed his discomfort with the most intense political controversy in which rap, as a cultural force in the island, has been involved, when, after the summer of 2002, a foster-home minor starred in a video that he directed for rappers Wisín and Yandel. The key point of this controversy was female representation, specifically speaking, a scene in which Yandel took a shower with the minor, and the lack of "measures" in the use of underage youth in the video. In this way, following the discovery of these "flaws," government attention, which began to focus on this previously ignored *underground*, centered on superficial aspects of the industry of rap imagery, with a strictly visual spirit, paying little initial attention to the lyrics, the circulation of which surpasses the broadcast of videos in the TV screens.[7]

Later on, Jiménez adds:

As the granddaddy of rap in video, Figueroa publicly accepted the "blame" of all creators of rap videos in the island for the hypermasculinity of the imagery, and claimed that "the controversy had in some way contributed to the rap industry," thanks to the "self-regulation measures" accepted by the industry to avoid future attacks. Yet, ironically, Figueroa's admission that rap had "lost its way" centered on lyrics; he forgot or misunderstood the reasons behind the initial debate, which were the surfacing of bare flesh and gender representation in videos, not the lyrics, which, apparently, the Puerto Rican legislative sector had not considered as objectionable as to go against them.[8]

Of course, lyrics, attire, and other forms of expression have served to articulate reggaeton singers' masculinities. But, following Jiménez's analysis, when it comes to gender, music videos endured as spaces of resistance throughout the period of the controversy. They reaffirmed themselves as expressions that, despite a decrease in their "hypermasculine intensity," continue to legitimate and naturalize the masculinities of reggaeton.

*   *   *   *   *

Even though Puerto Rico and Panama both claim to have originated reggaeton, Puerto Rican singers have garnered greater commercial recognition. Through their work, Daddy Yankee, Wisín and Yandel, and Don Omar, among many others, lay the foundation for a multifaceted market that today generates millions of dollars throughout the world. Many reggaeton performers trace their origins to poor neighborhoods or public housing projects in Puerto Rico, which underlines the music's link with subaltern classes. There are also others, however—such as Tego Calderón, Julio "Voltio" Ramos, and Héctor "El Father"—to name a few, who were raised in private *urbanizaciones* [subdivisions] and middle-class homes, and who incorporate into their projected images this "marginal" imaginary. On the one hand, this "incorporation" could be interpreted as a form of masquerade, which founds the lie in the "origins" of a genre that, at the same time, creates new forms of identification and appropriation for audiences. On the other hand, such strategies also serve to orient the public that consumes reggaeton toward registers that are not limited to "poor neighborhoods" or "housing projects."

When we compare the contents of earlier Puerto Rican commercial rap to those of reggaeton, we notice that the latter shies away from criticism of the system and social commentary to glorify the superiority of the "barriocentric macho."[9] In the case of reggaeton, this superiority is articulated from the very perreo, in which a woman swings her hips to the rhythm of the music while the male partner, standing right behind her, rocks slowly. In terms of discourse, reggaeton also reproduces a male domination,[10] one that enhances the figure of the man and situates him in a position of constant symbolic authority.[11]

This male domination may be noted in the gangster's logic, the violence, the *tiraera* (the clashes between groups of singers through song lyrics that, at times, include homophobic expressions), and the forms of seduction narrated in the songs. It is important to note that in most cases, these forms of seduction are practiced at the discos and occasionally involve third parties who, in some way, threaten the consummation of the sex act or the coming together of couples. The following verses of the song "Dale Don Dale" by Don Omar are a clear example of this practice.[12]

> Yo soy su gato.
> Ella es mi gata en celo.
> Quiere buscar rebuleo del bueno.
> Quiere fingir que no le gusta el blin-blineo
> y cuando canto, hasta abajo con mi perreo.
> Por ahí anda su novio en un fantasmeo.
> Me está que esta noche va a haber un tiroteo.
> Dile que yo ando con mi gato en el patrulleo.
> (Y al que se lamba, jurao' me lo llevo.)

I am her cat.

She is my cat in heat.

She's looking for a good fight.

She pretends she doesn't like the bling-bling.

But when I sing she rocks her hips

down to the floor with my *perreo*.

Her boyfriend is around like a ghost.

I think there's going to be a gunfight tonight.

Tell them I'm cruisin' with my cat.

(And the first to flinch, I swear I'll take with me.)

Moreover, in many reggaeton songs, the participation of women is circumscribed to dancing and fulfilling male sexual desire. Women's objectification within reggaeton eliminates almost all possibility of action and translates their presence into a prize or trophy that men exhibit, dominate, and manipulate. This is evident even in the songs of some female singers such as Ivy Queen, who, for example, in her song "Chika Ideal," presents herself as a lover willing "to bring along a friend" to the dance floor to satisfy her man's "fantasies" and answer (with her body) each time he wants to "call" her.

The representations of masculinity established by the songs, dances, and pretenses of reggaeton contribute to the genre's naturalization of a particular kind of man. Images of men in reggaeton are dominated by the use of sportswear, major-league baseball caps, designer jackets, and shiny jewelry, also called "bling bling"—an aesthetic drawn in part from contemporary, commercial U.S. rap/hip-hop. As such, the reggaeton man or barriocentric macho emerges from an exaggerated heterosexual masculinity that, in an immediate way, suggests fissures. And it's precisely these fissures that create space for such groups as Calle 13, whose hypermasculinity—mainly, as expressed by lead vocalist, Residente—denaturalizes the representations of the "barriocentric macho" routinely affirmed by reggaeton.

Created by a pair of foster brothers—René Pérez, a.k.a. Residente, and Eduardo Cabra, a.k.a. Visitante—Calle 13 revolutionized Puerto Rico's popular music scene rather rapidly, distributing the song "Querido FBI" (Dear FBI) via the Internet, releasing their debut album *Calle 13* (2005), serving as speakers for a government campaign to prevent stray bullets during the New Year's Eve in 2005, and celebrating their first massive concert within a year of the group's inception. Before discussing the relevance of each of these events, it's important to note that Calle 13 is a project loaded with humor, cynicism, social commentary, musical innovations, and new representations of masculinity.

The group's concept is implicit in its name. Both Residente, who writes all lyrics, and Visitante, the musical director or producer, grew up in middle-class neighborhoods. Since they had different parents, Eduardo visited René's home frequently, located on Thirteenth Street of the *urbanización* El Conquistador in Trujillo Alto, Puerto Rico. According to the duo, each time Eduardo wanted to enter the subdivision, he told the guard at the gate that he was "Visitante" (a visitor), and when René wanted to enter he said he was "Residente" (a resident). Perfectly compatible with the spirit of show business, the idea for the name of the group came from the street in which its main members spent most of their childhood, which today becomes a reference for many of their actions onstage. Some of the stories narrated in songs by Residente also come from the small urban universe of Thirteenth Street.

Calle 13 refreshened the repetitive character of reggaeton by incorporating the sounds of techno, *cumbia*, *batucada* (a Brazilian rhythm), reggae, and hip-hop, among others, with lyrics that address a mass audience through the promotion of reflection and political action in an innovative form. Constant references to Puerto Rico's popular culture, the use of metaphor, and an original approach to language are some of the characteristics that have caught the public's attention. The duo is often accompanied by a band of musicians called Los de Atrás Vienen Conmigo (The Ones in the Back Come with Me), a phrase used frequently when residents arrive home with friends and request the authorization of a guard to let them in. Using live instruments, most of which are percussive, the band brings a strong musical presence to the concerts of Calle 13. Residente and Visitante also include Ileana Cabra, PG 13, an adolescent who is one of their six other siblings. PG 13 sings backup vocals in some of the songs and usually plays Residente's counterpart on the stage.

Unlike most reggaeton acts, the main members of Calle 13 are college graduates. Residente holds a bachelor's degree in art, image, and design from the School of Fine Arts of Puerto Rico and a master's degree in computer animation from the Savannah (Georgia) College of Art and Design (SCAD). Visitante studied piano at the Music Conservatory in Puerto Rico and finished the bachelor's program in information systems at the Universidad de Puerto Rico. For several years, he belonged to Kampo Viejo, a reggae and ska band, and Bayanga, a batucada collective.

Both artists are considered white. Yet this has not been the reason for the distrust felt by other reggaeton artists—many of them also considered white. Rather, the problem is that Residente and Visitante grew up in neighborhoods linked to a different social class. In other words, they are *blanquitos de clase media* (middle-class white boys).[13] In response to this claim, Residente has tried to establish a bond with other acts by indicating that, in Puerto Rico, the middle class suffers as much or more than the lower class. He has been quoted in the press saying that the only thing differentiating him from other reggaeton performers is that he managed to study. In an interview with Rusell Rúa, Residente delineates this common condition:[14]

> The middle class is really fu . . . (cked), more than the lower class. We don't even have the financial aid and we are too rich to be poor, but too poor to be rich, and we are in the very ham of the sandwich. My mom sold clothing at school so that I could get an education[15]

The public statements by Calle 13, mainly from Residente, are set apart by their endorsement of populist politics and social equality. In the interview with Rúa, Residente adds that "education is free (in the sense that), you educate yourself buying books and reading them anywhere. You can educate yourself without money, and in the street you can also do it." The fact of having successfully graduated from college is another element that sets Calle 13 apart from the imaginary of reggaeton acts, since it reiterates their "difference," as many of the latter are school dropouts. However, Residente denaturalizes the masculine representations of reggaeton by stating that poverty is no justification to stop studying and that the educational process is not limited to the academic environment. Residente does not position himself as a victim of the system, since to him education is a phenomenon that may take place in an independent fashion and in any place.

The artist has also addressed gender. In his response to another inquiry by Rúa,[16] which questioned the gender roles proposed by his music—including the emphasis on an exaggerated masculinity—Residente stated that

> People shouldn't be conscious of the role they take on in terms of gender. They must do things 'cause they feel them and as they flow. Women can do things meant for men and men can do things meant for women. Here in Puerto Rico and (in the rest of) Latin America, in particular, it's hard to deal with gender.

These words evince that Residente is very conscious of the masculine constructions legitimized by reggaeton. Accordingly, one of his premises in terms of lyrics is, without a doubt, to denaturalize prevailing constructions of gender as well as sexuality. With regard to the latter, it's important to note that on June 4, 2006, Calle 13 performed during the Gay Pride Festival in Puerto Rico. There, Residente expressed his satisfaction in sharing the moment with the country's homosexual population. He described antigay prejudice as based upon "insecurities." In an interview with Mariela Fullana, Residente claimed:

> I feel happy to participate in an activity like this one. Sexuality is some-thing relative . . . . It's a right for people to choose, people have to be free . . . . [I] believe it has to do with the insecurity of many, you see, I am very sure of my sexuality and preferences, but it's tough for anyone insecure.[17]

"Sin Coro" is one of the songs by Calle 13 that shows the willingness to deconstruct the masculinities of reggaeton (by means of jokes, hyperbole, and implicit mockery). The song centers on Residente's rhyming capability and Visitante's musical skills. It includes a choir, the Tuna de Bardos (the Bards Ensemble) of the Universidad de Puerto Rico.[18] In "Sin Coro," Residente criti-cizes the self-representation of the reggaeton singer as barriocentric macho, threatening others by enacting gangster logic. While describing these vocalists' abilities to compose songs as mediocre and childish, he comments on how such images hide the "insecurities" of these subjects.[19]

[Y] dónde están los más jodones,
que no necesitan guardaespaldas
que tienen como 40,000 armas.
Más puercos que un guardia penal,
los (Jean-Claude) Van Damme
mezclaos con Steven Seagal,
que están más armaos que un arsenal,
con un corillo como de 20,000 soldados, todos agitados,
pero con lírica de chamaquito colgao de tercer grado:
"Qué pajó pai, que eh la que hay.
Reguetín, reggaetón, reggaetón, reguetain".
Están to's cruzaos, colgaos,
mal sincronizaos, desequilibraos . . .

[And] where are the big shots
who don't need bodyguards,
who have more than 40,000 guns.
More like pigs than a prison guard,
the (Jean-Claude) Van Dammes
mixed with Steven Seagal,
more armed than an arsenal,

with a crew of about 20,000 soldiers . . . all hyped up,
but with the lyrics of a flunked-out, third-grade kid:
"What's up man, how's it goin'.
Reguetín, reggaetón, reggaetón, reguetain."
They're all twisted, flunked, out of tune, crooked . . .

In his essay "Humor" (1927), Sigmund Freud contends that there are two ways to practice humor:

> It may take place in regard to a single person, who himself adopts the humorous attitude, while a second person plays the part of the spectator who derives enjoyment from it; or it may take place between two persons, of whom one takes no part at all in the humorous process, but is made the object of the humorous contemplation by the other.[20]

Based on this Freudian reflection, it is possible to argue that Residente incorporates the latter form of humor in his approach to reggaeton artists. In "Sin Coro," the object of Residente's humor is linked directly to the listening public's reception, contemplation, and enjoyment of the mockery. In this case, humor contributes to the denaturalization of reggaeton's masculine representations, which Residente identifies precisely.

Such prevailing representations are also questioned in the image projected by the main members of Calle 13. The journalist Marcos Pérez Ramírez describes the artists' appearance thusly:

> The duo in Calle 13 is not configured by two traditional rappers. Residente wears baggy pants and his arms sport more than five tattoos; he uses a white tank top and wears a "puca"-style beach necklace. There are no traces of a designer's jacket, with matching clothes and hat, nor of the emblematic bling bling—jewelry—favored by most of his colleagues. His hair is buzzed, with lines and marks that suggest designs, plus a nose ring. More than a rapper, he looks like a punk rocker from the eighties.
>
> On the other hand, Visitante is as inscrutable in person as the sound he produces. His curly hair is covered by a Rasta hat or a bus driver's hat, he wears thick, tortoise-shell glasses and has grown a thick beard, like a bass player from a funk band of the sixties.[21]

Pérez Ramírez's description thus illustrates how Calle 13's image differs markedly from the one usually attributed to reggaeton acts, which could be interpreted as a challenge to the aesthetic politics of other performers. This aesthetic "difference" is a form of representation similar to one popularized by singer Tego Calderón during the release of *El Abayarde*, his debut album in 2002. Calderón's peculiar image rearticulated the conventional attire of men in reggaeton by underlining his African roots with an "Afro" hairstyle and wearing clothing alluding to Santeria, such as baggy, light-colored shirts and pants made out of cotton, and accessories like beaded necklaces and bracelets. Although it sparked some reactions, however, Tego's aesthetic difference was accepted by his fellow reggaeton singers and was not perceived as defiance. This was so because it came packaged with a political discourse closer to other performers' "social origins" and with cultural references—like Santeria—to "barrio" populations, features that did not necessarily denaturalize reggaeton's barriocentric macho. In turn, the "aesthetic difference" of the members of Calle 13 counters the "barrio" image and upholds itself through a discourse that transcends middle-class imaginaries to suggest the possibility of social "equality."

ICE CREAM / I SCREAM

> Calle 13 is a slap in the face,
> a caress of daily truths, urban music,
> born and raised in middle-class subdivisions
> in Puerto Rico's metro area,
> straight from El Conquistador, Trujillo Alto.
> —*Reggaetón News*, November 29, 2005

> The origin of the spectacle lies in the world's loss of unity,
> and its massive expansion in the modern period demonstrates
> how total this loss has been.
> —Guy Debord, *The Society of the Spectacle*, 22

It was like a scream. On Friday September 23, 2005,[22] Puerto Rico woke up to the news that members of the United States' Federal Bureau of Investigation (FBI) had launched an operation in the town of Hormigueros to arrest Filiberto Ojeda Ríos, leader of Los Macheteros, the Boricua Popular Army.[23] Throughout the day the country's media offered fragmentary information, with press coverage limited by federal agents. By night, the outcome of the operation was evident to many: lacking any medical attention, Filiberto had bled to death from a wound resulting from an exchange of fire with FBI agents. On Saturday September 24, the news was confirmed.

Two days after the death of Ojeda Ríos, a song that sparked the nationalist spirit of some and criticism by others began to circulate via e-mail. The song was titled "Querido FBI."[24] As a visceral response to the death of Filiberto Ojeda Ríos, it was composed and sung by Residente, and it incited violence against the U.S. government. At the same time, the walls of many Puerto Rican cities were covered by graffiti repudiating the actions of the FBI. "FBI asesino" (Killer FBI) and "Filiberto vive" (Filiberto Is Alive), among many other messages, covered the empty spaces of the city with new writing, colors, and shapes to underline the historic moment for the island. This was the setting in which Calle 13 broke into the music world, defying decorum to broadcast a strident cry for rebellion, a call for uprising, and a claim to independence for the country under the title of "Querido FBI."

Using a hip-hop backing, Calle 13 produced a song that summarized their fleeting and immediate reaction to the event. The lyrics of "Querido FBI" begin by calling for the mobilization of various groups representing Puerto Rican society. Teachers, lawyers, firemen, mayors, drug traffickers, and politicians alike, raps Residente, are to be informed of the acts committed by federal agents against Filiberto Ojeda Ríos. From this initial account, Residente goes on to request the "activation" or setting into motion of the marginalized and subaltern groups of Puerto Rico.

In this call to action, it is significant that Residente includes groups who have not traditionally belonged—in the past or present—to the struggle for Puerto Rican independence. The followers of the independence struggle in Puerto Rico belong mostly to the middle and upper middle class; they are made up of salaried professionals, businessmen, academics, and students, as well as people who attended college in the sixties and seventies and experienced the excitement of multiple independence movements from those decades. Subaltern groups usually do not participate in these types of debates. Nevertheless, in "Querido FBI," these groups are urged to join the collective uprising.

> [Q]ue se activen La Perla, Lloréns, Barbosa, Manuel A., Caimito, Vista Hermosa, Covadonga, Camarones, Alturas, Torre Sabana, Villa Esperanza, Sabana Abajo, Villa Fontana, Gladiolas, Villa Carolina, el pueblo 'e Trujillo, Las Parcelas, San Just, Monte Hatillo, Canales, San José, Río Grande, Luquillo, Puerta e' Tierra, Santurce, Monacillos, urbanizaciones, caseríos: el FBI se ha metío en un lío. . . .

> [L]et's activate La Perla, Lloréns, Barbosa, Manuel A., Caimito, Vista Hermosa, Covadonga, Camarones, Alturas, Torre Sabana, Villa Esperanza, Sabana Abajo, Villa Fontana, Gladiolas, Villa Carolina, the

town of Trujillo, Las Parcelas, Saint Just, Monte Hatillo, Canales, San José, Río Grande, Luquillo, Puerta 'e Tierra, Santurce, Monacillos, *urbanizaciones*, projects: the FBI has gotten itself into a mess. . . . [25]

At the same time, this joining of forces implies the massification of Calle 13's message and its modes of representation from a place of difference—from a discourse that goes beyond a relationship with more "traditional" Puerto Rican rap and reggaeton, problematizing the masculinities established by this type of music.[26]

Though Calle 13 was gaining popularity among the Boricua reggaeton crowd thanks to the video of "Se Vale To-To" (Anything Goes), one of their first hits, the group wasn't yet established as a staple of the artistic scene at the time of the release of "Querido FBI." Given Calle 13's musical style, aesthetics, and language, reggaeton lovers were still skeptical about the duo's proposal. Only when "Querido FBI" began to circulate through the radio, Internet, and among Puerto Ricans did Calle 13 begin to enjoy a growing reputation. But this reputation didn't mean that Calle 13, and particularly Residente, were completely accepted by the world of reggaeton. This only happened when the singer became widely recognized as a voice defiant of authority and expressed the indignation of most Puerto Ricans regarding the events that led to Ojeda Ríos's death, a defiance and indignation projected through the social and antiestablishment character of hip-hop and which created a new space for the discourse of associated musical styles (like reggaeton). This happened despite the fact that, in Puerto Rico, there was and still is a significant hip-hop culture— represented by groups such as Conciencia Poética (later known as Intifada), SieteNueve, and Tráfico Pesado, among others—which had put forward convincing social proposals but which lacked public visibility. This visibility allowed Residente to become a "political leader" even before he was accepted as a reggaeton or hip-hop artist.

In November 2005, two months after the death of Ojeda Ríos and motivated by the success of "Querido FBI," Calle 13 released their eponymous debut album, *Calle 13*. On the cover is the profile of a woman licking a colorfully sprinkled ice cream cone (figure 1), clearly alluding to oral sex. The image shows a pierced nose and tongue, but not the woman's eyes. Generally speaking, women on the covers of recordings, in videos, or on stage at reggaeton concerts are voluptuous, provocative, and scantily clad.

When you open the cover of *Calle 13*, the same signs are there. However, the content demands new ways of understanding. It includes a picture of Residente and Visitante with a dwarf (Karla Sánchez) in a bathing suit and an ice cream cone in her right hand, suggesting that she's the woman from the cover (figure 2). From this point of view, the cover of Calle 13's debut album seduces and sparks the interest of the fan/consumer through the use of an image that evolves into a perceived erotic fallacy, a trick among friends. There's a certain perversity in this gesture, which is reinforced by the set of signifiers that activate the rest of the images in the cover (condoms, candies, toy soldiers, and colorful ice cream), demanding an interpretation from the public. This "lack of totality," this deliberate provocation into constant resignification, leads to the feeling that Calle 13 is a project in which identities are in flux, in which masking, acting, and fun decenter the message and increasingly distance it from the criteria that have articulated the idealized imagery of reggaeton. On this game of signifiers, Jacques Derrida suggests:

> If totalization no longer has any meaning, it is not because the infiniteness of a field cannot be covered by a finite glance or a finite discourse, but because the nature of the field . . . excludes totalization. This field is in effect that of *play*, that is to say, a field of infinite substitutions only because it is finite, that is to say, because of being an inexhaustible field . . . instead of being too large, there is something missing from it: a center which arrests and grounds the play of substitutions. One could say . . . that this movement of play, permitted by the lack or absence of a center or origin, is the movement of *supplementarity*.[27]

Other images that denaturalize masculine representation in reggaeton through a game of signifiers are evident in the back cover and inside the album. One includes Residente's grandmother, Flor Amelia, in common attire but carrying firearms; in the first one, a machine gun, and in the second, a pistol. Violence and sex, reggaeton's primary topics, are expressed in this context from a deliberately playful viewpoint.

From another perspective, in Puerto Rico the term *mamar* (to suck) alludes to oral sex or to when a person must acknowledge the superiority of someone or something with respect to a practice or skill. This game of signifiers and infinite possibilities and interpretations facilitates an understanding of the rest of the cover design of Calle 13's album, which in turn opens into the lyrics of songs such as "Cabe-C-O" (Head Nodding). This song's title is based on a game of words, another bout of signifiers and "lack of totality" that results in a particular rhythmic cacophony compatible with the beat of hip-hop. This song, the first one on the album, also establishes the form in which the audience must listen to music by Calle 13. It involves the body in a movement that, on one hand, alludes to head nodding in hip-hop, and on the other, to the

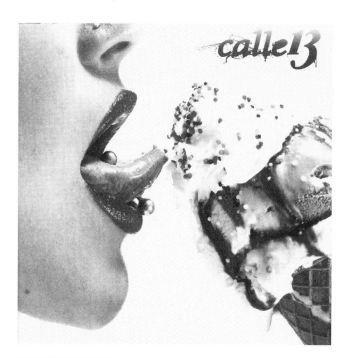

1. CD cover art, *Calle 13*, 2005.
2. CD inside art, *Calle 13*, 2005.

fact that other singers and MCs will have to "suck" the *flow* of Residente. "Cabe-C-O" introduces a set of signifiers that, if not listened to properly, if taken out of context, will only lead to a literal interpretation, solely pointing to a metaphor for oral sex.

In December 2005, the political visibility generated by "Querido FBI" led the group to collaborate with Puerto Rico's governor, Aníbal Acevedo Vilá, in a campaign to prevent shots from being fired into the sky during the New Year's Eve celebration. On this occasion, Calle 13 recorded the single "Ley de Gravedad" (Law of Gravity). In one of its stanzas, the song claims:[28]

> *¡Puerto Rico lo hace mejor!*[29]
> *¡Aquí en la isla del mar y el sol*
> *disparar para arriba es un vacilón!*
> *¡Ja, ja, ja, ja!*
> *Hasta que le dé una bala a tu nena.*
> *Ahí te va a dar pena, ahí tú lloras.*
> *No te hagas el macho ahora.*
> *Tú lloras.*
> *Cualquiera llora.*
> *Con tanta cara linda que hay en el barrio,*
> *Pa' que venga un brutosaurio[30] guillao de mercenario*
> *a cagar el arroz con dulce del vecindario.*

> Puerto Rico does it better!
> Here in the island of sun and sea
> to shoot into the sky is a joke!
> Hah, hah, hah, hah!
> 'Till a bullet hits your little girl.
> Then you will hurt, then you cry.
> Don't be tough now.
> You cry.
> Anyone cries.
> With so many cute faces around the neighborhood,
> 'till a *dumb-saurus*, pretending to be tough,
> comes to shit on the neighborhood's rice pudding.

The fact that Acevedo Vilá accepted Calle 13's assistance during the campaign ignited controversies, for many people could not understand how a singer that had incited violence against the FBI and the United States a few months earlier had the "moral weight" to now demand that people not shoot into the air during the New Year's Eve celebration. Calle 13's initiative was joined by other reggaeton artists—Tito "El Bambino," Magnate & Valentino, and Zion & Lennox, among others[31]—and various sectors of Puerto Rican society in a preventive campaign that produced important results.[32] In "Ley de Gravedad," Residente deals again with the denaturalization of reggaeton (and Puerto Rican) masculinities through humor, references to popular culture, and cynicism. The song claims that as a result of the shots into the sky, Residente will have to wear a "football helmet even to go shopping to the mall." On this instance, Residente also questions the Puerto Rican who feels more "macho" by shooting into the sky without considering the danger he causes to others. He even defies the popular saying "Real men don't cry." Once again, he does everything with a playful style that spreads to the song's music and incorporates sounds of the circus, techno, voice sampling, and hip-hop. In sum, it's another musical statement through which Calle 13 rearticulates and represents its performativities.

THE FALL(S) OF RESIDENTE

In Boricua rap, exaggerated manhood is brought close to its destruction.
—Félix Jiménez, *Las prácticas de la carne*, 122

Anyone whose goal is "something higher" must expect someday to suffer vertigo.
What is vertigo? Fear of falling?
No, vertigo is something other than fear of falling.
It is the voice of the emptiness below us which tempts and lures us, it is the desire to fall, against which, terrified, we defend ourselves.
—Milan Kundera, *The Unbearable Lightness of Being*, 59

For many years, the music videos of reggaeton imitated the style of U.S. hip-hop. Producers such as Héctor "El Flaco" Figueroa established an aesthetic in which images loaded with sex, violence, partying, and women in bikinis were common.[33] According to Wayne Marshall, "reggaetón tends toward partying and sex as primary subjects. Descriptions of sexual acts and female bodies alternate between explicit language and innuendo, and women rarely appear as anything other than objects of the male gaze."[34] The narratives of these videos reproduce the lyrics of the songs, as well as the singers' codes of masculinity. After the controversy sparked by senator Velda González in 2002, reggaeton videos softened their sexual content, though not their symbolic excess, which, as mentioned earlier, reproduces images of gangsters (many of them taken from U.S. rap), sexist and prejudiced against aesthetic, gender, and sexual difference. Nonetheless, Calle 13—Residente, in particular—again denaturalizes the representation of masculinity in reggaeton by performing in music videos in an austere and humorous manner, like a jester laughing at himself. Take, for example, the videos for the songs "Atrévete Te, Te" and "Chulin Culin Chunflay"—the latter recorded for the album *Voltio* (2005), with reggaeton star Julio "Voltio" Ramos. Residente falls down (physically) in both videos, showing how he attacks reggaeton's barriocentric macho from another perspective.

The interlocutor of "Atrévete Te, Te" is a supposedly intellectual girl who enjoys music by American rock band Green Day and English rock band Coldplay, and who Residente dares to dance reggaeton with him. The gist of the song is evident in the chorus.[35]

> *Atrévete, te, te salte del clóset.*
> *Destápate, quítate el esmalte.*
> *Deja de taparte, que nadie va a retratarte.*
> *Levántate, ponte hyper.*
> *Préndete, sácale chispas al starter.*
> *Préndete en fuego como si fueras un lighter.*
> *Sacúdete el sudor como si fueras un wiper,*
> *Que tú eres callejera, Street Fighter.*

> I dare you, you, come out of the closet
> Take it off, take off the nail polish.
> Don't cover yourself, no one is going to take a picture.
> Stand up, get hyper.
> Start up, make sparks come out of the starter.
> Set yourself on fire as if you were a lighter.
> Shake off your sweat as if you were a wiper.
> You belong to the street, Street Fighter.

Residente's implicit message is that the girl should take off her middle-class disguise to dance reggaeton, which, to a large extent, revives the metaphors of equality and freedom suggested in the previously quoted songs. A great number of the metaphors in the song present Residente in such a way that he is practically begging the woman to dance with him. This trope of seduction stresses the fact that the woman desired by Residente is not the same one "desired" in the songs by other singers of reggaeton, an aspect that is reiterated in the musical video of "Atrévete Te, Te" given the way that the women in the video articulate their approach to seduction from a place of indifference. Contrary to most reggaeton videos, in "Atrévete Te, Te" women are not begging for sexual action, but are provoking and inducing it through their games of seduction.

Nevertheless, another reading is possible. The fact that Residente insists that the woman dance with him might imply that she will not develop as an object of desire unless she accepts the invitation to dance (doggy style), which reveals a situation similar to that suggested in music videos by other reggaeton singers. More than questioning the masculine constructions that serve as a framework for the audiovisual productions of other acts of reggaeton, then, the music video of "Atrévete Te, Te" suggests a change in the form, an aesthetic —not a circumstantial—change. Hence, there is relevance in the falls suffered by Residente; these are falls that, in final instance, involve a way of problematizing these masculine constructions.

The video for "Atrévete Te, Te" opens with one of Calle 13's musicians playing a clarinet, which produces a noise similar to an alarm. The song combines the rhythm of reggaeton with the sounds of cumbia, which adds a festive character. The musician is sitting on the roof of a house and, when the camera pans out, it shows a Puerto Rican suburban urbanización. Following this introduction, we see the arms of a man (Residente) unloading newspapers from a truck. On the cover of the newspapers, we can see a photo of Residente and Visitante, as well as a headline that reads: "Salte del clóset" (Come out of the Closet). In Puerto Rico, as in other countries, the phrase "Salte del clóset" alludes to when a man or woman accepts or assumes his/her homosexuality publicly. But, in this case, Calle 13 enhance the popular meaning of the phrase to tell the women in the video to be "authentic," to enjoy reggaeton without any need of makeup or cosmetics, and that music is something that goes "into your guts and brings out the Taíno native in you." In other words, they have the innate desire to dance, which is also a part of Puerto Rican cultural heritage, and which in turn alludes to the relative nudity of Indians. In this way, Residente asks them to denaturalize their social condition, belonging to the middle class, and to assume by means of a game (just as he has done) their "true" cultural nature, so they may enjoy reggaeton while temporarily taking on a new identity.

Further on, we see Residente on a bike—an image that alludes to the music video of "En Peligro de Extinción" (On the Endangered List) by Tego Calderón and Eddie Dee—distributing newspapers in the urbanización, with interspersed shots of women with blond wigs and white dresses putting on their makeup. A moment later, these same young women come out of the houses dancing to the beat of music, while Residente stares at them in amazement. The video continues with the women watering plants and cleaning the windows of houses, when, all of sudden, Residente gets distracted watching one of them and falls off his bicycle. The woman does not pay attention to him and continues dancing indifferently. Residente keeps singing on the ground, while the women line up and dance together next to the rails of a bridge surrounding a road.

Residente's fall may be interpreted as a flash of vertigo, which describes the feeling of instability spurred by strong emotions—fear or desire, for example. Though the girl is dressed like the others—with a white dress and a blond wig— there's something that grabs Residente's attention, though the nature of the distraction is not clarified in the video. What is established clearly is that Residente likes the girl, which makes her the object of his gaze/desire and the protagonist of this audiovisual piece. The fall reformulates the position of men in the videos of rap and reggaeton. It clarifies that women, not men, lead the game of seduction. The fall is what allows Residente to get close to the desired woman the first time around, though at the end of the video she shares meat— quite literally—with him. Or as Kundera would put it, she forces him to face "the depth that opens beneath," that "seduces" him, and into which he jumps. This is what happens when, in the final scene—in which Residente is eating and drinking with some friends at a traditional Puerto Rican food kiosk—the women from the video come in dancing. The one that Residente likes stops in front of him, removes a piece of meat from his hand, and eats it.

Also exemplifying the denaturalization of reggaeton masculinities is the video of the song "Chulin Culin Chunflay," directed by Gabriel Coss and Israel Lugo. In this case, though, Residente is accompanied by Voltio. The video starts with images of Residente dressed like a priest, sitting next to Voltio and some other men, in what appears to be a Chinese restaurant or cabaret. A blond woman flirts with them while she dances onstage and then leaves. Residente stands up and races after her, only to be stopped by another woman, who seduces him. Meanwhile, Voltio sings to a female bartender at the bar, who throws a drink at his face.

The action then continues outside, where the singers become cops, as evinced by the blue light on the car they ride in. A new scene takes the plot back to the place from the beginning, but this time around the singers appear in stereotypical Chinese attire. Voltio wears dark shades and a lengthy moustache, and Residente wears a black wig and a tank top. They both talk at the table. An Asian woman walks toward them. She carries a knife hidden under the dish in her hands. Voltio throws a chopstick dipped in red sauce at an Asian man who is dining there, and the woman attacks Residente with the knife. The singer grabs the woman by the hand, and she kicks him. The camera focuses on the legs of Residente, who falls to the floor after the impact. Yet another take shows the woman loosening her hair and jumping on Voltio. He defends himself and uses a lock to spank her repeatedly. Three Asian men show up on-screen and Residente takes off his shirt like Hulk Hogan, willing to face them. In the back of the frame, we can see the blond from the beginning standing next to a door. Residente then goes into the restaurant's kitchen and faces a huge cook, whom he hits without causing any damage. The cook grabs Residente, throws him on a table and, once Residente falls on the floor, Voltio hits the man with two cooking pot lids.

The fight between the singers and the people at the restaurant, and Residente's first fall force the blond girl who has seduced him to acknowledge their presence. This fleeting appearance of the woman makes it clear that there is a certain gratification in all the absurd dynamics that take place around her and which, in some way, establishes a seductive dialogue between both parts. Residente's first fall is the result of a kick by the Asian woman, who, like a thump of desire, sends him to the ground, from where he rises beaten and bruised.

Just like the first one, Residente's second fall in the video leads him to a new scenic space. Following the clash, there is a new sequence of black-and-white images, in which Residente appears fighting the men he faced inside the restaurant. The camera angles highlight the fact that the men are fighting in a high place (a building's rooftop), which likewise might be a source of vertigo. But Calle 13's most distinctive fall is the last one, in which Voltio also goes along.

After the outdoor B & W sequence, we see the singers riding in a car and dressed like characters from *Miami Vice*. They stop at an alley, presumably to arrest a man who is there. Nevertheless, the man runs away and the singers urinate against a wall, which clarifies that their intention was not to arrest the man. While they sing, a group of youngsters armed with pipes and sticks surround them and beat them up. At this point, the song's hook goes: "Aquí está todo bajo control, *under control*" [Everything's under control over here, under control]. After a few seconds, while beaten, the singers stand up and try to flee, since the group of youngsters is still there. They get into the car's trunk, and the vehicle leaves at full speed while the blond—once again dressed in her nightclub attire—closes the video dancing in the street, outside, in a different setting from the one in which we saw her at the beginning.

"Chulin Culin Chunflay" makes direct allusions to the sex organs of men and women. Along the same lines, it describes—in the style that is common in reggaeton—the singer's attempt to conquer a woman and have sex with her. Nonetheless, Residente's falls, the ensuing beating he receives with Voltio, and the lack of success of his flirtations undermine these possibilities and, as a consequence, the masculine-dominance discourse presumably advocated by the song. In this last scene, the singers are apparently beaten because they are cops, predominantly male authority figures who, within the narrative space of this music video, appear consistently diminished.

CONFETTI

> Sometimes masculinity has nothing to do with it. Nothing, that is, to do with men.
> —Eve Kosofsky Sedgwick, "Gosh, Boy George, You Must Be Really Secure in Your Masculinity," 11

The theatricality with which Residente and Calle 13 present themselves in their music videos is reflected in their live performances. Up to this moment, the greatest example is their first massive concert, celebrated at Puerto Rico's José Miguel Agrelot Arena on May 6, 2006. The concert's stage featured decoration alluding to theater and circus productions, a concept similar to the one popularized on the island by CIRCO, a Puerto Rican rock band.[36]

An electric sign with the word "Circo" (Circus) as well as red-and-white canvases, made the stage look like a giant tent. The show included clowns, dancers, the participation of the Universidad de Puerto Rico's Tuna de Bardos during the singing of "Sin Coro" and "La Madre de los Enanos," actors, a magician, and a number of theatrical elements that maximized the contents of songs and made reference to Calle 13's music videos. For example, during the playing of "Atrévete Te, Te," Residente shared the stage with eleven dancers dressed like the women from the video. The same thing happened during "Chulin Culin Chunflay," which Residente sang with Voltio and in which they were both dressed in clothing similar to the one from the last scene of the video. Tego Calderón and La Sista, a female vocalist who is breaking ground in the circuit and whose musical formula mixes reggaeton and *bomba*, also appeared as guest artists during the event. And even though Vico C was not at the concert, a message by that artist, in which he acknowledged and endorsed Calle 13's talent among rap and reggaeton acts, was played on two giant screens.

A key moment of the concert was when a group of actors with FBI T-shirts appeared onstage and handcuffed Residente. The lights of the arena turned on, as if the show had finished. The audience was confused, since it did not know whether what was happening onstage was part of the show or not. Residente was removed from the stage, but minutes later he returned to sing "Querido FBI." PG 13 sang the song as a duo with Residente and, quite interestingly, she performed the parts with the strongest language.

PG 13's protagonism during the singing of "Querido FBI" is another form in which Calle 13 appears inclusive and causes ruptures within the customary masculinity put forward by reggaeton. Here, she is the female lead, the one who plays an active role and invites the audience to form part of the message conveyed by the song. Usually, Puerto Rican kids of PG 13's age are not involved (or are not interested) in the political discussions about the nation. They are not key players in this context. Along the same lines, PG 13's assuming an active role grants her some authority among her peers; she invites them to sing "Querido FBI" and join—as members of society—in the scream mediated by the song.

Calle 13's concert at the arena ended with "Atrévete Te, Te," which was followed by a rain of multicolored confetti. This fact, as well as the staging of their first big performance, reiterate the denaturalization of the masculinities of reggaeton. Unlike the concerts by Daddy Yankee, Rakim & Ken Y, and Don Omar, for instance, where the staging highlighted the male "supremacy" of the singers, Calle 13's presentation distinguished itself by opening the stage space to a large number of performers and artists in other disciplines. The group shared this space of representation with a great number of cultural expressions that nourish or intervene in "its" art. In turn, the presentation reaffirms Calle 13's disposition to articulate new identities in its formula and to allocate any resources available to the process. After all, sharing performative space with others is a way of playing with your "neighbors." It is akin to relocating Thirteenth Street of the El Conquistador urbanización in Trujillo Alto, where, just as in the rest of Puerto Rico, "Se Vale To-To" (Anything Goes).

OUT OF THE CLOSET?

The forms employed by Residente to model gender constantly denaturalize the representations favored in the legitimization and articulation of reggaeton's masculinities, hoping to build a "new man" for this musical genre from the stage. This is a man who problematizes the barriocentric macho to show his imperfections and fissures. This is accomplished through drama, masquerades, a game of signifiers, and humor, resources that Residente handles to his advantage in a clever fashion and which refer us to the role of the jester, who through his jokes expressed "truths" before royalty.

This process of denaturalization, however, also hides Residente's anxiety about acceptance. It is an anxiety reflected in his persistent alignment with subaltern sectors to which he does not "necessarily" belong and which demand certain social, educational, and cultural qualities that he lacks. This anxiety for acknowledgment—like that of a spoiled brat—causes his self-denaturalization. When he seeks to position himself as the voice of subaltern sectors through a cynical message—more political, more learned perhaps—he attains a position of superiority that gives him an advantage, not only among the other members of reggaeton but also among the populations he tries to address. He gives new meaning to his masculinity and, on top of that, changes it into a form of authority. It is a conduct similar to that of a political leader, who supposedly leaves behind his/her original conditions of life to turn into someone else; to become or "return to be" part of the "people," as Residente has stated frequently.

This rearticulation of the masculinities of reggaeton leads Residente—as a "political leader," a leader of the new politics of masculinities in reggaeton, and a leader of Calle 13—to uphold his proposal through a new mix of performative techniques. These are represented through the lyrics of his songs, his music videos, his answers to the press, his way of dressing, and the staging of concerts, among many elements that mold him as a "public" figure. As I mentioned earlier, up to this moment reggaeton does not contain substantial political or social proposals. Its representations are limited to describing the nature of the sexual desires, prejudices, symbolic articulations, and material aspirations of its singers, which—given their social condition—emerge from an emphasis on a streetwise, violent, and sexist orientation.

But Residente does not come from this context, so to him it's a game, one that, viewed in depth, he condemns from the inside, through difference, defying the imaginaries of the subaltern sectors as well as those of the upper and middle class. Yet, as the figure of the jester reminds us, this game is also a space to raise consciousness, a linguistic expression that allows Calle 13 to problematize the discourses that configure the sexual desires, prejudices, symbolic articulations, material aspirations, and representations of masculinities naturalized by reggaeton. It is the hypermasculinity of Calle 13, mainly of Residente, that deconstructs the reggaeton man to propose an ambiguous, fragmented, incomplete, contemporary man. A man so "manly" that he isn't a "Man." A man who pokes fun persistently at his own condition.

Full source for the essay's opening epigraph is Judith Butler, "Performative Acts and Gender Constitution: An Essay in Phenomenology and Feminist Theory," in *Performing Feminisms: Feminist Critical Theory and Theatre*, ed. Sue-Ellen Case, 279 (Baltimore: Johns Hopkins University Press, 1990). Full sources for the two epigraphs at the beginning of the section "Ice Cream/I Scream" are Reggaetón News, "Calle 13 sorprende a todos," Barrio 305, http://www.barrio305.com/reggaeton_news_calle_13.htm (accessed June 13, 2006); and Guy Debord, *The Society of the Spectacle* (New York: Zone Books, 1994), 22. Full source for the epigraph at the beginning of the section "The Fall(s) of Residente" is Milan Kundera, *The Unbearable Lightness of Being* (New York: Harper Collins, 2004), 59. The full citation for the section "Confetti" is Eve Kosofsky Sedgwick, "Gosh, Boy George, You Must Be Really Secure in Your Masculinity," in *Constructing Masculinity*, ed. Maurice Berger, Brian Wallis, and Simon Watson, 11 (New York: Routledge, 1995).

1. See Wayne Marshall, "The Rise of Reggaetón: From Daddy Yankee to Tego Calderón, and Beyond," the *Phoenix*, http://thephoenix.com/article_ektid1595.aspx, January 19, 2006. In this article, Marshall states that "dancehall reggae had already established a strong following in Puerto Rico in its own right by the early '90s, as popular songs by Jamaican deejays such as Shabba Ranks, Cutty Ranks, and Chaka Demus & Pliers helped to redefine the sound of contemporary club music. It was, in fact, a Shabba Ranks song, 'Dem Bow,' produced by Bobby Digital, which would lay the foundation for what became known as reggaeton."

2. In the early nineties, DJ Negro—one of the forerunners of rap in Puerto Rico—organized a contest at a disco called the Noise to identify new talents among rappers. The winners of this contest were Baby Rasta and Gringo, who, together with Don Chezina, Las Guanábanas Podrías, Maicol & Manuel, and Memo & Vale, among other singers, recorded the album *The Noise Uno: Así Comenzó el Ruido* (ca. 1994). At this point in time, DJ Playero had also produced several underground recordings; *Playero 37* was among the better known of the collection.

3. Nieve Vázquez, "La 'mano dura' ayudó a impulsar el reggaetón," *Primera Hora*, September 1, 2003, final edition.

4. Mary Ann Calo Delgado et al., "Más allá del perreo" (M.A. thesis, Universidad de Puerto Rico, 2003).

5. Law no. 140 establishes the "Citizen's Bill of Rights Regarding Obscenity and Child Pornography" (Carta de Derechos del Ciudadano ante la Obscenidad y la Pornografía Infantil). This law makes reference to the First Amendment of the U.S. Constitution to ratify that "obscene material and child pornography are not protected by said amendment and that representations and/or descriptions of indecent material within the mediums of radio and television accessible to children can be regulated." It also establishes a mechanism through which citizens can exercise their right that "radio and television" "not include that type of material and that the State provide the community

with greater guidance regarding the legal norms that apply to the diffusion or transmission of that material." Law no. 141, or the "Law of the Motion Picture Rating System," creates jurisprudence so that every establishment selling or renting movies places a visible announcement regarding its classification, according to the parameters adopted by the United States' film industry. Last, Law no. 142 creates the legal mechanisms for the establishment of an Office of Citizen Orientation against Obscenity and Child Pornography in Radio and Television, as part of the Department of Consumer Affairs in Puerto Rico (Departamento de Asuntos del Consumidor de Puerto Rico).

6. After the initial debate in the midnineties surrounding the musical genre, several of the main reggaeton recordings of the time followed a clean lyrics format. Two clear examples are *The Noise 3* (1998) and *The Noise 4* (1998).

7. Félix Jiménez, *Las prácticas de la carne: Construcción y representación de las masculinidades puertorriqueñas* (San Juan: Ediciones Vértigo, 2004), 133.

8. Ibid., 133–34.

9. The phrase "barriocentric macho" synthesizes the codes of masculine domination and representation that construct the male reggaeton subject in terms of image, gender, and discourse. In general terms, this synthesis results from a subject's identity organized through a constant reference to gangster logic, the objectification of women, and the almost total omission of messages that acknowledge the value of education. In addition, it includes its aesthetics, influenced by U.S. rappers.

10. To Pierre Bourdieu, masculine domination represents a crucial example for the understanding of symbolic violence. This domination is rooted in all cultural, social, and political practices. The French theorist establishes that this rooting naturalizes domination in such a way that it often goes unnoticed and gains hold of our subconscious. In order to fight it, Bourdieu proposes the denaturalization of domination in the symbolic circuit, through the exercise of representation. See Pierre Bourdieu, *Masculine Domination* (Stanford, Calif.: Stanford University Press, 2001).

11. To Jacques Lacan, the symbolic order is made up of everything that may be represented through language. It is through language that the subject can interact with others and understand the social laws that organize its processes of communication and desires, which Lacan calls the "Name of the Father." Lacan states, "It is in the *name of the father* that we must recognize the support of the symbolic function which, from the dawn of history, has identified his person with the figure of the law." See Jacques Lacan, *Ecrits: A Selection*, trans. Alan Sheridan (New York: Norton, 1977), 67.

12. "Dale Don Dale" from the album *The Last Don* (V. I. Music, 2003).

13. In Puerto Rico, the term *blanquito* is not necessarily conditioned by a person's racial origin. The term describes someone who belongs to a social class above marginal status or who lives in an urbanización, instead of a barrio. Calle 13's social "difference" becomes greater given the fact that Residente's father is a lawyer of moderate renown in Puerto Rico and his mother is an actress. Therefore, for the purposes of public perception, Calle 13 seems to be above the traditional middle-class population. The members of Calle 13 have been called "blanquitos" because they emerge from this context, sup-

posedly different from that of other singers. But, as I've pointed out earlier, other reggaeton singers share with Calle 13 the experience of growing up in urbanizaciones and also belong to a "different" social class. Still, the aesthetics of these other reggaeton singers—which Raquel Z. Rivera calls "barriocentric"—have saved them from criticism, since these are more related to performers that come from marginal sectors. This adds an aesthetic dimension to the application of the term *blanquito* to Calle 13, thoroughly supported by the eclectic image of these artists, which is explained at length further on in this essay.

14. Rusell Rúa, "Residente se canta igual a los reguetoneros, pero con estudios," *Primera Hora*, April 21, 2006, final edition.

15. Since it's within U.S. jurisdiction, Puerto Rico is eligible for federal financial aid in the form of welfare for its working classes. These forms of aid are called *los cupones*.

16. Rúa, "Residente se canta igual a los reguetoneros, pero con estudios."

17. Mariela Fullana Acosta, "Calle 13 sazonará su nuevo disco de temas fuertes," *Primera Hora*, June 12, 2006, final edition.

18. Translator's Note: A *tuna* is the musical equivalent of a college fraternity, coming from an old Spanish academic tradition. Social activity centers around music and performances by guitar and tambourine ensembles. Tunas are common in the college scene throughout Latin America and Spain.

19. *Calle 13*, CD (Sony International, B000BTITU8, 2005).

20. Sigmund Freud, "Humor," in *Art & Literature*, ed. Albert Dickson (Middlesex, England: Penguin Books, 1990), 427.

21. Marcos Pérez Ramírez, "Se la juega Calle 13," *El Nuevo Día*, April 30, 2006, final edition.

22. September 23 is a crucial date for supporters of Puerto Rican independence. It commemorates the Grito de Lares (the Lares Uprising), a revolt against the Spanish government—which then ruled the island. It started on September 23, 1868, in the town of Lares and lasted for a few days. Every year, hundreds of independence supporters meet at the town square in Lares to remember the event and reiterate their wish of independence for Puerto Rico. Filiberto Ojeda Ríos, leader of Los Macheteros, the Boricua Popular Army, sent a recorded message every year, which was played during the celebrations in commemoration of the Grito de Lares. During the late eighties, Ojeda Ríos was charged with the robbery of 7 million dollars from the Wells Fargo Bank. In 1989, he was declared innocent by a Puerto Rican jury but was required to wear an electronic leg bracelet, which he removed in 1990. After that, he remained at large for more than a decade. On September 23, 2005, he was killed by FBI agents when they tried to arrest him. The death of Ojeda Ríos generated indignation in many sectors of Puerto Rican society, who consider him a Puerto Rican hero and martyr.

23. Los Macheteros is a clandestine organization founded in the late seventies by the independence supporters Filiberto Ojeda Ríos, Juan Segarra Palmer, and Orlando González Claudio. It's dedicated to the promotion of the liberation of Puerto Rico from U.S. colonial rule through the use of force. See Latino Studies Resources, "Puerto

Rican Separatists," http://www.latinamericanstudies.org/epb-macheteros.htm (accessed June 19, 2008).

24. "Querido FBI" may be downloaded for free at http://pr.indymedia.org/news/2005/09/10155.php (accessed June 27, 2008).

25. The song makes reference to neighborhoods, projects, and towns of Puerto Rico inhabited by working-class populations.

26. Prior to the advent of reggaeton, the social content of Puerto Rican commercial rap did not necessarily deal with the island's political or colonial situation. Its content was limited to criticizing the conditions of poverty and the dynamics of oppressed sectors of the country. For the most part, reggaeton has dealt with politics only when its rhythm and singers have been recruited to create songs for political campaigns.

27. Jacques Derrida, "Structure, Sign, and Play in the Discourse of the Human Sciences," in *Writing and Difference*, trans. Alan Bass (London: Routledge, 2004), 289.

28. Shooting toward the sky during New Year's Eve is, unfortunately, a relatively common practice in Puerto Rico. It has caused injuries and deaths to adults and children. For this reason, in recent years government entities and civil society groups have organized campaigns to prevent these acts. The 2005 campaign was called "Las balas no van al cielo, los niños sí" (Bullets don't end up in heaven, children do). The single "Ley de Gravedad" was released as part of a public service campaign. I was unable to obtain any record label information

29. In 1993, Governor Pedro Rosselló appointed Luis Fortuño as head of the Puerto Rican Tourism Company. Fortuño developed a campaign to promote the island as a tourist destination with the slogan "Puerto Rico lo hace mejor" (Puerto Rico does it better), which had various Puerto Rican public figures as speakers, including the singers Ricky Martin and Chayanne.

30. In Puerto Rico, a *bruto* is a person with little intelligence or with rough manners. By using "brutosaurio" or "dumb-saurus," Residente animalizes these men and suggests that persons who shoot into the sky are brutos the size of a dinosaur.

31. See Miguel López Ortiz and Javier Santiago, "Valiosa aportación del reggaetón en ofensiva boricua contra las balas," Fundación Nacional para la Cultura Popular, http://www.prpop.org/noticias/ene06/reggaeton_ene04.shtml (accessed June 19, 2008).

32. According to data by the Policía de Puerto Rico, during the 2006 New Year's Eve there were no deaths resulting from shots into the air, and only two persons were injured by this sort of action. This number contrasts with data from the previous year, when ten injuries of this kind were reported during the New Year's Eve celebration.

33. Throughout 2001, Héctor "El Flaco" Figueroa was the producer of most of the reggaeton music videos filmed in Puerto Rico. Their strong visual content, evident in the music videos of Wisín and Yandel, Daddy Yankee, and Nicky Jam, among others, generated the 2002 legislative inquiry led by Senator Velda González to censor perreo.

34. Marshall, "The Rise of Reggaetón."

35. *Calle 13*, CD (Sony International, B000BTITU8, 2005).

36. CIRCO is one of the most popular rock bands in Puerto Rico. Its live perfor-

mances are well known for their conceptual incorporation of elements of *performance*, theater, contemporary dance, and the circus scene. The lyrics of its songs are poetic, and its music combines electroacoustic sounds, distinguishing them from other Puerto Rican and Latin American bands. One of CIRCO's main attractions is their front man, José Luis "Fofé" Abreu, who displays a particular use of language, metaphors, and a liberating discourse that proposes coming out of the closet and freeing passions. Fofé evinces, both at the artistic level and in terms of gender, a certain ambiguity. CIRCO's songs, which include the well-known hits "Un Accidente," "Cascarón," "Circosis," and "Historia de un Amor," among others, always carry sexuality to a fantastic environment. José Luis Colón, their manager, also handles Calle 13.

How to Make Love with Your Clothes On

Dancing *Regeton*, Gender, and Sexuality in Cuba

REGETON LYRICS: THE YUMA FACTOR.
THE BODY AS "CONVERTIBLE CURRENCY"

Havana 2005 and I am living in Vedado—that is, uptown—in an area that before the 1959 Revolution was mostly white and middle class, and which is now mixed socially and racially.[1] Between May and July almost every night, through my bedroom window, I hear one song played frequently by the people officially squatting in the half-finished building alongside. Each time the song comes on, they pump up the volume. I become aware of this song everywhere: in taxis, fast food restaurants, and bars, at house parties and on the radio. It's the song of the moment, and for a foreigner like me it has a lot of ironic resonance. It's called "A Ti, Te Gustan los Yumas" (Oh You, You Like Foreigners), and on the home-burned compilation I buy from a Cuban on the street one day, I learn from the minimal information on the paper sleeve (names of songs and artist only) that it is by Reana (an artist I have so far not managed to find out anything about). Its catchiness makes it stick in my memory immediately, particularly what I hear as the "diffidence" or irony of the female chorus as they sing the title line, "A ti, te gustan los yumas."

In Cuba *yuma* is the street slang used to refer to a "foreigner." Originally it meant a "Yankee," someone from the United States, but now it is used, often pejoratively, to refer to any foreigner.[2] Unequal access to the dual currency on the island (the Cuban peso and Cuban convertible peso, the latter having replaced the American dollar, which functioned as dual currency from 1993 until 2001) has led to a certain disdain verging on dislike of foreigners among Cubans. This implicit resentment is due to the fact that access or selling services to foreigners of any nature, officially or unofficially, is one good way of getting the convertible pesos, which Cubans need to get hold of. The text of the song discusses the impact of yumas while professing mutual love between a Cuban couple, "yo soy tu mangote . . . tu locote" (I'm your big mango, your crazy one). The "mutual love" of the text was reinforced by the regeton dance itself being danced between Cubans rather than between Cubans and yumas (seen on occasion, although few yumas dance regeton effectively since regeton moves are quite difficult for non-Latinos, as they require a lot of learning of body movements that for many Cubans begin within the first year of life). I see this regeton song as voicing similar sentiments to those expressed in the *timba* lament "La Bruja" written by José Luis Cortés of NG La Banda, which caused controversy and was effectively marginalized from the Cuban media in 1999, after protests from the Cuban Women's Federation. As a song, while it un-doubtedly expressed what could be interpreted as misogynistic elements, it was simultaneously a male lament at the sadness brought about by Cuban women preferring foreign men to Cuban men as a result of the implied dollar factor.

What struck me every time I heard "A ti, te gustan los yumas" in 2005 in houses, Cuban peso taxis, blaring from bars and the occasional fast food outlets, is the way the verse is sung by male hip-hop style rappers with clever rhyming verses over a prerecorded "background," while the chorus, sung by a group of female singers, sounds diffident—like a "shrugging shoulder"—as if liking a yuma or foreigner is a necessary evil, that is, voicing an attitude inherent to Cuban everyday life.

I found the yuma text really interesting because, confirming my own ethno-musicological research on timba dance music in the late 1990s in Cuba, song lyrics for dance music seemed to be functioning as newspaper articles and columns did in other cultures, acting as a barometer of Cuban everyday life, an essential way of finding out what ordinary Cubans think about what is going on politically, economically, and socially, particularly in the absence of an independent press. In the 1990s in a climate of *jinetera* service culture, the music scene was one of the most promising for Cubans to meet tourists and gain access to much-needed hard currency.

As a dancer I noticed the development of "new" dance moves involving the "solo" female body: the *despelote* (all-over-the-place) and *tembleque* (shake-shudder), and the *subasta de la cintura* (waist auction). These moves define a solo female dance style which involves fast undulating and turning or swirling of the area from below the shoulders and chest to the pelvis (as if one were Hula-hooping or belly dancing). Often accompanied by hand and body gestures mimicking self-pleasuring, in the 1990s it constituted a noticeable change in dance style, of women dancing to be "looked at" both by their partners, by other prospective partners, and by other spectators, using their body as a (their) major asset. This was in striking contrast to the more normative couple dancing.

In my opinion, the female body could be read symbolically as the "convertible currency" of the 1990s "Special Period," "exchanged" between Cuban male musicians and foreign men. I link these developments to attitudes toward, about, and among women at the time, arising from the responsibilities women assumed during the Special Period which gave them new authority. As I have written elsewhere, "lyrics were danced out in the music's shifting polyrhythms and structures which themselves form and mirror coital narratives . . . the dancing maps the complexities and contradictions of the new 'tourist' dollar economy."[3]

Timba is a driving dance music with a vital black Cuban dancing public.[4] Regeton, while danced by "white" Cubans, is similarly associated with a young, black Cuban population. As an ethnomusicologist, journalist, and someone who responds to the present scene in Cuba when I am there, my interest in regeton in 2005–6 stems from several important questions about music and dance: Why is regeton so popular and why now? What do regeton lyrics and dance moves suggest about gender and sexuality in Cuba; and about Cuban identity and local/global relations? And what kind of reading could be given to the way in which in regeton Cuban women were standing in front of their men with their backs to them, rather than facing them as in other dances?[5]

REGETON AND INFORMAL DISTRIBUTION NETWORKS

The music of "A ti, te gustan los yumas" is a regeton, that is, voices singing and rapping against a computer or machinemade "background" recording that Marshall calls "inherently hybrid . . . an industrial music . . . a high-tech product . . . based around recycled rhythms and riffs."[6] It was featured on various home-burned unofficial regeton compilations circulating in Cuba in 2005 that offered a mix of homegrown songs and Pan-Caribbean hits. Regeton production and distribution (like hip-hop and rap before, yet more so) is the result of new underground initiatives fostered by the arrival in recent years of computer hard- and software into the hands of individuals who for the first time in Cuban history have the opportunity to create and distribute their music independently of state networks, albeit unofficially and illegally.[7]

The regeton compilations I purchased on the street had an overlap of songs. One compilation with twenty tracks—identified by title only—had a cover sporting a white, blond topless model up to her thighs in the sea baring her bottom naked save for a thong. The other—called *2005: La Cocinita, Volumen 12, La Popola* (a reference to a song where a woman complains about her sore vagina)—sports a soft-porn image of a blond white female model kneeling by an Ahamay motorbike with the titles of eight of its twenty-two tracks scattered alongside. Asking dancers about its imagery, the response I received is captured by the remark of one male dancer: "Women love guys with motorbikes." Of the tracks offered inside, some nineteen include an artist's name. Most tracks are not Cuban in origin. The atmosphere of the disc is fast, upbeat and fun, with some witty introductions to songs, yet it has to be said that close scrutiny of the lyrics of many of the songs, be they non-Cuban or Cuban, leave little to the imagination. As a result, in Cuba the lyrics were often spoken of as "vulgar," while simultaneously the same song as an entity would be appreciated for having an irresistibly "good" dance beat which largely outweighed the impact of lyrics.

On this CD, numerous songs with titles like "Cógeme el Tubo" (Hold my tube) serenade sexual parts, various sore orifices, oral, doggy-style and, implicitly, anal sex. For example, DJ Emilio celebrates female body parts: "Mami dame chocha/quiero chocha chocha chocha" (Sweetie, give me pussy, I want pussy, pussy, pussy). The female chorus' response is "Estaré mi corazón" (I'll be there, my heart). A Los Gatos song implies a woman's insatiability for sex and includes lines such as "me gusta . . . chocha . . . este palo es para ti perra . . . te gusta que te pega y que te pasa brocha (I like . . . pussy . . . this stick is for you bitch . . . you like it to hit you and to brush you [the latter word "brush" has explicit sexual meaning concerning moving "the stick/penis" between orifices]). The point here is that while double-entendre is a strong feature of all Cuban music throughout the twentieth century from classic *trova* to *son* to *changüí*, most of it was and is, though, often witty innuendo with nothing explicit. In contrast, taken lightly, humorously or not, regeton lyrics are more often than not explicitly pornographic and challenging. A good example of this came one day in a regeton sung by a six-year-old into my microphone in response to the invitation to "sing me a song" (when regeton was far from the discussion). Her musician mother was visibly shocked when her daughter sang shyly, "Que me gusta suave suave" (I enjoy it slowly, gently). While there is no doubt that most Cubans enjoy regeton just to dance to and may ignore the words, when they do listen to the words of some songs they agree that lyrics and their subliminal meanings can be questionable when younger listeners are concerned. In 2005, as regeton became the music par excellence for school parties, home fiestas, and the all-important, coming-of-age fifteen-year-old *quince* birthday parties for girls, the genre came under scrutiny because of its lyrics and dance moves.

MARGINALIZATION OF REGETON

By March–April 2006 regeton was being officially marginalized. Articles in the press following a debate on regeton at a significant Young Communist movement meeting were particularly prominent and persuasive, stimulating private and public discussion. Both lyrics and dance movements came under fire, and cultural institutions reacted against regeton.[8] In response, regeton was defended by musicians, with the female singer Oneilys Hevora of the group Los Gatos, reportedly saying "mi música es para bailar, para disfrutar, para que muchos se diviertan" (my music is for dancing, for pleasure, for many people's enjoyment). Despite this, regeton's fate was sealed: "Está siendo sutilmente limitado en los medios de prensa; se aconseja que no se utilice en fiestas de centros de enseñanza y se filtra en las discotecas" (It is being subtly limited in the media and press; we advise that it not be used in parties at teaching institutions, and it is being filtered in discothèques).[9]

DANCING BACK TO FRONT (CHEEK-TO-CROTCH)

Regeton dancing is, as far as I know, the first publicly popular "back to front" dance in Cuba. It is a dance which sensualizes the bottom and pelvis in fetishistic fashion. Hitherto most couple dancing has been face to face, save for processional congas in Cuban carnival, which uses quite different dance movements. Talking to choreographers and dancers in Cuba, I found that Cuban regeton moves were seen to have precedent in Cuban dance history, rather than coming into Cuba from elsewhere, like some of the music itself.[10] Let me describe three moments of regeton dance.

IN SITU 1

Carnival in Santiago de Cuba in July 2005: a line of five girls are dancing regeton with their men, the men using the wall of a dark side street to lean back on to support them, while their women stand in front, with their backs to them. Wearing tight, figure-hugging clothing, they are making fast swirling undulations from chest to their pelvic area, bottoms stuck slightly outward, while their partners stand close behind them, their own pelvic area thrust forward, so that their partners are stimulating their presented crotches. The girls look straight out at a group of Cubans and non-Cubans dancing salsa in the beer bar in front of them. A lot of the time they look us straight in the eye, with occasionally smiling faces that imply, "I don't mind if you look at me; look at what I can do for my man." The eyes of their men, meanwhile, rove slightly diverted, inward looking, concentrating on what is happening, or exchanging glances as if slightly diffident to the whole process. While this may appear pure conjectural observation, asked what the experience was like, a Santiago Cuban male dancer told me, "Slowly, you often get to where you are about to 'come' when it is happening, it is amazing." As the dance appears to be "female" led, its performative attributes and conventions certainly set up vivid notions of gendered power relations.[11]

IN SITU 2

July 2005 and Santiago's premier folk-dance ensemble Cutumba are invited to the Tropicana, Santiago's top cabaret nightspot, along with their guests, a group of British tourists who are taking dance classes with them. The Tropicana in Santiago, as in Havana, has continued prerevolutionary traditions (reappraised in the 1960s–70s) of a nightclub with a big dance and music spectacle. Today this involves top university-trained dancers and musicians. On this specific night the public also includes a 60–70 person mixed-gender squad of Venezuelan sailors spending time visiting Cuba. Both male and female sailors are in their late teens and early twenties and are dressed in pristine white uniforms. After the live show, whose vividly exuberant finale of a pan-Caribbean celebration of dance symbolically affirms the significance of Petro-Caribe economic relations and government agreements between Venezuela, Cuba and other parts of the Caribbean and South America, the disco takes over. Within minutes, Venezuelan sailors are inviting Cutumba's British male and female guests to dance, but mostly the female guests.

On the dance floor while some couples dance salsa, several pairs of Venezuelan men begin to dance with women "sandwich" style between them, the women's colorful dresses between the white uniforms bringing home the sandwich metaphor. They are dancing close in, with a man back and front, bodies touching, one man swiveling his pelvic area and pushing against the woman's bottom, the other her front. In practically all cases the eye contact is homosocial between two men over the woman's head, acknowledging each other as they move. Occasional movements take the trio or one or the other of the men swiveling (corkscrewing) down the woman's body to a crouched semisquat, their head level either with the woman's midbottom or her crotch, to then move back up again. The music is regeton; the atmosphere is playful. One woman in such a sandwich is seen pushing both men front and back away from her trying to achieve a more "normal" dancing distance. Another tries to dance-squirm her way into freer space in vain.

Asked afterward how they felt, one of these woman said, "It started out fun and flirty then it got rather heavy and I felt cramped and heavily pressed into and 'used.' I used my arms to try to make them keep their distance, but that just seemed to add to their idea of 'fun.'" Given that dance floor etiquette prevails—that is, being courteously asked to dance and then thanked afterward, and more often than not being accompanied back to their seat—the actual sexual and emotional impact of the experience is "forgotten" in the moment, or at least not mentioned. The only "negative" message given by these women to the men to show that they did not exactly enjoy the experience is by declining to dance again.

The sandwich dance is reportedly part of various Caribbean TV programs in which a woman is covered with water so that when she dances in a sandwich between two men, wet patches on the men's clothes afterward reveal where their bodies have touched. Indeed such "wet" patches offer a simulation of the excretions associated with sexual activity, notably sweat and semen.

READING THE DANCE: DANCE AND PORNOGRAPHY, DANCE AND GENDER RELATIONS

Let us say dance example "In situ 1" is a publicly performed, symbolically masturbatory dance. "In situ 2," the sandwich dance, apes troilism and pornographic "split roasting," that is, a woman serving one man sexually while another man is having sex with her. In my view, both these dances have sexually explicit if not pornographic references. How then are these dances to be "read," if we take into account the opinion of dance scholar Judith Lynne Hanna, who writes, "Feelings and ideas about sexuality and sex roles (also referred to as gender) take shape in dance. These visual models of which dancer (male or female) performs what, when, where, how, why, either along, or with another dancer, reflect and also challenge, society's expectations for each sex's specific activities, whether dominance patterns or mating strategies."[12]

In nearby Puerto Rico, the *reggaetón* dance is called *el perreo* ("doggy-style" in Puerto Rican slang). Put *perreo* into an Internet search mechanism, and you are presented with a lot of "veiled" porn sites. To me, the relationship between doggy dancing and porn is direct and unequivocal. At the risk of entering muddy moral waters, there are issues to explore. How are we to read *regeton*, *perreo*, and "sandwich dancing" if we approach gender as performed identity? How are we to read them if we consider that in many societies the rules that discipline the use of the body in dance "constitutes not only a means of self-display for the individual but also and especially the traditional occasion for public relationships between men and women (as well as between persons of the same gender)"?[13] How do we interpret regeton if, as Hannah notes, dance rules symbolize the synthesis of ideas on the feminine, the masculine, and the "proper" interaction between genders (or within a single gender) that distinguish a given community at a given point in time?[14]

Without wishing to offer too deterministic an explanation, where does the back-to-front dance position come from? Can it be explained as anything other than simply another novel way of dancing? Other than folkloric explanations, no Cuban I spoke to could offer me a reason as to why this dance with these moves has emerged. Is it too mechanistic to suggest that the symbolic impact of the dance is a response to the fact that in the 1990s women came to the fore in managing the difficult economic and domestic situation of the Special Period, keeping families fed and together under severe economic duress, that the woman does indeed stand forward with her man behind her?

In 2006, Cuban professional dancers I talked to were keen to dispel any overreading of regeton: "Es un movimiento del cinturón, menea, circulando caderas y cintura sin mala intención. El hombre disfruta del movimiento sin mala intención . . . es una provocación al hombre pero sin pretensión del sexo; se puede 'conquistar el hombre' también" (It's a move of the waist, a swirl, circling the hips and waist without any bad intention. The man enjoys the movement without any bad intention [either] . . . it provokes the man but without any intention of sex; you can "conquer a man" in this way as well). While the "lack of any bad intention" may mean these dancers were hedging their response given the 2006 media outcry against regeton, their remarks fall within the etiquette of much Cuban public discourse expressed verbally, which tends to "qualify," to never slander anything and to avoid critique. When asked about "sandwich" dancing the response was, "No es costumbre en Cuba pero si en el Caribe . . . se baila pero tiene que ser con alguien que se conoce, en una fiesta cuando se conoce entre compañeros, sería dos hombres y una mujer o dos mujeres y un hombre, pero no es común." (It's not a custom in Cuba, but it is in the Caribbean . . . it is danced but only with someone you know, at a party when you know the friends, whether two men and a woman or two women and one man, but it isn't common.)

In March 2006 all-night filming is going on at the open-air ballroom of the holiday camp at Playa Blanco, down the coast from Santiago, for a DVD for the song "La Farándula" (The Night Life) by Salsa Chula, a Santiago-based orchestra trying to get official recognition at the time. The song and video celebrate the vibrant dance nightlife of Santiago and the dancers are a mix of professionally trained, state-salaried dancers and "street" (i.e., unsalaried) groups. The choreographic moves of male and female are encoded with regeton moves, and the song features vocals from male singer El Médico del Regeton (the "Doctor of Regeton," who is indeed a doctor in his daytime job). Talking with these dancers about regeton—including posing the question, "What's in it for women?"—I got these answers: that (a) it is fun, (b) it can be erotic for both parties as the man caresses his partner's body including neck, shoulders, hips, and buttocks. Women dancers stressed you would only dance it with your boyfriend or someone you knew well. It was mentioned that it was all about sex, and that occasionally when people danced regeton in the right place and time, sex might occur. The explanation given was that there are few places for young people to meet in private as most live with their families, often sharing a bedroom with another family member. In discussing privacy issues among young people, I was told there are rooms that can be rented for an hour for liaisons, but with money short, many young people prefer to congregate in parks with little or no lighting. That people do have sex in parks may not be desired behavior, but everyone knows it happens. "Where else?" one person remarked. Then a male dancer told me, "In regeton it is possible for the man to come in from the behind: as the woman lifts her skirt and bends over more, the guy drops to his knees, drops his zipper and he's in."

ANTECEDENT CUBAN DANCE MOVES

While the Cubans I interviewed claimed not to know where regeton's dance moves originated, it is clear that there are, in fact, antecedents in Cuba. I first saw a precursor to the body movements used by women for regeton in 1989 during the Havana Jazz Festival in the main seated concert area of Cuba's National Theater. In an aisle between sections of seats while others sat and listened, a girl with a red Lycra dress clinging to her frame, legs slightly apart, moved fast, swirling her bottom outward behind her while a steady stream of men took their turn to stand behind her. At a certain point, the man immediately behind her benefiting from her gyrations was "moved on" by a man standing at her side (friend, boyfriend, brother, lover, pimp?). This was a masturbatory service dance done proudly as if the woman's body was a glorious choice, a public expression of male and female libido.

In the early 1980s and through the '90s Pedro Calvo, then lead singer and dancer with Cuba's top group Los Van Van, would dance *sandunguera* style with women he pulled up onto the stage out of the audience, the whole thing encapsulated in the Los Van Van song "Sandunguera." Depending on the context, he would invite women, from preteen to middle age. While they swiveled their bodies facing him, often he undulated downward, going "down" on them so that his head and mouth at one point would be level with their crotch, a stylized direct reference to oral sex. In Cuba such public dancing behavior is not considered to transgress taboos; nor in my experience is it considered taboo when a young (female) child in her first twelve to eighteen months (not years) apes swirly pelvic and bottom movements. Rather, such precocity is applauded and celebrated: "aquí nos celebramos, es una gracia . . . cuando vemos un niño o una niña es novedoso para nosotros y pensamos que lo trae en la sangre de cuando pequeño" (here we celebrate that, as a gift, when we see a young girl or boy do it, it is a novelty for us, and we think they carry it in their blood). Thus, the sexual movements prominent in Cuban dance are part of normative learned behavior.

According to a Cuban choreographer I interviewed, some of the moves involved in regeton, despelote, and tembleque reference rumba, notably the *baile de yambú*, "donde la mujer tiene la fuerza, una oportunidad [de] mostrar su belleza, la coquetería con el hombre desplazado, se desplaza atrás de la mujer" (Where the woman has the power and opportunity to show her beauty and coquetry while the man relocates himself behind the woman). Other dances mentioned as possible sources for choreographic gestures are rituals of the Afro-Cuban Palo religion, *baile de makuta* and *de yuka*, "que es un baile en que el hombre y la mujer empiezan en frente pero después el hombre baila atrás de la mujer como algo picaresco amándola y haciendo gestos de un agradecimiento pero de atrás como un gallo" (which is a dance where the man and woman begin in front but then the man goes behind the woman in a picaresque way, loving her and making gestures of appreciation from behind like a cock).

Dances in Latin America since colonial times have included the stylized flir-tatious "cock and hen" couple dances known as the *zamacueca* and *cueca*, which exist under other names and in different forms in various countries. This dance usually leaves the women in a decisive position as to whether to be symbolically "possessed" or not, in similar ways to the *vacunao*, the "posses-sion" move in rumba. In the Colombian *cumbia callejera* the woman controls by carrying a handful of lit candles, which she holds in front of her lower waist in order to be able to see and fend off the man trying to conquer her. However, while these dances involve moves denoting symbolic attempts at sexual posses-sion, none of them is a back-to-front dance.

In Cuba, until the ongoing Young Communist–prompted discussion which began openly in December 2005, dance moves have rarely been spoken of as transgressive. Yet, as Charles Chasteen shows in his history of dance—which focuses on the emergence of tango in Buenos Aires, Argentina; *danzón* in Havana, Cuba; and samba in Rio de Janeiro—Brazil, transgressive dance is the key to dance history in Latin America.[15] He shows how social and gender inequalities and imbalances created the climate in which tango, danzón, and samba (which have all become "national" dances) emerged. Each was regarded as deeply transgressive at the time, and each shocked Western sensibilities with their explicitness. In Cuba, danzón—which appeared in the 1880s—was felt to have too much African influence as it brought the pelvic *requebro*, the breaking of natural vertical line body by a fast-hitting move frontally of the pelvis from male to female, as a mark of possession. Chasteen quotes a "Cuban social reformer" as writing "the dancers were pushing their thighs and hips together separated only by the women's wrinkled skirt."[16]

Unlike regeton, danzón (like tango and samba) was initially popular in bordellos, that is, with the "other" side of society, gradually making its way into the salon via upper-class men who frequented lower-class haunts and then brought the dance to private salons, where it became stylized and normative. While tembleque, despelote, and regeton moves did not develop in bordellos, they all developed in the climate of modern sexual flirtation and potential sexual liaisons between Cubans and Cubans, and (more significantly) Cubans and non-Cubans, in the heady atmosphere of Havana clubs in the 1990s when jinetera service culture and sexuality as "convertible currency" were prime.[17] As such, in comparable ways to tango and danzón, changing social relations are acted out on the dance floor. The difference with regeton per se post 2000 is that it is notably danced out between Cubans, especially in what are often referred to in Cuba as "barrios malos" (bad neighborhoods) which implies poor, marginal, and often, black. Thus, although regeton may not have emerged in bordellos, it is definitely identified in Cuba by Cubans with the "lower strata" of Cuban society.

Given the "official" message from the Cuban media that regeton is a questionable form, it is notable how regeton moves and music have been absorbed into hip-hop and other salsa hybrids. Officially regeton may be suspect but unofficially it will not disappear, protected by other hybrid forms and the performers who create it.

Indeed the cultural politics of the official Hermanos Saíz cultural associations, who encourage cutting-edge or youth music in Cuba, have it that there is "good" and "bad" regeton. While it is not within the purview of this essay to analyze racial issues, they are deeply relevant in Cuba; "banning" dance popular with black Cubans as a form of social control has been an integral part of Cuba's cultural history since before the nineteenth and twentieth centuries.[18] While racial equality has been state ideology since the 1959 Revolution, racial difference is articulated in everyday conversation by the description of subtle gradations of skin color when referring to family and friends, often in a deprecating and self-deprecating manner.

CONCLUSIONS

I would like to conclude with a series of questions: In the twenty-first century, given its "back to front" positioning and intrinsic sexuality, does regeton pose a serious set of postfeminist questions? And, historically, did other dances— including danzón, son, rumba, tango, and samba—also pose such issues before they were "cleaned up"? Is the bottom line that the values embraced by both sexes are "male" values? Does analyzing new dance moves that have been incorporated into regeton in Cuba reveal that they signify different sexual values embraced by a new generation of women? Do dances that accentuate sexual movements give women a "sense of power" from the idea that they are in control, turning their man on, capable of being what men want? Sexual attractiveness, "showing of your assets" at all times, seems to have become more of a norm, confusingly tied up with confidence and self-esteem.

Is regeton as a dance empowering for women? Can it be empowering to one generation and not another? To me its message is, "I am a woman and I am here to serve men's needs, when I choose!" However, as both song lyrics and the dance are familiar to and copied by preteen and prepubescent teenagers as well as teenagers, is the subliminal message of this dance, a foreplay dance acted out in public, the sexual "domestication" of women into traditional "service" roles, in other words, that a woman's role is to serve her man? Is it a dance in which Cuban women are telling their men they still serve them even if they have to face and at times interact with foreigners and other men?

I would argue that reggaetón in general, as both a Cuban and Pan-Latin phenomenon, has serious issues attached to it. In the global context of the increased availability of pornography mostly consumed by men; increased media use of soft porn images in advertising to the extent that soft porn is considered as normative; increased sexual trafficking of young women throughout the world; information that anal sex and doggy-style sex are part of an increasing AIDS climate with anal sex with women (or men) as the "ultimate male fantasy"; information that sex workers get paid most for unprotected anal sex, leading to higher incidence of HIV—given all this, is it possible that behind regeton/reggaetón fun is a less positive reality? Or am I being an old prude? Reggaetón, we are reliably told by a leading British Sunday newspaper, will soon be the subject of a Hollywood film. Perhaps in the same way Hollywood bastardized and cleaned up tango with its Rudolph Valentino films in the 1920s and '30s, reggaetón dance and lyrics will be "cleaned" up, made palatable for the mainstream media perhaps with the swirling butt of Jennifer Lopez! But, I would argue, the deeper issues for women, feminist or not, remain.

NOTES

The title "How to Make Love with Your Clothes On" (Cómo hacer el amor con ropa) is taken from a report on articles about *reggaetón* published in the Cuban *Juventud Rebelde* newspaper early in 2006. See http://www.terra.com/ocio/articulo/html/oci61067.htm (accessed July 7, 2007). An earlier version of this essay appears as Jan Fairley, "Dancing Back to Front: *Regeton*, Sexuality, Gender and Transnationalism in Cuba," Middle Eight, Dance Issue, *Popular Music* 25, no. 3 (2006): 471–88. In Cuba, *regeton* is known on the street as *regeton/regetón*, occasionally *reguetón*. Officially in and outside Cuba, it is now also known as *reggaetón*. In deference to the orality of Cuban culture, I use *regeton* when talking only of Cuba as this was the first spelling I saw on a homemade poster, and *reggaetón* for outside Cuba. Translations of Spanish-language quotations are my own.

1. I write this essay from the point of view of being a white British female interdisciplinary trained researcher with a Ph.D. in ethnomusicology working as a writer

and broadcaster, who has been observing the Cuban music and dance scene since 1978. The interviews cited in this essay were conducted in Cuba between 2005 and 2006. As an "outsider," or "yuma," in Cuba, my perspectives are my own, as are any unwitting prejudices.

2. While Cuba receives limited tourists from the United States, there are a small number each year. More significantly, Cuba receives U.S. cultural production through the comings and goings of the Cuban diaspora from the United States, and via TV programs from the United States and Americas via legal and illegal satellite dishes. The term *yuma* in Cuba originally defined North Americans or those who symbolize a "North American" lifestyle, i.e., exhibiting material wealth through indicators such as clothes and possessions and the ability to travel in and out of Cuba by means of their own capital. In Cuba today, *yuma* is used to refer to all foreigners. Nevertheless, it remains for many Cubans an embarrassing term if used face to face; i.e., it has a pejorative inflection, bound up with the service culture of "jineterism." For more on "jineterism," see Jan Fairley, " 'Ay Díos, Ampárame' (O God, Protect Me): Music in Cuba during the 1990s, the 'Special Period,'" in *Island Musics*, ed. Kevin Dawe (Oxford: Berg Publishers, 2004), 91.

3. Fairley, " 'Ay Díos, Ampárame,'" 92.

4. See Vicenzo Perna, *Timba: The Sound of the Cuban Crisis* (Aldershot, England: Ashgate, 2005).

5. I do not use the Puerto Rican / U.S. term *perreo* to describe regeton in Cuba as this term was not used at all when I carried out this research, and, as far as I have been able to ascertain, it is not commonly used in Cuba. As a frame for this study, I refer to Helmi Järviluoma, Pirkko Moisala, and Anni Vilkko, *Gender and Qualitative Methods* (London: Sage Publications, 2003). My conclusions move beyond their work.

6. Wayne Marshall, "The Rise of Reggaetón: From Daddy Yankee to Tego Calderón, and Beyond," *Phoenix*, January 19, 2006.

7. While regeton is by no means the first non-Cuban music to circulate in Cuba, I would argue that it has circulated in much wider form than rock, rap, or even hip-hop largely because of the means of circulation—i.e., burned CDs sold illegally on streets rather than circulating among musicians and aficionados—and due to it being primarily perceived as party dance music.

8. "Censuran al reggaeton en Cuba, dicen que es 'peligroso,'" *Terra*, http://www.terra.com/ocio/articulo/html/oci61067.htm (accessed July 7, 2007). "Cuerpos muy pegados . . . como hacer el amor con ropa" (Bodies stuck together . . . like making love with clothes on) was the description of reggaeton dance moves in a *Juventud Rebelde* newspaper article.

9. *Terra*, http://www.terra.com/ocio/articulo/html/oci61067.htm (accessed July 7, 2007).

10. Similar movements can be found elsewhere in the Americas (e.g., in sound system carnival *blocos* in Brazil, "wining" in Trinidad, Jamaican dancehall moves, and "freak dancing" in the 1990s in the United States).

11. Järviluoma, Moisala, and Vilkko, *Gender and Qualitative Methods.*

12. Judith Lynne Hannah, as quoted in Tulia Magrini, ed., *Music and Gender: Perspectives from the Mediterranean* (Chicago: University of Chicago Press, 2003), 6.

13. "Dancing provides a faithful expression of the most diverse and nuanced meanings, since its rules specify who can take part in the dance and how the body is used . . . allowing or denying specific forms of bodily contact, and regulating other aspects in such a way as to highlight shared ideas on what constitutes an acceptable physical relationships in the public sphere." Ibid., 6.

14. Ibid.

15. John Charles Chasteen, *National Rhythms, African Roots: The Deep History of Latin American Popular Dance* (Albuquerque: University of New Mexico Press, 2004).

16. Ibid., 20.

17. Fairley, " 'Ay Díos, Ampárame.'"

18. Robin Moore, *Nationalizing Blackness: AfroCubanismo and Artistic Revolution in Havana, 1920–1940* (Pittsburgh: University of Pittsburgh Press, 1994).

PART VI
REGGAETON'S POETICS, POLITICS, AND AESTHETICS

GALLEGO (JOSÉ RAÚL GONZÁLEZ)

TRANSLATION BY JUAN FLORES

Chamaco's Corner

Los chamacos no se van de la esquina ni a tiros.
Los chamacos siempre están enesa esquina.
Los chamacos se arrebatan en la esquina también.
Los chamacos hablan de política, de trucos,
de salsa vieja, de nuevayol, de grafitis, de las mámises,
de los camarones que anoche
les violaron sus derechos.
Los chamacos hablan del bambalán
que les tumbó el quiosco, hablan de presidio,
de los socios ausentes que picharon pa' locos,
de lo triste que quedaron cuando se fue Paula C.
De que los ricos van pa' arriba
y los pobres vamos pa' bajo,
de que esto es una encerrona disfrazá de felicidá
y más na' pana mío.
Los chamacos se lamentan
por la irrepentina muerte del tecato favorito
del barrio nuestro de cada día.
Los chamacos se amanecían en la esquina
celebrando la ocasión de aún estar vivos,
hablán de sus biejas, de la raíz que tiene la noche,
delos que han matado y quisieran volver a revivir
y volver a matar, que ojo por ojo se paga en la calle,
que cada santo obliga'o tiene su misa.
Rompe en frío el más cercano a mí
Y pago el tax sentimental que nos une.
Los chamacos hablaron deun subterráneo

en la esquina en donde se bailan
rumbas de alma adentro,
dijeron de una venta de collares preparados,
hablaron de la novia del novio asesinado
con un poco de explotaera de casco.
La escoltaron hasta un lugar estipulado
y vacilaron pero siempre vacilaron.
Los chamacos se fueron de la esquina a tiros.
Los chamacos calentaron el punto, están a fuego
Y no piensan jugársela fría,
ni pa' dios.

Those guys don't leave the corner even when shots are fired.
Those guys are always on that corner.
Those guys get high on the corner too.
Those guys talk about politics, about tricks,
about old salsa, about nuevayol, about graffiti, about fine ladies,
about the cops who violated
their rights last night.
The guys talk about the shithead
who messed up their spot, about doing time,
about the missing partners who didn't pay them no mind,
about how sad they felt when Paula C split.
About how rich people move up
and we poor folk go downhill,
about how this is a dead end dressed up as happiness
and that's about the size of it my man.
Those guys are saddened
by the dragged-out death of the junkie
who is the all-time favorite of our 'hood day in and day out.
Those guys would wake up on the corner
celebrating the occasion of still being alive,
talking about their ole ladies, of the deep roots of the night,
of the ones who they killed and want to bring back to life
so they could kill them again, of how in the streets it's an eye for an eye,
and every saint eventually gets his day.
The one closest to me breaks into a cold sweat
and I wind up paying the sentimental tax that binds us together.
Those guys talk about a subway

on the corner where you can dance
rumbas from your inner soul,
they told about a sale of handmade necklaces infused with spiritual powers,
talked about the girlfriend of the boyfriend who was murdered
with a little blow of the mind.
They escorted her to an agreed-on place
and had a great time every time.
The guys left the corner when shots were fired.
The guys heated up that spot, they're on fire
and have no intention of taking that risk,
not even for god's sake.

Editors' Note: This poem served as the introduction to Daddy Yankee's 2000
debut album El Cartel de Yankee.

Salon Philosophers

Ivy Queen and Surprise Guests Take Reggaetón Aside

For the occasion of Panama's centennial, the honorary queen of the festival in San Miguelito hoped to cool down and, in her words, baptize the audience with a bottle of water. Before dousing the crowd, however, preparations needed to be made. Martha Ivelisse Pesante, better known as the singer Ivy Queen, pointed her long ornate fingernail toward a woman in the audience and said, "Tú no quieres que se te joda el blower negra, ¿verdad? Yo tampoco. Yo tengo el pelo malo. Te lo juro, yo soy blanca pero tengo pelo malo" (You don't want me to fuck up your blow-out, *negra*, am I right? I wouldn't want that either. I have bad hair. I swear to you, I'm white but I have bad hair).[1] Far from the wet T-shirt shenanigans common to outdoor concerts, this aside offers a provocative entry point into reading reggaetón, especially as it comes from the genre's heralded queen. I hesitate to address her by this royal moniker and not because of the validity of the title. To subject her to this honorific is to also in some ways subject her to a perpetual takedown. The miring of these superlatives on musicians too easily makes them instruments for genres' cock-fights, too readily sets them up as the standards by which everything else must be kept real. Given that these royal titles can only be held one at a time, the music's makers are understood as temporary, interchangeable, replaceable. And of course, in the case of women musicians, these titles position them as the singular exceptions to the male rule.

I begin this essay with Ivy Queen's aside for its unique ability to swerve reggaetón's charted course, both musical and critical. Its uniqueness lies in its confrontational bent, but also in its potential to go unnoticed. It is not part of a song, but a moment of quick improvised banter that takes place off the set list and outside the studio space. As such, it is one of those wonderful outlaw moments that can be taken up when constrained by the laws of genre.[2] The aside pulls the rug out from under what is thought to govern reggaetón: the audiences, locations, and practices it is said to encompass. Beyond corrupting any assumed sense of market, the aside is a compelling example of what broadening the terms of the musical can make possible. It enables us to read and hear music as that which goes beyond songs and/or praxis. It is a thread of performance—if and when it is picked up—that allows for movement into critical and creative places often lost from reggaetón's range of sight and sound.

This essay takes up a few such moments, or to borrow a term from Barbara Johnson, surprises. Johnson argues, "The impossible but necessary task of the reader is to set herself up to be surprised. No methodology can be relied on to generate surprise. On the contrary, it is usually surprise that engenders methodology."[3] Here I extend Johnson's "necessary task" not only to the realm of performance, but to a way of being in the world. To set oneself up for surprise would mean abandoning that quantitative thrust behind having to know everything, what she calls the "comforts of mastery." Uncomfortable, unpredictable, but always-present surprises put any methodology into productive crisis. But the surprise is not waiting to be discovered by you, the critic, so that it can be made visible and valuable to scholarship. To remain open to surprise is not about an excavation, but an inclination. You must be prepared (if you aren't already) to assume an already heard, danced, and lived agent on the move.

To simply call Ivy Queen out for reproducing shame over her African roots by the use of *pelo malo* is too easy. A few things must nevertheless be stated from the outset. The phrase "pelo malo"—the discursive dread(s) of Africa in the Americas—does indeed signal the violence of value that has long been assigned to phenotypic racial marks. This gesture of presumed affiliation might too readily rely on shorthand to approximate the lived realities of dark-skinned Latinas, those for whom racial passing is not a choice. Her qualifier "soy blanca" could be read as a distancing, a recognition of her option to pass, or both at once. Perhaps it collapses the specific processes of racial formation experienced by a New York—born but island-raised Boricua, and the woman in the audience, presumably Panamanian from San Miguelito.[4]

What's more, this aside evokes a phenomenon in reggaetón that acknowledges racial signifiers—both physical and musical—only through their refusal. As one example: in the video accompaniment to N.O.R.E.'s "Oye Mi Canto," that most audible global hit, you'll come to find that "it doesn't matter your race 'cause today you're Latino" is a straight-up falsehood—and only convenient for that feel-good, last-line-of-the-verse chiming in so common to anthems. This refusal of race as a rallying cry outs a particular strain of pan-*latinidad* that will affirm African ancestry so that it can also subjugate it. This kind of recognition or refusal has long put certain women's bodies at the service of a global pan-Latino ethos. In the case of "Oye Mi Canto," the women are light skinned, wear bikinis inspired by the flags of their respective nations, and grind on a beach. This is but one dangerous enactment that has gone down in the vexed interstice that Raquel Z. Rivera has theorized as "between blackness and *latinidad*."[5]

You might have gathered that there are all kinds of precedents already in place for reading reggaetón.

I would like to take what Ivy Queen does in this aside elsewhere. To skew it from the above course might first mean noting the vital countertradition of having to occupy descriptives such as "pelo malo" from the inside: to make them sound, and yes, actually mean, terms of endearment and recognition. It is also to acknowledge "pelo malo" as a banal descriptive: for getting a blow-out does not necessarily mean that you are eliminating the ancestors with every downward pull of the round brush. Without relaxing the precedents of her remark, its delivery comes with a tenderness that does not subjugate Africa in the Americas, but instead involves it as a vital and assumed part of her performance. There might not be that assumed and flattened experience of race in the aside, but (and not unrelated) a sharing of what feels like lifetimes spent in hair salons. That it is a comment that shares those private processes between women in a very public way strongly corrupts the idea of male-dominated spaces of reggaetón, a mythos that upholds men as the drivers of the music, its reception, which is to also say, its *perreo*.[6] And anyway, one look at the black studded leather belt strapped around Ivy Queen's pelvis is enough to disrupt those secure assumptions of penetration.

The aside puts the audience of mostly women and girls who flank the stage and sing along with Ivy Queen aboveground, especially when they all laugh hard in response. This is not a mosh pit, a site from which to launch your panties at a male MC, or a gutter for a potential crowd surge. There is no hooliganism here. The youngest girls look up, their eyes wide, beautiful, and visible even as they fall way below bodies that tower over them. Young boys recite the songs from memory. Mothers have their toddlers gathered to their waists as they dance. It is their inspiration for this calling out that I am able to read, by which I mean hear, some different spaces within reggaetón. There is the actual fact of the location of San Miguelito, a place that borders the fractured isthmus. In this performance, underrecognized legacies of West Indian migration are made a central and fundamental part of reggaetón's aesthetics.

This location bears the traces of those who have historically brought their own cadences to Panama. They might have arrived to work an actual cut into the landscape, but they also bore deep musical cuts that have augmented the performance repertory of the Americas. These modulations contribute their own particular signals to what Daphne Brooks has poetically named "the middle passage wall of sound."[7]

Ivy Queen gives us a few locations here that engender and amplify different receptive worlds. Thus far, we have the import of Puerto Rico and New York to the site of San Miguelito with all of the implications that migratory path carries. But then we are given the referent of the salon. The salon has been historically and inaccurately imagined and dismissed as a bourgeois, chenille-draped space of frivolity. However, salons have long existed as vital noninstitutional gathering spaces for women, or more broadly, as noninstitutional spaces of learning. The salon might mean the crowded tumble around a family's bathroom mirror, one that relies on intense mathematical coordination when one blower is on hand (to say nothing of what the circuitry can actually handle). The salon can also mean an actual *peluquería*, the translocal repository of salon culture, with all the implications that space carries.[8] However understood, through surfacing the specter of the salon in the duration of the performance, Ivy Queen resurrects many ghosted locations behind reggaetón, and of Latina/o music generally.

The implicit mention of the salon recognizes the work it takes before women go public. This getting-ready time is not without its pain nor is it without its pleasures. While it is absolutely important, what is made visible here, goes beyond simply looking good. In San Miguelito and elsewhere, women are not solely spectators of reggaetón's commercial spectacular enterprise. The outing of the salon is a reminder that women get ready and prepare to enter spaces of live performance, especially as spectators, whether we're talking about getting a blow-out, outfit coordination, brushing up on history, shoe selection, selecting points of argument, and overall psychic preparation. They are not simply found bent over with their backsides in the air. The women that flank this or any stage are not passive spectators present in order to get discovered at the scene of "liveness." Roxanne Shante puts it best on the current single by Basement Jaxx: "Your hair's done, just bust a move."

On a more literal level, Ivy Queen makes visible the salon as a formative and specific site of women's musical publics. The salon can be a crucial, alternative venue that has as much a part of musical circulation as bars, cabarets, and bodegas. Ivy Queen signals that time and work that goes down in the beauty salon, where all kinds of things are done and said under the sonic blasts of blow-dryers. She makes audible the listening and the talking that gets done even in the midst of chemical processes and acetone, the grind of a manicurist's drill, and the music that blasts from a small radio hung up in a corner.[9] Even if there is no radio, music is still being made and publics are still being developed. No, of course she does not want to ruin those hours and money spent; she does not want to fuck up the blow-out.

I am now brought to Ivy Queen's thundering voice as it emerges in both her speaking and singing. Her voice signals other genealogies of women vocalists from Latin/a America. Its grumble reminds us of others who have so bravely and unapologetically resided in or dipped into the lower reaches of the vocal range. Myrta Silva, Toña la Negra, Freddy, La Lupe, Lisette Melendez, and Judy Torres are all part of the vocal lineage that leads to Ivy Queen.[10] Her voice has a deep sound and withholding, a quality that comes from keeping things locked up in your chest, a place where you've temporarily stuffed a few things so you don't explode. It has the kind of hoarseness that sounds like having to constantly speak above things. This "above" might be the noises of the salon, your friends embroiled in serious *chisme* (gossip), the undermiked area in the background, the frequencies of male producers.

Ivy Queen's husky intervention cannot be lost here, because it cuts a critical seam into those ubiquitous and wheedling choral refrains replete in much of reggaetón. To say nothing of its rampant misogyny, it cannot be denied that reggaetón allots little to no space for women's voices. When heard in recordings, women performers usually lay down a "dame/dale" response to a phallocentric call. These responses are made manifest via choral begging that modulates between a request of "dame" (give me) and a demand "dale" (go ahead) of the male vocalist. In certain instances, "dale" can also be heard as an indirect request (give her) as when the singer refers to herself, removed, in the third person. The omnipresence of the dame/dale responsive is such that it could provide quantitative fun for a parlor game. How many can you think of? Two exemplary moments of this can be found in Wisin and Yandel's "Rakata" as "Papi dame lo que quiero" (Papi give me what I want); and in Hector El Bambino's "Dale Castigo" as "Dale perro, dame castigo" (go ahead *perro*/punish me).[11]

These responses cannot be utilized as a litmus test to gage whether the women are really "in control" or not. Nor can we make any kind of assumptions about the modes of reception that might take place during their iteration, recorded or otherwise. The commands that surface via these choruses become reoccupied in all kinds of creative and expansive ways, whether enacted on a dance floor, a bedroom, or both. To engage either/or questions that revolve around some facile sense of women's "agency" turns any critique of genre's conventions into a problem (and not accidentally, a women's problem) that can be figured out and solved with a quick corrective. There are, to my mind, more pressing dilemmas. The vocal uniformity of these choral retorts across an impressive number of tracks, the fact that they exist *only* in the responsive address, and their lack of poetic play are but a few of the conventions that demand further analysis. Most pressing of all: I would like to be able to address the women vocalists who perform in the songs above by name, but they are not credited in the liner notes.

I don't want my calling out the recurrence of the dame/dale responsive to prohibit the flow of surprise. Instead, I'll use it to trouble those stable notions of how descent and dissent can function in feminist musical genealogies. While noting credit where credit is due is an essential (and essentially difficult) part of the effort, feminist genealogies should not only be about epistemologically outing the work of women musicians. How women are actually represented and made vocally present in recording is only part of the process. A genealogical project must also hear women's publics and other unseen, though nevertheless felt, traces imported into the music itself. By import, I not only mean through the actual recordings but also those receptive worlds that have long lived alongside them.

I was once visiting Los Angeles and stuck in traffic on Sepulveda. To my left I saw two gothed-out Salvadorean teenage boys who were singing along and bumping to the melancholic chorus of R.K.M. and Ken-Y's "Down," a song that can waver even the most seasoned broken heart. This scene might not be anything out of the ordinary, especially considering reggaetón's vast spatial and cultural reach. These two Salvadoreños offered a dynamic surprise, even in the smog-choke of four o'clock traffic. They sang along to the rounded out *ao*'s of the song's lyrical lines. For example, Ken-Y sings *despertado* (woke up) as *depertao*, *desorientado* becomes *desorientao*, and so on. The tidal texture of Caribbean Spanish, with its strain of winsome pronunciation, facilitates a rounding out of words. It is a linguistic habit, comfort, and affective beeline. To sing along with this specificity of accent, with a certain tone and rhythm to the hurt of teenage love, did much more than offer easy proof of pan-latinidad. This recourse to the ballad (a vast, impassioned, and underanalyzed realm in reggaetón) picks up a set of musical conventions, and not only those that get performed in the recording. They sang along with knitted brows and their faces upturned. I've enacted that knitted brow and upturned face before, and I've usually done it when singing along to Lisa Lisa and Nayobe. In other words, it is time to starting thinking about the tethered relationship of freestyle to reggaetón.[12] It is time to start putting Latino/a musical genres that too easily get discarded (analytically and otherwise) into conversation.

Were I lecturing the foregoing, this would be the moment a student might pop their hand up and ask, "Isn't this too much?" Or I might start to hear those "what the——?" giggles. As educators, we're never quite sure if they're talking about the performance in question or our affective relationship to it. Either way, this question and these giggles are necessary interventions: *Is* it too much to ask of an aside in performance to carry the weight of such heavy history? To bear the demands of genocide, slavery, and misogyny? To use an aside to move through multiple geographical locations, and the ways of being and loving enacted there? Freestyle *again*? Or is it too much to employ Ivy Queen, or any performer for that matter, as the hatchet-woman against genre? While her oeuvre is not safe from critique and deserves further analysis, this is not the work I do here.[13]

Instead, I would argue that it is through the route of the salon that we can hear Ivy Queen's aside as a pedagogical moment. Her import of the salon to the stage reminds us (as I mentioned above) that it is also a noninstitutional site where other, unsanctioned modes of learning and preparation take place. By tossing off an aside in this forum, she puts it to public contestation and analysis. We can liken it to part of the trajectory of teaching and learning that happens when huddled around that bathroom mirror, peluquería, or what have you; and to the advice, insults, and jokes that take place there. A few lessons are required: you learn to take your turn, find ways to tweak the hierarchy, and call each other out with humor. You learn to recognize yourself in the other, however resistant you or the other might be. The critical unfurling made possible by Ivy Queen's aside reminds us that we must and can make do with what we have at hand, especially when we are trying to think deeply about performance. And ultimately, it reveals some of the difficult and challenging work that surprise actually demands of us. No, it isn't too much; it is not enough.

This work can be downright hard when we take on performance that too many people (or ourselves) so readily dislike. The challenges are acute when working with music that gets pulled over for its repetitive, "same old, same old" aesthetic. These noise complaints accuse reggaetón of reproducing at too fast a rate; it is another musical instance that has ignited brown panic over the sound waves. For now, the work can require a necessarily combative stance to address the grievances of the recently urbanized professional classes for whom reggaetón too often rattles their floor-to-ceiling windows. The work also comes with visceral disappointment when you see and feel men land-grab musical space. It is also a challenge to engage reggaetón as it is already understood as a passé failure, an already dead genre. This ethos was noted in *Latina* magazine's May 2007 issue by the byline "Can [Calle 13's new CD] save reggaetón?" But, then again, reggaetón can also give you hope for a broader dream of longevity. Perhaps it will exceed the locations it is allowed to operate in. It is doing so already, especially when we are given a peek at Ivy Queen's long term vision: "If it's up to me, I'd like to be like Celia Cruz. . . . She was singing at her own tribute concert!"[14]

The stakes of making do with surprise means finding the potential in moments when the thing you're studying and all that it stands for have no value in the eyes of scholarship. This judgment of value might stem from a generational prejudice, hostility to pop culture, and the continued refusal of historical sites of Afro-latinidad. By making do, I superficially mean what a critic must do when little formal literature exists on a subject, when there are few women practitioners around; when you don't want to become part of a properly funded project; when you want to place something into a trajectory that would otherwise be lauded as yet another decontextual and dehistoricized "boom" or "explosion." But most crucially, I'd like to think more about making do with the surprise of that palpable energy (made through murmuring and squirming in seats) once you've made even slight mention to reggaetón in the classroom. Playing an aside such as this in the official place of the classroom models the necessary import of the noninstitutional stuff of salons into the ways we teach and learn.

Students have brought reggaetón to us. For many of them it is their musical here and now. As such, they insert a collective aside to a syllabus packed with Latina/o content. When they alert me to some of the genre's locations, they also at the same time alert me to where they are currently occupied (or preoccupied). Their citations of reggaetón allow us to listen to how they spend some of their time. They reveal themselves in reggaetón in moments in which they are trying to meet formalized demands, say, when they decide to write final papers in urgent tones on their attendance at Don Omar's messianic performances or La Bruja's tricky navigation of sex-positive themes in "Mi Gatita Negra." More often than not, they tend to mention reggaetón's suggestive reception outside the realm of proper requirements. They work through their relationship to reggaetón in the form of asides not only during class time, but mostly in office hours, those temporal margins of official school.

One student worked packing boxes in a factory where (among other things) he had to navigate his privilege in higher education, while also being one of the sole students of color in his program who had to work for a living. As he did so, he packed to the beat with mostly second-generation Latinos who learned to speak Spanish from reggaetón's repetitive choruses. Other students share the pearls of all that intimate time spent in the virtual outer reaches looking for company or a way out. This was how I was introduced to Prosas, one of the many lesbian groups working in reggaetón. The Dominicana Sargenta G founded this group after she was honorably discharged from military training for a tour in Iraq. This important, queer seed—another bold, creative trace laid down by what Karen Tongson has termed the "dykeaspora"—continues to alter reggaetón.[15] That reggaetón can provide refuge after a body is withdrawn from the front lines of war is something that demands our attention. By dropping in these surprises from their intimate worlds, students demand that we tune in to reggaetón's dynamic receptive worlds. These asides from our students are opportunities to do away with our own "comforts of mastery" and breathe much needed life into the course of their, by which I also mean our, fields of study.

I hesitate to perform that conclusory recourse to the pragmatic, so often found in pedagogical declarations (though not in Ivy Queen's). A question remains: What can you do to set yourself and the classroom up for surprise? Johnson offers the following advice, "Obviously, in a sense, one cannot. Yet one can begin by transgressing one's own usual practices, by indulging in some judicious time-wasting with what one does not know how to use, or what has fallen into disrepute."[16] I read Johnson's "judicious time-wasting" as affording yourself and your classroom the time to think hard about what is around and is not going away. Allow the time in seminar for more replays. Resist fading the track out before it is over. Submit something to an anthology—writing about a most cherished, though necessarily neglected, side project—when you should be writing a book in order to secure employment. Replay Ivy Queen's performance to the point where you feel like you could identify many of the audience members by name and what they were wearing that night. Take pause to recognize how hard your student has to work and still not be allowed to register for classes. Steal a minute to hold up traffic and notice how the Caribbean announces itself in California. Remember when looking up to others getting their eyebrows and mustaches waxed meant that one day you would be able to take on the world in a new way. Go out and listen to reggaetón in ways that you are not supposed to, as music that can engender asides.

NOTES

I'd like to acknowledge my students, especially Sandy Isabel Plácido, Pricilla Leiva, Tanya Martínez, Evania Vásquez, and Gonzalo Venegas for their righteous critical voices. I'm grateful for that late night of much-needed inspiration from Paola Fernández and Rita. Thanks to Irene Cara for singing me through the final stages. I'm especially indebted to Christine Bacareza Balance, Vincenzo Amato, Licia Fiol-Matta, José Esteban Muñoz, Jim Stoeri, and Shane Vogel for their enthusiasm and feedback. And finally, I dedicate this essay in loving memory to Camilla McGrath and her most formative salon, where so many have learned to take their turn, find ways to tweak the hierarchy, and call each other out with humor. Translations of Spanish-language quotations are my own.

1. "Blow-out" is the phrase used to describe hair that has been blow-dried straight. The aside is taken from *Ivy Queen: the Original RUDE Girl . . .* , DVD (Real Music Inc., Universal Music Latino, 2004).

2. I refer here to Derrida's essay on the legislative function of genre. He writes, "As soon as the word 'genre' is sounded, as soon as it is heard, as soon as one attempts to conceive it, a limit is drawn. And when a limit is established, norms and interdictions are not far behind: 'Do,' 'Do not' says 'genre,' the word 'genre,' the figure, the voice, or the law of genre." Jacques Derrida, "The Law of Genre," trans. Avital Ronell, *Critical Inquiry* 7, no. 1 (autumn 1980): 55–81.

3. Barbara Johnson, "Nothing Fails like Success," in *A World of Difference* (Baltimore: Johns Hopkins University Press, 1989), 15.

4. There is a vast and rich critical literature keen to the relationship between racial formation, phenotypic signifiers, and popular culture, especially around Puerto Rico and its diaspora. See Frances Negrón-Muntaner, "Barbie's Hair: Selling out Puerto Rican Identity on the Global Market" and "Jennifer's Butt: Valorizing the Puerto Rican Racialized Female Body," in *Boricua Pop: Puerto Ricans and the Latinization of American Culture* (New York: New York University Press, 2004); Raquel Z. Rivera, "Butta Pecan Mamis," in *New York Ricans from the Hip Hop Zone* (New York: Palgrave Macmillan, 2003); and Frances R. Aparicio, *Listening to Salsa: Gender, Latin Popular Music, and Puerto Rican Cultures* (Middletown, Conn.: Wesleyan University Press, 1998).

5. In her book, Rivera provides the useful hermeneutic "between blackness and *latinidad*" to rethink the terms of blackness as primarily Afro-American. She puts these seemingly stringent systems of signification into productive flux. Rivera, *New York Ricans from the Hip Hop Zone*.

6. In reggaetón's parlance, *perreo* means doggy-style dancing. It has been a term widely debated in terms of its origin and actual definition. In Puerto Rico in 2001 and 2002, e.g., it became a contested object of definition in the legislative realm. These debates reached a crux via the failed campaign launched by the senator Velda González to ban its public performance. I'm grateful to Lena Burgos-Lafuente for this insight.

7. Daphne Brooks, "Time Out of Mind: TV on the Radio's Diasporic Data Tapes &

the ReMixed Code(s) of *Cookie Mountain*" (paper presented at the annual meeting of the Experience Music Project, Seattle, April 2007).

8. There is an equally vast and rich critical literature on Latina beauty salon culture. Ginetta Candelario offers some of the most definitive scholarly work on the subject, specifically on Dominican beauty salons in New York City. See Ginetta Candelario, "Hair Race-ing: Dominican Beauty Culture and Identity Production," in *Meridians* 1, no. 1 (2000): 128–56. Also see Candelario, *Black behind the Ears: Blackness in Dominican Identity from Museums to Beauty Shops* (Durham, N.C.: Duke University Press, 2007). For a perspective on salon cultures in Puerto Rico, see María Isabel Quiñones Arocho, "Beauty Salons: Consumption and Production of the Self," in *None of the Above: Puerto Ricans in the Global Era*, ed. Frances Negrón-Muntaner (New York: Palgrave, 2007), 109–28.

9. Here I am thinking of Deborah Pacini's work on the spaces of *colmados* (grocery stores) as important sites of reception for *bachata*. Her work recovers much of the demanding material to be found in those locations that might get kicked off of ethnography's dependable maps. See Deborah Pacini Hernandez, *Bachata: A Social History of A Dominican Popular Music* (Philadelphia: Temple University Press, 1996), 28–29.

10. There has been a wonderful upsurge of feminist genealogical work in Latina/o musical criticism. I am particularly grateful for Frances R. Aparicio's now foundational essay "La Lupe, La India, and Celia: Toward a Feminist Genealogy of Salsa Music," in *Situating Salsa: Global Markets and Local Meaning in Latin Popular Music*, ed. Lise Waxer (New York: Routledge, 2002), 135–60. Also formative is Licia Fiol-Matta's work on transnational circuits of Latina musicians, "The Black Diva and Other Female Figurations in 'Latin Music'" (public lecture, New York University, March 9, 2005). For a closer reading of Aparicio's essay, see my work on Graciela in "'Una Escuela Rara': Havana Meets Harlem in Montmartre," in *women and performance: a journal of feminist theory* 16, no. 1 (March 2006): 27–49.

11. Both songs are featured on Luny Tunes 2006 collection *Mas Flow 2.5* (produced by Luny Tunes, Mas Flow Studios). Luny Tunes is Francisco Saldaña and Victor Cabrera, one of the most successful production teams in reggaetón. It might seem unfair to place the burden of this critique squarely on Luny Tunes in this essay, particularly as their oeuvre is much more imaginative and diverse than many give them credit for. However, as two of the most visible producers and artists in reggaetón, they are representative of these practices that run the gamut of reggaeton's practitioners.

12. For more information, see the chapter "Latin Freestyle: with her black liquid eyeliner in her hand," in my doctoral dissertation. Alexandra T. Vazquez, "Instrumental Migrations: The Transnational Movements of Cuban Music" (Ph.D. diss., New York University, 2006), 175–227.

13. For a comprehensive and excellent scholarly review of Ivy Queen, see the perceptive work of Jillian M. Báez, "En Mi Imperio: Competing Discourses of Agency in Ivy Queen's Reggaetón" in *Centro Journal* 18, no. 2 (fall 2006) 63–81. Báez is especially engaged with the gendered performance and reception of Ivy Queen. Her project of

"writing IQ [Ivy Queen] into history as a female music producer," in particular, is part of the vital initiative needed to imagine what she provocatively terms "reggaetón feminism."

14. This quote is taken from the cover of *Latina* magazine, May 2007.

15. For more on Karen Tongson's "admittedly cheeky" neologism, see her article "JJ Chinois's Oriental Express, Or, How a Suburban Heartthrob Seduced Red America," *Social Text* 23, nos. 3–4, 84–85 (fall–winter 2005): 207.

16. Johnson, "Nothing Fails like Success," 16.

WELMO E. ROMERO JOSEPH

TRANSLATED FROM THE SPANISH BY RAQUEL Z. RIVERA

From Hip-Hop to Reggaeton

Is There Only a Step?

This question is constantly on my mind, and sometimes the answer seems to me a simple "yes." But when I try to do reggaeton, thoughts of this sort come to my mind: "Welmo, don't be ridiculous. Why would you do that to yourself?" or "Remember you'll have to rhyme like they do." It's because of those internal mental battles that I write this reflection. I want to know if, for me, the decision to get into reggaeton is only a simple step. Is it as easy as asking the DJ to change the *beat*?

If I had to change up my rhyme scheme so I can "azotarle el c*u*lo contra el m*u*ro" [slam her ass against the wall] or "pedirle acción mientras sudo pasión entre sábanas blancas eh oh, eh oh" [ask her for action as I sweat passion among white sheets, eh oh, eh oh], then I don't think I can do it. A step that maybe has been easier to take for rappers such as Tego Calderón, Eddie Dee, or Vico C has become for me an internal battle where I have to struggle with my prejudices against reggaeton and my belief that hip-hop is the last bastion of verbal skill and blow-your-mind rhymes. Perhaps that's my problem: my love for hip-hop and for the crafting of stimulating rhymes is not compatible with music industry formulas and its quest for clones that facilitate the exploitation of urban music.

> *Sólo llama al 1-800-raperos de moda*
> *Te creamos un rapero en 24 horas*
> *Echa un chin de bling, bling*
> *Un pianito de Cepillín*
> *Pal de jeans con g-string*
> *Y en nombre MC Payazín*
> *No es que yo sea el mejor*

Es que tú eres el peor
Y si de peor se trata
Entonces eres el mejor
Se soltó la lengua del negro
Dominando el liriqueo en la zona
En cuarentena por el brote de raperos
(2006)

Just call 1-800-trendy rappers
We'll create a rapper for you in 24 hours
Mix a little bling bling
With a piano like Cepillín's
A few jeans with g-strings
And baptize him MC Payazín
It's not that I'm the best
It's just that you're the worst
And if it's about being the worst
Then you're the best
Unleashed is now this black man's tongue
Mastering the lyrics in the zone
That's been quarantined because of the rapper epidemic

In order to write this reflection, I have to tell the story of my relationship to hip-hop and reggaeton, two genres that I call distant cousins. I remember that around 1993, I started to record without even thinking about selling my musical product or getting a contract with a record label. I started recording out of artistic need, ten years after first falling in love with that music genre called rap where you could rhyme over anything. My first rhymes were recorded over dancehall beats with hip-hop hooks (for example, Cutty Rank's "A Who Seh Me Dun (Wake De Man)" and Super Cat's "Ghetto Red Hot" with a hook based on A Tribe Called Quest's "Scenario" and Ol' Dirty Bastard's "Shimmy Shimmy Ya"). I was able to make these first recordings thanks to my man K.I.D. in a small room in Barrio Obrero, where we would turn off the light to create a serious and rugged atmosphere. My method of selecting beats has always been very visceral, so I just felt that these *melcochas* worked well.[1]

Little by little I started distancing myself from dancehall reggae, and I let myself be completely seduced by hip-hop, more because of its beats than its lyrics. I have never been able to understand 100 percent of the lyrics by African American rappers. I know who they are and their styles, but I only manage to catch loose phrases, unless I actually read the lyrics. For me, what they were

1. Welmo E. Romero Joseph. Photo by Abey Charrón (2005).

saying was not as important as how they were flowing over the beat. That bass in your chest, that furious loop in your face accompanied by the current code of the barrio:

> *Barrio Obrero quiero que alzes tu bandera ya*
> *Para que todos luchen y hablen por la paz*
> *Pues se me va a hacer difícil entender*
> *Que un hijo mío salga y no vuelva jamás*
> *Y a través de esto puedo comprender*
> *Que el nombre del lugar no dice*
> *Si este es bueno o malo*
> *Sino el que vive allí, así que ten cuidado*
> *A la hora de ponerme tu etiqueta*
> (1993)

Barrio Obrero I want you to raise up your flag
So that everyone will struggle and speak for peace
Because it will be hard for me to understand
That a son of mine goes out and never comes back

And through this I can understand
That the name of a place doesn't tell you
If it's good or bad
Only those who live there, so be careful
When you put a label on me

Before speaking about my first encounters in the early nineties with what we call today reggaeton, I have to say that, for me, Puerto Rico is a type of musical vacuum cleaner. It sucks up everything, but it doesn't hold in what it sucks up. It spits it out in its very unique way. The same thing probably happens in other places but, frankly, "Puerto Rico lo hace mejor."[2] That's how it happened with reggaeton.

History took a turn in the early nineties, after Jamaican dancehall achieved Top 20 status in radio stations like X-100, I-96, and KQ 105 and thanks to the *marquesina* party DJs (those responsible for spreading the music in an *underground* fashion).[3] I remember that on Saturdays I would go to the *caserío* Las Casas so Macho would cut my hair.[4] It didn't matter if I was going to fix my "flat top" or get a shape-up, what made the experience intense was listening to the new songs of the artists Cutty Ranks, Shabba Ranks, Chaka Demus, Super Cat, and Capleton, among others, on tapes that cost a few dollars. And if I said earlier that I didn't understand African Americans' lyrics, never mind Jamaicans'. Still that music begged for jean-to-jean friction.

This all quickly changed when Panamanian dancehall came onto the scene, mostly using Jamaican artists' instrumental tracks and even adopting the same melodies for the lyrics. Music by El General, Nando Boom, and Pocho Pan got into my hands behind my mother's back. As the parties kept happening, the Panamanian voices started being substituted with Boricua voices: Oh Shit! *Underground* arrived!

Wiso G and Ranking Stone, Chezina, Rey Pirín, Falo, Frankie Boy, Daddy Yankee, Maicol & Manuel, Baby Rasta & Gringo were some of the voices back then. In the beginning, most *underground* artists used the same vocal melodies and beats as the Jamaicans. Even though the lyrics were not faithful translations of dancehall, at least they carried the tune. Initially I thought: "Well, they're probably doing that now because they're just starting out." But time kept ticking by, and I started thinking that the issue was that the artists lacked originality.

About the topics . . . what can I say? A bit of lead over here, a bit of ganja over there, and a lot of sex. They were topics that back then were being exploited in the mass media like any other merchandise, underneath the umbrella of artistry and the slogan "we give audiences what they want." These lyrics did not represent danger for me because the quasi-dictatorial upbringing of my Haitian mother, Andrea, kept me and my brother, Raúl, in the margins of the marginality of living in Barrio Obrero, Santurce, Puerto Rico (and don't you dare look at me wrong!).

And what was I doing musically during those years of *underground*? I was writing just for myself, excited because I had found a musical canvas to experiment with my "dropping science" or "dripping science" (in the vein of Pollock)—hours and hours of writing, delivering and memorizing, accompanied by my mighty beatboxing or rhyming over other rappers' songs. Having been exposed to dancehall reggae, Haitian *kanpa*, merengue, salsa, rap from Vico C's era, and *underground*, gave me the melodic approach that I like so much for the hooks and the verses of songs. It was 1995 and I had started studying at the University of Puerto Rico in Río Piedras. I would work on my lyrics between classes, or sometimes in class when it was as slow and boring as an intravenous drip made of asphalt. Anything could inspire lyrics. I remember a hook that said:

> *Aquí me encuentro solo y feliz*
> *Desde Barrio Obrero viajo a la Iupí*[5]
> *Con mi socio Angel Suárez, Raúl y David*
> *No brincamos los portones, tenemos* ID
> (2005)

> Here I am alone and happy
> From Barrio Obrero I come to the U.P.R.
> With my man Angel Suárez, Raúl and David
> We didn't jump over the gates, we have our ID

This text came up after observing during my first semester at the university the small number of black students on campus. Where did they go once they graduated high school? "Please Welmo, drop the drama. Here in the island we are all Boricuas." "Sure man. Now tell me one about cowboys."

The new information that I got through the books I devoured at the School of Social Sciences served as the foundation for creating lyrics where I tried to explain to myself the things happening around me with respect to the barrio, my negritude, my relationship to women, and so on. It was a way to take academic information to the street. Back then I saw the street and academia as two spaces in opposition, spaces constantly fighting over the definition of what was "real." Today I see them as a beast with two heads—the same body but two different brains. Before my eyes, a world of information opened that served as the scaffolding to develop my lyrics. Texts by Martín Baró, short stories by Julio Cortázar and Jorge Luis Borges, among others, provided necessary references for my ideas:

El sol aún no sale y la alarma sicodélica
Se clava en mis tímpanos diciendo: ¡Es lunes!
Mi mente sólo piensa en sudor y los afanes
ALERT LIKE FUNES[6]
Atrás quedan mis planes
Mis manos no responden a estímulos neurales
Sino que sólo siguen los marcados patrones
Que dan la eternidad a la cadena de ensamblaje
Trabajo que no quiero, cuestiono y odio
Basado en la extrema dependencia de un salario
Contradictorio en su naturaleza
Opciones reducidas en cuanto a las creaciones
Si me quito de obrero paso a ser de los millares
Que dan la formación a poblaciones marginales
O ejército de reserva que el orden bien conserva
Necesarios en caso de la aparición de huelgas
O sea, siempre hay alguien que espera mi despido
Listo pa' someterse, en fuerza convertirse
(1996)

The sun is not out yet and the psychedelic alarm
Stabs itself into my eardrums saying "It's Monday!"
My mind can only think of sweat and worries
ALERTA COMO FUNES
My plans get left behind
My hands don't respond to neural stimuli
They only follow the patterns
That give eternity to the assembly line
Work that I don't want, that I question and hate
Based on the extreme dependence on a salary
Contradictory by nature
Reduced options when it comes to creation
If I stop being a worker I become one of the thousands
That make up marginal populations
Or the reserve army that ensures order

Necessary in the case of strikes

In other words, there's always someone waiting for me to be fired

Ready to submit and become part of the force

As all these preoccupations circled in my head and my rhyme notebooks, reggaeton kept marching from marginality to the public eye, despite censorship attempts by the state. Each news item about the confiscation of music in record shops or about the explicitness of the lyrics or video images served as free public relations for the genre. I thought maybe all that was happening would push rappers to create texts and visual proposals that were more complex, less stereotypical. But that was not the case since one thing that has been clear for the rappers of *underground*, reggaeton, *dembow*, and *perreo* is that "you have to give audiences what they like"—the phrase typical of the world of entertainment. Maybe that would have been the best moment for me to launch my career. I don't know, maybe I should have gone to Playero, DJ Eric, or Nico Canadá and offer a bit of "melaza para la yale."[7] I know I could have done it, but I wasn't interested. Who knows if today I would have been MC Rabadán, like I was called by my friends Beibito and Cholo from Cantera.

As *underground* got stronger, I kept getting deeper and deeper into hip-hop. In my comings and goings in events related to hip-hop was where I met groups that, like myself, carried their thoughts on the tip of their tongues: Gunzmoke, No Mel Syndicate, Conciencia Poética, Mad Steelo, 65 de Infantería and Mito, among others. Each one flowed with their particular stylistic proposal in an environment of respect and where artistic ego did not exist, or at least did not manifest itself like it does today. The guiding thread of conversations in those spaces was hip-hop; many times we talked about *underground* as the greatest trash of the musical scenes in Puerto Rico.

In these events the few women who attended were going out with the protagonists; perhaps there might be a B-girl or a female graffiti artist, and one or two groups of inseparable girlfriends who enjoyed the music that the DJ played. I don't know if this happened because of the lack of interest of women in participating as protagonists in one of the hip-hop elements, or if it was the great presence of testosterone that didn't permit the opposite sex to get on the mic and in front of the audience. However, I've noticed that the whole reggaeton movement, since its beginnings under a different name, clearly established that its lyrics were directed toward women. While the call to pleasure was direct in *underground*, in hip-hop we would fight each other over who had the better flow or pointing out the *cabrones* responsible for the majority of social ills.

After the last attempt at censorship in 2002 by the State and its Horsewo-man of the Apocalypse, Senator Velda González, the perreo "sacó su colita al aire" [started holding its tail high up in the air].[8] The beat of *underground* slowed down its tempo, and rappers started changing up their lyrics. The strident notes coming from the barrios and caseríos that scared the state so much when they first came out started softening themselves to take advantage of the promotional opportunities offered by those same people who initiated the hunting spree. Perreo let go of its transgressions so that it could join in the dance convoked by the musical market that years earlier described the genre as one by *cacos* and for *cacos*.[9] The classist dimension of the term was eventually sucked out like grease in a liposuction so that, from then on, being a caco was cool.

The foregrounding of asses on the TV screen was not precisely what both-ered me most about the genre. For me, the problem was that the only bodies being sexualized were those of females; male bodies didn't see the light, as usual. At least the explicit verbal images gave you a path to walk down on if you wanted to discuss the whys of the lyrics; they were like a guide to get to know how young people spoke about sex and street violence produced by drug traffic.

Little by little, thick female bodies with a high concentration of melanin (videos of Nico Canadá or DJ Eric's *La Industria* series) were substituted for runway models that seemed to come straight from a modeling agency (video "La Gata" from *Playero 42*). The new aesthetic was skinny bodies, an aesthetic where "lo blanquito fashion"[10] was mixed with "lo stripper dominatrix." Little by little the barrio disappeared from the videos, giving way to the disco or the photography studio as a neutral space where the social classes could mingle and *perrear*, at least until each one had to return to their particular reality. As perreo kept transforming itself, I clung even tighter to hip-hop as my life jacket. I was unhappy with the formulas, the lack of lyrical elaboration. Verbal skill no longer mattered, and almost all the artists sounded the same.

Even though the new popularity of perreo dominated the media, I had great opportunities to do what fulfilled me. The same year when the debates sur-rounding perreo and Senator Velda González began, I was asked to be part of the yearly Christmas documentary sponsored by Banco Popular. *Raíces* was the title of the special that year dedicated to narrating the history of *bomba* and *plena* from the mouth of singers, dancers, musicians, visual artists, and ethno-musicologists. I came in as the narrator for the special, to the sounds of hip-hop that also integrated plena's and bomba's acoustic drums, *cuás*, and mar-acas. That caused a huge scandal! People criticized my participation or, more specifically, the inclusion of hip-hop in a documentary that presented two of the musical manifestations of our Puerto Rican identity—an identity which, for me, is as well defined and absolute as a chameleon's skin.

This helped in getting my name to circulate in advertising agencies, non-profit institutions, schools, and university circles which understood rap to be another form of expression and a link between the generations. That's how I started to rap for commercials of everyday consumer items. Every time they called, I would say: "I'll go but I warn you that I do hip-hop and not reg-gaeton." I would utter that phrase right after introducing myself. Then I would be asked, from the other side: "And what's the difference?" When that moment came, I would flaunt my indestructible beatbox skills and, when I was done, the person would have a blank look on their face or would say: "Now I understand. So what I want you to do is do that thing you do to advertise this product."

One time they called me to be part of a public service campaign for the Alianza para un Puerto Rico sin Drogas [Alliance for a Drug-Free Puerto Rico]. This nonprofit organization wanted to present a music video that addressed the use of firearms among young people. I wrote the lyrics in collaboration with a young rapper who had lived the experiences of violence and incarceration at a young age. The music part of the project was put in the hands of Eliel (Don Omar's producer). After recording our parts, we left the studio with the agreement that the beat would be 50 percent reggaeton and 50 percent hip-hop, like it used to be during the times of *underground*.

The day we were going to film, as I usually do in these types of projects, I ask for the playback so I can practice the lyrics. When the song comes out I realize that the 50 and 50 has turned into 100 percent reggaeton. Damn it! For a few seconds I had the silly idea of complaining, but I knew I wouldn't be able to solve anything. I simply decided that the lyrics were more important than the beat at that point, and I just did it. To this day, even thought I still see the commercial and feel weird listening to myself over a reggaeton beat, I think the message was well received. That's what I get from young cats who sing the lyrics when they see me. If at the end of the day what I want is to be heard, why is it so difficult for me to accept reggaeton in my creative process?

Sometimes I think it's because of the monotonous rhythm. Many may say that hip-hop is monotonous too, but at least there are many drum patterns that give me a feeling of variation. I think that as long as the approach to beat making is similar to salsa, where there are a lot of musical layers in conversation, then I will like the results. I think that as long as I don't feel that visceral sensation that stimulates me when I hear a hip-hop beat I like, I won't do a reggaeton song.

It's not that I dismiss reggaeton: I even jumped up from the sofa when I saw the presentation of "Quítate Tú pa' Ponerme Yo" from Los Doce Discípulos at the 2005 Latin Grammys. That was a special moment because I felt a connection with the rappers and the images of the salsa musicians they wore on their shirts. Aside from that song and about five rappers more, the rest is fluff. What happens is that I just don't feel it and, when I do feel it, I enjoy listening to it more than I do creating it. When a reggaeton song steals my attention, it is because the rapper did a play on words different from the usual and in combination with a beat with samples—even if it uses the same percussive pattern as always—that are closer to the production of a hip-hop beat, such as Tego Calderón's "Guasa Guasa" or Ñejo's "No Quiere Novio."

Reggaeton has covered a space that in the most underground of hip-hop is reserved only for B-boys and B-girls: the dance space. I understand that we have to aim our work toward the feet. I don't always identify with the vibe of hip-hop in English, and I can't deny that the *dembow* hypnotizes. And, in most cases, it hypnotizes until they start rapping and that's when I change the radio station. If making reggaeton suggests that laziness I perceive in composing rhymes, then I will stay on this side, on the side of hip-hop my way, among MCs who wrongly understand music as a language that often can get to places where words can't, MCs that understand music as a "pure" essence not contaminated by the same industry that boxes it in. In the world of music they are talking about the fall of reggaeton. Nowadays the genre is saturated. Nowadays people think anyone can rap.

> *¿Del hip hop al reggaetón un paso es?*
> *Si fuera tan fácil ¿por qué tanto stress?*
> *Yo no me he ido*
> *Siempre he estao aquí*
> *Aquí en lo mío*
> *No el medio pero en serio*
> *En este asunto, mucho papagayo*
> *Y pocos puntos, lucho contra*
> *Lo que escucho, mucho loco junto*
> *Le doy vuelta al acertijo y termino*
> *Más perdío, paro y respiro, vuelvo a lo mío*
> *Un poco escribo, y sigo lo que dicta el latido*

El tiempo pasa y al igual que el olvido
Toca a mi puerta para ver si me rindo
¿Del hip hop al reggaetón un paso es?
Si fuera tan fácil ¿por qué tanto stress?
(2007)

From hip-hop to reggaeton, is there only a step?
If it were that easy, then why so much stress?
I haven't left
I've always been here
Here doing my thing
Not in the center but committed
In this scene, there's a lot of parrots
Few good points, I struggle against
What I hear, too many crazy ones together
I try to solve the riddle but I end up
Even more lost, I stop and breathe, return to my own
I write a little and I follow what the heartbeat dictates
Time goes by and just like that which escapes memory
Knocks on my door to see if I give up
From hip-hop to reggaeton, is there only a step?
If it were that easy, then why so much stress?

NOTES

Welmo is a hip-hop artist born, raised, and living in Puerto Rico. This essay's endnotes are the translator's.

1. A melcocha is a mixture of ingredients where the result is sticky and sweet.

2. "Puerto Rico does it better" was the slogan of a campaign launched by the Puerto Rican government's Tourism Company in the 1990s. Welmo is here referencing his own song "Puerto Rico Lo Hace Mejor," a sarcastic take on the government's self-congratulatory slogan.

3. In Puerto Rico, marquesinas or carports of private homes have been important venues where youth have gathered to party.

4. A caserío is a housing project.

5. "Iupi" or "U.P." is a common nickname for the University of Puerto Rico.

6. "Funes el memorioso" ("Funes the Memorious") is a short story by the Argentine writer Jorge Luis Borges.

7. "Molasses for the girls" was an ever-present phrase in the *underground* music of the time.

8. This is a play on the canine reference of the term *perreo* (doggy style).

9. *Caco*, a term that literally means "thief," started being used in the 1990s in Puerto Rico to refer to fans of *underground* or reggaeton.

10. *Blanquito*, literally meaning "little and white," is a racial/class term applied to the elite. "Lo blanquito fashion" refers to the trends dominant among blanquitos.

Black Pride

Just this morning, I was listening to radio host Luisito Vigoreaux talking about a movie project that I am working on which co-stars Mayra Santos Febres and he was saying, "Her? She's starring in it?" Questioning her Black beauty.

I remember, too, when Celia Cruz died, a newscaster, thinking she was being smart, said Celia Cruz wasn't black, she was Cuban. She was pretty even though she's black.

As if there is something wrong with being black, like the two things can't exist simultaneously and be a majestic thing. There is ignorance and stupidity in Puerto Rico and Latin America when it comes to blackness.

In Puerto Rico, Spike Lee's *Malcolm X* was only shown in one theater and unlike all the other movies shown here, there were no subtitles. It's as if they don't want the masses to learn.

But it's not just here—in Puerto Rico—where I experience racism. When I lived in Miami, I was often treated like a second class Boricua. I felt like I was in the middle—Latino kids did not embrace me and African American kids were confused because here I was a black boy who spoke Spanish. But after a while, I felt more embraced by black Americans—as a brother who happens to speak Spanish—than other Latino kids did.

Because I am well known, sometimes I forget the racist ways of the world. But [when] I travel to places where no one knows Tego Calderón, I am reminded.

For instance, when I travel first class, the stewardess will say, "Sir, this is first class," and ask to see [my] ticket. I take my time, put my bags in the overhead, sit, and gingerly give them my ticket, smiling at them. I try not to get stressed anymore, let them stress themselves.

And the thing is that many white Puerto Ricans and Latinos don't get it. They are immune to the subtle ways in which we are demeaned, disrespected.

They have white privilege. And I've heard it said that we are on the defensive about race.

Those things happen and it's not because of color, Tego, but because of how you look, how you walk, what you wear, what credit card you have. Then, they spend a couple of days with me, sort of walk in my shoes, and say "Damn negro, you are right."

When I check into hotels and use my American Express, they call the credit card company in front of me saying the machine is broken. This happens a lot in U.S. cities but it's not because there is more racism there; it's because they don't know me. When I'm in Latin America, I am known, so it's different. That is not to say that there is less racism. The reality for blacks in Latin America is severe, in Colombia, Venezuela, Peru, Honduras. . . .

Puerto Rican (and Latin American) blacks are confused because we grow up side by side with non-blacks and we are lulled into believing that things are the same. But we are treated differently.

My parents always celebrated our history. My dad always pointed things out to me. He even left the PIP (Pro-Independence Party) because he always said that *los negros* and our struggle was never acknowledged.

Maelo (Ismael Rivera) and Tite Curet did their part in educating and calling out the issues. Today, I do my part but I attack the subject of racism directly.

It makes me so happy to see Don Omar call himself "el negro" and La Sista celebrate her blackness. Now it's in fashion to be black and to be from Loíza. And that is awesome; it makes me so happy. Even if they don't give me credit for starting the pride movement, I know what I did to get it out there.

Young black Latinos have to learn their story. We also need to start our own media, and forums and universities. We are treated like second class citizens. They tell blacks in Latin America that we are better off than U.S. blacks or Africans and that we have it better here, but it's a false sense of being. Because here, it's worse.

We are definitely treated like second class citizens and we are not part of the government or institutions. Take, for instance, Jamaica—whites control a Black country.

They have raised us to be ashamed of our blackness. It's in the language too. Take the word denigrate—*denigrar*—which is to be less than a negro.

In Puerto Rico you get used to it and don't see it everyday. It takes a visitor to point out that all the dark skin sisters and brothers are in the service industry.

It's hard in Puerto Rico. There was this Spaniard woman in the elevator of the building where I lived who asked me if I lived there. And poor thing—not only is there one black brother living in the penthouse, but also in the other, lives Tito Trinidad. It gets interesting when we both have our tribes over.

Black Latinos are not respected in Latin America and we will have to get it by defending our rights, much like African Americans struggled in the U.S.

It's hard to find information about our people and history, but just like kids research the newest Nintendo game or CD they have to take interest in their story. Be hungry for it.

We need to educate people close to us. I do it one person at a time when language is used and I am offended by it. Sometimes you educate with tenderness, as in the case of my wife, who is not black.

She's learned a lot and is offended when she sees injustices. She gets it. Our children are mixed, but they understand that they are black and what that means. My wife has taught her parents, and siblings, and they, in turn, educate the nephews and nieces. That is how everyone learns.

This is not about rejecting whiteness; rather it's about learning to love our blackness—to love ourselves. We have to say "basta ya," it's enough, and find a way to love our blackness. They have confused us—and taught us to hate each other—to self-hate and create divisions on shades and features.

Remember that during slavery, they took the light blacks to work the home, and left the dark ones to work the fields. There is a lot residue of self-hatred.

And each of us has to put a grain in the sand to make it into a movement where we get respect, where we can celebrate our blackness without shame.

It will be difficult but not impossible.

As told to Sandra Guzman
© NYP Holdings, Inc.

FRANCES NEGRÓN-MUNTANER

TRANSLATED FROM THE SPANISH BY MARITZA HERNÁNDEZ

Poetry of Filth

The (Post) Reggaetonic Lyrics of Calle 13

From its emergence in the 1980s, the musical genre known today as reggaeton has been generally regarded as cultural trash by the state, the majority of intellectuals, and most of the so-called general public. This is the case because (in no particular order), reggaeton speaks to what good taste considers garbage —that is, the genre's main subject is sexuality in its most carnal dimensions; and, also, because until now it has been mainly associated and consumed by a "trashy" group with little social prestige, the Puerto Rican lower classes.

But since there is no real contradiction between trash and culture, this dichotomy is of little use when it comes to appreciating the significant impact of reggaeton. Although critics have repeatedly characterized the genre as being pure noise without any aesthetic value—"filth and degeneration posing as art,"[1] to be exact—reggaeton's cultural record is nothing short of impressive. Not only has reggaeton produced a new sound by fusing black Atlantic genres such as dancehall reggae and hip-hop; it also constitutes the most important verbal event that has taken place in (and from) Puerto Rico in the last two decades.

"RAISE THE VOLUME OF THE SATANIC MUSIC"

While it might surprise a few, this claim about the importance of reggaeton's verb has, as Spanish rap pioneer Vico C would say, a "base and a foundation."[2] Similar to other Afro-diasporic forms such as rap, reggaeton is constituted by an extravagant poeticness; a faith in the spoken word as a means to create imaginative and affective worlds through rhyme, repetition, and alliteration. Moreover, the verbal events of reggaeton performers—more commonly known as concerts, compact discs, or radio play—have a broader audience than any other type of artistic practice based completely or partly on the word, including literature. The way that some reggaeton stars even find themselves in the position of adding cultural capital to the island's traditional literati is evident in that well-known writers such as Mayra Santos and Mayra Montero are currently collaborating with artists on various projects, including reggaeton versions of classics like Gustave Flaubert's *Madame Bovary* and Franz Kafka's *The Metamorphosis*.[3]

It is not, however, until the emergence of the alternative music duo known as Calle 13 (13th Street) that reggaeton articulates a poetic rupture within and beyond the genre's boundaries. Hailed as the first "intellectual" group of reggaeton by no less than the *New York Times*, Calle 13 is made up of two half brothers, Residente (Resident) and Visitante (Visitor). With his ten tattoos, vanilla biceps and naughty-boy face, Residente, a.k.a. René Pérez Joglar, is the group's singer-songwriter and frontman. A man of few words and a beard, Visitante, otherwise known as Eduardo José Cabra Martínez, is the pair's producer, composer, and key music man.[4]

According to various newspaper stories, Calle 13 adopted these stage names because since the brothers did not grow up together, when Eduardo would visit René, he would identify himself to the gated community's guard as a "visitor" on the way to see a "resident." The significance of these aliases, however, goes well beyond their particular biographies. By adopting them, Calle 13 calls attention to global forms of community founded on physical mobility and affinity, as well as critiques the middle classes' fear of the urban poor, a theme that will serve as subtext to one of the group's first hits, "Atrévete Te, Te."

Despite Calle 13's strong identification with the "street," the duo is known not for conventionally popular or populist lyrics, but for making language itself their artistic battlefield. In contrast to the other great poet of reggaeton, Tego Calderón, Residente's rap typically produces such perplexity among listeners that some journalists have turned to providing more familiar analogies and thick descriptions of their style as a way to make it more accessible to reggaeton fans. While Jordan Levin, a *Miami Herald* music critic, for instance, has described Residente's lyrics as "a whirlwind of rhythms and rhymes . . . along with the rat-a-tat-tat of exhortations and puns, words and ideas ricocheting off each other,"[5] Juan Carlos Pérez-Duthie, an independent journalist, calls Calle 13's verbal artistry a "crude, fascinating, violent and delirious collage . . . as if Quentin Tarantino had taken Kill Bill to an alternative reggaetón world."[6] Although these descriptions cannot fully account for a typical

Calle 13 intervention, the references to "puns" and "collage" do provide important leads toward understanding why the group differs from most, if not all, contemporary reggaeton acts: their unmistakable surrealist tendencies.

"WATCH HOW IT FLOATS, MY HEAD"

One of the most influential movements of the twentieth century, surrealism today is mostly associated with the painting of artists such as Salvador Dalí, Max Ernst, and René Magritte. Since the movement's origins in the 1920s, however, surrealists defined themselves not simply as constituting an "an aesthetic doctrine," in historian Robin D. G. Kelley's words, "but an international revolutionary movement concerned with the emancipation of thought."[7] Surrealism's political orientation had much to do with its immediate historical context: World War I, a conflict that produced over 40 million deaths and "shell shock," or the loss of sight and memory that afflicted numerous combat soldiers. A response to the devastation of World War I, the surrealist movement was bent on addressing the reasons why neither science, nor the humanities, nor logic protected Europeans from this brutality. Influenced by the psychoanalysis of Sigmund Freud, who insisted that the truth of human behavior was evident in those activities that revealed the unconscious such as dreams, the surrealists devoted themselves to liberating people from their destructive impulses through the imagination and the fulfillment of the childhood desires critic Henri Peyre called "joy, for risk and play."[8]

From the point of view of form, Calle 13's lyrics are explicitly surrealist, and are characterized by the juxtaposition of incongruent images, the use of non sequiturs, black humor, and automatic writing or "out loud monologue."[9] From the mouth of Residente, who defines himself as "the spider that spoils language," words follow one another as if we were listening to a recording of the rapper's most intimate thoughts, intertwined with television ads and any verbal accident of the immediate environment.[10] An example of these elements at work is "La Hormiga Brava" (The Feisty Ant), in which Residente aims the following blanks at a woman he is trying to seduce:[11]

> *Deja las penas, no te arranques las venas*
> *Que usted se ve bonita con esa diadema*
> *Ese colillón está que bota flema*
> *Se empató el juego en la novena*
> *Usted es la reina de la verbena*
> *Usted me llena, tamaño ballena*

Forget your worries, don't root out your veins,
You look beautiful with that diadem
That wedgie in your butt is ready to spit out phlegm
The game got tied on the ninth
You are the queen of the fair
You fill me up, like a whale.

The effect of "novelty" or "freshness" often attributed to Calle 13's lyrics is also produced by the surrealist technique of "overloading the system."[12] With the purpose of avoiding the clichés of everyday speech, music, history, and literature, Calle 13 breaks down linguistic structures and substitutes words by their extended definitions or associations in order to liberate them from their mimetic, social, and moral charge. In this way, if the average reggaeton singer refers to a desired woman's buttocks as an "ass," Residente attempts to impress her by saying that she possesses "esos dos cachetes llenos de musculatura" (two cheeks full of muscles)[13] or a "zona nalgable acojinable" (cushiony buttocky zone).[14] And if the typical rapper says, "Hoy es noche de sexo, voy a devorarte nena linda" (Tonight is for sex, I'll eat you up, pretty babe),[15] Residente counterattacks with "Yo quiero beber agua de ese pozo/chocolatoso/ embriagarme con tu caldo de oso" (I want to drink water from your well/all chocolaty/get drunk on your bear broth).[16]

In addition, Calle 13 bets on what founding surrealist writer, André Breton, called the "image," or "the fortuitous juxtaposition of two terms" which produce sparks when they come into contact like saying "arroz pegao, dominicanos en balsa" (crispy rice, Dominicans on rafts") to evoke Puerto Rico.[17] Even if most of the duo's songs ultimately tell a brief tale, centered on Residente's unfulfilled desire for a woman, what listeners tend to remember is a succession of unexpected, and often humorous images that incite linguistic disorder and "verbal rebellion" to anyone who listens.[18] Serving as a classic example are the lyrics from "Atrévete Te, Te" (Dare To-To), where Residente describes the midsection of a certain "señorita intelectual," or "miss intellectual," in the following terms: "Ya se que tiene el área abdominal/que va a explotar/como fiesta patronal/que va a explotar, como Palestino" (I already know that your abdominal area is/ready to explode/like a Patron Saint feast/ready to explode/like a Palestinian").[19] As other surrealists, Calle 13's use of humor is not an afterthought but an essential resource that makes René-Residente/Joglar-Juglar (jester) a "satirical poet" (comical and satyr-like), whose comic license allows him to attack the so-called common sense that sustains the dominant social order.

Furthermore, Calle 13 shares the surrealist impulse to offend "bourgeois" morality and expose their hypocrisy. This convergence is particularly useful in understanding the role of sexuality in the group's poetic discourse. Even though the media has harshly criticized reggaeton for its vulgarity in sexual matters, Residente's invitation to "mount" his "sail (boat)" and "insult the entire world,"[20] is no more explicit than the writings of canonized surrealists, as suggested by the title of Louis Aragon's novella *El coño de Irene* (*Irene's Cunt*) (1927). In both cases, the emphasis on sexuality has less to do with a lax morality or lack of "education" as reggaeton critics contend than with a rejection of social hierarchy and the established order, a stance that is clearly articulated in "Cabe-C-O,"[21] a self-reflective ode to their own music:

> *Aquí no hay reglamento*
> *Aquí no hay juramento*
> *No hay gobierno*
> *No hay coroneles*
> *No hay sargentos*
> *A tu coraje échale pimiento*
> *Este movimiento no lo cancelen*
> *Esto es pa' que tus piernas se rebelen*
> *Todo esto es pa' que tus orejas vuelen*
> *Todo esto es pa' que el tiempo se congele*

> There are no rules here
> No oaths here
> No government
> No colonels
> No sergeants
> Put pepper on your anger
> This movement won't be cancelled
> This is for your legs to rebel
> This is for your ears to fly
> This is for time to freeze over

The classic surrealists and Calle 13 then share as much an aesthetic as a political project. In the broadest terms, if surrealism had the goal to liberate the imagination from social and artistic conventions, reggaeton, in the words of cultural critic Raquel Z. Rivera, was originally "identified by its participants with a street-oriented, vernacular, spontaneous and uncensored mode of expression."[22] Literarily, both practices are founded on the premise that words have the capacity to create utopias, imaginary places "in which all the objects that language can create may naturally exist" yet "no particular known object should be allowed consistency."[23] The common desire to destabilize conventional meanings and to imagine alternative social orders makes the wordplay of the surrealists and Calle 13 not only a new form of expression but something significantly more ambitious and radical: "a form of mental liberation."[24]

"AND IF YOU DON'T UNDERSTAND ME, YOUR MOMMA'S THE FAT ONE"

At the same time, Calle 13's surrealism differs from the European kind. If Breton and his close collaborators had to "create" surrealist conditions and situations in postwar Europe, Calle 13 (as those other surrealists of the Americas—Frida Kahlo, Wifredo Lam, Richard Wright, and Aimé Césaire) is the product of a historical moment and a geopolitical context in which the surreal—that is, the juxtaposition of arguably incongruous elements—is not an exception but everyday reality.[25] In this sense, what Calle 13 offers his "modelno" (modern) listeners, as Residente would say, is not a new version of the surrealist project. Rather, the group recycles and incorporates world surrealist discoveries onto a popular poetics that given its themes, politics, and style could be called *poesía de porquería*, or "poetry of filth."

In part, Calle 13's poetry of filth is a call to rethink what so-called urban music can be, underscoring the capacity of language and the fusion of musical genres to make up alternative worlds. Yet, even further, it is a political proposition that redefines the postreggaeton poet as a new intellectual figure whose main function is to humorously manage, renew, and radicalize corporeal, cultural, political, and media garbage.[26] This accounts for why in Calle 13's world, the only truly enjoyable things in life are "puerco, sucio, como de inodoro" (filthy, dirty, as from a toilet).[27] And, also, why the enemies of enjoyment and desire are not identified with any particular nationality (say, American visitors) or a social class (say, upper-class residents) but with the more universal "puercos," or "pigs," those despicable beings (not always cops) that sell themselves to the highest bidder and/or abuse the weakest. "Como robarle el desayuno a un tecato," Residente raps, "eso es de puerco" (Like stealing breakfast from an addict/that is pig-like).[28]

Aesthetically, the trash that grounds Calle 13's poetry is reggaeton itself. As Residente once told a *Latina* magazine reporter, Calle 13 will mostly be remembered for having transformed reggaeton at a time when it was "doing the same garbage (porquería)."[29] By *porquería*, Residente specifically refers to the fact that in order to supply the market, most of the music produced, especially after Daddy Yankee's global hit "Gasolina," used the same rhythm and the same lyrical repertoire of "I-want-you-mami" clichés. In order to renew reggaeton, or in Residente's terms, run over "tu mierda con mi Super Trooper" ("your shit with my Super Trooper")[30] Calle 13 broke the rules of the commercial game by transforming the verbal and musical expectations of the public and turning reggaeton's mainstream porquería into a different poetics.

To the trash that is reggaeton, Calle 13 adds a long list of discarded cultural references that, having been forgotten or hurled into the dumpsite of memory, have become the equivalent of symbolic garbage. While Residente's rap often articulates a strong anticonsumerist ideology (or what one could call leftist theoretical waste), he also concedes that under certain circumstances, media excess can be used as a fertilizer for new expressive uses and the invention of other cultural worlds. To this end, Calle 13 stores and deploys a wide range of references produced by mass culture, including, in no particular order, Conan the Barbarian and Jean-Claude Van Damme; a Roberto Roena music jam, and Chayanne; P. Diddy, Freddy Kenton, and Ricky Martin; Cheech and Chong, King Kong, and James Bond; El Invader, Darth Vader, and the Pink Panther.

Thematically, the poetics of Calle 13 center on the filth of the body and the trash of desire. Although media industry fans still wonder why the group indulges in "so much *porquería*," the attention to the body and its biological functions is not fortuitous.[31] As other surrealists, Calle 13 identifies rebellion with articulating the wildest of desires and realizing the most intimate of fantasies. In addition, this emphasis is part of a long tradition of symbolic insurrection—from the Renaissance writer François Rabelais in his novel *Gargantua and Pantagruel* to the DJs of Jamaican dancehall—that through word, image and/or music exalt the body as a living organism to celebrate "the victory" of the people over static social hierarchies and death.[32] This is why Calle 13's body is always eating "without cutlery, like Vikings,"[33] spitting "phlegm,"[34] "pissing territory," and "getting it on."[35] Similarly, the body serves to underline the core "primitiveness" of human beings ("come on, you animal"[36]); the fact that no matter the abundance and material "progress" that each of us may suffer or enjoy, humanity in general is subject to the same basic needs of hunger, sexuality, defecation, and urination.

The body's filth is not, however, only thematic; it is also an epistemology, a distinct way of knowing and acting in the world. Not surprisingly, bodies nourished with bad intentions produce excrement that reveals their core filthiness as human beings. In the song "Pi-Di-Di-Di,"[37] for instance, Calle 13 demonstrates this very principle when Residente stages an encounter between himself and hip-hop entrepreneur P. Diddy, when the latter presumably visited Puerto Rico in search of local talent to exploit:

> *Lo puse a escupir agua de piringa por los pantalones*
> *Empezó a botar azúcar negra por los calzones*
> *Y hasta por las medias botando mojones*
> *Mojones color verde oliva; sí, color verde oliva*
> *Lo que caga la gente fina por comer platos de comida*
> *De $50.00 pesos pa' arriba . . .*

> I made him spit watered-down swill through his pants
> He started to leak brown sugar through his underwear
> And even his socks were shitting turds
> Green olive turds, yes, of a green olive color
> The kind that classy people shit for eating entrées
> of $50.00 or more . . .

In opposition to the spoiled milk of corporate interests, Residente celebrates and feasts on the popular body, the "iron fortified cream" that "combines egg, with yolk puree of oatmeal."[38]

To bodily filth, Calle 13 adds the garbage of desire, the "library of sexy and fresh things" that "smell." This is evident in songs such as "Mala Suerte," a duo with Spanish rapper La Mala Rodríguez, where Residente declares that "este sudaca quiere tener sexo con caca/kinky, peludo como Chubaca" (this *sudaca* wants to have sex with shit/kinky, hairy like Chewbacca).[39] Although the sexual explicitness of much of Residente's rap has led some listeners to collapse Calle 13's surreal poetry with the misogynist lyrics of early *underground* songs— "Malditas Putas," by Guanábanas Podrías, for example—the duo's erotic imagination greatly differs from the classic reggaeton corpus. Residente certainly indulges in some sexist garbage of his own by locating masculinity in "los cojones" (the balls), and condoning an ambivalent homophobia in which he wants the whole world to "suck" his creative juices while the "cocksucker" is portrayed as a particularly despicable character. Yet, it is no less true that Calle 13's lyrics make fun of the pretense that sexuality is a heterosexual male arena and that men can be completely successful in fulfilling women's desires. If most reggaeton songs, exemplified by Daddy Yankee's "Gasolina," include a chorus of female voices begging "papi, give it to me, papi," Residente self-represents as a poor desiring man at the mercy of women who insist that "tú no sabe, no sabe na'" (you have no idea what a woman wants).[40] In this regard, Residente, despite all his glibness and licentiousness, is more of a daydreamer whose creative possibilities are precisely founded in the insufficiency of language to verbalize and satisfy his desires.

"GOOD MORNING, PUERTO RICO/IT'S LIKE 12-SOMETHING"

Even though sexual desire is the main subject of Calle 13, Residente's rap is also symptomatic of the trash of politics, the garbage of the press, and TV filth—an emphasis that underscores the intimate relationship between the physical body and the body politic. Even in "La Ley de Gravedad" (Law of Gravity), a song commissioned by the island's government, Calle 13 uses a by-now mythical publicity slogan "¡Puerto Rico lo hace mejor!" (Puerto Rico does it better!) to criticize the practice of firing bullets into the air—the "stray bullets" that claim a dozen lives during the New Year's festivities. Violating the consensus that Puerto Ricans are "hospitable and peaceful" (like the Taínos, pre-Conquest inhabitants of the island), Calle 13 ironically links the slogan to the problems that concern most citizens: "Drugs, violence and much alcohol/Puerto Rico does it better!"[41]

Through turning publicity trash into trashy commentary, Calle 13 calls attention to the surreal porquería of living in twenty-first-century Puerto Rico. And what, exactly, does this crappiness consist of? For Calle 13, it is about racist practices and class hierarchies that despite social movements aimed at overthrowing them are camouflaged and reorganized, but not eradicated. It's about the political corruption invading every pore of the body politic—"Soy pana de los cocorocos/de Toledo, de Acevedo/Tengo comprao to' los jueces" (I'm tight with all the big shots/From Toledo to Acevedo/I've bought all the judges)—that results in everyday life "shit" like an incompetent government, a biased press, and bad public services.[42] It's also about a political subordination of the Puerto Rican elites to Washington, D.C., that produces the excremental excess of the FBI's killing fugitive Filiberto Ojeda Ríos, leader of Los Macheteros (Ejército Popular Boricua) on September 23, 2005, as addressed in Calle 13's first song "Querido FBI" (Dear FBI).[43]

In this song, which succeeds like no other in incorporating the surrealist practice of a spontaneous monologue—having been written, produced, and disseminated via Internet only thirty hours after the assassination of Ojeda Ríos—Residente seems to literally spit his words, as if he was possessed by the most unbearable political poison:

A to' los federales los escupo con diarrea
Me dan náusea, me dan asco
Yo sé que estoy perdiendo los cascos
Por culpa de ustedes, jodíos brutos
La Calle 13 está de luto

I spit on all the feds with diarrhea
They make me nauseous, disgust me
I know I'm losing my marbles
It's your fault, fucking animals
That Calle 13 is in mourning

Here, as in other Calle 13 tracks—such as the more recent "Pa'l Norte,"[44] an ode to Latin American immigrants—physical and figurative spitting appears as a vital political act. Although many have understood "Querido FBI" as the group's most political intervention for its mention of a proindependence leader, and criticism of the U.S. federal government, the song's greatest political contribution may well be the centrality given to disgust and verbal insurrection as critical forms of social protest.

In other words, "Querido FBI" is not a traditional leftist "call to arms." Despite lines such as "I swear on my mother I'll *dress up* like *machetero*/and tonight I'll strangle ten sailors," Residente's main "explosion" is not of bombs but "of *style* in the name of Filiberto Ojeda Ríos" (my italics). Residente also raps that he will "dress up" as a machetero, not that he intends to actually be one. In this sense, songs such as "Querido FBI" and "Tributo a la Policía," a devastating critique of police brutality in Puerto Rico, are not manifestos offering specific policy directions. Instead, they are uncontainable bursts of expression struggling to bring forth a new political body.

"DARE TO, TO"

With Residente, the reggaeton poet acts as a surreal part of the body politic's digestive system. Calle 13 thus takes on what cultural critic Juan Duchesne Winter has called "sewer-mouth" discourse and redirects it to other ends.[45] If Duchesne Winter defines the sewer-mouth process as the tendency of the state and media to devour every ideology as a strategy to stay in power without changing anything, Calle 13 envelops itself in social waste, and stirs the "personal like vaginal fungus" to destabilize reigning discourses.[46] Like Aimé Césaire's marvelous cannibals, the members of Calle 13 eat public discourse, swallow it, and above all spit it back in the face of those who detest them.

Furthermore, the verbal art of Calle 13 recognizes that the best thing to do with porquería—be it filth, trash, garbage, or shit—is to push it out like a *gargajo* (a ball of phlegm) in order to show how power operates not only through the state apparatus but also, and even more effectively, "through all of our being," as literary critic Suzanne Roussy once put it.[47] By reconceptualizing politics in this way, Calle 13 implies that the biggest challenge facing all of us is not colonialism or the global order as such. Rather, it is something simultaneously simpler and more complex: how to creatively and humorously handle the crap of which we are irremediably made, and the enormous amount of physical and symbolic waste that falls upon us each day.

From the utopian "no place" of music that Residente calls "real," Calle 13 then imagines a different political space, one that differentiates between those who "pee themselves laughing" from those who "shit themselves from fear." It is in this context that their hit "Atrévete Te, Te"[48] can be understood as a call for liberation directed to anyone who listens, but above all to the Puerto Rican middle class, the so-called miss intellectual whose heady "show" of racial and class superiority does not allow her to enjoy her body and "bailar por to'a la jalda" (dance down the hill) with the rest of the reggaeton nation. As Residente eloquently puts it:

Atrévete Te, Te, salte del clóset
Destápate, quítate el esmalte
Deja de taparte, que nadie va a retratarte
Levántate, ponte hyper
Préndete, sácale chispa al starter
Préndete en fuego como un lighter
Sacúdete el sudor como si fueras un wiper
Que tú eres callejera, street fighter

Dare to-to, get out of the closet
Unwrap yourself, take off the polish
Stop hiding, no one will photograph you
Get up, get hyper
Turn on, get a spark off the starter
Get on fire like a lighter
Shake off your sweat as if you were a wiper
You are from the street, you're a street fighter.

At the end of the day, Calle 13 seems to say with complete surrealist conviction, the only true insanity is not to lose control but to give up on what we want. For life may be crappy, yet it's a poetic crap, a very good crap, like spitting diarrhea on the FBI.

NOTES

Translator's Note: In Spanish, the title reads as "poesía de porquería." Because the word *porquería* does not have an exact equivalent in English, throughout the essay, I have used the words *garbage, waste, crap, filth,* and even *porquería* itself to convey the many meanings of this term. The word implies contempt, worthlessness, and dirtiness.

Sources and translations for section-heading quotations:
"Raise the Volume of the Satanic Music" is from Calle 13, "El Tango del Pecado," *Residente o Visitante,* CD (2007). In Spanish, "Súbele el volumen a la música satánica."
"Watch how it floats, my head" is from Calle 13, "La Hormiga Brava," *Calle 13,* 2005. In Spanish, "Mira como flota, mi cabeza."
"And if you don't understand me, your momma's the fat one" is from Calle 13, "La Madre de los Enanos," *Calle 13,* CD, 2005. In Spanish, "Si ustedes no me entienden, tu mai es la gorda."
"Good morning, Puerto Rico/It's like 12-something" is from Calle 13, "La Madre de los Enanos." In Spanish, "Buenos días, Puerto Rico/Son como las 12 y pico."
"Dare-to-to" is from Calle 13, "Atrévete Te, Te."

1. See Raquel Z. Rivera's essay in this anthology, "Policing Morality, *Mano Dura Stylee*: The Case of Underground Rap and Reggae in Puerto Rico in the Mid-1990s."
2. Quoted in Raquel Z. Rivera, "Will the 'Real' Puerto Rican Culture Please Stand Up? Thoughts on Cultural Nationalism," in *None of the Above: Puerto Ricans in the Global Era,* ed. Frances Negrón-Muntaner (New York: Palgrave Macmillan, 2007), 217–31.
3. Please see Juan Carlos Pérez-Duthie, "Junte de literatura y reggaetón," *Primera Hora,* February 17, 2006, http://www.mundoreggaeton.com/foros/noticias/116-calle-13-reforma-regeaton.html (accessed July 25, 2007).
4. *New York Times,* Monday, October 29, 2006.
5. See Jordan Levin, "Calle 13: A Reggaeton Revolution," *Daily Collegian,* February 21, 2006, http://media.www.dailycollegian.com/media/storage/paper874/news/20 06/02/21/Entertainment/Calle.13.A.Reggaeton.Revolution-1620747.shtml?norewrite20 0603302237&sourcedomain=www.dailycollegian.com%253Cbr%253E/ (accessed July 25, 2007).
6. Pérez-Duthie, "Junte de literatura y reggaetón." In Spanish: "Un 'collage' crudo y fascinante, violento y delirante . . . un 'comic book' de clasificación X convertido en cancionero urbano, como si Quentin Tarantino hubiera llevado su Kill Bill a un mundo de reggaetón alternativo."
7. Robin D. G. Kelley, *Freedom Dreams: The Black Radical Imagination* (Boston: Beacon Press, 2003), 5.

8. Henri Peyre, "The Significance of Surrealism," *Yale French Studies* 1, no. 2 (fall–winter 1948): 41.

9. André Breton, *Manifiesto del surrealismo*, http://www.ideasapiens.com/textos/Arte/manifiesto%20surrealismo.htm (accessed July 25, 2007).

10. Calle 13, "El Tango del Pecado."

11. Calle 13, "La Hormiga Brava."

12. Joseph Halpern, "Describing the Surreal," *Yale French Studies* 61 (1981): 94.

13. Calle 13, "El Tango del Pecado."

14. Calle 13, "Se vale to-to," in *Calle 13*, CD (Sony International, 2005).

15. Wisin and Yandel, featuring Aventura, "Noche de Sexo," *Pa'l Mundo*, 2005.

16. Calle 13, "Suave," in *Calle 13*, CD (Sony International, 2005).

17. Breton, *Manifiesto*.

18. Armand Hoog, "The Surrealist Novel," *Yale French Studies*, no. 8 (1951): 17–25, 19.

19. Calle 13, "Atrévete Te, Te," in *Calle 13*, CD (Sony International, 2005).

20. Calle 13, "El Tango del Pecado."

21. Calle 13, "Cabe-c-o," in *Calle 13*, CD (Sony International, 2005).

22. Rivera, "Policing Morality, *Mano Dura Stylee*."

23. Halpern, "Describing the Surreal," 96.

24. Breton, *Manifiesto*.

25. For a discussion on this subject, see Frances Negrón-Muntaner, ed., *None of the Above: Puerto Ricans in the Global Era* (New York: Palgrave, 2007).

26. Calle 13, of course, is not alone in this role. For a parallel analysis of writer Don DeLillo as "waste manager," see Jesse Kavadlo, "Recycling Authority: Don De Lillo's Waste Management," *Critique* 42, no. 4 (summer 2001): 384–401.

27. Calle 13, featuring La Mala Rodríguez, "Mala Suerte con el 13," in *Residente o Visitante*, CD (Sony International, 2007).

28. Calle 13, "Ley de Gravedad," single, 2005.

29. Damarys Ocaña, "You Say You Want a Revolution?," *Latina* (May 2007): 120–23. Spanish in the original.

30. Calle 13, "Cabe-c-o."

31. Writer and producer Anjanette Delgado, interview by author, Miami, May 12, 2007.

32. Quoted in Wikipedia, "The Grotesque Body," http://en.wikipedia.org/wiki/Grotesque_body (accessed July 25, 2007). Also see Mikhail Bakhtin, *Rabelais and His World* (Bloomington: Indiana University Press, 1993). I thank Celeste Fraser Delgado for pointing out the link between the grotesque body and dancehall.

33. Calle 13, "Eléctrico," in *Calle 13*, CD (Sony International, 2005).

34. Calle 13, "La Madre de los Enanos." In Spanish, "un gargajo con flema/color límber de crema." A "límber" is frozen syrup water or juice in a plastic cup.

35. Translator's Note: "Metiendo mano" is a widely used expression that could mean having sex, joining the action, or getting things done.

36. Calle 13, "Vamo' Animal," in *Calle 13*, CD (Sony International, 2005).

37. Calle 13, "Pi-Di-Di-Di," in *Calle 13*, CD (Sony International, 2007).

38. Calle 13, "La Crema," in *Residente o Visitante*, CD (Sony International, 2007).

39. Calle 13, "Mala Suerte," in *Residente o Visitante*, CD (Sony International, 2007).

40. Calle 13, "La Hormiga Brava."

41. Calle 13, "La Ley de Gravedad."

42. Calle 13 with Tego Calderón, "Sin Exagerar," in *Residente o Visitante*, CD (Sony International, 2007). In Spanish, "Soy pana de los cocorocos/de Toledo, de Acevedo/ Tengo comprao to' los jueces."

43. Calle 13, "Querido FBI," single (2005).

44. Calle 13, "Pa'l Norte," in *Residente o Visitante*, CD (Sony International, 2007).

45. Juan Duchesne, "Vieques: Protest as a Consensual Spectacle," in *None of the Above: Puerto Ricans in the Global Era*, ed. Frances Negrón-Muntaner (New York: Palgrave, 2007), 87–97.

46. Calle 13, "La Madre de los Enanos." In Spanish, "Más personal que el hongo vaginal."

47. Cited in, Robin D. G. Kelley, "A Poetics of Anticolonialism," *Monthly Review* 51, no. 3 (November 1999): 1–18, 3, www.monthlyreview.org/1199kell.htm (accessed June 18, 2008).

48. Calle 13, "Atrévete Te, Te."

BIBLIOGRAPHY

Selected Sources for Reading Reggaeton

Allen, Ray, and Lois Wilcken, eds. *Island Sounds in the Global City: Caribbean Popular Music and Identity in New York*. Urbana: University of Illinois Press, 2001.

Báez, Jillian M. "En Mi Imperio: Competing Discourses of Agency in Ivy Queen's Reggaetón." *Centro* 18, no. 2 (fall 2006): 63–81.

Baker, Ejima. "A Preliminary Step in Exploring Reggaetón." In *Critical Minded: New Approaches to Hip Hop Studies*, ed. Ellie M. Hisama and Evan Rapport, 107–23. Brooklyn: Institute for Studies in American Music, 2005.

Baker, Geoffrey. "¡Hip hop, Revolución! Nationalizing Rap in Cuba." *Ethnomusicology* 49, no. 3 (2005): 368–402.

——. "*La Habana que no conoces*: Cuban Rap and the Social Construction of Urban Space." *Ethnomusicology Forum* 15, no. 2 (2006): 215–46.

Calderón, Tego. "Black Pride." *New York Post (Tempo)*. February 15, 2007.

Calo Delgado, Mary Ann, Raquel Delgado, Lourdes Figueroa, and Lennith López. "Más allá del perreo." Master's thesis, Universidad de Puerto Rico, Río Piedras, 2003.

Caramanica, Jon. "The Conquest of America (North and South)." *New York Times*. December 4, 2005.

——. "Grow Dem Bow." *Village Voice*. January 10, 2006.

Castillo-Garstow, Melissa. "Latinos in Hip Hop to Reggaeton." *Latin Beat*. March 2005.

Cepeda, Raquel. "Riddims by the Reggaetón." *Village Voice*. March 28, 2005.

Chang, Jeff. *Can't Stop Won't Stop: A History of the Hip-Hop Generation*. New York: Picador, 2005.

Cooper, Carolyn. *Noises in the Blood: Orality, Gender, and the "Vulgar" Body of Jamaican Popular Culture*. London: Macmillan, 1993.

——. *Sound Clash: Jamaican Dancehall Culture at Large*. New York: Palgrave Macmillan, 2004.

Corbett, Sara. "The King of Reggaetón." *New York Times*. February 5, 2006.

Dinzey-Flores, Zaire. "From the Disco to the Projects: Urban Spatial Aesthetics and Policy to the Beat of Reggaeton." *Centro* 20, no. 2 (fall 2008): 34–69.

Flores, Juan. 1992–93. "Puerto Rican and Proud, Boyee!: Rap, Roots and Amnesia." *Centro* 5, no. 1 (1992–93): 22–32.

——. *From Bomba to Hip-Hop: Puerto Rican Culture and Latino Identity*. New York: Columbia University Press, 2000.

——. "Creolité in the 'Hood: Diaspora as Source and Challenge." *Centro Journal* 16, no. 2 (fall 2004): 283–89.

Forman, Murray, and Mark Anthony Neal, ed. *That's the Joint!: The Hip Hop Studies Reader*. New York: Routledge, 2004.

Giovannetti, Jorge L. "Popular Music and Culture in Puerto Rico: Jamaican and Rap Music as Cross-Cultural Symbols." In *Musical Migrations: Transnationalism and Cultural Hybridity in Latin/o America*, ed. Frances R. Aparicio and Cándida F. Jáquez, 81–98. New York: Palgrave Macmillan, 2003.

González Acosta, Karla F. "El rap underground en Puerto Rico y la libertad de expresión." *Revista Jurídica Universidad Interamericana de Puerto Rico* 37, no. 1 (September–December 2002): 191–208.

Gurza, Agustin. "When the Fad Goes Fizzle." *Los Angeles Times*. April 16, 2006.

Jiménez, Félix. *Las prácticas de la carne: Construcción y representación de las masculinidades puertorriqueñas*. San Juan: Ediciones Vértigo, 2004.

Kenner, Rob. "Dancehall." In *The Vibe History of Hip-hop*, ed. Alan Light, 350–57. New York: Three Rivers Press, 1999.

Manuel, Peter, and Wayne Marshall. "The Riddim Method: Aesthetics, Practice, and Ownership in Jamaican Dancehall." *Popular Music* 25, no. 3 (2006): 447–70.

Marshall, Wayne. "Hearing Hip-hop's Jamaican Accent." *Institute for Studies in American Music Newsletter* 34, no. 2 (2005): 8–9, 14–15.

——. "The Rise of Reggaetón: From Daddy Yankee to Tego Calderón, and Beyond." *Phoenix*. January 19, 2006.

——. "We Use So Many Snares." In *Da Capo Best Music Writing 2006: The Year's Finest Writing on Rock, Hip-Hop, Jazz, Pop, Country, & More*, ed. Daphne Carr and Mary Gaitskill, 260–71. New York: Da Capo Press, 2006.

——. "Routes, Rap, Reggae: Hearing the Histories of Hip-Hop and Reggae Together." Ph.D. diss., University of Wisconsin, Madison, 2007.

Miranda, Carolina. "Daddy Yankee, Reigning Champ of Reggaeton." *Time*. May 8, 2006.

Mitchell, Tony, ed. *Global Noise: Rap and Hip-Hop Outside the USA*. Middletown, Conn.: Wesleyan University Press, 2001.

Moris García, Raúl. *El rap vs. la 357: Historia del rap y reggaeton en Puerto Rico*. N.p., n.d. [2005].

Negrón-Muntaner, Frances, and Raquel Z. Rivera. "Reggaeton Nation." NACLA *Report on the Americas* 40, no. 6 (November/December 2007): 35–39.

Pacini Hernandez, Deborah. "A View from the South: Spanish Caribbean Perspectives on World Beat." *World of Music* 35, no. 2 (1993): 48–69.

Pereira, Joseph. "Translation or Transformation: Gender in Hispanic Reggae." *Social and Economic Studies* 47 (March 1998): 79–88.

Rivera, Raquel Z. "Rap Music in Puerto Rico: Mass Consumption or Social Resistance?" *Centro* 5, no. 1 (1992–93): 52–65.

———. "Del underground a la superficie." *Claridad*. February 10–16, 1995.

———. "Rap in Puerto Rico: Reflections from the Margins." In *Globalization and Survival in the Black Diaspora: The New Urban Challenge*, ed. Charles Green, 109–27. Albany: State University of New York Press, 1997.

———. "Rapping Two Versions of the Same Requiem." In *Puerto Rican Jam: Rethinking Colonialism and Nationalism*, ed. Frances Negrón-Muntaner and Ramón Grosfoguel, 243–56. Minneapolis: University of Minnesota Press, 1997.

———. "Cultura y poder en el rap puertorriqueño." *Revista de Ciencias Sociales*, no. 4 (January 1998): 124–46.

———. *New York Ricans from the Hip Hop Zone*. New York: Palgrave Macmillan, 2003.

———. "Reggaeton: The Rise of the Boricua Underground." *Urban Latino*, no. 46 (2003): 31–32.

———. "Entrevista a Tego Calderón." *Centro* 16, no. 2 (2004): 272–81.

———. "Will the 'Real' Puerto Rican Culture Please Stand Up?: Thoughts on Cultural Nationalism." In *None of the Above: Puerto Ricans in the Global Era*, ed. Frances Negrón-Muntaner, 217–31. New York: Palgrave Macmillan, 2007.

———. "Between Blackness and Latinidad in the Hip Hop Zone." In *A Companion to Latina/o Studies*, ed. Renato Rosaldo and Juan Flores, 351–62. Malden, Mass.: Blackwell, 2007.

Santos, Mayra. "Puerto Rican Underground." *Centro* 8, nos. 1 and 2 (1996): 219–31.

Scholtes, Peter. "Reggaeton Animal." *City Pages*. November 22, 2006. http://citypages .com/databank/27/1355/article14906.asp (accessed July 25, 2007).

Schloss, Joseph G. *Making Beats: The Art of Sample-Based Hip-Hop*. Middletown, Conn.: Wesleyan University Press, 2004.

Spady, James G., H. Samy Alim, and Samir Meghelli, ed. *Tha Global Cipha: Hip Hop Culture and Consciousness*. Philadelphia: Black History Museum Press, 2006.

Stolzoff, Norman. *Wake the Town and Tell the People: Dancehall Culture in Jamaica*. Durham, N.C.: Duke University Press, 2000.

Triviño, Jesús. "Spanish Fly." *Source*. March 2004.

CONTRIBUTOR BIOGRAPHIES

GEOFF BAKER received his Ph.D. in colonial Latin American music from Royal Hollo-way, University of London. He was appointed Leverhulme Research Fellow in the same university in 2003 and lecturer in music in 2005. He is working on a book on Cuban hip-hop and reggaetón for Duke University Press.

TEGO CALDERÓN is a hip-hop and reggaeton artist born in Puerto Rico in 1972. He has been hailed as "reggaeton's leading innovator" by the *New York Times* and "reggaeton's Bob Marley" by *Rolling Stone*.

CAROLINA CAYCEDO was born in 1978 in London, and lives and works in Puerto Rico. She responds to the effects of global capitalism with an artistic practice rooted in processes of communication, movement, and exchange. She has exhibited worldwide, including at the Whitney Biennial 2006 (New York); J'en Reve, Cartier Foundation for Contemporary Art (Paris); and the Venice Biennial 2003 (Italy).

JOSE DAVILA currently works as a content editor for Fania Records and writes for the *Village Voice*, *Vibe*, *Houston Press*, *Dallas Observer*, *Miami New Times*, and the *Broward New Times*. Davila is the former host of the reggaeton broadband show *Barrio 305* and lives in Miami Beach.

JAN FAIRLEY is an independent scholar who works as a music writer, journalist, broadcaster, and lecturer. An Honorary Fellow of the Institute of Popular Music, University of Liverpool, she has been researching in Cuba since 1978 and in various parts of South America (Chile, Argentina, Bolivia, and Peru) since 1971. A member of the editorial board of *Popular Music* (CUP) since 1988, she is at present book reviews editor. Her most recent scholarly publication is " 'Ay Dios, Ampárame' (O God, Protect Me): Music in Cuba during the 1990s" in the book *Island Musics* (Berg Publishers, 2004) edited by Kevin Dawe. She has worked extensively for BBC radio and writes on music for *Songlines*, *fRoots*, the *Scotsman*, and the *Guardian* newspapers.

JUAN FLORES is professor at the Department of Social and Cultural Analysis at New York University. His books include *The Diaspora Strikes Back: Caribbean Latino Tales of Learning and Turning* (Routledge, 2008); *From Bomba to Hip-Hop: Puerto Rican Culture and Latino Identity* (Columbia University Press, 2000); and *Divided Borders: Essays on Puerto Rican Identity* (Arte Publico Press, 1993).

GALLEGO (JOSÉ RAÚL GONZÁLEZ) is one of the most prominent poets of Puerto Rico's literary *generación del noventa* ('90s generation). Author of two critically acclaimed books, *Barrunto* (Editorial Isla Negra, 2000) and *Residente del lupus* (Editorial Isla Negra, 2006), his poetry has been featured in numerous reggaeton recordings, among these, Daddy Yankee's debut album *El Cartel de Yankee* (2000) and in *Eddie Dee: 12 Discípulos* (2005). His debut album was released in 2007 by VI Music and is titled *Teatro del Barrio* (2007).

FÉLIX JIMÉNEZ, a visiting scholar at Columbia University, is professor of communications and cultural studies at Universidad del Sagrado Corazón, Puerto Rico. He has written for the *Nation,* the *Village Voice*, and the *Washington Post,* among other publications. He is the author of *Vieques y la prensa* (2001; PEN Club of Puerto Rico's Book of the Year) and *Las prácticas de la carne* (2004).

KACHO LÓPEZ has directed videos for Daddy Yankee, Tego Calderón, Don Omar, Voltio, Ednita Nazario, and many others. He has twice won the Latin People's Choice Award, once for Daddy Yankee's "Gasolina" and once for Ricky Martin's "Tal Vez." His videographic work has also been nominated for several other prestigious awards, including Best MTV2 Video 2005 for Daddy Yankee's "Gasolina."

MIGUEL LUCIANO received his M.F.A. from the University of Florida. His work has been exhibited at the Brooklyn Museum; El Museo del Barrio, New York; the Bronx Museum of Art; the Chelsea Art Museum, New York; the Newark Museum, New Jersey; and the Jersey City Museum; as well as internationally at the Ljubljana Biennial in Slovenia, San Juan Poligraphic Triennial in Puerto Rico, and Zverev Center for Contemporary Art in Moscow. His work has been reviewed in the *New York Times*, the *Village Voice*, *Newsday,* and the *Utne Reader.*

WAYNE MARSHALL has taught courses on popular music and technology, world music, hip-hop and reggae, and ethnomusicological theory and method at Brandeis University, the University of Chicago, Brown University, and the Harvard Extension School. He has published scholarly articles and reviews in *Popular Music, Latin American Music Review, Interventions, Callaloo,* and the *World of Music* while writing for a broader audience via such outlets as *XLR8R* magazine, the *Fader,* and the *Boston Phoenix* as well as on his blog (wayneandwax.com), from which a post on reggaeton was selected for the *Da Capo Best Music Writing 2006* anthology.

FRANCES NEGRÓN-MUNTANER is a filmmaker, writer, and scholar. She is the author of *Boricua Pop: Puerto Ricans and the Latinization of American Culture* (2004 Choice

Outstanding Book), and editor of several books, including *None of the Above* and *Sovereign Acts*. Among her films are *Brincando el charco: Portrait of a Puerto Rican* and *For the Record: Guam and World War II*. She currently teaches Latino and Caribbean literatures and cultures at Columbia University.

ALFREDO NIEVES MORENO is associate dean of the School of Communications at the Metropolitan University and a former professor of theoretic foundations in communications at Universidad del Sagrado Corazón, Puerto Rico. He has published articles on contemporary culture in *El Nuevo Día* and *Claridad*. He is a regular collaborator for the music column at *Diálogo*, newspaper of the University of Puerto Rico, and worked as coeditor of the architecture magazine ENTORNO. Currently editing his first book, *Las mecánicas del pájaro: Para ver y audiover el cine de Hitchcock*, he was also a contributor for the book *La cultura material del deseo: Objetos, desplazamientos, subversiones* (2007).

IFEOMA C. K. NWANKWO is associate professor of English at Vanderbilt University. She is the author of *Black Cosmopolitanism: Racial Consciousness, National Identity and Transnational Identity in the Nineteenth-Century Americas* (University of Pennsylvania Press, 2005), "The Art of Memory in Panamanian West Indian Discourse" (*PALARA*, 2002), and a number of other comparative studies of U.S. African American, Caribbean, and Latin American literature that have appeared in journals such as *American Literary History*, *Cuban Studies*, *Radical History Review* and the *Langston Hughes Review*. Her current projects employ ethnographic as well as literary-criticism and cultural-studies methodologies to explore Inter-American encounters in the realms of identity, cultural memory, and language. Among these projects are a multi-faceted public Humanities initiative focused on Panamanian West Indians at home and abroad, a special journal issue on Afro-Latin Americans of West Indian descent, and an edited collection (with Mamadou Diouf) on Afro-Atlantic expressive cultures.

DEBORAH PACINI HERNANDEZ is an associate professor of anthropology at Tufts University, where she teaches Latino studies courses and directs the American and Latino Studies Programs. She is coeditor of *Rockin' Las Americas: The Global Politics of Rock in Latin/o America* (University of Pittsburgh Press, 2004) and the author of *Bachata: A Social History of a Dominican Popular Music* (Temple University Press, 1995) and numerous articles on Spanish Caribbean and U.S. Latino popular music.

RAQUEL Z. RIVERA, Ph.D., is a researcher at the Center for Puerto Rican Studies at Hunter College, New York. She is the author of *New York Ricans from the Hip Hop Zone* (Palgrave Macmillan, 2003) and various scholarly articles. A freelance journalist, her articles have been published in numerous magazines and newspapers, among these *Vibe*, *One World*, *Urban Latino*, *El Diario / La Prensa*, *El Nuevo Día*, *Claridad*, and the *San Juan Star*. She blogs about reggaeton in reggaetonica.blogspot.com.

WELMO E. ROMERO JOSEPH was born in Puerto Rico in the 1970s to a Dominican father and a Haitian mother. He embarked on a rap career in 1994. His first CD was titled *negroporvenir* (2000), and it landed him the opportunity to narrate through rap rhymes *Raíces* (2001), a yearly musical special filmed by Banco Popular. His EP *Adelanto* (2005) fused samples and live instrumentation; and his third musical production, *Abre los Ojos* (2005), was released for free download on the Internet.

CHRISTOPH TWICKEL lives and works in Hamburg, Germany, as a freelance journalist. Author of *Hugo Chávez: Eine Biographie* (Hamburg: Edition Nautilus, 2006), he has also been writing about Latin America and Afro-Latin music since the early 1990s for various newspapers and magazines. Under the alias Basso Profundo, he is a club and radio DJ. His radio show airs on www.byte.fm every Saturday at 10 am EST/18 CET.

ALEXANDRA T. VAZQUEZ is an assistant professor in the Center for African American studies and the Department of English at Princeton University. Vazquez is the author of *Instrumental Migrations: The Critical Turns of Cuban Music* (under contract with Duke University Press), and with Ela Troyano, a coeditor of a forthcoming anthology on La Lupe. She has written on Graciela, "the First Lady of Afro-Cuban Jazz," in *women and performance: a journal of feminist theory*. Vazquez is also part of the triumvirate that is ohindustry.com.

INDEX

Brazilian funk, 190–91
Brewley M.C., 139, 141, 252; "Nena Sexy,"
35, 141
bultrón, 31
Bustamante, Pucho, 81, 95
Byron, Melanie, 210

Cabrera, Victor (a.k.a. Tunes), 143,
310n11. *See also* Luny Tunes
Calderón, Tego: *bachata* in, 143; *bomba*
and folk forms of, 23; Calle 13 and, 272;
censorship of, 162n51; childhood of,
255; creativity of, 62; "Dominicana,"
144, 161n42; Dominican vs. Puerto Rican identity and, 152; *El Abayarde*, 143,
207, 261; "En Peligro de Extinción,"
269; "Guasa Guasa," 321; hip-hop influence on, 27; Luny Tunes and, 143;
"Métele Sazón," "Pa' Que Retozen,"
143; as musical role model, 211; Panama
and, 31–32, 69n35, 96; as poet, 328; on
race, 10, 47, 324–26; Romero Joseph
on, 312; in Sierra Leone, 14, 216–17, 222,
225; in *Time* magazine, 239
Calle 13: aesthetic "difference" of, 260–61;
"Atrévete Te, Te," 268–71, 273, 328, 330,
337; "Cabe-c-o," 264, 266, 331; *Calle 13*
(2005), 263–64, 265; "Chulin Culin
Chunflay," 268, 270–72; concert of,
272–73; "El Tango del Pecado," 327; innovations of, 257; as "intellectual"
group, 328; irreverence of, 62; "La Hormiga Brava," 328–30; "La Ley de Gravedad," 266–67, 278n28, 335; "La Madre
de los Enanos," 272, 332, 335; "Mala
Suerte," 334; "Pa'l Norte," "Tributo a la
Policía," 336; "Pi-Di-Di-Di," 333–34;
"poesía de porquería" of, 332–33;
"Querido FBI," 256, 261–63, 266, 273,
278n25, 335–36; race and, 276n13–
277n13; self-criticism of, 274; "Se Vale
To-To," 263; "Sin Coro," 259–60, 272;

social commentary of, 258; surrealism
of, 329, 337–38; *Voltio* (2005), 268
Calvo, Pedro, 289
calypso, 11, 23, 31, 68n31, 79, 86, 88, 107
Capleton, 315
Caribbean, the: aesthetics of, in reggaeton 3, 113; "authentic" vs. "commercialized," 171; Barbados, Trinidad,
Tobago, 84; 3:2 cross-rhythms in, 6;
Cuba, 185; Dominican Republic, 145;
Jamaica, 24, 29–30; *melaza* and, 46;
merengue and, 140; Miami and, 212;
migration and, 48, 66, 201; musical exchanges in, 11, 68n31, 135, 139, 171–72,
182–83; New York and, 32–33, 36; Panama and, 31, 79, 81, 83; pride about, 215;
4/4 pulse with 3 + 3 + 2 cross-rhythms
in, 23, 29; race in, 71, 136; reggaeton
criticisms in, 165; in reggaeton's
origins, 5, 8, 21, 28–29; reggaeton's
popularity span in, 61, 282; scholarship
on, 12–13; Spanish dialects of, 305, 308;
Tego Calderón and, 143; television
in, 286
Caterine, 86
Caycedo, Carolina, 14, 216, 217n2
C&C Music Factory, 82, 104
censorship, state control: art vs. reality
and, 111, 118–19; class and, 121–25; in
Cuba, 180–81, 189, 284; reggaeton and
underground culture wars and, 9;
dancing and, 177; dissent against, 117;
in the Dominican Republic, 146,
162n51, 230, 245; mainstream vs. "underground" and, 114; marginality and,
121–25; Morality in Media and, 38, 111,
115, 253; in Panama, 82–84, 93–94, 102,
106; of *perreo* in Puerto Rico, 130, 253,
278n33, 309n6, 319; power and, 126–29;
as "public relations," 318; in Puerto
Rico, 275n5–276n5; "Pu Tun Tun" and,
160n28; race and, 121–25, 291; as target

censorship (*cont.*)

of, 61; *underground* and, 38, 73n69, 112–13, 116, 120, 253

Central America. *See* Latin America

Centro de Investigación de la Música Cubana (CIDMUC), 167–68, 170, 173, 176, 180–81, 197n29

Chaka Demus (and Pliers), 315; "Murder She Wrote" (1992), 26

Cheb, 83, 107n3

Chezina. *See* Don Chezina

Chicho Man, 31, 82, 95, 97

Chosen Few: El Documental (2004), 10, 26–29, 34, 55, 58–59, 69n35, 72n53, 147–48

chutney-ton, 62

CIRCO, 272, 278n36–279n36; "Un Accidente," "Cascarón," "Circosis," "Historia de un Amor," 279n36

Clark, Rodney, 81

class. *See* social class

clothing. *See* aesthetics, performative

club, dance anthems, 49

cocolos vs. *roqueros* (salsa vs. rock fans), 7, 139

Coco Man, 95

Cold Crush Brothers, 104

Coldplay, 268

Colombia, reggaeton in, 76n92, 82

Colón, Panama (city, province), 31, 81, 83–84, 93–94, 99, 102, 106, 108n8

commentary, in lyrics (cultural, political, social): about "street" identity, 114–15, 144, 268, 298, 328; "barrio-centric," 276n9, 277n13; "battle of ideas" in Cuba and, 193–94; Calle 13 and, 256–58, 273–74, 334; censorship and, 118–21; on corruption, 25, 38, 335; dancehall "culture wars" and, 6–7; of dancehall vs. roots reggae, 25; dissent and, 106; on excess, 231–32; grassroots expression and, 149–50; politics vs. pleasure

in, 175–76, 185–86, 193–94; raps for politicians and, 92; reggaeton's shift in, 49–50; Renato's, 94; romantic, 85; Romero Joseph's, 317–19; shift in reggaeton's, 49–50, 60–61; socially conscious, 175; surrealist, 331; Tego Calderón's, Residente's, 63; in *underground*, 111–12, 116–17, 122–30, 125, 252; of *underground* vs. mainstream, 113; urban settings in, 47; youth- and class-inflected, 46–47

commercialization: Calle 13 and, 333–34; consumerism and, 215–16; co-optation and, 48; Cuba and, 161, 165–67, 171, 184, 188–89, 199n51, 199n52; dance music and, 197n24; El General on, 105; "Gasolina" (Daddy Yankee) and, 3, 19; gender and, 255–56, 303; globalization and, 194–95; Glory and, 231, 244–45; hip-hop and, 38, 56, 59, 186–87, 211; Ivy Queen and, 239; of meren-rap, 140–42; *Meren-Rap* and, 34–36; Puerto Rico and, 157, 173, 238–39, 253–54; reggae and, 96; *reggaeton* as term and, 253; in reggaeton's development, 21, 49–52, 54, 157; sexuality and, 49, 73n69, 139, 190; social content and, 278n26; style and, 49, 144, 185; *underground* and, 37, 113–14, 121–22; U.S. music industry and, 56

compa, Haitian. *See* konpa

compilations: children-oriented, 61; communal flavor of, 250n9; *Dancehall Reggaespañol* (1991), 32; of discrete songs, 51; home-burned, 280, 282–83; *Meren-Rap*, 141; of Panamanian dancehall, 81, 85; recording careers helped by, 237

concerts, live performances: affective relationships to, 306; of Calle 13, 256–57, 272–74; CD "buzz" and, 179; of Cubanito 20.02, 187; of Don Omar, 307; of El General, 105; El Roockie in,

85; Havana hip-hop festival (2002), 186; hip-hop, 140, 183; of Ivy Queen, 249, 300, 302, 308; in Miami, 209; mixtapes and, 42; *quinceañeras*, 92, 101, 284; reggae, 7; "Reggaeton a lo cubano," 182; Reggaeton Summerfest (2003), 147, 152; of Tego Calderón, 152, 211; *tunas*, 259, 272, 277n18; as verbal events, 328–29; of Vico C, 140; of Wisin and Yandel, 2; women in, 232, 263, 288

Conciencia Poética (Intifada), 263, 318

Conjunto Quisqueya, 140

Cooper, Carolyn, 191, 193

Correa, Miguel, 140

Cortés, José Luis, NG La Banda: "La Bruja," 281

Crespo, Elvis, 140, 154, 156

crime, 25, 116, 121–22, 137

Criminal Minded (Boogie Down Productions, 1987), 66n15

critiques about reggaeton: "banality" and, 193; in Cuba, 165–68, 193, 195; dance vs. political music and, 197n24; defenses and, 327–28; formulas and, 319; "Gasolina" and, 19; hip-hop and reggae sales and, 60; lack of aesthetic merit and, 9; lyrics and, 66n12; monotony and, 306, 320; "polka reggae" and, 15n16, 74n78; representational limits and, 274; sexism and, 63n1; surprises and, 301; women's global standing and, 291–92

"crunk," Atlanta-based, 5, 200–201, 209, 212n2

crunkiao (El Crunkiao), 12, 200–201, *202*, 203–4, 208–11

Cruz, Celia, 307, 324

Cuba: Cuban Women's Federation, 281; dance and, 288; foreigners in, 280–81; Jamaican migration to, 30; Miami and, 202; public discourse in, 287; Puerto Rican reggaeton in, 168, 170–73, 177, 185; rap and, 165, 167, 169–70; rap as "transcendent" in, 174; reggaeton as postprotest music in, 191; reggaeton's development and, 12; reggaeton's popularity in, 161, 166, 282, 293n7; reggaeton vs. hip-hop in, 9, 165, 185; *son* and, 156; Special Period in, 177, 188, 191–94, 197n29, 282, 287

Cubanito 20.02, 165, 168, 170, 181, 184–85, 187, 191; "Mátame," 166; *Tócame*, 183

Culture Club: "Karma Chameleon" (1984), 53

cumbia, 8, 62, 257, 269, 290

Curet, Tite, 325

Cutty Ranks, 32, 46, 315; "A Who Seh Me Dun" (1993), 26, 313

Cypress Hill, 27, 43, 206

Daddy Yankee (a.k.a. Raymond Ayala): *Barrio Fino* (2004), 146; on *Billboard* awards show, 250n11–251n11; *bomba* and, 64; "Brugal," 144; "Chamaco's Corner" and, 299; *crunkiao* and, 201; Cuba and, 179; Dominican Republic and, 161; Don Omar and, 250n8; *El cartel de Yankee*, 12, 299; El Chombo and, 74n70; as foundational to reggaeton, 50, 207, 211, 239, 254; Glory and, 229, 235, 247; internationalization and, 236; Miami and, 210; Pitbull and, 204; Renato on, 96; Romero Joseph on, 315; "Rompe," 238; synth effects in, 53; *Talento de Barrio*, 247; "Todas las Yales," 53; United States and, 209; videos of, 278n33. *See also* "Gasolina"

dance: Americas' similarities in, 20, 293n10; anthems and, 19; "back-to-front," 287–88; breakdancing, 5–6, 29, 177; as central to reggaeton, 29, 67n23; in "Chamaco's Corner" (Gallego), 298; Cuba and, 178, 197n29, 281, 284; *dem-*

dance (*cont.*)

bow and, 29; expressiveness of, 176, 295n13; feminist view of, 13; *Meren-Rap* and, 34; Miami and, 203; nondance vs. music for, 174–75, 197n24, 199n52, 321; in "Oye Mi Canto" video, 59; Panama and, 101–2; Puerto Rico and, 269; *sandunguera*-style, 289; sexualized, 1, 13, 49; social relations and, 291–92; tempos for, 24; "transgressive," 290; U.S. popularity of, 61; in videos, 270. *See also perreo*

dancehall (dancehall reggae, *ragga*, or "raggamuffin"): allusions to, 53; crossover hits from, 50; female "slackness" in, 191; in *The Flow* (DJ Nelson), 55; hip-hop and, 66n14; lyrics of, 74n71; marginality and, 123; melodies from, 20, 37, 43; Panama and, 31, 81, 92; Puerto Rico and, 112, 121–22; as reggae subgenre, 5; reggaeton's connection with, 24–26, 29, 49, 51–52; rhythms from, 29; Romero Joseph on, 313, 315–16; roots reggae vs., 6–7, 15n10; Spanish-language, 70n36; symbolic insurrection in, 333; *underground* and, 21, 36, 40, *41*, 46, 252. *See also reggae*

Dancehall Reggaespañol (1991), 32–34, *33*. *See also reggae en español*

Danger Man, 70

danzón, 290–91

Davila, Jose, 9, 12

dembow (*dembo, denbo*): applied to reggaeton's precursors, 8; in Cuba, 195n1; Danilo Orozco on, 183; description of, 20–21; as early name for reggaeton, 4, 36–37; explanations of, 65n6, 72n54; grafting onto, 49; hip-hop combined with, 43–44; as localized term, 40; Luny Tunes and, 55, 57; in Miami, 207–8; resignification of term, 38–39; Romero Joseph on, 318, 321; Tego Cal-

derón and, 207; in "Todas las Yales" (Daddy Yankee), 53. *See also boom-ch-boom-chick*

Dem Bow riddim (Bobby Digital's): as central to reggaeton, 56; "Dembow 2004," 39; DJ Playero and, 72n57; "Ellos Benia" and, 72n55; explanations of, 20, 65n6, 72n54; extensions beyond, 62; Jamaican influence and, 90; in *The Noise 9*, 53; *Playero 38* and, 42; Puerto Rico's localized, *40*; in *Reggaeton Sex*, 54; sampling and, 45–46; as set of tools, 39; snares and, 21; in *underground* mixes, 38

"Dem Bow" (Shabba Ranks, 1991): *Dem Bow* rhythm and, 20, 38, 66n13; explanations of, 65n6, 72n54; idea of "bowing" in, 38; instrumental from, 39; in Panama, 95

"Dem Bow" (Wisin and Yandel, 2003), 39, 96

Demphra, 86

despelote, 176, 289–90

Dicky Ranking, 70

digital software, tools: Cuban music and, 170, 172–74, 282; Fruity Loops, 19, 52–54, 56, 75n85; Luny Tunes and, 56; *reggaeton* term and, 51; style changes through, 51–52; *underground*'s mainstreaming and, 48–49; "vamp and machine in one" and, 232

Dirtsman: "Hot This Year," 26

distribution of music. *See* production, distribution of music

DJ Adam, 71n45

DJ Anqueira: *Innovando*, 234

DJ Blass, 3, 49, 51–52, 54, 56, 71n45

DJ Coyote, 38, 72n53

DJ Dicky, 71n45

DJ El Niño, 51, 57

DJ Emilio, 283

DJ Eric, 71n45; *La Industria* series, 319

El Chombo, 69n35; *Cuentos de la Cripta*, 81, 95, 98n8; "Papi Chulo," 74n70
El Comandante, 28
Elephant Man, 50
El General (Edgardo Franco): "Borinquen Anthem," 82; on calypso, 88; dancehall emulation by, 32; "El Caramelo," 82; Jorge Oquendo and, 141; "Las Chicas," 82; "Muévelo," 79, 82, 105; naming of, 82, 102; in New York, 103–4; Panama and, 29, 34, 99, 100–102, 106–7; on Panamanian *plena*, 69n35; photo, *100*; as reggaeton founding figure, 99, 207; Romero Joseph on, 315; "Son Bow" (1991), 39; touring by, 105; Vico C and, 67–68n34. *See also* "Pu Tun Tun"; "Te Ves Buena"
Eliel, 320
El Imperio (compilation), 81
El Médico del Regeton, 288
El Roockie, 70; "Falta Otro en el Barrio," "Grave Error," 85
Elvis Manuel, 171
ethnicity: Dominicans in Puerto Rico and, 137–38, 149–51; hip-hop vs. reggaeton and, 9; intersections of, with class, race, gender, 13; *latinidad* and, 27; in Miami vs. New York, 202; musical expression and, 10; in New York, 150, 152; race and, 10, 149–50; relationships and, 156; strategic mobilization of, 24; tensions around, 9. *See also* race

Fab 5: "Mini Mini," 32
Fairley, Jan, 12–13, 196n9, 197n29
Falo, 315
fashion. *See* aesthetics, performative
Fatal Fantasy series (DJ Joe): *Fatal Fantasy 1* (2001), 54; *Fatal Fantasy 3* (2002), 57
Fat Joe and the Terror Squad, 27
Figueroa, Héctor "El Flaco," 253–54, 267, 278n33

Flores, Juan, 47–48, 124, 157
Fornaris, Danny, 62
Francheska, 28, 139–41
Frankie Boy, 315
Freddy, 304
"freestyle," Latin, 34, 200, 203, 208–9, 212n2, 306, 310n12
Fruity Loops (software), 19, 52–54, 56, 75n85
Fulanito, 142

Gallego (José Raúl González): *Barrunto*, 12
gangs, 85, 252, 255, 259, 268, 276n9
Garvey, Marcus, 81, 84
"Gasolina" (Daddy Yankee): alternating snares in, 71n46; as anthem, 2; as commercial apex, 3, 146; cultural influences in, 19–21; Daddy Yankee's career and, 161n46; female begging in, 334; as global hit, 333; Glory's chorus in, 230–32; Luny Tunes and, 56; in Panama, 96; petroleum in interpreting, 64n5; Pitbull and, 209; techno synths of, 48–49
Gem Star, 148
gender: "agency" and, 305; Bourdieu on, 276n10; Calle 13 and, 258, 260, 263–64, 267–69, 269, 272–74, 335; in "Chamaco's Corner" (Gallego), 298–99; Cuba and, 179, 197–98n29; Daddy Yankee and, 20; dance and, 176, 216, *221*, 285–88, 291–92; debates about, 1, 60; female availability and, 233; feminism and, 13, 305, 310n10, 311n13; Glory and, 229–35, 243; Glory vs. Ivy Queen and, 241, 245; hair salons and, 301n8, 303; heterosexuality and, 334; Ivy Queen and, 239–40, 242; in Jamaican dancehall, 191; liner notes and, 305; masculinity and, 115, 253–54, 255–56, 259, 273, 276n9; misogyny and, 120, 129, 281; musical space and, 307; Panama and, 86; pan-

Latin ethos and, 302; as performed identity, 287; PG13 (Calle 13's) and, 273; Puerto Rico and, 236, 238; racialization and, 58; *reggae en español* and, 97; in reggaeton's production, 236–37; Romero Joseph on, 318–19; in salsa, 120–21; sexism and, 9, 63n1, 128, 134n60, 268; spectatorship and, 303; stereotypes of, 49; tourism and, 282; visual style and, 215; women's labels and, 250n1. *See also* sexuality

Giovannetti, Jorge L., 7, 11

global, transnational music industry: Cuba and, 171, 174, 181, 188; El General and, 79; local control vs., 61, 183; Luny Tunes and, 57; Miami and, 210; Puerto Rico and, 8; reggaeton's popularity and, 328; "transnationalism from below" and, 47; *underground*'s success in, 252; "underground to mainstream" shifts and, 48

Glory (Glorimar Montalvo Castro), 249–51; "Duro Duro," 234; as foil, 19, 229–30; as "Gangster Kitten," 234, 250n1; *Glou* (2005, 2006), 230, 243, *243*; as "*It* voice" in reggaeton, 231; Ivy Queen compared with, 239, 242, 247, 249; "La Popola," 163n72, 230, 245–47; *La última noche*, 247; "Perreo 101," 244–45; in politics, 250n10; solo image of, 234–36, 240–45, 248–50; "Suelta como gabete" chorus of, 237–38; as verbal robot, 232–33

Gold Disc Records, 32

González, Isai (a.k.a. Jibba Jamz), 202–3

González, Velda (Puerto Rican senator), 130, 253, 267, 278n33, 309n6, 319

graffiti, 5–6, *41*

Gran Omar, 236, 240

Green Day, 268

guaracha, 124

Guasabanga. *See* Wassabanga

Guerra, Juan Luis, 74n83, 155; *No Es El Mismo Ni Es Igual* (2000), 148

Gunzmoke, 318

Haila, 181

Havana: "battle of ideas" and, 169, 192–93; "bedroom studios" in, 179; Casa de la Cultura in, 181; cultural policies in, 189; dance in, 177, 197n29, 280; hip-hop/rap in, 165, 186; *jineterismo* in, 176; musical training in, 172–73; Puerto Rican reggaeton in, 172; reggaeton distribution in, 178, 198n32; reggaeton-rap fusions and, 197n21; in reggaeton studies, 167; reggaeton types in, 168; reggaeton vs. rap in, 183–84, 187–88, 196n8; U.S. radio broadcasts and, 195n1. *See also* Cuba

Heavy Management, 204

Hector and Tito, 96, 235

Hector El Bambino: "Dale Castigo," 304

hip-hop (rap): rap vs., 5–6; antiestablishment character of, 263; B-girls, B-boys in, 318, 321; "bling-bling" and, 256; Calle 13 and, 257, 262; *crunkiao* and, 201; Cuban, 198n49; dancehall and, 8, 25–26; Dominicans and, 138, 145, 147; in *El Abayarde* (Tego Calderón), 143; electronic backgrounds and, 172; in *The Flow* (DJ Nelson), 55; Latin, 28, 200, 202, 205, 206, 209; Lisa M on, 142; marginality and, 123–24, 193; marketing tools from, 59; "meren-rap" project and, 34–35, 140–42, 145–46; Miami and, 12; *Playero 38* and, 42; Puerto Ricans and African Americans in New York and, 157; Puerto Ricans and Dominicans in New York and, 147–48; Puerto Rico and, 112, 113, 121–22, 252, 278n26; race and, 1; reggae and, 15n10, 26–27, 37; reggaeton collaborations with, 152; as reggaeton precursor, 23;

hip-hop (*cont.*)

reggaeton's decline in, 51–52, 144; reggaeton vs., 9, 165, 169–70, 183, 189–90, 194–95, 211, 321; rhyme and speechlike flows from, 20; rhymes and speechlike flows from, 312, 319; Romero Joseph on, 312–13, 316, 318–21; sampling in, 42–43; success of, 50; tempo of, 67n23; *underground* and, 36, 37, 40, *41*, 45–46; Vico C and, 28–29, *29*, 95

homosexuality, 129, 134n60, 258–59, 269, 308, 334

humor, satire: Calle 13 and, 256, 264, 267–68, 274, 332, 337; in Cuban reggaeton, 283; Freud on, 260; Ivy Queen and, 302, 306; reggaeton vs. rap and, 186; Residente and, 63; Romero Joseph and, 322; surrealism and, 329–30

"hurban" music, 2, 57–59. *See also* "urban music"

hyphy, Bay Area, 5

Iglesias, Enrique, 207

instruments: accordion, 147, 160n38; acoustic drum, *cuá*, maracas, 319; bass drum, 39, 53, 66n11; drum machine, 212n2; *güira* scraper, 141; guitars, 42–44, 57–58, 75n85, 143–44, 160n38; keyboard, piano, 6, 32, 35, 39, 56, 57, 94, 143–44, 160n37, 208, 257, 313; kick drums, 19–20, 23, 25, 29, 39, 43–44, 49, 52–55, 212n2; live, 257; saxophone, 42, 52, 141, 160n38; snares, 19–21, 23, 25, 29, 36, 43–44, 49, 52–54, 63, 71n46; *tambora*, 141; *tambores*, 205; *timbal*, 39. *See also* digital software, tools; synths from techno, trance, rave, club

intertextuality, 42, 44, 46

In the House magazine, 58, 79n53

Ivy Queen (Martha Ivelisse Pesante), 306–9; Career Achievement Award of, 249; "Chika Ideal," 256; concert aside

by, 300–304, 306, 309n1; *The Diva Chronicles* concert, 249; *En Mi Imperio* (1997), *The Original Rude Girl* (1999), 239; *Flashback* (2005), 98n7, 240; as foremost female star, 239; Glory compared with, 230, 241–43, 247; Gran Omar and, 236, 240; long-term vision of, 307; Luny Tunes and, 143; "makeover" of, 240, 242; Panama and, 90, 95, 96–97; "Reggae Respect," 95, 98n7; Renato on, 97; scholarship on, 310n13; "Te He Querido, Te He Llorado," "La Mala," 143; "Yo quiero bailar," 240–41

Jamaica: Cuba and, 186–87, 195n1; dancehall in, 6–7; dancehall vs. roots rhythms from, 24; El General on, 107; "flip tongue" rapping and, 42; "Latin" vs. influences from, 23; migration from, 29–30, 34, 66n15, 68n25; New York and, 26, 32–33, 47, 107, 66n15; Panama and, 31, 53, 80; patois and, 8, 82, 101; race and, 325; in reggaeton's development, 11, 24, 149; *stylee* term from, 131

Javia, 150

Jay-Z, 211

jazz, 42, 124, 186, 288

Jhosy and Baby Q, 148

jíbaro music, 11, 139

Jiménez, Félix, 12, 163, 253–54, 267, 276n7

Johnson, Linton Kwesi, 24

Jossie Esteban, 141, 155

Jossie Esteban y La Patrulla 15, 140

Juanes: "Camisa Negra," 162

Junior Ranks, 83

Kelly, R., 62

Ken-Y: "Down," 305

Kid Frost, 27

Killa Ranks, 83

klezmer, 62
konpa, 23, 316
Kool G Rap, 26
kwaito, 190, 196n8

La Bruja: "Mi Gatita Negra," 307
La Charanga Habanera, 181
La Diva, *33*
Lady Ann, *87*, 97; "Anina es mi nombre,"
    "Déjalo Que Aprenda, Mama,"
    "Quiero Sentir un Hombre," 86
La Fabulosa, 81
La Factoria, 82, 97
La Kalle, 2, 59–60
La Lupe, 304
La Mega, 81
language. *See* lyrics; Spanglish; Spanish
    language
Las Guanábanas Podrías, 275n2; "Mal-
    ditas Putas," 120, 334
La Sista, 23, 272, 325
Latin America: critiques of reggaeton and
    perreo in, 165, 188, 197n24, 216; El Gen-
    eral's popularity in, 104; gender in, 258;
    Latin rap and, 27; Miami and, 202, 210;
    migration and, 2, 30, 86, 200, 336; mu-
    sical exchanges in, 21, 68, 139, 173;
    "petro-Caribe" relations and, 285; race
    in, 10, 47, 60, 71n49, 324–26; reg-
    gaeton's origins and, 5, 76n91; reg-
    gaeton's popularity in, 3, 61; religion
    in, 86; Renato's popularity in, 89, 93,
    97; salsa in, 139; "traditional music"
    from, 9, 85, 277n18; "transgressive"
    dance in, 290; "YouTubosphere" of, 58,
    75n87. *See also* Caribbean, the; *lati-
    nidad*; "tropical" music forms; *specific
    countries*
latinidad (Latinness): Afro-, 307; Carib-
    bean pride and, 215; hip-hop artists
    and, 27–28; as inherent in reggaeton,
    23; in marketing, 59; "Oye Mi Canto"

and, 59, 302; pan-, 8, 10, 58, 61, 149, 292,
    305; pan-Caribbean, 285; race and,
    309n5; "Reggaeton Latino" shift and,
    36, 49–50, 57–58, 60, 144
Latin pop, 2–3, 34, 50, 61, 85, 207
Latin rap, Latin hip-hop, 23, 27–29,
    67n18, 139, 145, 200, 202, 204, 206,
    209–11
Lavoe, Héctor, 105, 231
LDA, 148
Lee, Spike: *Malcolm X*, 324
Lil' Jon, 209, 212n3
Lisa Lisa, 305
Lisa M, 28, 139, 140–42, 252; "El Pum
    Pum," 35, 141
Lito y Polaco, 207
Little Lenny, 33, *33*; "Punany Tegereg,"
    32, 35
López, Kacho, 14, 216
Lord Cobra, 31, 88, 107
Lord Panama, 31
Lorna: "Papi Chulo" (2003), 74n70, 86
Los Aldeanos, 175; "Repartición de
    Bienes," 166
Los de Atrás Están Conmigo, 257
Los Doce Discípulos: "Quítate Tú pa'
    Ponerme Yo," 321
Los Gatos, 283–84
Los Hermanos Rosario, 140; "Bomba,"
    163n71
Los Macheteros, Boricua Popular Army,
    14, 215, 220, 261, 277n22–277n23, 335
Los Paisanos, 175
Los Tres Gatos, 168
Los Van Van: "Sandunguera," 181, 289
Lovindeer: "Babylon Boops," "Don't
    Bend Down," 93
Luciano, Miguel, 14, 146, 215–16, 216n1
Luke Records, 204, 208
Luny Tunes (production team): devices
    of, 56–57, 310n11; formation of, 143; as
    foundational to reggaeton, 55, 62, 149;

style, 163n71; debates about, 139, 154–56, 159n23; Dominicans in Puerto Rico and, 135, 140; hybrids, fusions with, 152; interethnic collaborations on, 148; Luny Tunes and, 57, 143; "meren-rap" project and, 34–35; piano riffs of, 143; rapping over beat of, 146; as reggaeton precursor, 8; reggaeton rhythms in, 62; rhythms of, 23, 141; Romero Joseph on, 316

"meren-rap," "merenhouse": after popularity of, 70n43; in Dominican Republic, 145–46; hip-hop in Puerto Rico vs., 35–36; Jorge Oquendo's project with, 34, 141–42; Orquídea Negra on, 145–46; as reggaeton precursor, 22

Meren-Rap (recording), 70n41, 141, (1991) 34–36; *Meren-Rap II*, (1993) 141, 160n26

Miami: competition in, 211; *crunkiao* and Spanish music in, 200; Daddy Yankee and Don Omar in, 250n8; dancehall in, 82; Latin influences in, 208; New York and, 201–2, 203; Pitbull's success and, 204; reggaeton in, 205–6; reggaeton vs. hip-hop in, 9; reggaeton vs. other Latin music in, 209–10; Spanish language and, 207; *305* symbol in, 200, 211; Tego Calderón in, 324

Miami bass ("booty music"), 5, 200, 203–4, 208–9, 212n2

Mighty Sparrow, 107

migration: bachata and, 57; circular patterns of, 22, 30, 71n48; diasporas and, 5, 37, 48, 163n67, 293n2, 309n4; of Dominicans, 135–37, 150, 163n67; El General and, 79; Family Reunification Act and, 136; "geographical other" and, 47; hip-hop's narratives and, 157; island-to-island, 135; of Jamaicans, 29, 66n15, 68n25; from Latin America, 2; Luny Tunes and, 55–56, 135, 143; to Miami,

200; of Panamanians, 91, 106; of Puerto Ricans, 150; race and, 60; reggae and, 31; in reggaeton's history, 21; rural-to-urban, 86; transnational, 13; *underground* recordings and, 113; West Indian, 302

Miller, Karl, 32, 108n5

Minneapolis, 76n92

Mito, 318

mixtapes: circulation of, 35; collaboration in, 73n59; commercial market vs., 51; decline in, 51; of DJ Blass, 3; of DJ Joe, 53; of DJ Negro and DJ Playero, 40; intertextuality of, 44–45; of Jorge Oquendo, 160n36; length of, 71n45; by The Noise, 43; promotional videos for, 47; as Puerto Rican practice, 207; in Puerto Rican stores, 253; snares in "Gasolina" and, 21; techno in, 54–55

monetary compensation: album sale figures and, 1–2; Cuba and, 161n44; El General on, 103, 105–6; El Roockie on, 85; Glory's solo image and, 247; in Panama, 81–82, 98n9; in Puerto Rico, 315; reggaeton's success and, 254–55; for reggaeton vs. other Latin genres and, 211; Renato on, 93, 96

Mr. Vegas, "Pull Up," 212n3

musical style, devices: "breakdowns" in, 64n2; call-and-response, 230, 304; collage and layering, 32, 36, 42–44, 52, 62, 180, 320, 329; duos and, 237–38, 250n9; scratching, 94; shifting semitones and, 19–20; slight pitch changes, 32, 46, 74n76, 205; tempo and, 67n3, 69n35, 82, 209, 319; verse-chorus-verse form, 51, 53

música negra ("black music"): decreased emphasis on, 10, 50, 57; as early term for reggaeton, 36; nationalization, commercialization, and, 48; in *Playero 38*, 43; to "reggaeton latino" shift, 59–

P. Diddy, 334

Pacini Hernandez, Deborah, 8, 12–13, 48, 70n41, 73n68, 74n80, 75n83, 198n34, 198n49, 310n9

Panama: Colón–Panama City rivalry in, 83, 106, 108n8; dancehall in, 25; "Gasolina" in, 64n5; Jamaica, United States, and, 24, 92; Jamaica and, 29, 30, 53; migration from, 91; musical hybrids, fusions in, 70n35; music distribution in, 93–94, 100–101; musicians from, 31–36, 69n34, 69n35–70n35, 74n70, 79–88, 95, 97, 145, 315 (See also El General; Renato); New York and, 32–34, 47, 79, 82, 99, 103–4; popular music in, 31, 68n31; Puerto Rican influences in, 96; reggae en español in, 81–83, 90, 95; reggae in, 8, 68n32, 69n35, 81–88, 99; reggaeton's development and, 4, 10–11, 29, 34, 65n7, 79–80, 149, 254; San Miguelito, 300–303; sound systems in, 93, 101; West Indians in, 89

Panama Canal, 29–30, 79, 83–84, 91–92, 98n4, 99

Panama City, 31, 81–83, 85–86, 91–92, 99–100, 106, 108n7

Panama Music Corp., 82

pan-Latin/pan-Latino identity, 3, 8, 36, 48, 50, 58–59, 61, 144, 149, 292, 302

Papá Humbertico, 175, 186

Papo Record, 184–85

Paul Wall, 216–17, 225

Pérez Prado, 208

perreo: baile del perrito, 155; "barrio-centric macho" and, 255; in Cuba, 171, 197n29; feminist view of, 13; focus on, 49, 54; male domination and, 302; música del perreo term and, 130; photos, 221; as pornographic, 286; as Puerto Rican and U.S. term, 293n5, 309n6; in Puerto Rico, 130, 216, 253, 275n5,

278n33, 318–19; pun on term, 319, 323n8; reggaeton with, 1

petróleo, 31

PG13 (Ileana Cabra), 257, 273. See also Calle 13

Philip, Louis (Wicho), 98

Phillips, Kathy, 97

Picón, Milton, 115, 118, 132n15, 253

Pincay, Eloy: "Xiomara la Pipona," 94

Pistas de Reggaeton Famosas (Flow Music, 2005), 39

pistas (tracks), 19–22, 25, 36, 39, 44, 52–53, 56, 72n57

Pitbull (Armando Perez), 201–2, 204, 207, 209–11, 212n3; "Culo," 50, 212n3; "305 Till' I Die," 200

Plátano (Iván Rodríguez): Baja Panties parties and, 203; "Como Duele," 208; dembow and, 207–8; "Helicoptero," 200, 202; Miami competition and, 210; Pitbull and, 204; on reggaeton, 201; reggaeton's benefits to, 211

Playero series: Playero 41: Past, Present, and Future (1998–99), 52, 73n59; Playero 42, 319; Playero 37 (ca. 1991/1992), 40, 41, 42, 149, 252, 275; Playero 38 (ca. 1994), 40, 41, 42, 114; "Raagga Mix to Mix" (Playero 38), 42. See also DJ Playero

plena (Panamanian), 31, 69n35, 81, 101, 105, 107n1

plena (Puerto Rican), 8, 23, 34, 66n12, 124, 319–20

Pocho Pan, 315

Polaco, 27

polka, 15n16, 20, 74n78

poverty: Calle 13 on, 258; in Cuba, 291; criminalization and, 133n32; dancehall and, 25; in Dominican Republic, 145, 155; of Dominicans in Puerto Rico, 136–38; in neighborhoods of origin, 256; in Puerto Rican rap, 278n26; in

and, 84; *reggae en español* and, 9, 98; reggaeton and *underground* and, 9; in reggaeton's promotion, 36; Romero Joseph on, 316, 319; social struggle and, 39; in Spanish Caribbean, 136; stereotypes of, 49; strategic mobilization of, 24; "street" identity and, 59; Tego Calderón on, 324–26; transnationalism and, 47; in *underground*, 46; visual style and, 215. *See also* ethnicity; *latinidad*; *música negra*

radio: in Cuba, 187, 195n1; El General and, 103; Glory and, 247; "hurban," 58; La Kalle, 59–60; MCs, DJs, and, 71n47; merengue and, 153; in Miami, 145, 203, 210; in Panama, 82, 84, 90, 93; in Puerto Rico, 315; race and, 324; reggaeton's popularity and, 2, 211, 329; in San Juan, 38; style "friendly" to, 51

Raekwon, 216

raï-ggaeton, 62, 76n91

Rakim and Ken Y, 273. *See also* R.K.M. and Ken Y

Ranking Stone, 37, 122; "Castigo," 233, 315

rap: definitions of, 5–6; as early term for reggaeton, 4. *See also* hip-hop

rap en español, 28, 139, 145

raperos, 133n35

Rastafarianism, 7, 8, 25, 81–85, 88, 102–3, 106–7

Rasta Nini, 83–84, 106

R&B, 5–6, 19, 31, 35, 42, 50, 56, 58, 59, 89, 91, 98, 208

Reana: "A Ti, Te Gustan los Yumas," 280–82

regaeton. See reggaeton (term)

regeton: as Cuban spelling, 292. *See also reggaeton* (term)

reggae: applied to its precursors, 8; Calle 13 and, 257; changes to, in Panama, 31; dancehall vs. roots, 6–7; definitions of, 5; global heyday of, 31; hybrids with

hip-hop, 37; in Panama, 81–88; Panamanians and, 69n35; Puerto Rico and, 69n35, 113; as reggaeton name source, 4; as reggaeton precursor, 23; roots, 6–7, 15n10, 25, *26*, 31; soca influences on, 69n35; as term for *reggaeton*, 74n73; versioning in, 42–43

reggae en español: Dancehall Reggaespañol (1991) and, 32–34, *33*; in Dominican Republic, 145; Jamaican reggae and, 4; in New York, 12, 67n18; Panama and, 4, 69n34, 81–83, 95; Puerto Rican vs. Panamanian roots of, 34, 96; in Puerto Rico, 252; racial commentary and, 9; as reggaeton precursor, 8, 22; in San Juan, 42; as trans-Caribbean genre, 11

Reggae Sam (Everett), 82, 94, 102, 105–6

"reggae/ton," 22, 28, 31, 34, 38, 65n8. *See also reggaeton* (term)

reggaetón. See reggaeton (term)

reggaeton, history of, 21–22, 36, 49–52, 54, 135, 149, 152–57, 158n1, 183, 230, 255, 307. *See also* space

reggaeton cristiano, 61

Reggaetón News, 261

Reggaeton Niños (2005), 20, 61, 64n4

Reggaeton Sex series (DJ Blass), 3, 49, 51, 54

reggaeton (term): applied to its precursors, 8; commercialization and, 253; early use of, 49, 51; future of, 61; narrow vs. broad meanings of, 62; Puerto Rico as "reggaeton nation" and, 130; spelling of, 3–4, 292

reguetón: APLE's dictionary proposal for, 4

"re-licks," "do-overs," 32, 44–45, 69n34

Renato (Leonardo Renato Aulder): childhood of, 91; on discrimination, 98; El General on, 101–2, 105; as founder of *reggae en español*, 89; innovation by, 92–94; on Jamaican influences, 90; "La

Renato (Leonardo Renato Aulder) (*cont.*)
   Chica de los Ojos Café" (1985), 89, 94–
   95; "Me Voy a Viajar," 93; Panama and,
   12, 80, 82, 86; on Panama's versatility,
   97; photo of, *90*; on Puerto Rican influences, 95–96; R&B and, 98n5; "The
   D.E.N.I." (1984), 93
Renato y las 4 Estrellas, 31, 79
Residente (René Pérez Joglar), 63, 256–
   60, 262–64, *265*, 266–75, 276n13,
   278n30, 328–37
"reuse," 43, 45, 73n62
Reyes, Sandy, 155
Rey Pirín, 315
rhythms/meter: backbeat and, 6, 29;
   breakbeat and, 70n42; cadence of *underground*, 252; 3:2 clave, 39, 205, 208;
   3:2 cross-rhythms, 6; dancehall's 3 + 3
   + 2 cross-rhythm (*bomb bomp*), 20, 25,
   25, 43–44, 54, 62; downbeat and, 6, 21,
   25, 64n2; galloping figures, 32nd note
   flourishes, 21; hip hop's duple divisions, 6; I-V ("oompah-style") bassline, 20, 54; of reggaeton vs. hip-hop,
   28–29; roots reggae's "one drop," 25;
   salsa and merengue syncopations, 52;
   "skanking" keyboard accent, 6, 35. *See
   also boom-ch-boom-chick*
Richie Ricardo, 89
"riddims": *Bam Bam*, 21, 43–46, 53–54, 56,
   62; *Coolie Dance*, 212n3; definition of, 6;
   *Drum Song, Poco Man Jam, Real Rock,
   Stalag, Tempo*, 46; *Fever Pitch*, 44, 46, 53;
   Pounder, 90, 95; versioning and, 15n11,
   15n20, 32. *See also Dem Bow* riddim
Rivera, Ismael (Maelo), 120, 231, 325; "Si
   Te Cojo," 121
Rivera, Raquel Z., 7, 9–10, 12–13, 16n21,
   27, 37–38, 67n18, 71n50, 75n86, 137, 151–
   52, 157, 159n21, 160n35, 163n67, 163n70,
   164n77, 277n13, 302, 309n4, 309n5, 331,
   338n1, 339n2

R.K.M. and Ken Y: "Down," 305
rock music: alternative, 205; in Calle 13
   video, 268; CIRCO and, 272; in Cuba,
   179–81, 293n7; "GQs" and, 161n48; in
   Puerto Rico, 171, 178; *rock en español*,
   62; *roqueros* and, 7, 139; in Soviet
   Union, 189–90; as umbrella term, 62
rocksteady, 8
Roc La Familia, 2
Rodríguez, La Mala: "Mala Suerte," 334
Rodríguez, Silvio, 179
Romero Joseph, Welmo E.: in commercials, 320; on dancehall in Puerto Rico,
   7; on Dominicans in reggaeton, 150,
   159n23; on hip-hop preference, 9, 312–
   13, 318, 320–22; photo, *314*; "Puerto
   Rico Lo Hace Mejor," 322n2; in *Raíces*
   special, 319–20; on reggaeton in Puerto
   Rico, 12; university studies of, 316–17;
   untitled hip-hop verse, (1993) 314–15,
   (2005) 316, (2006) 312–13, (2006) 317–
   18, (2007) 321–22
roots reggae. *See* reggae
Rosario, Toño, 140–41, 153, 155
Roxanne Shante, 303
Rubén DJ, 252
Rude Girl (La Atrevida), 33, *34*
Ruiz, July, 148
rumba, 124, 289–91, 299
Run DMC, 26

sabor, 5, 24
Saldana, Francisco (a.k.a. Luny), 74n81,
   143, 150, 160n32, 310n11. *See also* Luny
   Tunes
salsa: in "Chamaco's Corner" (Gallego),
   297–98; criticisms of, 140; in Cuba,
   285; debates about, 164n75; gender in,
   120–21, 231; history of, compared,
   15n18, 156–57; hybrids of, 291; Luny
   Tunes, DJ Joe, and, 57; in Miami, 209;
   in Panama, 97; Plátano on, 203; in Pu-

130, 156, 237, 275n5–276n5, 319; *Rap City*, 26; Romero Joseph's nonprofit video and, 319–20; *The Roof*, 210; "sandwich" dancing and, 286; Univision, 2, 59; *Yo! MTV Raps*, 26, 42

tembleque, 289–90

Tempo, 58

Tenor Saw, 46

Terror Fabulous: "Action" (1993), 44

"Te Ves Buena" (El General, 1990), 32, 35, 79, 82, 105, 141

Thompson, Dennis "the Menace": version of *Dem Bow* by, 39

timba, 167–70, 172, 174–77, 181, 190–91, 194, 281–82

Tito El Bambino, 238, 267. *See also* Hector and Tito

Toña la Negra, 304

Tony Bull, 83

Torres, Judy, 304

Tosh, Peter, 7

tourism, 176, 179, 191–92, 278n29, 280–82, 285, 290, 293n2, 322n2

tracks. *See* pistas

Tráfico Pesado, 263

trance, 19

Triángulo Oscuro, 187

Tribe Called Quest, A: "Scenario," 313

Tricks (Joel Prenza), 203–4

Trinidad, 31, 88, 107, 293n10

Triple Sexxx, 49

"tropical" music forms: Afro-Latin identity and, 23; clave, *tumbao* and, 208–9; definition of, 64n2; later use of, 48; Latin form without emphasis on, 59; Lisa M on, 141–42; Luny Tunes and, 56–57; "merenrap" project and, 34–36; overemphasis of, 8, 15n15, 19; as reggaeton description, 5, 23; *sabor* and, 24; stereotyped images from, 144; "transgressive" dance in, 290

Tuñón, Héctor, 89, 93

Tupac Shakur, 205

"Tu Pun Pun." *See* "Pu Tun Tun" (El General, 1990)

Twickel, Cristoph, 8–9, 12–13, 68n31, 80

2 Live Crew, 208

2005: La Cocinita, Volumen 12, La Popola, 283

underground (Puerto Rican): censorship of, 116, 254; dancehall "versions" and, 21; distribution of, 113; as elusive term, 113; as grassroots, 142; hysteria about, 117–18; as localized term, 40; lyrics in, 119–20; "mainstream" and, 48, 131n12; marginality and, 112, 115, 121–26; market position and, 38; "meren-rap" project vs., 35, 142; "Molasses for the girls" phrase in, 322n7; power and, 126–30; precensorship, 114; Puerto Rican-ness and, 42; as Puerto Rican "underground" rap and reggae, 111–12; in Puerto Rico, 7; as rap-reggae fusion, 37; as reggaeton early name, 4–5, 36; as reggaeton precursor, 9, 134n60, 252; reggaeton's boundaries with, 131n1; in *Reggaeton Sex*, 54; Romero Joseph on, 315–16, 318, 320; San Juan and, 38–39; as trans-Caribbean genre, 11; versioning and sampling in, 45–46, 72n56

Union of Young Communists (Cuba), 166, 183–84, 187–88, 192–94, 284, 290

United States: *bachata* in, 57; criticisms of, 262, 266, 277n22, 336; Cuba and, 195n1, 197n21; dancehall in, 25, 50; Glory's popularity in, 245; migration to, by Dominicans, 135–37; migration to, by Jamaicans, 30; music production and, 155; narratives about, 63; Puerto Rico and, 275n5, 277n15; reggaeton's development and, 3, 4, 61; television broadcasts from, 293n2; *underground* in, 113 *urbanizaciones* (subdivisions), 255, 257, 262–63, 269, 276n13

"urban music," 185, 200, 208, 252, 261, 312, 332

vallenato, 8

Vargas, Wilfrido, 89, 155

Vazquez, Alexandra T., 4, 12

Velcro, 144

"versioning," 6, 11, 21, 31–32, 34, 38–39, 42–45, 57, 69n34, 77n55, 92

Vico C: Calle 13 and, 272; "De la Calle," 114–15, 131n13; "dirty language" and, 114–15; El General and, 67–68n24; as foundational to reggaeton, 28–29, 207; as hip-hop artist, 6, 327; Jorge Oquendo and, 140–41; "La Recta Final," 28; *Meren-Rap* and, 36, 141; Panama and, 90; "Para las Chicas Que Le Gusta El Sex," 95; Puerto Rico and, 139, 252; reggaeton description by, 5; Renato on, 95, 97; Romero Joseph on, 316; on tempo, 67n23

videos, music: Calle 13's, 263, 268–74; censorship and, 118, 130, 318–20; of Cubanito 20.02, 187; dancehall, 26; Dominican culture in, 144; Héctor Figueroa's, 253–54, 267, 278n33; hip-hop style in, 267; "hypermasculine" content of, 253–54; *The Noise 6*, 47; *The Noise 7*, 28; "Oye Mi Canto," 49, 59, 301; reggaeton's circulation via, 215; Romero Joseph in, 320; Salsa Chula's, 288; Tego Calderón's, 10; underage youth in, 254; women in, 58, 232, 253–54; on YouTube, 75n87

Villalona, Angelito, 155

violence: Calle 13 and, 264; in "Chamaco's Corner," 297–98; as dancehall theme, 25; firearms and, 84–85, 255–56, 264, 267, 278n28, 278n32, 297–98, 315, 320, 335; in lyrics, 255–56; in Panama, 84–

85; Romero Joseph on, 314–15, 320; in *underground* lyrics, 116, 125, 128–29, 139, 252, 315; in videos, 267

Visitante (Eduardo José Cabra Martínez), 62, 256–57, 259, 263, 265, 328. *See also* Calle 13

vocal styles: *American Idol*, 50, 56; "choral begging," 304; crooning R&B, 58; Cuban "flow," 170; dancehall-inflected, 35; emotional, 143; "flip-tongue," 36, 42, 70n44; Glory's, 235; Ivy Queen's, 242, 304; nasally tinged, 20, 54; "off-key," 46, 74n76; speechlike, 6; "squawking," 82; tongue twister, 86

"Voltio" Ramos, Julio, 201, 255, 268, 270–72

Walsh, Martha, 104

Wao, 81

Wassabanga (Guasabanga), 92, 101

Wayne Wonder, 50

Whitney, Marva: "Unwind Yourself" (1967), 42

Wila Rose, 97

Wilfrido, 155

Wisin and Yandel, 2, 254, 278n33; "Dem Bow" (2003), 39, 96; "Rakata," 304

Wiso G, 315; *Sin Parar* (1994), 114

women. *See* gender

Wu Tang Latino, 2

Wyclef Jean, 239

Xtreme, 58

Yellow Man, 92

Ying Yang Twins, 204

youth: censorship of *underground* and, 111–12, 115, 118–19, 122–27; criminalizing of, 133n32; in Cuba, 167–68, 170–71, 178–81, 186, 193, 198n32, 291; dancehall and, 25; Dominican, in Puerto Rico, 138; generational debates and, 60; Jamaican culture and, 30; in Miami, 205; in Panama, 98; PG13 and, 257, 273; power and, 127–29; in Puerto Rico, 319; rap and, 139, 320; reggae and, 7–8; in reggaeton scholarship, 307–8; teeny-boppers, 56; *underground* and, 35, 37, 42, 47

Zion and Lennox, 267
Zona de Guerra, 81
zouk, 23

See the contributor biographies for more information
on this volume's editors.

Wayne Marshall has taught at Brandeis University,
the University of Chicago, Brown University, and the
Harvard Extension School.

Deborah Pacini Hernandez is an associate professor
of anthropology at Tufts University.

Raquel Z. Rivera is a researcher at the Center for
Puerto Rican Studies at Hunter College, New York.

Library of Congress Cataloging-in-Publication Data
Reggaeton / edited by Raquel Z. Rivera, Wayne
Marshall, and Deborah Pacini Hernandez.
p. cm.—(Refiguring American music)
Includes bibliographical references and index.
ISBN 978-0-8223-4360-8 (cloth : alk. paper)
ISBN 978-0-8223-4383-7 (pbk. : alk. paper)
1. Reggaetón—History and criticism. I. Rivera,
Raquel Z. II. Marshall, Wayne, 1976– III. Pacini
Hernandez, Deborah. IV. Series: Refiguring
American music.
ML3532.5.R44 2009
781.64—dc22   2008048053